Marriage Certificate

This certifies that on _____ 19____
I united in *HOLY MATRIMONY*

Mr. _____

   of _____

            and

M _____

   of _____

at _____
   (city or town)   (state)

   *Being duly authorized to perform marriage
ceremonies in the state named*

Signed _____
                      minister

Address _____

Witnessed by

_____

_____

"What therefore God hath joined together, let not man put asunder."
—Matt. 19:6

Family Record

1. Name _____
   Date of birth_____Converted_____Died_____

2. Name _____
   Date of birth_____Converted_____Died_____

3. Name _____
   Date of birth_____Converted_____Died_____

4. Name _____
   Date of birth_____Converted_____Died_____

5. Name _____
   Date of birth_____Converted_____Died_____

6. Name _____
   Date of birth_____Converted_____Died_____

7. Name _____
   Date of birth_____Converted_____Died_____

8. Name _____
   Date of birth_____Converted_____Died_____

THE HOME

—COURTSHIP, MARRIAGE, and CHILDREN

A Bible Manual of Twenty-Two Chapters
on the Christian Home

By
Evangelist John R. Rice, D.D., Litt.D.

SWORD OF THE LORD PUBLISHERS
Murfreesboro, Tennessee   37130

Printed in U. S. A.

CONTENTS

other words, sex instinct is an automatic matter. It is
... of the most powerful of all human instincts, and... ...
... stronger than any instinct except that of self-preservation.
... We must remember that many matters and habits of this
... themselves on without the will, just as a drunkard ...
... take a glass of beer and then be absolutely unable to

PREFACE

Much free advice is given about how to make marriage happy and successful. Some of this advice is good, some of it is bad, some of it is frivolous and incidental. Husbands and wives are exhorted to divide up the money evenly so there will be no quarrel, or to agree on a budget, each one to have his own part for his personal expenses and the rest of the income apportioned to definite needs. Husbands are advised to bring home flowers and candy to the wife. The wife is told that if she expects to hold her husband's love she must put on a fresh dress before he comes from the office, and meet him with a kiss. Some writers tell wives to appear to concede the husband's every request but to guide him quietly into her own way unnoticed by the unsuspecting male. The husbands are told that if they will take their wives out dancing or to the theater, their marriage will turn out happily. Wives with philandering husbands are advised to laugh off the indiscretions of their mates, and husbands are told that they must not be jealous if they want their wives to continue to love them. That kind of twaddle fills the advice columns in the newspapers and books on marriage and the home.

"Never force your will on a child. To do so may break down his self-respect and cause him to live a frustrated life the rest of his days!" advises some maiden lady who never had a child. Another columnist thinks that the boy should call his daddy "Bill" and the girl should call her mother "Susie," and that will make everything lovely in the home! Those who have trouble in the home are advised to see a psychiatrist. The counselors speak as if the integrity and happiness and spiritual welfare of the home depend on no more than a flower in a woman's hair or a bit of rouge on her cheek or on simply deciding to have a financial budget or on a man's bringing home a box of candy. These incidentals are well enough in their place, but sensible people ought to know that what is wrong with godless homes goes deeper than that. Where, oh, where is there honest, intelligent, practical teaching from the Word of God on how to have a successful, prosperous marriage, rear godly children, and make home a bit of Heaven on earth? Certainly we need more such teaching.

There are a few good books on the home, but they do not usually deal with the great issues concerning the home which are discussed in the Bible. It is all well enough to tell husband and wife to stay sweethearts, and that everybody must talk nicely in the home and say, "Please," and "Thank you"; that husbands must be courtly and keep on wooing their wives, and that wives must be soft-spoken and dress up for their husbands. But home problems are deeper than that and the needs of perplexed and troubled and sinning husbands and wives are greater than that. People need a Bible manual on home and marriage and children and worship and discipline and godly living in the home. These are some of the reasons I have made an honest effort to give plain Bible teaching on the problems of marriage and home in these pages.

In this volume I do not claim any special wisdom. I simply profess to be God's preacher, trying to tell what He says in His Word about some holy matters, with practical applications. If readers will receive the book kindly—overlooking, because of the honest motive that prompted me to write it, the shortcomings therein—I shall be eternally grateful. Many men could do much better what is here attempted than can I. But I do long to help people to live before God in the home and make home a bit of Heaven on earth, and I shall earnestly pray God to bless these chapters to that end.

All over America I have preached on the home. Family altars have been started. Wives have humbled themselves and submitted themselves to their husbands as unto the Lord. Parents have set out to make their children obey, to teach them to work, to win them to Christ. Fathers have given up habits that were a bad example before their children. Some have surrendered to Christ in order to have their homes like that about which I have preached. The results of my preaching on these themes give me great encouragement. I have found that people want to know what the Bible says on the problems of the home. If people read this book with as kindly an interest as that shown by multiplied thousands who have heard me speaking on such themes, the book will do much good. My preaching on some of these themes has been used of God to prevent divorce in homes. It has been used to win many souls to Christ. May God grant His favor on the message in print to the same ends!

There are parts of the book that will be thought by some

fine, old-fashioned people to be shockingly plain. My explanation of such plain talk is that the Bible itself is plain and the problems are weighty problems, and the need is great everywhere. On every hand are books in plain language concerning marriage, but without the Christian viewpoint, and often definitely anti-Christian. So I believe there should be plain talk, from a Bible standpoint, in chaste language and with a fervent heart, to help people with these problems. Young people have asked me, young married couples have written me from all over America for information and counsel on the problems related to a happy marriage and home: courtship, birth control, divorce, and kindred themes. Christian people ought to have a clear, straight answer that they can understand, one backed up by the Word of God. I have tried to give that answer.

These chapters have been written under very great pressure, and they need more rewriting than I could give. On a train between Chicago and Boston, one chapter was dictated on a machine. Another chapter was partly written in longhand in LaGuardia Airport waiting room, en route by plane from Boston to Chicago. More of that chapter was written on the plane, and it was finished at home. Another chapter was written in longhand as I flew between Oklahoma City and Chicago. In hotel rooms in Boston; in Guthrie, Oklahoma; and in Spokane, Washington, some chapters were dictated. The dictated records were then mailed to my office in Wheaton, Illinois, to be transcribed while I carried on revival campaigns in various cities. The obviously great need for the book compelled me to write it, though under great difficulties, and I trust that kindly readers will judge the book leniently and get what good they can from it. May God bless to His glory the toil, prayers, and tears that have gone into the book. The price I have paid in labor and care has been heavy. If God smiles upon it I shall rejoice.

To my assistant, Miss Lola Bradshaw, for proofreading the entire book and making many suggestions, I owe most fervent thanks. Other friends who read certain chapters and gave kindly counsel deserve my thanks which are gratefully given.

I close with the prayer that the homes where this book comes may see many days "as the days of heaven upon the earth" (Deut. 11:21), as is the promise of God for the homes that teach and keep His commandments.

JOHN R. RICE

November, 1945

CHAPTER I

Marriage and Home

"And the Lord God said, It is not good that the man should be alone; I will make him an help meet for him."—Gen. 2:18.

"Marriage is honourable in all, and the bed undefiled: but whoremongers and adulterers God will judge."—Heb. 13:4.

"And he answered and said unto them, Have ye not read, that he which made them at the beginning made them male and female, And said, For this cause shall a man leave father and mother, and shall cleave to his wife: and they twain shall be one flesh? Wherefore they are no more twain, but one flesh. What therefore God hath joined together, let not man put asunder."—Matt. 19:4-6.

Someone has said that the three sweetest words in the English language are mother, home, and Heaven. These three words center around the middle one. No one thinks of mother without thinking about home. And home itself ought to be a picture, a reminder, of Heaven. Nearly everybody who ever thinks about Heaven thinks about loved ones whom he expects to meet with there. So the home is rooted in the heart's tenderest devotion and memories and aspirations of every normal person.

In Psalm 68:6 the Scripture says, "God setteth the solitary in families." That means that one of the great blessings God gives is the home and the family. How much better it is that the unit of the family should exist, with its tender ties, with its safe protection, with its sure provision for those who could not stand alone. A chicken is able to pick its own food, with a little supervision and protection by the mother, soon after it is hatched out of the shell. And in a few weeks' time the chicken does not need a mother at all. Even a kitten or a puppy is soon able to eat and go without the parent's protection and care. But a baby should be fed, normally, at the mother's breast for ten or twelve months, and then must be provided for and protected and fed and clothed long years before the child is able to care for his own needs and live his independent life. God evidently extended the growing period for children so that they could be in a home and there be molded and protected and taught and developed in the bosom of the family. Thank God that we are not out scratching for our own food in a few weeks' time as a baby chick is! God's great mercy has provided this boon, this comfort, this privilege to human beings; He "setteth the solitary in families." What a sweet provision of God for us all is the home!

Some people live solitary lives after they are grown. Some few people, misanthropic and subnormal in social instincts, seem to be content to live alone after they are grown. But to the poorest and weakest child ever born God gives the privilege (if things work out as they should) of life in a home to start his career in this world.

It is said that John Howard Payne never knew in his adult life the comfort of a home, yet he was all the more able to write that throbbing, heart-wringing song, "Home, Sweet Home."

Mid pleasures and palaces, though we may roam,
    Be it ever so humble, there's no place like home!
A charm from the skies seems to hallow us there,
    Which seek thro' the world, is ne'er met with elsewhere.
Home! home! sweet, sweet home;
    There's no place like home, there's no place like home!

An exile from home, splendor dazzles in vain;
    Oh! give me my lowly thatched cottage again;
The birds singing gaily, that come at my call;
    Give me them with that peace of mind, dearer than all.
Home! home! sweet, sweet home;
    There's no place like home, there's no place like home!

How sweet 'tis to sit 'neath a fond father's smile,
    And the caress of a mother to soothe and beguile;
Let others delight 'mid new pleasures to roam,
    But give me, oh! give me the pleasures of home.
Home! home! sweet, sweet home;
    But give me, oh! give me the pleasures of home!

To thee I'll return, overburdened with care,
    The heart's dearest solace will smile on me there;
No more from the cottage again will I roam,
    Be it ever so humble, there's no place like home.
Home! home! sweet, sweet home;
    There's no place like home, there's no place like home!

As I go up and down the land and preach on the home in my revival campaigns, I find to my surprise and sadness that most people have forgotten this old familiar American classic. Most people can remember neither the words nor the melody, except perhaps a part of the chorus. It is not so easy for me to forget. I am away from home, week after week, most of the year, one year following another. That is a part of the sacrifice which an evangelist makes for the Lord. But knowing all the heart-hunger, all the loneliness, all the unsatisfied needs and longings of the heart of one who is away from home, I find that old song a holy and beautiful thing; and my heart sings it over and over again. Home, home, sweet, sweet home, "be it ever so humble, there's no place like home."

A home necessarily involves a marriage. For some men to live together is not a home. For two or three or four girls to have an apartment together while they go out and each makes her own living, is not really a home. Sometimes where a father or mother is taken away and one parent remains with the children, the place is a home partly because of the memories of the sweet communion of two companions, joined in heart and body and life and hopes and ambitions; yes, and joined together in the birth and rearing of their children. The blessing on such a home where one companion has already gone to Heaven is that the fragrance of the marriage remains, in some sense, with the children and with the bereaved mate. I say, it takes a marriage to make a home.

Let us consider, then, in this chapter some things about the nature of marriage.

I. Marriage Is Ordained of God

Only a fool would make fun of marriage. Surely only a thoughtless scatterbrain or a perverted wretch would talk and think lightly of the institution of marriage. Marriage, I say, was ordained of God.

It was in the Garden of Eden that God Himself planned the idea of marriage. Genesis 2:18 says, "And the Lord God said, It is not good that the man should be alone; I will make him an help meet for him." God made the kind of a man who needed a wife. God knew his heart's needs and his physical needs, and so God declared it was not good for a man to live without a wife. God made Eve, because she was needed, because she would fulfill the natural longings and would fit in with the natural and normal happy life of Adam. Marriage was ordained of God.

We find a tender gentleness in the story given in Genesis. In Genesis 2:21-25, we find, "And the Lord God caused a deep sleep to fall upon Adam, and he slept: and he took one of his ribs, and closed up the flesh instead thereof; And the rib, which the Lord God had taken from man, made he a woman, and brought her unto the man. And Adam said, This is now bone of my bones, and flesh of my flesh: she shall be called Woman, because she was taken out of Man. Therefore shall a man leave his father and his mother, and shall cleave unto his wife: and they shall be one flesh. And they were both naked, the man and his wife, and were not ashamed."

It was God who brought the woman to Adam. It was God who told them the meaning of marriage. And they loved each other at once, and beautifully, so that the Scripture says, "And they were both naked, the man and his wife, and were not ashamed." It was to these two, Adam and Eve, the first wedded couple, that God gave the command, "Be fruitful, and multiply, and replenish the earth, and subdue it" (Gen. 1:28).

Thus we may rightly say that God Himself made man and woman for each other; made them for marriage. And we may say that God Himself performed the first marriage ceremony in the Garden of Eden. Marriage, then, is a holy and beautiful thing, an institution ordained and planned by Almighty God for man's good and happiness, and for God's own glory.

The Lord Jesus Himself added His blessing to marriage by endorsing the Genesis account of the creation of man and woman for each other, and the first marriage, and God's principle of marriage there taught. Jesus said, "Have ye not read, that he which made them at the beginning made them male and female, And said, For this cause shall a man leave father and mother, and shall cleave to his wife: and they twain shall be one flesh? Wherefore they are no more twain, but one flesh. What therefore God hath joined together, let not man put asunder" (Matt. 19:4-6). The Lord Jesus Himself endorsed marriage as a holy and divine institution.

It is significant that when the Lord Jesus, our Saviour, came into this world, He was born into a home. It is true that Jesus was not conceived of natural generation. He did not have a human father. Joseph did not beget Jesus. The virgin birth of Christ is clearly stated a number of times in the Bible, and only unbelievers and non-Christians—those who do not accept the authority of the Bible, those who do not believe Christian doctrines—deny the virgin birth of our Lord. Yet Jesus was born in a home. Mary and Joseph were betrothed, engaged to be married, and God told Joseph, before the baby Jesus was born, to take Mary as his wife. In Matthew 1:18-25 we are told how Joseph, the troubled and distressed sweetheart, dreamed and God sent an angel to him to say: "Joseph, thou son of David, fear not to take unto thee Mary thy wife; for that which is conceived in her is of the Holy Ghost" (Matt. 1:20). And we are told, "Then Joseph being raised from sleep did as the angel of the Lord had bidden him, and took unto him his wife: And knew her not till she had brought forth her firstborn son: and he called his name JESUS" (Matt. 1:24, 25).

So it turned out that Jesus had not only a mother, but He had a home. Joseph was to Him like a father. Luke tells us how the Lord Jesus, when He was only twelve years old, went with "his parents" to Jerusalem (Luke 2:41, 42). Of course, Jesus regarded Joseph as legally His father, actually His foster father. Jesus had the care of a human father, though Joseph was not really His father. Jesus had the blessing of a home. Luke 2:51 tells us that the boy Jesus, even after His startling answers and questions before the doctors at Jerusalem, "went down with them, and came to Nazareth, and was subject unto them" (Luke 2:51).

How Jesus honored the home and made it a holy institution by choosing to be born into a home and to live in a home! The relationship of Joseph and Mary is all the more honored and glorified because while they had each other and loved one another tenderly, to them was committed the care of the Lord Jesus Christ, God's own Son, come to live on earth among men as a man. They cared for Him as a baby, and He nursed at a mother's breast. They fed Him, protected Him, washed Him, taught Him. They took Him to the synagogue at Nazareth. They took Him to Jerusalem to worship at the passover time. And Jesus loved them and was subject to them. Jesus had a home. Not much is said about the first thirty years of the life of the Lord Jesus on this earth, but enough is said to make us know that He lived in a human home and thus forever glorified home and marriage.

Marriage is of God, a divine institution. Those who speak of "holy matrimony" speak aright, for matrimony is holy.

Marriage is the oldest human institution. We may read back in the dusty files of history and find ancient human governments, but they did not begin in the Garden of Eden. Not till after the flood did God institute human government and make men accountable to enforce the law. Human government is not as old as marriage.

The church, congregations of believers, goes back to the times of Christ; the Jewish nation as a separated people with forms of worship given by God goes back far beyond that to Mount Sinai; but public worship, church organization and service—these are not as old as marriage. Neither the church nor human government (both of them divinely given) are as old as the sacred institution of marriage given by God in the Garden of Eden.

How remarkable it is that marriage was first intended for perfect men and women! Adam had never sinned when God made him a wife because, as God said, "It is not good that the man should be alone." Even perfect, sinless people, holy people, so virtuous and good that God Himself could come and walk with them in the garden and talk with them intimately and delight in their sweet and holy fellowship, such holy and sinless beings as Adam and Eve were in the Garden of Eden yet found marriage right and proper and helpful. Those who would say slurring things about marriage and about the relation of husband and wife are wicked and foolish people who disregard the holy character of marriage. No wonder God could say to us through the book of Hebrews, "Marriage is honourable in all, and the bed undefiled: but whoremongers and adulterers God will judge" (Heb. 13:4).

Some books on sociology taught in high schools and college teach that marriage is a product of evolution. They tell fantastic tales of some time before history began when marriage came slowly into being. (Then, so these God-haters would have us think, men and women were only half-human and half-ape.) These deniers of the Bible say that originally men and women ran together in hordes and lived promiscuously without any honest and permanent mating of man and wife. But it is significant that all of this is an invention, without one single shred of evidence. Nobody has any historical account of any such time or any such place when there was no marriage as it is known today. Those who believe that marriage is a product of evolution think so only because they want to think so. They think so without evidence. They think so without reason. The real reason such people believe that marriage is a product of evolution is that they hate the Bible and hate God and do not want to believe that marriage is an institution which God Himself gave according to the Bible. They do not want a binding, Bible marriage. They do not want to give an account to God. They do not want to repent of their sins. So they make up a fantastic tale, and try to make it plausible, in order to bolster the foolish doctrine, or guess, of evolution. They deliberately want to leave God out of their plans, and so they would like to believe that marriage is not of God but is simply the outgrowth of evolution.

Some people actually do not want to be bound by vows of marriage. They want easy divorce when lust is somewhat satisfied, when the fires of passion burn low. They do not want to regard marriage as a responsibility. They do not want to obey the laws of God. They do not want to accept the responsibilities of children. They advocate birth control, or companionate marriage, or easy divorce. But the simple truth is that not one shred of evidence in history indicates there was ever a time when men did not know marriage as we have it today, in the best cases the union of one man and one woman, bound together by solemn obligations in a holy institution.

It is true that because men and women are sinful they have not always lived up to their own ideals and to their own conceptions of what is true and proper in marriage. But marriage as an institution has endured from the first man and the first woman until now. It will endure until mankind in this flesh lives no more on this planet.

How foolish it is to believe that there was a time that men were not even as sensible as some animals are today! Many beasts mate for life, in something like a true marriage. It is said that lions mate for life. Some kinds of birds mate for life. There seems to be a true affection, a true sense of responsibility, an instinct for permanent mating.

If that be true among some of the higher animals, how much more is it true that God Himself has ordained marriage for mankind. It is a holy, a divine institution. We have no right to change God's laws concerning marriage. No one can ever disobey them without danger and terrible hurt to himself and to society.

There have always been perversions of marriage. There have been cases of polygamy. There have been times of great spiritual darkness and wickedness in not keeping the laws of God about marriage as well as about other matters of morality. But mankind was made for marriage, and marriage was made for mankind, by the plan of an infinitely loving and wise God.

II. Why Should People Marry?

There are many sensible reasons, reasons embedded in the need and consciousness of the human race, which make marriage desirable and proper, as the usual thing.

First of all, mankind needs fellowship.

Marriage is intended of God to be the answer to a lonely heart and to supply fellowship and comfort and joy. God said, "It is not good that the man should be alone." Do you think that for a man to have his stomach full of food satisfies all the highest and best in man? Do you believe that for a man to have the needs of his body supplied is all that is required? Obviously no. Man needs fellowship. If a woman cooks, she cannot enjoy her cooking unless someone else who loves her eats it. Many women who live alone almost starve themselves because they cannot enjoy cooking and cannot enjoy eating when there is nobody to cook for and nobody to eat with. Fellowship, after all, is more important.

Why should it please a man that he is wise if there is no one to hear his wisdom? Why should it please a man if he is brave when there is no one to protect and no one to praise his courage? And what would it matter to a woman if she could sing beautifully if there were no one who loved her to hear her sing?

The Saviour sent out His disciples two by two. He sent the seventy the same way, two by two. On the great missionary journeys we find that Paul and Barnabas went together; then Paul and Silas. This only illustrates the fact that companionship is an essential, not only for our happiness but for our usefulness. And the Scripture tells us how Jesus said, "Again I say unto you, That if two of you shall agree on earth as touching any thing that they shall ask, it shall be done for them of my Father which is in heaven" (Matt. 18:19). You see, even in prayer one can do better if he has help. God is more likely to hear the prayer of two people than the prayer of one.

When two people walk together, if one stumbles the other can hold him up. If one be discouraged, the other can encourage him. If one be hurt, the other can help him. Two people can sleep together warmer than if one sleeps alone. Two hearts together can be more cheerful and happy than either of them alone. You see, man, or woman, necessarily needs fellowship. At very best it is lonely enough in this world. At very best there are many of the secrets of the heart, the longings, the aspirations, the memories, the burnings of conscience that one cannot tell anybody. Oh, how each of us needs someone dear and sweet and near, loving and forgiving and understanding and believing, to share with us!

Marriage supplies the need of fellowship. The man who has a true wife who loves him and believes in him can face the world and not be afraid. How many times a noble preacher has preached the Gospel in the face of scorn and disbelief and even abuse and persecution, but has done it boldly and even happily, because he knew there was one nearby who loved and understood and believed in him and his message and held him up in prayer! You see, in the very nature of mankind is written the need for marriage. Marriage is for fellowship and comfort.

In the common language of the people, a wife or a husband is often spoken of as "my companion." That old English usage of the term really pictures what a husband or a wife is. God intended marriage to furnish a companion for the heart. That is one reason why people need to marry.

Second, people should marry for a partnership.

You see, a man is wonderfully built for the work that God has for him to do. But a man may be ever so strong in doing *his* work, and yet he may have clumsy fingers for threading a needle or dressing a baby. How often men have been astonished when they brought a bride to the home that was prepared ahead of time to see what deft changes a woman's fingers made in the home! An embroidered doily on a table here, a vase of flowers there, a dainty curtain, a neat arrangement here and there; and, lo, the home is different! You see, men and women are not alike and each needs the other for partnership.

How many men there are who have tried to live alone.

Sometimes on the plains of West Texas cowboys have
"batched"—which means they lived as bachelors, doing their
own cooking, living in abodes without a woman. I can tell
you from seeing many such a bunkhouse, many such a cook
shack, many such a ranch home in West Texas, that man was
not made to live alone. Man needs the help of a good
woman. A home is not a home without a woman.

In countless apartments over the nation two or three
girls—secretaries, stenographers, department store clerks—
live by twos or threes, together. They make their toast and
coffee in the morning over the little burner, they eat their
meals together at night perhaps. Though they have all the
dainty things that woman's fingers prepare for a home, it
may be, yet they must go out through the day and toil to
make a living for themselves. And when women live alone
they have trouble with the furnace. They do not know what
to do when a window sticks. And they always feel certain
limitations out in the world of commerce. There is a place in
business for a woman as an assistant to man, but any woman
who runs a business of her own, who meets the world on its
own terms, often feels her frailty, often feels the need for
stronger hands and shoulders and a bolder brain than her
own. I am not disparaging the gifts and the abilities that
women have. I simply say that women are only women and
men are only men. God intended that they should work together in a partnership.

In the pioneer home there was need for strong arms and
hands to fell the trees and clear the land and till it. There
was needed boldness for protecting the home against the In-
dians, courage to supply the larder with the wild meat. But in
the cottage there was a need for daintier fingers to rock the
cradle, to do the sewing and the cooking. And there was need
for a tenderer heart, for a woman's genius and a woman's
devotion and a woman's loyalty. You see, for the sake of
partnership, marriage is necessary. A man is only half a man
if he is not married. A woman is certainly less than a complete woman who is not married. God made man and woman
to work together, and no one is at his best who does not have
his work complemented by a partner of the other sex. It is
true that in business, and sometimes in Christian work, the
ideal and the best work is done by men and women working
together. But in marriage, even more than in business or in
the professions or in Christian work, men and women are

made to toil together and to divide their labor according to their gifts and capacities and inclinations. How wise, how good was God to provide the institution of marriage that the best both in man and woman could be brought out, and that their toil should have the best reward and the best fruitage!

Third, marriage is a necessity because of biological need.

God Himself has formed in human beings a certain sex capacity for marriage and love and home and mating. God Himself has given a hunger, a biological necessity that presses men and women toward marriage. That urge is a holy one. It is normal. It is right. I have heard Christian people speak of sex desire as if it were an evil and wicked thing. I have heard people speak of the normal biological necessity that people feel and call it by an evil name, "lust." It is true that sex desire can be perverted, can be unholy and wicked, but it is not normally so. Men are made for marriage. Women are made for marriage. God intended that men and women should look forward to mating. Love, courtship, marriage, mating, child-bearing—these are the normal futures of normal men and women. We ought to realize that the biological necessities of sex are created in men and women and that for good. Sex is holy.

It is true that sex desire can be perverted. It is true that sex, as flaunted by the moving picture screen, as regaled in the cheap magazines, as indulged in by lewd and immoral and godless people, can be a terrible trap for souls, a God-dishonoring evil. But let us remember that God Himself made man, and God made woman and made them with an innate desire the one for the other. That is one reason for marriage.

In I Corinthians 7:1, 2 the Scripture says, "Now concerning the things whereof ye wrote unto me: It is good for a man not to touch a woman. Nevertheless, to avoid fornication, let every man have his own wife, and let every woman have her own husband."

You see that to avoid fornication is one of the reasons for marriage. The bodily desire which is natural and proper, ought in usual cases, to result in love and marriage at the proper time and in the proper way.

Again in the same chapter, I Corinthians 7:9 says, "But if they cannot contain, let them marry: for it is better to marry than to burn." People ought to marry, as a general thing, to avoid the unrest, and avoid the temptation, and avoid the sin, that often comes when people are frustrated in their natural urge of sex.

I do not mean that Christians cannot live happy, noble, continent lives; for they can. Everybody in the world is intended to remain continent and self-possessed until the proper time comes for marriage and the proper mate appears and until the proper and conventional safeguards are met. Certainly honorable, good people can remain continent and can live separate from the opposite sex when that is necessary. And for some people that is necessary all their lives. In such cases, certainly, any man and woman can have grace to do right and live right. Christians who ought not to marry can have peace and joy and victory day by day. Yet the Scripture is clear that in ordinary cases, to avoid fornication and to avoid the burning of unfulfilled desires, marriage is proper.

We ought not to think of this biological urge, this sex necessity, as calling simply and only for mating. There are many secondary characteristics of this heart-hunger and body-hunger of sex. A man wants to hear a woman's voice. He wants the ministrations of her kind fingers. He wants to hear her laugh and her chatter. And so a woman feels the need to lean on a man, to depend upon him, to praise him and be praised by him. All of this is part of the sex urge that God has put in a man or in a woman. It is normal and right. A man is so made that he needs a woman. A woman is so made that she needs a man. In ordinary cases this biological urge is a reason for marriage.

Fourth, most people ought to marry for the propagation of the race; for the bearing and rearing of children.

To Adam and Eve in the garden God commanded, "Be fruitful, and multiply, and replenish the earth" (Gen 1:28). Again after the flood God repeated that command to Noah and his descendants, "Be fruitful, and multiply, and replenish the earth" (Gen. 9:1). You see, according to the Scripture, to multiply is a duty of mankind. It is God's plan that the race should be propagated. It is a solemn duty, a duty to God and a duty to society, to propagate the race.

I know that those who advocate birth control often tell how the increase of population means the increase of misery. But according to all the best authorities, the increase of good Christian marriages—honorable, godly, scriptural marriages—does not bring misery, but good. Big families are happier than small families. How infinitely better off is the home that has children than the home that does not have children.

God intended that a woman's womb should bear children. God intended that a woman's breast should give suck to little ones. God intended that a woman's arms should cradle tiny bodies, and that a woman's voice should croon to them the love songs and lullabies that all women instinctively seem to know. God put this urge, this burden on the little girls who play with their dolls. Women are intended to be mothers. Their bodies are made for motherhood. Their natures are made for motherhood. Their highest and best joy will come as mothers in ordinary cases.

So men are intended to be heads of families. Men are to know something of God's august might and of God's holiness and God's righteousness as they administer wisely the home over which God has made them head. Every man was made to be a husband and a father. In the very nature of a man are capacities never released until he has a home and family. I recall in my early ministry as a preacher I felt more richly and deeply my burden for preaching when I had children of my own. How rich, how noble, how blessed are the aspirations, the sense of responsibility, the holy heart-searchings of one who has become a father! You see, God intended men to be fathers.

So people ought to marry, generally, and they ought to marry partly as a matter of duty, partly as a matter of fulfilling holy destiny in propagating the race.

In I Peter 3:7 God tells us how a man and wife enter into the mysteries and miracles of creation in marriage. "Likewise, ye husbands, dwell with them according to knowledge, giving honour unto the wife, as unto the weaker vessel, and as being heirs together of the grace of life." Man and woman, when united in marriage and in godly mating, are "heirs together of the grace of life." God says to a man and to a woman, "I will let you join Me in the creation of a tiny creature. I will let you bring into the world not only a little body but an immortal soul." How wonderful that a man and a woman in mating and in marriage may be partakers with God in the mysteries and miracles of creation itself! That is the destiny of marriage. So, generally speaking, marriage is a holy duty and responsibility, a way to propagate the race and to fulfill the command of God as well as to fulfill the call that is innate in the bodies of men and women and in their natures.

Fifth, people ought to marry because they fall in love.

Certainly people should never marry who do not love. It is true that falling in love is not enough reason for marriage. No matter how much you love someone, it would be foolish and wicked and disastrous to marry that one unless certain other requirements were met. All these homes that are broken by divorce—do you think that they were not established on love? I say that love is not enough. We will deal further with that later. Yet, certainly, love is essential to a happy marriage, and when people love as they ought, that is a compelling reason for marriage.

I remember the long four years when I wrote a letter to my sweetheart almost every day, except those few months that we were in school together and when I could see her daily. I never read a book that blessed me but that I wanted her to read it. Usually I sent the book to her with my notations on the margin of the pages. I never ate pleasant fruit but that I wanted her to share it. I never smelled sweet flowers but that I wanted her to have their fragrance. Oh, love is a compelling thing. I longed and dreamed for the time to come when we could live together and never be parted any more. I wanted her in my sight. I wanted to hear her voice. I wanted to share her joys and help bear her sorrows, this beloved of mine. Love is a compelling reason for marriage, and people ought not to marry unless they love one another. But God sends love, if it be a holy love, and if it be approached according to His will. Love is one reason for marriage.

From these things let us conclude that in ordinary cases God intends men and women to marry and that in most cases marriage is the happiest way of life, provided it be marriage according to God's will, marriage with His blessing.

III.   Marriage Is the Most Intimate Human Relationship

In poetry and song through the ages men have made much of the love of a mother. On Mother's Day every year, cards are sent by the millions with loving verses, ascribing to mother all the highest virtues, all the tenderest sentiments. Many times people say that, "The best friend you will ever have is your mother." But I want to press on the heart of every reader that the most intimate and precious human relationship is not that of mother and child. It is the relationship of husband and wife.

Mother's love is very tender. It is a miracle of God's mercy that He gives to each of us a loving mother. My own mother has been in Heaven since before I was six years old, and I have missed her with a loneliness unspeakable. How I long to see her! How glad I am that she talked to me about the Lord, that she called me her "preacher boy," that she gave me to God when I was born and made me promise, as she lay on her deathbed, that I would meet her in Heaven! I thank God for the tender ties between a mother and her child.

But after all, there are many limitations to the mother-child relationship. For one thing, it is mostly one-sided. The mother loves the child when her love cannot adequately be returned. The mother gives; the child takes. That is not an equal relationship. After awhile, the mother's heart is often broken by the fact that the child's love turns elsewhere to other companions, other friends, and at last to a permanent mate. You see the mother-child relationship has a tendency to degenerate and become less binding. Children move away from home. The tie of a mother's love cannot hold the boy who learns to love a girl and wants to marry her. You see, mother's love has its human limitation. Great and sweet as it is, the mother-child relationship is not the most intimate, not the most precious, not the most blessed.

Often, in fact, mother-love is selfish. Often mother-love would keep for herself the young life that ought to be spent on the world. Boys and girls ought oftentimes to leave home and go out in the world to find other duties, other homes, other mates and companions. That is God's ordained law. Mother-love often regrets it, for mothers are only human after all, and mother-love is circumscribed by many selfish motives and desires and by limited vision, in the very nature of the case. Mother-love is not the greatest of loves. The mother-child relationship is not the sweetest nor the most intimate nor the most blessed relationship.

How strong is the love of some brothers! Stop and think among those you know of brothers who have been very near to one another. Sometimes it is a brother and a sister who are bound together so closely. Especially is this often true of twins. Sometimes there is a deep kinship of mind and heart between friends. You think of David and Jonathan, of Damon and Pythias. But the friendship of brother for brother is not the closest human tie. The relationship between friends is not the nearest and dearest, not the most intimate nor the most precious.

In the very nature of the case there are certain reticencies necessary and inevitable between people of the same sex. The most intimate men friends do not discuss certain things freely. These ties are not the closest. These loves are not the deepest. These understandings are not most all-inclusive.

No, the most intimate human relationship is that of husband and wife. The dearest love is that of the husband for his wife and of a wife for her husband. I think that properly, as illustrated in the Scriptures, a man ought to be a stronger character and thus ought to be capable of a richer, deeper love than the wife. I mean that a husband represents Christ and should love his wife "even as Christ also loved the church, and gave himself for it" (Eph. 5:25). And the wife is to love her husband as the church is to love Christ and is to be subject to him. In any case, the Scripture says that the wife is "the weaker vessel" (I Pet 3:7). But be that as it may, the relationship of husband and wife should be the most intimate, the most precious, the dearest and best in all human experience.

When God made Adam and Eve and brought them together, and gave Eve to Adam as a bride, the Scripture tells us then that "they were both naked, the man and his wife, and were not ashamed" (Gen. 2:25). That indicates how intimate is the relationship of husband and wife. Theirs should be and may be, if they are wholly devoted one to the other, if they are as fully surrendered to marriage and the home as they ought to be; theirs may be the most tender and beautiful understanding with no intimacies withheld, with no embarrassment over perfect oneness of mind and heart.

Marriage love and marriage intimacy is so great that the Scripture says that "they twain shall be one flesh."

The mating of a man and woman is so intimate that surely any man with any decency, any woman of sense can see it is proper only for people who are mated for life and who have given themselves wholly one to another.

Sometimes a tender and gentle girl, modestly reared and protected, may feel a sense of shame when she comes to the marriage bed. She may feel that there is something unholy, something indecent, about the marriage relationship. That is not true. And all of our teaching, and all of our attitude on this matter of marriage ought to be so holy and so scriptural that people would come to marriage with a sense of holy devotion. The marriage joys are holy joys. It is not wrong for a woman to give herself to her husband without reserve. It is not wrong that a husband should give himself to his wife without reserve. It is not wrong that they, the man and the woman, may be naked before each other and unashamed.

In fact, the ideal of marriage is that every woman's heart should be open, that she should seek to have her husband share all of her thoughts and dreams and aspirations. Likewise the husband should so love his wife and be so devoted to her that she may understand all his heart. The intimacies of marriage ought to be blessed and sweet.

Necessarily this attitude about marriage would demand purity and cleanliness. What man who is licentious and evil, a breaker of his marriage vows, a chaser after wicked women, would feel free to tell his wife all his heart? What woman who is rebellious and unsurrendered, unwilling to keep her marriage vow of obedience, and unwilling to go where her husband goes and live where he lives and work to please him as a "help meet"—what such rebellious woman would feel like taking her husband into all her heart? Such people have not truly married in their hearts when they do not give themselves, unashamed, wholly to their companions.

A man and a woman who marry should not only consider themselves legally as one flesh but they should so love one another, so mold themselves each to the other's needs and loves and desires and capacities that they actually become one. They can be one in their minds, one in their plans, one in their loves, and one in their understanding, as God gives grace and makes the marriage real.

There have been many very foolish and unscriptural things said about marriage. I have read the ravings of some writers who said that married women were living in "legal prostitution" because they felt obligated to surrender their bodies completely to the will of the husband in the marriage relationship. And some have even very foolishly taught that the sin of Adam and Eve in the garden was in the marriage relationship. How far-fetched, how unscriptural, how far from the truth are these vain human imaginings!

First Corinthians 7:3-5 says, "Let the husband render unto the wife due benevolence: and likewise also the wife unto the husband. The wife hath not power of her own body, but the husband: and likewise also the husband hath not power of his own body, but the wife. Defraud ye not one the other, except it be with consent for a time, that ye may give yourselves to fasting and prayer; and come together again, that Satan tempt you not for your incontinency."

Do you see how completely marriage makes husband and wife one? The wife does not have authority over her body. That authority belongs to her husband. The husband does not have authority over his own body. That power belongs to the wife. And the Scripture plainly commands, "Defraud ye not one the other, except it be with consent for a time, that ye may give yourselves to fasting and prayer; and come together again, that Satan tempt you not for your incontinency." You see, God puts no fence between a husband and wife. God puts no limit to the intimacy of a holy union. God has no restrictions on the marriage bed. The wife belongs to her husband. The husband belongs to his wife. It is no sin that they regard themselves as one, and the pleasure of one is to be the joy of the other. God puts no limit on the marriage relationship of a husband and wife.

I want you to see that marriage is the most intimate human relationship, so that two people actually become one in God's sight and grow more and more to be one in their wills, their beliefs, their habits, their understanding, their joys and sorrows.

This intimacy of the marriage relationship is so great that necessarily marriage ought to be a permanent relationship. Nobody but a prostitute could feel free to give herself to the arms of one man and then another, while the first man was still alive. The marriage relationship is so sacred, the relation of husband and wife so intimate, that marriage ought to last until death alone breaks it. That is the teaching of the Scripture. And that also is the plain implication of the nature of marriage itself. So intimate, so complete is this union of a man and woman in marriage that the union ought never to be broken except by death. How wicked to defile such a sacred and beautiful union! And what sorrow and grief will be the portion of those who think lightly of marriage and of its obligations and joys and privileges!

CHAPTER II

Courtship and the Dangers of Petting

"Blessed are the pure in heart: for they shall see God."—
Matt. 5:8.

*"Intreat . . . the elder women as mothers; the younger
as sisters, with all purity."*—I Tim. 5:1, 2.

*"Flee also youthful lusts: but follow righteousness, faith,
charity, peace, with them that call on the Lord out of a pure
heart."*—II Tim. 2:22.

*"That every one of you should know how to possess his
vessel in sanctification and honour; not in the lust of concu-
piscense, even as the Gentiles which know not God."*—I
Thess. 4: 4, 5.

Courtship of young people before marriage is natural. It
would certainly be silly for people suddenly to marry without
ever having paid any attention to one another or without
having found themselves mutually attracted and happy to be
together. A normal period of getting intimately acquainted,
of wooing the affections and of being won, is proper and
right. However the false idea has now become very common
in America that courtship means necking and petting, hugs,
kisses, and fondling. Actually petting is not normal; it is most
likely to substitute an animal sex desire for a holy and beautiful love and to confuse passion for love. Petting is such a
perversion of courtship, such an unholy and dangerous thing
for young people, that we feel a book on marriage and the
home from the Christian viewpoint must deal honestly with
this problem.

Courtship should naturally include the following elements:

1. Being together. People who might want to link themselves together for a lifetime ought to have some time in
each other's company to get well acquainted and to see
whether or not they enjoy one another.

2. Certainly they should talk together. Of course, there
should be some light conversation, but certainly there should
be some very serious talk. No man wants to marry a girl
without knowing what she thinks, what are her principles and

31

convictions. And how could a girl really love any man until she knew what were his aims and ambitions? One of the dangers of petting is that it shuts off serious talk and preoccupies young people with the physical so they do not put their comradeship on the mental and spiritual plane.

3. Courtship should have letters. First, young people feel the need for an intimacy in which the whole world cannot share, and letters are private. Second, one can learn more about another's character and culture by a letter than by long hours of conversation. The handwriting, the spelling, the niceties of expression all reveal what the writer is much better than casual acquaintance and conversation show. Many firms require that applications for positions must be in writing. So naturally young people like to write letters ranging from the note saying, "How about tennis at 4:30?" to the more serious letter of courtship. But let letters be decent and sincere so that they will not, if ever made public, cause shame.

4. Young people should appear in public together. First, in the early teens youngsters will pair off a bit at parties and picnics and at their homes under proper chaperonage, of course. Later, mature young people may go places together without chaperonage provided the distance is short or the trip made in a public conveyance, and provided, of course, that they come in at decent hours and that there is no opportunity for scandal to hurt a girl's name, and no unusual temptation.

5. Young people should enjoy things together: music, tennis, badminton, ping-pong, picture taking, the public lecture, the band concert, or, where custom permits, Christian services. In our home town only engaged young people sit together at the morning church services, but other couples attend the young people's meeting together or sit in the evening service together. Certainly there should be no hand-holding, no whispering during Christian services. But young men and women need to be together in the normal pursuits and pleasures of life if they are going to know one another well enough to become engaged and to marry.

6. Keeping company, or the normal courtship, does not require much physical contact. The friendly hand-clasp, a girl's hand upon her escort's arm in the evening darkness, his helping her across a muddy place—such casual contacts are enough for people who are not engaged.

When young people have learned to love one another and have definitely committed themselves to marriage and a life partnership, some chaste caresses should be permitted, but there should be yet restraint and modesty.

The movies, the dance, the fad for nudity, and the shameless uncovering of the bodies of women and girls lead to necking and petting. And necking and petting are the last step before adultery. I think we might say that cases of criminal attack and rape occur without petting, fondling and embracing, and perhaps some cases of adultery with professional prostitutes do. But adultery rarely or never occurs between ordinary, decent people who want to do right, except through fondling, kissing, and embracing, touching the bodies or seeing the exposed bodies of the ones with whom the sin of adultery is committed. Necking and petting are, in countless cases, the road to adultery, a road that soon turns downhill, where people slide, even against their wills, perhaps, to horrible sin. And all the other factors that lead to necking and petting, fondling and caressing between people who are not married, are leading straight toward adultery. Strip tease and leg shows, bathing suits which unduly expose the body, particularly women's bodies, magazine stories and pictures that turn the mind specially toward love-making, the movies, the embrace of the dance—these lead to sex desire and so to necking and petting. All these have broken down the modesty and natural inhibitions of purity, have even broken down the sense of respectability and decency, till on every bathing beach, in every darkened movie theater, on front porch swings, even on the dance floor and (most deadly of all) in automobiles far from chaperones, young people make free with each other's bodies, hug, kiss, and fondle each other. They pet when there is no pretence of actual love nor holy intention to marry. They do it promiscuously, as shamelessly as the mating of promiscuous barnyard animals. They cheapen holy love, they prostitute holy instincts, they arouse the passions of their bodies and inflame lust in their minds. Then in countless millions of cases they take the next step, one that naturally follows, and commit the scarlet sin, adultery.

The Bible on Caresses

The Bible frequently mentions caresses as proper and beautiful expressions of love. Christian men of the Bible often are said to have kissed one another. We suppose such a kiss was on the cheek. The noblest men in some European countries embrace one another and kiss each other on the cheek as an expression of love or admiration. So they did in Bible times. So Jacob kissed his father Isaac (Gen. 27:27). So Jacob and Esau kissed each other (Gen. 33:4). So Joseph kissed his brethren (Gen. 45:15). So Jonathan and David kissed one another (I Sam. 20:41). So David kissed his son Absalom (II Sam. 14:33). So Absalom kissed the men of Israel and stole away their hearts from King David (II Sam. 15:5).

Among New Testament Christians, the embrace and the kiss were frequently used as an expression of brotherly love. A most touching scene is that described when Paul came to Miletus, and there gathered to meet him were the elders of the church at Ephesus. Paul perceived that he would never see them again, so these godly men, with tears, fell upon Paul's neck and kissed him (Acts 20:37). And five times in the New Testament, Christians are commanded to salute or greet one another with a holy kiss, or the kiss of brotherly love (Rom. 16:16; I Cor. 16:20; II Cor. 13:12; I Thess. 5:26; I Pet. 5:14). We suppose that in most cases, if not in all cases, it was intended that Christian men should greet Christian men with a kiss, and Christian women should greet Christian women so. But at least we are to understand that caresses and affection were encouraged, with proper conventions. They are the normal expressions of loving hearts when under proper safeguards.

Under the safeguard of ties of blood the kiss between men and women is often proper, for example, the kiss of father and daughter. So Laban kissed his married daughters and his grandchildren (Gen. 31:55). Jacob kissed his cousin Rachel (Gen. 29:11). No doubt that first kiss was on the basis of kinship. Yet from that day they seemed to love one another and later married. Thus we see that strong bonds of natural affection, safeguarded by character and the sense of responsibility, make kisses proper between father and daughter, mother and son, and in other cases where there are strong ties of blood and where sex attraction would be properly curbed.

The Saviour seems to have been pleased with the affection of John the apostle who put his head on Jesus' breast. He was also greatly pleased when a poor, fallen woman who came to Him for forgiveness, kissed His feet repeatedly, wept over Him and then dried His feet with the hair of her head (Luke 7:36-50).

It has long been the custom in some circles that when a godly pastor reads the marriage ceremony for a bride who has grown up in his church, that he should give her a kiss of congratulation and love, a chaste kiss upon the cheek as a father might. And surely in cases of long friendship, the pastor who may have led to Christ and baptized the little girl, now grown to womanhood, might without offense or wrong so express his love and well wishes. And so might others, in reverence, be blameless about such a caress. I remember when long years ago I went to the army during World War I and a godly woman kissed me on the cheek in the place of the mother who had long before gone to Heaven. Under proper safeguards and obeying sensible conventions, caresses may be proper and good.

I am saying that caresses ought to be beautiful and blessed, they ought to come from the heart, they ought never to lead us wrong but make us richer and happier and stronger to do right.

But since caresses are intended to be holy and beautiful things, they should be safeguarded like all holy things. The story of drunken Lot committing incest with his two daughters shows that when alcohol breaks down the natural restraints of parental love, caresses may be shameful. The story of Amnon, his love and shameful rape of his half sister, Tamar (II Sam. 13:1-14), shows that even between brother and sister there needs to be a proper reserve to avoid temptation and sin. The truth is, of course, that wicked and licentious men or women may make unholy and vile that which ought to be sweet and noble and pure.

Married Love and the Petting of Husband and Wife

The Bible gives us a beautiful exposition of chaste and holy married love. The Song of Solomon tells the story of a bridegroom and a bride. I believe the book pictures the love of Christ for His church and the church for Christ. But it certainly also pictures the love, the ecstasy, and the mutual joy of a young couple whose love has now led to matrimony. In the Song of Solomon every bridegroom can find some of his own holy exultation over the beauty of his bride's body and the sweetness of her surrender. Solomon, we think, is pictured as the bridegroom. And this is the way he spoke:

"Behold, thou art fair, my love; behold, thou art fair; thou hast doves' eyes within thy locks: thy hair is as a flock of goats, that appear from mount Gilead. Thy teeth are like a flock of sheep that are even shorn, which came up from the washing; whereof every one bear twins, and none is barren among them. Thy lips are like a thread of scarlet, and thy speech is comely: thy temples are like a piece of a pomegranate within thy locks. Thy neck is like the tower of David builded for an armory, whereon there hang a thousand bucklers, all shields of mighty men ... Thou art all fair, my love; there is no spot in thee."—Song of Sol. 4:1-4, 7.

And again the bridegroom says:

"How beautiful are thy feet with shoes, O prince's daughter! the joints of thy thighs are like jewels, the work of the hands of a cunning workman. Thy navel is like a round goblet, which wanteth not liquor: thy belly is like an heap of wheat set about with lilies. Thy two breasts are like two young roes that are twins. Thy neck is as a tower of ivory; thine eyes like the fishpools in Heshbon, by the gate of Bathrabbim: thy nose is as the tower of Lebanon which looketh toward Damascus. Thine head upon thee is like Carmel, and the hair of thine head like purple; the king is held in the galleries. How fair and how pleasant art thou, O love, for delights! This thy stature is like to a palm tree, and thy breasts to clusters of grapes. I said, I will go up to the palm tree, I will take hold of the boughs thereof: now also thy breasts shall be as clusters of the vine, and the smell of thy nose like apples; And the roof of thy mouth like the best wine for my beloved, that goeth down sweetly, causing the lips of those that are asleep to speak."—Song of Sol. 7:1-9.

This is holy ground. These Scriptures ought to be read reverently; and such love-making, of course, is for husband and wife. It is proper and is evidently God's plan that a husband should be proud of the beauties of his wife's body, that she should be "all fair" to him. But the picture here given would be defiled and unholy if it represented mere lustful fondling and petting between two people who are not given to each other for a lifetime, two people whose bodies have not become one flesh, two people who have not promised themselves wholly to each other.

I think it proper also to mention here how the Scripture pictures the bride as feeling toward her husband.

"Let him kiss me with the kisses of his mouth: for thy love is better than wine ... A bundle of myrrh is my wellbeloved unto me; he shall lie all night betwixt my breasts. My beloved is unto me as a cluster of camphire in the vineyards of Engedi. Behold, thou art fair, my love; behold, thou art fair; thou hast doves' eyes. Behold, thou art fair, my beloved, yea, pleasant: also our bed is green. The beams of our house are cedar, and our rafters of fir."—Song of Sol. 1:2, 13-17.

"He brought me to the banqueting house, and his banner over me was love. Stay me with flagons, comfort me with apples: for I am sick of love. His left hand is under my head, and his right hand doth embrace me."—Song of Sol. 2:4-6.

Of the right kind or pure, married love, Song of Solomon 8:6, 7 says,

"Set me as a seal upon thine heart, as a seal upon thine arm: for love is strong as death; jealousy is cruel as the grave: the coals thereof are coals of fire, which hath a most vehement flame. Many waters cannot quench love, neither can the floods drown it: if a man would give all the substance of his house for love, it would utterly be contemned."

This love is as strong as death. This love cannot be quenched by water nor drowned by floods nor bought by all the substance of one's house. But it must be pure, married love with each of the mates given wholly to the other and with their love undefiled by sin, for "jealousy is cruel as the grave."

The Scriptures given above are the inspired Word of God. They are holy, they are good. They should be read reverently. Dr. Scofield says: "Nowhere in Scripture does the unspiritual mind tread upon ground so mysterious and incomprehensible as in this book, while the saintliest men and women of the ages have found it a source of pure and exquisite delight. That the love of the divine Bridegroom should follow all the analogies of the marriage relation seems evil only to minds so ascetic that marital desire itself seems to them unholy."

Absolute freedom of caresses and love-making and fondling are proper within marriage. "Every good gift and every perfect gift is from above, and cometh down from the Father of lights, with whom is no variableness, neither shadow of turning" (Jas. 1:17). In the Garden of Eden Adam and Eve, who were as pure and sinless as the angels of God, were naked and were not ashamed (Gen. 2:25).

But all this is clearly intended for married people, and it is certainly wicked and vile when the petting, caressing and fondling are matters of unholy lust, uncurbed, characterless animalism, instead of proper, sanctified, married love.

It is obviously intended that intimate love-making and petting are to lead to sex relations. And that means that such intimate petting and fondling are for married people.

It is also quite clear from the Scriptures that kisses and caresses, when outside of marriage, often lead to adultery.

For example, Proverbs 7 tells how a simple youth, void of understanding, is led into sin by an harlot. "So she caught him, and kissed him, and with an impudent face said unto him ... Come, let us take our fill of love until the morning: let us solace ourselves with loves" (Prov. 7:13-18).

So kisses and flattery and the enjoyment of a woman's body may be expected to lead to adultery.

In Proverbs 5:15-23 the Scripture gives these plain words:

"Drink waters out of thine own cistern, and running waters out of thine own well. Let thy fountains be dispersed abroad, and rivers of waters in the streets. Let them be only thine own, and not strangers' with thee. Let thy fountain be blessed: and rejoice with the wife of thy youth. Let her be as the loving hind and pleasant roe; let her breasts satisfy thee at all times; and be thou ravished always with her love. And why wilt thou, my son, be ravished with a strange woman, and embrace the bosom of a stranger? For the ways of man are before the eyes of the Lord, and he pondereth all his goings. His own iniquities shall take the wicked himself, and he shall be holden with the cords of his sins. He shall die without instruction; and in the greatness of his folly he shall go astray."

Here we are plainly told that certain privileges of petting are for the married couple only and nobody else. "Rejoice with the wife of thy youth. Let her be as the loving hind and pleasant roe; let her breasts satisfy thee at all times; and be thou ravished always with her love," says the Lord. Such intimacies are reserved for the husband and wife. Otherwise they are likely to lead to adultery and bring the curse of God.

And several times God speaks of fondling of the breasts as

a part of the sin of whoredom or adultery. For example, Ezekiel 23:8-21.

In Deuteronomy 22:28, 29 God's Word gives the punishment that shall be meted out in this particular case of adultery, "If a man find a damsel that is a virgin, which is not betrothed, and lay hold on her, and lie with her, and they be found; Then the man that lay with her shall give unto the damsel's father fifty shekels of silver, and she shall be his wife; because he hath humbled her, he may not put her away all his days." But hardly noticeable in this King James translation of the Bible is an indication that petting or for a man to handle the body of a woman precedes and often leads to adultery. The Hebrew word *taphas,* which is here translated *lay hold on,* is translated once *to hold,* three times is translated *catch,* and eight times it is translated *handle!* The word used here about a man's laying hold on a girl is primarily "to handle." And the *handling* would naturally lead to adultery, as this verse indicates.

Another striking provision of the Mosaic law is given in Deuteronomy 25:11, 12, which says, "When men strive together one with another, and the wife of the one draweth near for to deliver her husband out of the hand of him that smiteth him, and putteth forth her hand, and taketh him by the secrets: then thou shalt cut off her hand, thine eye shall not pity her."

Could there be any stronger evidence of the danger and wickedness of men and women outside of wedlock taking liberties with each other's bodies?

Sex Passion and Bodily Desires When Encouraged Often Overwhelm Reason and Override the Will

It is well to remember that sex is of God. God prepared the bodies of men and women so each would feel a need for the other, and so both, united in holy marriage, might have part in the reproduction of the race. Nature, by God's plan, has so arranged that the wholehearted love of man and his wife will lead them to sex intercourse and the conception of children. In other words, God planned that in the natural course of events all normal marriages would properly and automatically result in children. So love-making stirs sex desires. But when, outside of marriage, sex desire is stimulated by petting, it may overcome all restraints. Modesty, Christian rearing, purity of heart, good intentions, will power—all these may be broken down before the force of aroused sex desire.

In other words, sex instinct is an automatic matter. It is one of the most powerful of all human instincts, and is said to be stronger than any instinct except that of self-preservation. We must remember that many matters and habits of life carry themselves on without the will. Just as a drunkard might take a glass of beer and then be absolutely unable to control his desire until he was dead drunk, so men and women or young people who play with the sex feeling by petting and fondling one another and by hugs and kisses, are likely to find themselves swept off their feet and led on into the actual sin of adultery which they never planned. When people trifle with the human body, then sometimes bodily passions take control and are stronger than the will, stronger than character.

We must remember that this is as true about women as about men. It is as true about good men as it is about bad men. Sex desire, strongly aroused, is often practically beyond control. The fact that the desire, when directed toward anyone but one's own married mate, is sinful and dangerous may be ignored just as the danger and sin of drink, or of dope-taking are ignored when a deep-seated craving has been aroused by long habit, but the sin and the danger are there, nevertheless.

The best Christian in the world, if he is not a good enough Christian to keep from petting, may not be a good enough Christian to keep from adultery.

Lust may be as powerful if aroused by a casual acquaintance as if it were a holy desire between man and wife. And just as the drunkard may make tearful promises and sign pledges and vow he will never grieve his wife by drinking again, but then, if he takes one glass of beer, may plunge into drunkenness and ruin again; so a man or woman may break all their vows and forget all their promises and all of their pure love for somebody else under the blinding, soul-paralyzing effect of an aroused sex desire.

A young woman attended a dance with her sweetheart to whom she was engaged to be married. After dancing several times with a high school friend, whom she did not love, she and he both became deeply aroused, and they were led into the scarlet sin. Weeping, she told me later that she did not love that young man but that she still loved the boy to whom she was engaged to be married. She had been utterly swept off her feet by physical instincts which are perfectly normal, instincts which all normal people have, but which should never have been aroused to any strong degree except in marriage and by her own husband.

Sex is a gift from God. It is meant for our happiness and our good. It is meant to tie husband and wife together in mutual love and devotion through a long life. It is meant to result in happy families and beloved children. But when perverted and used wickedly, contrary to God's commands, sex can become the most deadly enemy of any man or woman and lead to horrible ruin.

Petting Prepares the Body for the Marriage Relation

Petting, as the term is often used among young people, referring to the intimate fondling and embracing which cause strong sex excitement, is intended only for mates. Normally, the body prepares itself for its various functions. For example, the sight and smell of food causes the blood to go to the stomach of a hungry person and starts saliva to running in the mouth and gastric juice in the stomach, to digest food. Fear causes certain glands to secrete extracts which, in the blood prepare the body for violent action. Fear causes the eyes to dilate to see any danger. Fear automatically causes the breathing to be deeper, and the body takes in more oxygen, preparing to fight or run. So petting stimulates the body to prepare for the sex act. Blood vessels are enlarged near the sex organs and they are filled with blood, become larger and more sensitive, increasing sex desire. Certain glands are stimulated to discharge secretions. In the man the semen is produced more rapidly, and millions of germ cells are prepared. The condition of the body then cries out for mating. The heart beats faster, the breathing may be deeper. This condition is caused by hugs, kisses, and such necking, spooning or petting as are customary among young people. It is caused by the close physical contact of the dance. It is also caused when the mind and imagination become centered on sex matters, as in observing a sex movie or reading sex stories, seeing nude pictures, or the exposed bodies of the opposite sex.

And this stimulation, particularly in the case of the man, is

not temporary. The large amount of the sex fluid produced in
the male organs has a tendency to cause recurring sex desire
until it is released, either in a sex union, or in self-abuse, or
in a "wet dream." Wet dreams coming oftener than a few
weeks apart are likely caused by extra sex stimulation.

Even the memory of petting continues to stir the imagination and sex desire long afterward.

All thoughtful married people know that what I say here is
true, and young people who have indulged in petting and
have carefully analyzed what took place, know there is terrible temptation in petting.

Other Harmful Results of Petting Besides Adultery

Though petting often leads to adultery and brings great
danger to all who indulge in it, there are other very harmful
results. If you, by God's mercy, are not led into the scarlet
sin by petting, these other results may cost you much in the
future.

First, promiscuous petting and fondling of others now may
lose much of the sweetness of marriage later on. Much of the
beauty of marriage is that it is new and fresh, enjoyed by two
alone. What man, after he has examined the bodies of other
girls or women, has fondled them, handled them, hugged
them and kissed them, can come to his wife with the same
holy awe and reverence and joy as if he had lived pure and
clean and had saved his body and his sex interest wholly for
her? On the other hand, do you think any man will enjoy the
charms of his wife as well if he knows that she has been handled, fondled, caressed and had her passions aroused by the
petting of a number of other men? No doubt, petting before
marriage tends to make marriage insecure. No doubt, many
are divorced because there was no sweetness, no holy soul-
union in marriage. The early experiences of married life
ought to bind husband and wife together forever in mutual
love and respect and delight. They ought to grow to feel that
they were each made for the other and for no one else, and
that each holds a place in the other's heart and life and experience that no one else ever has held or could hold. If marriage does not mean certain exclusive rights, then why should
men and women feel themselves bound by marriage? Petting
before marriage certainly sometimes leads to divorce after
marriage.

Second, petting often loses a girl a good chance to marry happily. Even though men may be tempted, and may tempt girls to pet, often men of high ideals are then disgusted with the girls who allow themselves to be pawed over. Women and girls who have no respect for their own bodies often lose the respect of the men with whom they pet. From long association with men and young men, I know, and hundreds of cases prove, that men will sometimes go with a girl whom they would not marry, and will pet with girls whom they would not marry under any circumstances. Any sensible man is bound to feel that if the principal attraction a girl has is her body, she would not make a steadfast and desirable wife. And men often feel that a girl who will pet would go farther. What man wants to marry the girl that he feels might have committed adultery with any man she allowed to fondle her body?

Again, petting leads to many hasty and unhappy marriages. Sometimes after petting has led to adultery, young people who do not really love each other feel forced to marry. Recently a woman told me how she had hated her husband for many years. They went too far in their petting. Aroused desire led to adultery, and she felt bound to marry him, though after their sin she did not respect him and always blamed him for it. How many unhappy homes are so caused! Or petting may lead to such strong sex desire that it is mistaken for love. Many times people seem madly in love. Yet when the honeymoon is over they find they have almost nothing in common. They do not enjoy each other's company. *Sex appeal alone is the poorest basis in the world for a happy marriage!* Even the European plan where parents plan the marriages of young people who do not yet love each other, but who learn love after marriage, in the long run proves much happier than marriage based on sex passion only. A mate chosen for good family, beauty of character, and personality, is much more apt to make a happy home than one chosen for temporary sex appeal. Of course, the ideal way is that people should learn to love each other before marriage, but that this love should be based principally on character, on real admiration and unity of interests and plans, and sanctified by a clear sense of God's leading and blessing. When a marriage is based simply on the sex passion which is aroused in petting, when beauty wanes, or the mate seems to become common, that which bound the marriage together is gone, and either party may be attracted to an outsider, as happens in many, many cases, and a broken home results. Marriages which simply follow sex passion are not likely to be happy nor successful marriages.

Besides, there is great bodily harm in the stimulation of petting which arouses sex passion but does not satisfy it. Often inflammation results in both men and women. The constant arousing of desire may result in self-abuse, causing guilty consciences or even nervous breakdowns sometimes. With men there is often a serious loss in semen which depletes the physical strength and sometimes affects the mind. In middle life many men suffer from prostate gland trouble, requiring a serious operation, because of prolonged sex stimulation in youth, such as petting brings.

One of the most lamentable results of petting is that sex matters come to absorb the mind, to draw it away from wholesome pleasures and work and duties. Ordinary pleasures lose their attraction to people who give themselves to petting. I have known men who developed a state of mind in which every look at a woman was a lustful one, and who all through the day talked of sex matters among their friends. Evil thoughts and a habit of dwelling upon obscene matters may last for years. Many, many Christian men have told me that an improper stirring of sex passions and dwelling on sex matters in youth had left them with a recurring of evil thoughts long later which took much praying and often much sorrow to overcome.

Sex, when properly used, is blessed of God and results in happiness and health and usefulness for both men and women. But when perverted, and when sex desires are aroused by illegitimate fondling and petting of the opposite sex, great harm may result.

Some Rules About Love-Making to Avoid Sin

Friendship, comradeship, enjoying the fellowship of the opposite sex, is proper for girls and boys of all ages, and for grown men and women whether married or not married. But love-making is another matter. I believe that these rules will be helpful.

1. *Be honest and sincere.* The acts of love are always improper and wicked when they are insincere. When a boy and girl kiss, and when the kiss is a lie, then it is a sin. When they act like people who are married, or like those who have al-

COURTSHIP AND THE DANGERS OF PETTING   45

ready pledged themselves each to the other until death, and
when that is not the real feeling and intention of their hearts,
then their love-making is a lie. It is insincere and wicked. The
love of two good friends does not demand liberties each with
the other's body. If you are not married, then do not act as if
you were married. If you do not plan to marry, then do not
act as if you plan to marry. Any petting or fondling on insincere grounds is wicked and dangerous.

If you take the liberties that are intended only for married
people, with one to whom you are not married, you are hy-
pocritical and insincere, you are saying things you do not
mean, you are acting things which are a lie. The Scripture
commands, "Provide things honest in the sight of all men"
(Rom. 12:17).

2. *Keep the Golden Rule as given by our Saviour in Matthew 7:12: "Therefore all things whatsoever ye would that
men should do to you, do ye even so to them: for this is the
law and the prophets."* When a boy and girl pet and arouse
sex passion and so take the road that leads toward the scarlet
sin, they should remember that several other people are involved and deeply concerned in what they do. That girl has a
brother. Young man, are you treating that Christian brother
right? Are you willing for others to treat your sister as you
are treating another man's sister? That girl has a father and
mother who love her dearly, and they would probably be
deeply grieved if they knew their daughter's feet were so near
the brink of adultery. When you have daughters of your own,
will you want them treated as you are treating someone else's
daughter?

More important still, that girl with whom you pet expects
to marry. There is somewhere a man who will become her
husband. How will he feel if he learns you have taken liberties with the woman who becomes his bride? Well, how do
you feel yourself about the girl you hope to marry? Would
you just as soon she came to you secondhand after other
men have hugged her, kissed her, fondled her body, aroused
her passions and led her to the brink, or even over the brink,
of the scarlet sin? Is there a single man who reads this who
does not want his bride to come to him virgin pure in her
thoughts and passions as well as in the actual matter of mating? I have asked this question of hundreds of young men.
I have never yet met a young man who preferred that his
wife had been handled by other men, petted, fondled, em-
braced, aroused by other men. If a man wanted that kind of

a wife, of course, he would go to a bawdy house to find one. But men want pure wives. Men, when they come to marry, even if they themselves have not been all they should have been, still want their wives to be virgin in mind and heart as well as in body, virgin regarding the endearments and privileges which normally belong only to husbands and wives.

Young man, if, you take liberties with a girl someone else is to marry, when you would not want others to take liberties with your own future bride, then you are not keeping the Golden Rule. You are cheating. You are sinning grievously against a man, even if you do not know who he is, who would have a right to call on God to punish you for your sin.

And young woman, you should keep the Golden Rule, too. Do not do with someone else's future husband what you would not want them to do with your future husband.

3. The third rule I suggest is this: *Judge yourself by the same standards you hold up for others.* Jesus said, "And why beholdest thou the mote that is in thy brother's eye, but considerest not the beam that is in thine own eye?" (Matt. 7:3). If the most respected Christians you know should pet, as worldly and sinful young people pet, men taking liberties with women's bodies, fondling, embracing, arousing sex desire, would you think it right? Would you think that would be right for preachers? Would it be right for your mother, with another man besides her husband? Would not you feel that that was poor Christianity if responsible Christian people, married people as well as single people, preachers as well as lay leaders, petted as some young people do? Well, Jesus said to judge yourself by the same standard with which you judge others. If it is wrong for others, it is wrong for you. If it is wrong for preachers, it is wrong for church members. If it is wrong for married people (with others not their mates), it is wrong for single people.

4. The next rule is this: *Always be a good example to others.*

God requires Christian young people to set a Christian example. First Timothy 4:12 says: "Let no man despise thy youth; but be thou an example of the believers, in word, in conversation, in charity, in spirit, in faith, in purity." Young people are to be examples in purity! You are accountable for those about you. We are commanded to provoke one another to good works (Heb. 10:24). And Romans 14:13 commands us, " ... but judge this rather, that no man put a stumblingblock or an occasion to fall in his brother's way." Ro-

COURTSHIP AND THE DANGERS OF PETTING   47

mans 14:15 says, "But if thy brother be grieved with thy
meat, now walkest thou not charitably. Destroy not him with
thy meat, for whom Christ died." Romans 14:21 says, "It is
good neither to eat flesh, nor to drink wine, nor any thing
whereby thy brother stumbleth, or is offended, or is made
weak." If your example would lead others to do wrong, then
it is a sin. Or if your act grieves the consciences of others,
then the Scripture makes it clear you have sinned. Speaking
of meats offered to idols, the eating of which was not necessarily wrong in itself, Paul says:

*"But take head lest by any means this liberty of your's be-
come a stumblingblock to them that are weak. For if any
man see thee which hast knowledge sit at meat in the idol's
temple, shall not the conscience of him which is weak be em-
boldened to eat those things which are offered to idols; And
through thy knowledge shall the weak brother perish, for
whom Christ died? But when ye sin so against the brethren,
and wound their weak conscience, ye sin against Christ.
Wherefore, if meat make my brother to offend, I will eat no
flesh while the world standeth, lest I make my brother to offend."*—I Cor. 8:9-13.

If your example causes others to do that which grieves
their consciences, to them it is a sin and God holds you guilty
for the harm you have done your brother.

I have letters many times from people who were led into
petting by others, though it offended their consciences and
though those who followed others into sin thereby lost the assurance of the Lord's presence and the joy of His power. Is
your example good or bad when you pet? If you are honest
with yourself in answering that question, you will save years
of smiting conscience and a sense of defilement to others who
might be led astray by following your example.

5. *The Christian's body should be kept sacredly for God
who dwells within.*

The Christian young person has a special reason to be
careful about misuse of bodily passions. His body is the temple of the Holy Spirit of God who dwells within. First Corinthians 6:13-20 warn us, "The body is not for fornication, but
for the Lord" (vs. 13), that "Your bodies are the members
of Christ" (vs. 15), that sex sins are special sins against the
body as no other sins are (vs. 18). Then we are given the
plain command: "What? know ye not that your body is the
temple of the Holy Ghost which is in you, which ye have of

God, and ye are not your own? For ye are bought with a price: therefore glorify God in your body, and in your spirit, which are God's" (vss. 19, 20).

But even unconverted young people, and older ones, must remember that they are not brute beasts to live as animals, revelling in sex passion promiscuously without lawful and holy bonds, without sacred fidelity to a God-given mate. For we are made in the image of God. Christ had a human body like ours. How wicked to debase ourselves and defile our bodies with unholy lust, deliberately inflaming sex passion like whoremongers and harlots, when we are made in the image of God.

Again in I Corinthians 10:31 we are commanded: "Whether therefore ye eat, or drink, or whatsoever ye do, do all to the glory of God." Does petting, arousing sex passion, honor God in your body?

6. *Do nothing that would hinder your prayer life, your spiritual happiness, your joy in the Lord.* In Ephesians there is a long passage beginning with verse 17 of the fourth chapter and continuing through verse 20 in the fifth chapter which has to do with the Christian's joy and power. After naming many sins, Ephesians 4:30 tells us: "And grieve not the holy Spirit of God, whereby ye are sealed unto the day of redemption." Then follows a list of other sins, and Ephesians 5:3 says: "But fornication, and all uncleanness, or covetousness, let it not be once named among you, as becometh saints." And verse 5 says: "For this ye know, that no whoremonger, nor unclean person, nor covetous man, who is an idolater, hath any inheritance in the kingdom of Christ and of God." Then Ephesians 5:11, 12 tell us: "And have no fellowship with the unfruitful works of darkness, but rather reprove them. For it is a shame even to speak of those things which are done of them in secret." The shameful things that young people do in the dark, "the unfruitful works of darkness" related to fornication, grieve the Holy Spirit, and Christians are commanded to have nothing to do with them. Then in Ephesians 5:18 we are commanded: "But be filled with the Spirit."

It will make a difference when you pray. For Timothy, a Christian young man, was commanded, "Flee also youthful lusts; but follow righteousness, faith, charity, peace, with them that call on the Lord out of a pure heart" (II Tim. 2:22). Can you "call on the Lord out of a pure heart" if you do not "flee youthful lusts"? And Timothy was commanded to intreat the younger women "as sisters, with all purity." That certainly shows that he could not please God by fondling them, kissing them, embracing them till both he and they were sexually aroused and their minds defiled with desire.

Marriage is holy and there is no blame, no defilement, no sin in the love-life of husband and wife who reverently remember that they belong to each other and to God. But how the Holy Spirit must be grieved when His temples, our bodies, are defiled by necking and petting! No Christian can maintain his spiritual prosperity who so sins against his body and against others and against God.

A young woman wrote to me telling how she had lost the joy of the Lord and felt guilty and defiled after she had been a party to petting. Many others have told me, in substance, the same thing. To give way to the excitement of physical lust in petting grieves the Holy Spirit.

Tell me, is it as easy to pray after your passions have been inflamed and your conscience defiled by necking and petting? Oh, young people, above all things, I beg you to strive to keep a good conscience before God and not to grieve the Holy Spirit of God who lives within your body!

7. *Do nothing that would hinder your Christian testimony!* If others knew all you do, could you win them to Christ? Would they believe in your sincerity? And if you should try to win to Christ those with whom you pet and arouse desires that are dangerous and evil, would you have power from Heaven to help you? Oh, if one soul should go to Hell because you had ruined your testimony, because you had acted in a way unbecoming a Christian, how terrible that would be! Paul said, "For though I be free from all men, yet have I made myself servant unto all, that I might gain the more" (I Cor. 9:19). Anything to win souls! And again he says, "I am made all things to all men, that I might by all means save some" (I Cor. 9:22). By all means in the world Paul sought to save some. In the same chapter he continues, "And every man that striveth for the mastery is temperate in all things. Now they do it to obtain a corruptible crown; but we an incorruptible. I therefore so run, not as uncertainly: so fight I, not as one that beateth the air: but I keep under my body, and bring it into subjection; lest that by any means, when I have preached to others, I myself should be a castaway" (I Cor. 9:25-27).

Paul says that others who take part in athletic competition

are temperate in all things so they can win in the Olympic games and earn the crown of laurel leaves. And should not a Christian be temperate, carefully keeping his body in subjection, so he may win the soul-winner's crown when "they that turn many to righteousness" shall shine "as the stars for ever and ever," according to Daniel 12:3? So Paul, after preaching to so many, watches lest he should be laid on the shelf, useless to God for soul winning because he does not control his bodily passions and desires!

Oh, young Christian, do not lose your testimony by giving way to carnal desires! Do not let some dear soul for whom Christ died go to Hell because you petted one who is a wicked lost sinner!

Suggestions for Engaged Couples

When two people have come to know that they sincerely love each other and that as a result of this permanent and tested love they plan to marry, certainly they would not act as if they were strangers nor as if they were casual friends. I believe that honorable and earnest Christian people, when engaged, would naturally expect some caressing in most cases, but this need not always be so. Under proper conventional safeguards I believe good people would usually not begrudge engaged lovers their holding hands and an honest good-night kiss. Yet some of the happiest couples I have known never even kissed each other until after marriage. But engaged couples need to hold themselves to strict account. They are not married, and they ought not to act as married people. They have need to observe certain decencies and certain restraints in their love-making. Those who truly love one another can wait for a little while to enjoy each other fully after marriage.

When engaged couples fondle each other overmuch, the stimulation of sex desire may make them very unhappy. It is foolish to arouse, strongly, desires which we have no right to satisfy. On the other hand, engaged couples who tempt themselves may fall into the great sin of adultery. Though they are engaged, yet the adultery is a great sin and sometimes has heartbreaking results.

A young man sadly told me of the breaking of all his plans for the future. He loved a beautiful girl, and she loved him. But in their freedom each with the other their aroused bodily passions overcame them. Not waiting for marriage they abused their love in the scarlet sin. And then love died. He told me that each of them was so shamed and heartsick and so lost respect for each other that their love altogether disappeared and marriage was impossible. So, young people, if you want happy marriage, then while you are engaged be moderate and decent. See that no critic can ever hint later that you were impure before marriage. See that there is such reverence, each for the other's body, that marriage will be all the sweeter because of your present loving restraint. See that your love-making be so modest that it does not unduly arouse passions, but only expresses affection in a way that would not grieve the blessed Holy Spirit of God, and in a way that you will never have cause to regret, and in a way of which you will never have cause to be ashamed.

If by petting and too much intimacy engaged couples are led into the scarlet sin, even if they go on and marry, it will probably be the cause of constant grief. The husband when angry may accuse the wife of having been impure before marriage. And each may feel that the other was so weak in character that he or she may have likewise sinned with others, or would have done so if strongly tempted. The only way to the best happiness in marriage is in continence and honorable self-control and decent love before marriage.

We have written plainly and at some length on this subject of petting, believing that millions of young people who sin and are tempted to commit the scarlet sin after the customary petting might be saved heartbreak and much trouble and sin if they be lovingly and intelligently warned.

Be Charitable; Do Not Judge Harshly

I feel that older people need here a special warning. Many who read this message are older people. Your eyes are opened more than the eyes of many young people to the dangers of sex sins. Sometimes Christians who were licentious and vile in their early lives before they were saved, now think they see every kind of wickedness in young people who simply follow the easy but dangerous and wrong customs of the world, having never been taught what petting may lead to. Certainly petting and love-making are far more wicked when deliberately planned to lead to adultery than when ignorant young people, unwarned, do not mean more than good fellowship and friendly affection. Promiscuous petting among young people is still deadly dangerous and wrong, however innocent the intentions. But we do wrong to be bitter and accuse of wicked *intentions* those who, it may be, have never entertained the idea of adultery and would be surprised to know their danger.

Younger people, and those older people whose minds are defiled with a wicked past and wicked thoughts, must likewise be careful not to judge others. God sees the heart. Good doctors, often Christian men, may, having become accustomed to the care of women patients, operations, and childbirth, find themselves disciplined till they are not specially tempted by necessary contact with the opposite sex in professional duties. That would demand high ideals, a good conscience, and a clean mind. Should we think evil every time relatives embrace at parting? One of the most modest women I know, a remarkable, Spirit-filled soul winner. one night, after long pleading and teaching, won a man to Christ as his wife joined in the entreaty; and then she hugged the man in joy when he was saved. It was unusual. In a younger woman, dealing with a stranger, the embrace would have been out of place. It might have been hurtful, and would have, at least, been subject to unfavorable comment. But in that godly woman, so wholly given to soul winning, none present thought it anything but the natural reaction of joy over a sinner won after much pleading. I wanted to embrace him too. Age has a tendency to cool the passions of youth if people live cleanly. When minds are pure and kept in holy restraint, people are kept more easily from sin.

I have said the above lest polluted minds set out to make evil of every act by innocent people. If we ourselves are clean in heart we can help others to see the danger in promiscuous petting and necking, but we would sin greatly if we set out to judge the hearts of others, accusing them of intentions they may not have, and of sins they may not have committed.

Oh, young people, let us so live that the blessed Spirit of God within us will not be grieved, so we will not be led into grievous sin nor tempt others to sin, and also so we may not cause others to be offended or to stumble, and Christ's cause be hurt.

As a minister of Jesus Christ I send this message out with prayer that it may bless many.

CHAPTER III

Principles of a Successful and Happy Marriage

I. *Christians Are to Marry Only Christians*

II. *Christians Should Have the Direct Leading of God About Marriage Plans*

III. *A Successful Marriage Must Be Based on Genuine Heart Agreement of the Couple Who Marry*

IV. *Those Who Want a Happy, Successful Marriage Should Accept a Bible Standard for the Marriage and the Home*

V. *Successful Marriages Are Those That Are Made "for Better or for Worse," and "Until Death Do Us Part"*

VI. *The Successful Marriage Should Have the Blessing of Children*

VII. *Genuine Love Is an Essential of a Happy Marriage*

VIII. *An Honorable Engagement Tends to Promote a Happy, Successful Marriage*

IX. *A Public Christian Wedding Is a Good Start Toward a Happy Marriage*

Marriage is intended to be happy. By reading the account of God's dealing with Adam in creating a wife for him, it is obvious that God intended marriage for happiness. The Scripture says: "Whoso findeth a wife findeth a good thing, and obtaineth favour of the Lord" (Prov. 18:22), and " . . . a prudent wife is from the Lord" (Prov. 19:14). Proverbs 31:10-12 has some earnest words from God about the prize a man has who has found a good wife. "Who can find a virtuous woman? for her price is far above rubies. The heart of her husband doth safely trust in her so that he shall have no need of spoil. She will do him good and not evil all the days of her life." The plain implication of this Scripture is that marriage tends to happiness, when a good man marries a good woman.

Isaac must have been lonely when his mother died. When Abraham sent his servant into the far country to find a bride for Isaac, and Rebekah returned with the caravan, we are told that "Isaac brought her into his mother Sarah's tent, and took Rebekah, and she became his wife; and he loved her:

and Isaac was comforted after his mother's death" (Gen. 24:67).

Marriage ought to be happy. If marriage is what God intended it to be, it will be happy and prosperous and successful and permanent.

Now since marriage is a divine institution and the oldest in the world, since marriage is ordained of God, there ought to be rules and principles laid down in the Bible for a happy, prosperous marriage, and that is true. Those who heed the clear teachings of the Word of God may marry happily and live happily, though they may have troubles and temptations incident to any life on this earth. There are certain added responsibilities and cares that are brought on by marriage and the responsibilities of a family. But nevertheless God's Word tells us how to have happy marriages, successful marriages, when love stays sweet and clean, when hope springs eternal in the human breast, when there are days of comforts in the midst of the cares and the burdens of life. Marriage if according to the Word of God can be a happy and beautiful venture, a *bon voyage*.

What are these Bible principles that show how to live a happy, successful married life? I will give some of them here. May God give us grace to take them to heart.

I. Christians Are to Marry Only Christians

Nothing more important can be said on the question of marriage, it seems to me, than that Christian people should marry only Christians. Marriage is a divine institution, a holy trust from God. The duties of a marriage necessarily involve Christian character. No one can really be the best husband or the best wife who is not willing to follow God's plan for a home. How could anyone be a good father or a good mother of children who does not know and does not love God? And how could anyone keep his vows of marriage adequately, spiritually, who does not love God and does not plan to please God?

The relationship of husband and wife is so intimate, so dear, as well as so permanent, that there is certain to be a continual heartache and a continual clash of will and purpose between the husband and the wife when one is saved and the other is lost.

At first, the attraction of love is so great that each dreams the other is his perfect ideal. The proverb well says that, "Love is blind." Many a Christian girl has married an unsaved man and in her foolish heart thought, "After we are married, he will never drink again. He says he loves me so much he will go to church with me. He is so dear and good and lovable, surely all he needs is to join the church." Such girls have found later to their deep distress that they married an ungodly man. The devotion of love to a wife is not strong enough to make a good man out of one who does not love God. No Christian girl is ever safe to marry an unsaved man. No Christian man is ever safe to marry an unsaved girl. Such marriages do not usually turn out well and happily. They never turn out happily except when God in His great mercy helps one mate to win the other. How often that never comes to pass! And how often, if it does come, it comes only after years of heartache and trouble and sin and burden!

On this matter, II Corinthians 6:14-16 says: "Be ye not unequally yoked together with unbelievers: for what fellowship hath righteousness with unrighteousness? and what communion hath light with darkness? And what concord hath Christ with Belial? or what part hath he that believeth with an infidel? And what agreement hath the temple of God with idols? for ye are the temple of the living God; as God hath said, I will dwell in them, and walk in them; and I will be their God, and they shall be my people."

You see, a saved person and an unbeliever cannot have real fellowship. "What fellowship hath righteousness with unrighteousness?" They cannot have real communion, for "what communion hath light with darkness?" You see, there is an innate and fundamental difference in the life and character and heart attitude of one who is saved and one who is lost. One loves God and the other despises Him. One has trusted Christ for salvation, the other has rejected Him.

There can be no real concord between a Christian and an unconverted sinner, because, "What concord hath Christ with Belial?" Or again the Scripture says, "What part hath he that believeth with an infidel?" (The word infidel here is simply the Greek word for unbeliever.)

How can a married couple live in agreement day by day, one saved and the other lost? For verse 16 says, "And what agreement hath the temple of God with idols? for ye are the temple of the living God; as God hath said, I will dwell in them, and walk in them; and I will be their God, and they shall be my people." A saved person has the indwelling Spirit of God who abides in his body, and that is the one great central fact of his life. Whether you know it or not, whether you are always conscious of it or not, if you are a converted person, a child of God, the Spirit of God dwells in your body and your body is the holy temple of God. How wicked, how certain to lead to heartache it is when a Christian turns this temple of God over to the control and whim of an unconverted child of Satan! You see, the marriage of a Christian with an unbeliever is essentially unfitting and wicked.

So Christians should never marry those who are unsaved. And preachers should not take part in such marriage ceremonies, in which one party of the marriage claims to have been converted and the other does not claim to have been converted. Such marriages grieve God and are certain to bring unhappiness.

In I Corinthians 7:39 the Scripture speaks of the marriage of widows: "The wife is bound by the law as long as her husband liveth; but if her husband be dead, she is at liberty to be married to whom she will; only in the Lord."

It is all right for a widow to marry again after her husband is dead. But it must be remembered that she is free to marry "only in the Lord." No woman, whether maid or widow, is free to marry except in the Lord, if she be a Christian. Saved people ought not to marry unsaved people. It is an unequal yoke. It is certain to lead to sin and heartache and unhappiness.

Solomon, the wisest man who ever lived, with a divinely given wisdom, yet sinned in this matter in marrying an unconverted woman. In II Chronicles 8:11 we are told, "And Solomon brought up the daughter of Pharaoh out of the city of David unto the house that he had built for her: for he said, My wife shall not dwell in the house of David king of Israel, because the places are holy, whereunto the ark of the Lord hath come." How foolish for any man to marry a woman who was not fit to come to the house of God, not fit to come where the ark of God had been brought!

The sad story of Solomon's fall into sin is told in I Kings 11. Verses 1-4 say: "But king Solomon loved many strange women, together with the daughter of Pharaoh, women of the Moabites, Ammonites, Edomites, Zidonians, and Hittites; Of the nations concerning which the Lord said unto the children of Israel, Ye shall not go in to them, neither shall they come in unto you: for surely they will turn away your heart after their gods: Solomon clave unto these in love. And he had seven hundred wives, princesses, and three hundred concubines; and his wives turned away his heart. For it came to pass, when Solomon was old, that his wives turned away his heart after other gods: and his heart was not perfect with the Lord his God, as was the heart of David his father." You see, even Solomon, the wisest man who ever lived, could not resist the temptation that was brought on by his marriage to ungodly heathen women.

In Nehemiah's day when a remnant of Israel was brought back from captivity and when they intermarried with the heathen people round about, Nehemiah told them of their sin and used Solomon as an illustration of the fearful results that come to people who are God's and yet marry ungodly people.

If you love God and believe the Bible, if you are a converted child of God, and if you want a happy, successful marriage, then certainly you must not marry a lost person. To do so would be sin and would surely bring unhappiness.

II. Christians Should Have the Direct Leading of God About Marriage Plans

A Christian can have the leading of the Holy Spirit in the matter of marriage plans. Every young man should prayerfully seek to find God's will about his wife. Many Christian young men have prayed God to give them a wife. Many Christian young women have prayed God to select their husbands. How often it has turned out happily. If a Christian ought to be able to pray about anything, he surely ought to be able to pray for wisdom from God on this matter. Young people should be taught to pray very much about marriage and not to go ahead without the clear leading of God.

"He that followeth me shall not walk in darkness, but shall have the light of life" (John 8:12). In John 16:13 Jesus said, "Howbeit when he, the Spirit of truth, is come, he will guide you into all truth." Surely the Holy Spirit can enlighten the heart and mind of a Christian and show him the will of God about marriage plans.

So it is important that a young man or woman should not cling to his own will. One should be willing to say, "Lord, I give up my sweetheart if she is not the woman You have for me." Every girl ought to be able to say, "Lord, I do not want any man who is not the husband You have selected for me. If I feel the pull of love toward him, then, Lord, You overcome it and help me to learn to love the man that I ought to marry."

I feel that God answered and led me in my decision as I walked up and down a country road one night, asking Him if the girl I loved was the right one for me.

I was deeply moved when visiting Bob Jones College as Mrs. Rice and I stood in the parlor before a great picture of Christ and heard behind us a young couple in prayer. They had met in the closing days of the commencement week to say good-bye for the summer. They thanked God for the love He had given them and asked Him to have His perfect way in their plans. I believe that God is glad to give guidance to those who wait upon Him and are willing to take His will when it is shown to them. Every Christian can have clear leading from Heaven about marriage plans. If one reads this who is not quite sure of the will of God, then wait on Him and pray. If there is an unrest, a sense of unease and fearfulness, then wait on God until that is settled before you say, "Yes," to the plans made for marriage.

III. A Successful Marriage Must Be Based on Genuine Heart Agreement of the Couple Who Marry

The Bible standard for marriage is that "they twain shall be one flesh" (Matt. 19:5).

How often marriage goes on the rocks and lives are blighted because people married only for 'love.' Love alone is a very poor basis for a happy and successful marriage!

That may sound strange to Americans who have gotten all their conception of love and marriage from the moving picture screens and from current novels. Nevertheless, the wisdom of the ages proves that what I say is true. Love alone is not a good basis for marriage.

Of course, I mean that the attraction that one person may have for another naturally is not enough for marriage. If love is to include agreement about all great essential matters of life, a oneness of mind and heart, then, of course, love would be in itself the one all-covering requirement for marriage. But usually what people call love is not that at all.

It is true that there is a certain magnetic physical attraction which some men and some women have for each other. It is not likely that people usually learn to love and marry the one person who would have for them the greatest physical attraction. Some women have more attraction for any given man than some other women would have. But this physical attraction is certainly not enough upon which to base a happy marriage.

Those who marry principally on the plane of physical attraction often find that they have joined themselves in wedlock to a person who is wholly different from them, one with whom they cannot be happy. Fires of passion soon burn lower. Sex attraction is a fleeting thing, and at best is by itself an unsatisfactory thing, so that the woman who was once very attractive to you may later be hateful. The man who once so thrilled you, may become abhorrent to you.

Let me illustrate what I am saying. In some unusual cases a white person and one of Negro blood become attracted to each other sexually. In some publicized cases, white women have married Negro men and professed to be devoted to them. The newspapers once told how some 4,000 Negro soldiers in the United States Army had, while in Europe, married white women, and now they seek to bring these white wives back to the United States. I am not now talking about the results to society, the unrest and harm that such mixed marriages give. Those sex attractions, or what most people call love, may be present; but that is not enough to make happiness. Actually, people who are reared with entirely different environments, who grow up with a different set of values, different ideals and different companions, will find that they are not happy together. They are not really of one mind and heart. Those two have not become one flesh. Any such marriage is wrong and doomed to misery and unhappiness.

Sometimes a Catholic and a Protestant, each of them equally sincere, fall in love. Such marriages do not usually turn out very happily. They have entirely different conceptions on important matters, deep-seated prejudices, traditions, and convictions that differ widely. Such people are not of one mind and one heart. In a spiritual sense they often cannot well become "one flesh." Perhaps a Catholic wife insists that the baby should be sprinkled by a priest, and feels that she is duty bound to rear the child in the Catholic faith. Perhaps the Protestant husband loves his wife devotedly but is not willing for the child to be reared as a Catholic, to be taught to pray to the Virgin Mary and to the saints, to wear a rosary, and to study in a parochial school or convent. Perhaps the Catholic wife feels duty bound to go to the priest in confession concerning the most intimate details of her life and thought. Perhaps her Protestant husband feels that such confession is essentially wrong, and he resents the idea of his wife's being questioned by another man, perhaps on the most intimate details of her married life and of her thoughts. I say that there is not in such a couple the fundamental agreement, the oneness, that makes for happiness.

If one mate is a worldly Christian who sees no harm in the picture shows, the dance, in cocktails, and in gambling, and the other mate is a fervent Bible-believer, a separated Christian who believes that he ought to keep himself apart from worldliness and sin; how can such a couple be happy? They are not fully agreed. They are not of one mind and one soul.

Suppose the husband wants children and feels that this is the normal and right issue of marriage, and suppose his wife feels that the bearing of children involves too much burden and responsibility and she does not wish to do it. They have not come to a clear agreement and are not one.

If a couple really expects to be happy and to be prosperous in their marriage, they should make sure that on important matters they are in agreement. On matters of conscience, on the matters where happiness necessarily is entailed, then those who marry should be of one mind. That truth is involved in the nature of marriage itself and in the Bible requirement that the husband and wife become one.

IV. Those Who Want a Happy, Successful Marriage Should Accept a Bible Standard for the Marriage and the Home

Remember that the Bible tells how to have a happy home. Then those who want a happy home should set out to follow the Bible. The home where the Bible is read daily, where there is family worship, and where God's Word is taught to the children, where thanks are given at meals and little children are taught to pray kneeling at Mother's knee or by their beds, is likely to be a happy home.

After settling that Christians should marry only Christians, I think that no single matter is of such vital importance for a happy home as this setting up of the home on a Bible standard. Where the Word of God is read and followed, where prayer is regularly made by husband and wife together, where the little children are taught about God, where God is taken into the family life in a real way, that home is almost certain to be a happy one. How could it be otherwise?

But a Bible standard for the home would mean that a husband should set out to be the head of the home and take the responsibility before God which is given him in the Word of God. He should remember that his wife is the weaker vessel, and he should give honor to her, "giving honour unto the wife, as unto the weaker vessel, and as being heirs together of the grace of life," as I Peter 3:7 commands. He should feel he is God's deputy. He should take the responsibility of leading out in matters of morals, in religion, in the example of the Christian life before the children, and in exercise of authority and discipline. A wife who accepts the Bible standard for a Christian home would necessarily set out to be subject to her husband and to obey him, as is so many times commanded in the Bible. See Genesis 3:16; Ephesians 5:22-31; I Peter 3:1-7; and other Scriptures.

Happy is the young couple who finds ahead of time God's plan for the home and sets out to follow it.

V. Successful Marriages Are Those That Are Made "for Better or for Worse," and "Until Death Do Us Part"

Marriage is not intended as a brief experiment. One should never enter marriage except with the wholehearted vow that it is for a lifetime and that the marriage is to be broken only by death. Those who feel that they can be married and if they do not get adjusted, if they are not compatible, if they do not "make a go of it," they can then get a divorce and try someone else, are headed for heartbreak and ruin. That is no attitude of mind that God can bless. That is no adequate arming to meet the problems of marriage. No, those who marry are dishonest and cannot mean their marriage vows if they do not set out to make this marriage a permanent matter.

Every girl should have this in mind: "If my husband turns out to be a drunkard, I must live with him until one of us dies. If he beats me, I must love him still and obey him and be his wife and bear his children and wait on him when he is sick and keep my vows until death parts us." Every man who marries ought to say in his heart: "This is my wife, the only wife I will ever have, at least until death separates us. I must love her, whether she deserves it or not. I must love her and keep her as my wife whether the beds are made, whether the meals are attractive, whether her tongue is sharp or not. This marriage is for better or for worse. This marriage is to last until death shall part us." Nobody has a right to marry on any other basis. To do so is to invite disaster. One is not truly married in his heart (though of course the marriage is binding in the sight of God as well as in the sight of man) who does not mean business enough to intend and vow that the marriage shall last until death.

When poverty comes, when sickness comes, when youth has fled away, when the personal attraction of husband and wife has gone, then it will often take more than a high-hearted experimental attitude to guarantee the permanence and happiness of the home. A holy resolution to be all that the marriage vows involve is absolutely essential to a happy and successful marriage. Marriage is permanent. When marriage is not permanent, then the hearts of those who enter it are adulterous and dishonest, and the vows are unholy and insincere in the sight of God.

No doubt many hasty marriages would be prevented if it were clearly understood that this is the one chance for happiness in marriage and we must make this good or live in misery. The foolish propaganda to make divorce easy and to withdraw the odium that has attached to it encourages many people to marry who are not fit to marry, who are not committed to the principles involved in the marriage vows. Let it always be understood among Christians that marriage is to be permanent and that a marriage cannot be broken decently by anything but death. That attitude in itself will go far toward insuring a happy marriage.

VI. The Successful Marriage Should Have the Blessing of Children

Psalm 127:3-5 says: "Lo, children are an heritage of the Lord: and the fruit of the womb is his reward. As arrows are in the hand of a mighty man; so are children of the youth. Happy is the man that hath his quiver full of them; they shall not be ashamed, but they shall speak with the enemies in the gate."

Couples who do not have children are more apt to have divorce. Statistics in every divorce court in the country show that couples who are not willing to have children are more likely to find their marriage gone on the rocks than those who follow the plan of God and have children.

Children give the husband and wife something in common. They make something worth living for, worth maintaining the marriage and home for. What man is there who wants to give up his children? No normal man, no man of high ideals and noble instincts. What woman is there who would be willing to bring her little children up without a father and without the protection and care and provision that fathers ordinarily give and ought to give? No normal woman. Many times a home has been saved by one child. And how much more when there are several children in the home is there a tendency to maintain the home, to overlook differences, to talk them out and plan about them and pray about them until peace is restored in the home.

Little tiny baby fingers hold fathers and mothers together. It is not so important to a wife that her husband scolded her or was heartless and cruel in some matter if her mind is set on the little one and the future of the little one. She can well realize that her own feelings are not so important. What man is there who thinks as much of his own pleasure if he really loves his own little children and thinks and plans for their welfare? One of the essentials that helps to guarantee a happy home is the coming of little children. Let every home then plan for children. Let every engaged couple talk it over ahead of time and agree that their marriage will be a marriage in truth and will expect the normal fruit of marriage, that is, little children sent from God to bless the home and bind the hearts of father and mother together forever.

It is true that there are sometimes happy homes where God has not seen fit to send little children. But certainly these homes would be happier if children were there. Many times the very presence of little children in the home keeps the marriage from going on the rocks.

VII. Genuine Love Is an Essential of a Happy Marriage

Ephesians 5:25 says, "Husbands, love your wives, even as Christ also loved the church. . . ." Titus 2:4 says that older women are to teach younger women "to love their husbands." Happy, successful marriage must have mutual love in it.

I should like to make a distinction between sex attraction and true love. Sex attraction may be a *part* of love, but it certainly is not all of any true love that is fit for marriage.

One of the dangers of the modern way of petting and necking is that young people may become attracted to one another physically and may be rushed off their feet into an engagement without any real love one for the other. Just the attraction of animal-like bodies is not enough to guarantee a happy home. There ought to be a genuine respect and admiration of husband for wife and wife for husband.

In fact love may usually be depended upon to come, when other factors are properly cared for. The European custom and South American custom of marriages that are planned by the parents of the bride and groom has often proved itself most successful. When a girl has a beautiful character, when she comes from a good home, when she has been properly reared and disciplined and educated, and when she has a normal and Christian attitude toward marriage and its responsibilities, she will make a good wife. In fact it is not hard for a normal and honorable man to love such a woman. Love ought to follow and usually does follow when such marriages are made with Christian people and on high standards of honor and character.

I am not advocating that we do away with love. I think we ought to expect a genuine love to be one of the great essentials to make every marriage happy. But certainly we ought to make sure that that love is based on character, a genuine admiration and understanding of one mate for the other.

Young people who enjoy each other's presence when they neck and pet, but cannot sit apart from each other and talk about things near to their hearts and be happy each in the other's presence, will find that they probably do not have true love. They are only attracted sexually and physically one to the other. That is not a safe basis for marriage.

Young people who cannot enjoy each the other's letters without the immediate physical contact of touch, had better beware. People who truly love one another can enjoy being together even when they do not touch one another. There ought to be a genuine enjoyment, a fellowship, a partnership that does not depend on sex attraction.

Of course, people who love one another will want to caress

one another. And love properly will include this desire to have the kisses and caresses of the one who is loved. But it is not true love fit for marriage, it is not the kind that will help to guarantee happiness, if the love does not go much deeper than physical attraction.

Young man, do you love a young woman because she is good, because she is kind? Do you love her because she has such a sweet voice, because she is musical? Do you love her because she is such a devoted Christian, so eager to serve God? Do you love her because she has pity for those in trouble, because she has laughter and a light in her eyes, and a quick mind? Do you love her because she has real Christian qualities? If so, then that is the kind of love which ought to be in every true marriage.

Young woman, do you love your intended husband because he is strong, because he is brave, because he is sensible? Does he have the kind of character that you would admire in your own brother or father? Does he seem to you the wisest young fellow you ever saw? Do you like the way he stands up straight, like his strong body, like his kindness to his mother and his gentleness to old people? Are you proud of his Christian character, his faithful, clean life, his ambition and plans for the future? If so, then that is the kind of love upon which happiest marriages are built. To be sure, the one you love should be personally attractive to you, but make sure that mere coarse animal attraction is not the sum total of love that guarantees success and happiness in marriage.

I suggest that each of you check up carefully on the family of the one you plan to marry. Young man, is the girl's mother a lovable woman? Do you admire the way she keeps house, do you admire the way she talks, do you admire her character? Well, it is very likely that the girl you are about to marry will be like her mother. You do not think so now. It may be that you are deeply attracted by the girl. When she turns out to have the kind of character and to be the kind of homemaker and housekeeper and wife that her mother is, stop and consider whether or not she will please you then. Real love ought to be based on what people really are, not on animal attraction.

Young woman, before you marry that young man, I suggest that you stop and consider. Do you admire his father? Do you want the kind of a man that his father is? Do you find that altogether aside from the attraction the young man has for you personally, he is a most admirable and desirable young man, judged by his family, his associates, his work in school, his job, his treatment of others, his devotion to Christ? Make sure that the love is really a love of character, a love of personality, instead of mere fleshly attraction. Then if God gives the personal attraction too, you may feel assured that love is on a safe and honorable basis that is lasting and will help to guarantee a happy and successful marriage.

VIII.   An Honorable Engagement Tends to Promote a Happy, Successful Marriage

Becoming engaged is a very serious matter. There are certain conventions of decency which civilized people expect in this matter. One who observes certain rules of honor and Christian character in the matter of an engagement to be married is well on the way to a happy and successful marriage.

First of all, let the engagement be genuine. If you do not expect and fully intend to marry, then you are not truly engaged. Young people who have a passing infatuation for each other and who want to take liberties that only engaged people are allowed, are sinning against each other and themselves and helping to unfit themselves for marriage. No young man should propose except on an honorable intention to marry, an intention which is based upon genuine love and admiration, and is the result of mature thought and prayer. And no girl should accept such an engagement and promise herself to a man or permit any claim of engagement until she feels genuinely sure he is the only man for her and until her heart's love and devotion have been truly given to him. An engagement should be genuine, a contract to marry which is sincere and with every intention of fulfillment.

Second, an engagement should not be too short. People who become engaged ought to have a few months, under ordinary circumstances, in which to know each other better. They ought now to be more frank with one another, and ought each to become better acquainted with the other. Some time for perfect understanding now may show that the engagement was a mistake. On the other hand, it may make the contracting parties even more sure of their love and even happier in their marriage.

Third, engagements should not be an excuse for unseemly

liberties and license. Engaged couples are not married. If they have no reserve, if they exercise no normal and decent restraint, they are likely to become disgusted one with the other, and love is likely to seem a tawdry and tarnished thing. Young engaged couples, I urge you to be restrained and decent, and have no regrets. Particularly let me give this warning. In these free and easy days when young people have very little chaperonage (and God pity us, very little teaching!), sometimes young people feel that they belong to one another and they take the liberties that belong only to married people. I remember that a young man told me with a broken heart how he had loved a girl with all the devotion of his heart. They planned to be married. Both had put the other first, and it seemed an ideal match. But the engagement was long, and they petted each other freely, and desire overcame them, and they fell into sin, the scarlet sin. Then, instead of loving each other, their love turned to disgust. He never wanted to see her again. He told me how all the dreams of his life had been wrecked on the altar of unseemly desire. Young people, if you want to maintain love, then be sure you observe the rules of decent society. The privileges of husband and wife do not belong to engaged couples. Adultery is a shameful, hateful thing, and that is what your sin will be, if you do not restrain yourself.

Again and again people have told me how they were guilty of adultery before they married, and ever after there was the stain on their consciences. One woman told me how she had hated her husband for more than twenty years because he led her into adultery before they were married. A man told me how he had lost all love for his wife, in fact had never respected her fully, because she had allowed him to take the privileges of a husband when he was not yet a husband. The love that he had had for her had been devoted and had involved all the honorable passion of his young heart, but he could never forget the shame that had darkened that love. I warn you now that sin committed in time of engagement will come out to haunt you later in marriage. In God's name and for the sake of your own happiness, young engaged couples, do not commit this sin. And do not go far enough with caresses to unduly stir the passions and desires that you have no right to fulfill until you are married.

An honorable engagement is one of the essentials of a happy, successful marriage.

Let me say frankly now that when a young couple is engaged and when either comes to feel that the engagement was a mistake, it is far better to break the engagement than to go on and marry. A young man had better break the girl's heart now by telling her frankly that he doubts his own love, doubts the wisdom of this marriage, than to make her miserable for many years, not being able to love her as she would desire. Of course, no honorable man wants to jilt a girl and no nice girl wants to jilt or break the heart of any man. But it is better to talk things over frankly, better to come to an understanding and to break the engagement if need be than to have a life of unhappiness because of haste now, or because of a sense of necessity to carry out prearranged plans.

Sometimes a little season apart to pray and plan and wait on God will settle the whole matter satisfactorily. Just now I think of a missionary couple, wonderfully happy in Africa, who came to doubt the wisdom of their engagement and for a season broke it. But as they waited and prayed, God led them together again and they have been a beautiful example of married happiness.

I think just now also of a farmer who after his engagement had a great doubt arise in his heart. Did he truly love this girl to whom he had given his hand and promised his heart's devotion for a lifetime? But after an absence of some time, they were together again, and he found her beautiful beyond his remembrance of her, and found her more lovely and fascinating than he had ever dreamed. Their marriage has been wonderfully happy now for more than twenty years.

IX. A Public Christian Wedding Is a Good Start Toward a Happy Marriage

Bible marriages referred to in the New Testament were marked by public, honorable announcement and ceremonies as we see by the marriage at Cana which Jesus attended, and by His parable of the ten bridesmaids, wise and foolish, in Matthew 25:1-13.

Runaway marriages are not as often happy as are marriages with the approval of relatives and friends.

Marriages, when the ceremony is conducted by the justice of the peace or a judge, are not as often happy and more often result in divorce than marriages in a church. For many reasons it is advisable to have a Christian marriage ceremony with the loved ones and friends about. Such a wedding should be openly, publicly announced.

Sometimes a home wedding may be preferable, but in any case a minister of the Gospel should perform the ceremony. The marriage should be publicly announced ahead of time with invitations to those who are expected to be present. Then announcements should be sent to other friends who would not be invited. The whole matter ought to be a publicly acknowledged contract. Every good man is proud of his bride. Every woman who marries ought to be proud of the husband she marries. A marriage is a contract between two individuals. But it is of profound importance to society. The community ought to be taken into account. Loved ones and friends ought to be present with their prayers and blessing. Let us make much of weddings. Let us count them as a Christian ceremony. Let us enter into the holy vows of marriage with prayer and high resolve and holy responsibilities publicly acknowledged. Church weddings are worth what they cost.

When two young people have announced their engagement, when they have come together publicly in the presence of many friends and loved ones and there have taken solemn vows, when they are now on record for better or for worse to live together until death shall part them, it is more likely that they themselves have taken the matter seriously, that they know their own minds, than if it were a hastily planned adventure in a runaway marriage or in a marriage quickly brought about by a justice of the peace.

Before great crowds of friends and relatives people do not take lightly such holy vows. Let us count marriage as a matter of great importance to society. Let it be done with holy pride and public acknowledgment of devotion. That adds stability and dignity to marriage and tends toward happiness and permanency.

CHAPTER IV

Some Things That Should Delay Marriage

"Art thou loosed from a wife? seek not a wife."—I Cor. 7:27.

An unhappy marriage can be very much worse than no marriage at all! All over America men and women have told me that they made a great mistake in marrying when they did, or in marrying the persons they married. At very best, marriage is not for everybody. Paul said, "I say therefore to the unmarried and widows, It is good for them if they abide even as I. But if they cannot contain, let them marry: for it is better to marry than to burn" (I Cor. 7:8, 9). In the preceding verse Paul, after wishing that all men were single as he was, says by the Holy Spirit, "But every man hath his proper gift of God, one after this manner, and another after that." So some men would do well if they never married, as would some women. Life will be happier and more useful for some if they do not marry at all. For millions of other people, married life will be a miserable failure and much worse than no marriage, if they do not take time and precaution to marry the right person and marry with the right viewpoint.

So, we may set it up as a piece of sound advice that no one should be in a hurry to marry. The old proverb has sage wisdom: "Marry in haste; repent at leisure." And to countless hasty young people who married contrary to the advice of wiser people, this adage has been quoted: "You have made your bed: now you must lie in it." Marriage itself is not a certain key to happiness. Under some circumstances marriage can be the most miserable state in the world. Let no one marry hastily, then, and let every intelligent person take time for grave consideration and adequate preparation for this most solemn step of marriage.

Certain conditions are most favorable for a happy and successful marriage. Therefore, intelligent people ought to wait until these happy conditions are met so that marriage may be happy and successful and the home a bit of Heaven upon earth.

I.   Wait Until You Are Old Enough to Marry

Some people are old enough for marriage sooner than others. I remember a young man who married at nineteen. He had been out of school several years. He had served an apprenticeship as a cowhand on a big ranch and already owned a ranch of his own. He had already learned to work, learned to save money, was regarded as a grown man in the community, with good business judgment and steady character. When he married at nineteen, no one felt he was too young.

I know another man who when he was nineteen married a girl of fifteen. They moved out to West Texas, made their home, grew their family. They were happy in their home life, they became well-developed Christians, they prospered in business, and all their children were sent through college. However, neither the man nor his wife had finished high school when they married. In those early days few schools of high school grade were available. Obviously they are not good examples for the present generation. The man had been at work several years when he was nineteen years old. The girl who married at fifteen had long been accustomed to cooking for a large family, knew how to make her own clothes, was accustomed to hard work, and was seriously prepared in mind for the business of a home and family.

Actual statistics prove that teenage marriages fail more often than marriages in the early twenties. Now many states require a man to be twenty-one years old and a girl to be eighteen years old before they can marry without parental consent, and some states have an older standard than that.

Maturity of mind, experience and training are factors to be considered. In industrial districts and among young people who would not go to college or take further training beyond high school, marriages will be at a somewhat younger age than among families whose children go to college or take special business or professional training after high school. Families whose living standards are higher require their young people to wait for marriage until advanced education has been completed and when the income of the young husband is larger.

Ordinarily I would say that young men ought not to marry younger than twenty-one and girls ought not to marry younger than eighteen. In cases where college training is involved, or where the husband will go into a profession like medicine, the law, or the ministry, marriage ought oftentimes to be delayed so as not to hinder.

But child romances are not the basis for a happy marriage. Children in their teens usually do not know enough to select a satisfactory mate for life. Wait until you know more of each other, know more of other men and women, know more of the world. Wait until you have maturity of judgment and know what you want.

Isaac was forty years old before he got married (Gen. 25:20). His marriage was a particularly happy marriage. Many others of the happy marriages in Bible times and in modern times have been by people who waited until they were old enough to know their own minds, old enough to take up and carry well the responsibilities which marriage entails.

II.   Wait for Love

Multiplied thousands of young people, I am persuaded, marry before they have time to be really in love.

Girls often accept the first proposal of marriage they get. It goes without saying that in such a case a girl finds her suitor somewhat interesting and attractive or she would not have gone with him long enough to receive a proposal of marriage. But many girls are naturally fearful of having to live a lonely, single life. They want security, they want a home, they want a husband and children. I believe this is particularly a temptation of girls who have had to work hard for a living or girls who are not happy in the home of their fathers and mothers and who think marriage will be a release from drudgery, a way to happiness and a security for old age. Often, according to Dorothy Dix, such girls do not love their husbands, do not make their homes happy, and are not prepared for the inevitable sacrifices which are required in wifehood and motherhood. But any girl had better wait some years, if need be, keep her job, drink her glass of milk and eat her sandwich on a lunch-counter stool, and hold on to her ideals and dreams until the right man comes along, one she can love with all her heart.

Often young people, in the fashion of the day, neck and pet and mistake the animal passion of sex desire for love, and so marry to find that they are not happily mated, that they have nothing in common, and that a rich and beautiful love, necessary for the best happiness in marriage, is utterly lacking. That warns us, first, that necking and petting may blind us to the lack of true love; and, second, that young people should know each other well and be sure of a holy love one for the other, which is composed partly of admiration, partly of enjoying one another's company, partly of unselfish devotion of each toward the other, and only partly of physical attraction.

Sometimes young people fancy themselves in love and get engaged, when some months of constant association prove that they are not fitted for one another and that they do not truly love one another as husband and wife should love. In such case, it is far better that they should break the engagement, whatever temporary embarrassment or hurt it might bring, rather than to go ahead with the marriage which is so likely to prove unhappy. People ought not to marry without love.

A beautiful, talented girl, a devoted Christian, was engaged to be married when twenty-two or twenty-three years old, after she had graduated from college. Yet there was not perfect assurance that the marriage anticipated was the will of God. The man to whom she was engaged was a good man, a useful man, with nice personality. But friendship, even admiration, was not enough for marriage; and reluctantly she broke the engagement to wait for God's best blessing and the fullness of love. As she did postgraduate work, her hand was sought in marriage by a talented and attractive man of highest character. The best days of her maidenhood were passing by and she was rapidly passing the marriageable age, as it is generally considered. Yet she was not willing to marry, for a home and security, a man whom she admired but loved only in a measurable degree. After prayer she waited. After college, graduate school and three years of teaching, she met exactly the man God had in mind for her. Her heart was perfectly satisfied. Their love ripened beautifully. Each had met the ideal long cherished and found the love long anticipated. Now she is the wife of a devoted minister, wonderfully happy, and certain that she is in the will of God. It paid to wait for the fullness of love.

III. Wait to Know Each Other

Short engagements are dangerous. They often do not turn out happily. Young people should not become engaged until they have known each other well for long months, or, better yet, years. Then they should not marry for several months, at the very least, so that they may be better acquainted with one another and may each carefully weigh the character of his or her beloved and see if their engagement fits in with the plan of God.

Love at first sight? It sometimes really happens, I think, but rarely. I had dinner last Sunday with a couple, wonderfully happy, who married forty-five days after they first met each other. But they were members of the same church, each investigated the other's family, and the character of each was unusual. More often it happens that so-called "love at first sight" is only a passing infatuation. On better acquaintance the beloved object proves not to be what one thought. What the young man fell in love with was not the girl as she was, but the girl he imagined her to be. What the girl fell in love with was not the young man she met, but her ideal of a young man, which she hoped and thought this young man would meet. So the first attraction, the love at first sight, so-called, should always be put to the test of further acquaintance. A more mature love based on character, based on a real understanding of one another's personalities can properly grow out of the first attraction if it is well based.

Hasty marriages are always dangerous. Any man who would enter the profession of medicine and bind himself for a lifetime to that profession, with no more preparation, no more consideration, no more acquaintance with the facts involved than many young people have before they get married, would be counted a fool. Any man who sailed to a foreign shore as a foreign missionary within a month of the time the idea first entered his head, and with no more preparation and no more consideration of the facts than some young people have in getting married, would certainly be on the verge of disaster. Any girl who took on a sudden whim the vows of a nun, lifetime vows shutting her off from the world, would be very silly. So any young couple who marries without taking time to know one another well and without proving that their love is deep-seated and based on genuine admiration, compatibility of character and personality, and attraction of the spirit instead of only animal-like sex attraction, is very foolish. A very large percent of hasty marriages end in divorce and heartbreak. No couple should marry without waiting until they know one another well and until their mutual love has brought deep-seated conviction that they will be happy together for a lifetime and would not be happy apart. Real love must be based upon what people are, what one knows another to be, based upon deep-seated admiration and devotion. Any marriage based upon a sudden whim, based upon the attraction aroused in an evening at the dance, based on the thrill of a good-night kiss after drinking wine maybe, or based on an evening's necking in a parked car, is certainly a foolish marriage. And people who enter marriage that way are fools who should expect disaster. Disaster is certainly likely to come to any such ill-considered and hasty marriage.

Many states require three days' delay after filing intention to marry. The idea is to thwart sudden marriages by half-drunken young people, by those who take marriage as a prank, and by those who run away from home and marry without parents' knowledge or consent. Hasty marriages are evil. Wait until you know one another better!

IV. Wait Until Moral and Spiritual Problems Are Settled Happily

Many a woman has married some man "to reform him." Then through her heartache she found that she had less opportunity to reform her drunkard husband after she had married him than she had had before. It is folly of the worst kind for any person ever to marry another whose moral standards are not already thoroughly acceptable. No girl is safe to marry a man who drinks until he has for at least a year proven his reform by leaving liquor absolutely alone. Girls, do all the reforming you ever plan to do before you marry! And the same advice is good for young men. If the girl does not already fit your moral standards, she will not be likely to do so after you are married. Such problems should be settled before marriage.

Any man who will not quit alcoholic drink totally and consistently for the girl he loves, before he marries her, is almost certain not to do it after he already has her as his wife.

Some Christian reads this who is engaged to be married to one who is not a Christian. You devoutly hope that your beloved will come to know your Saviour, will be converted and live a devoted, Christian life. But the only time to make sure about that is before marriage. All over America are women married to ungodly husbands, women whose lives are made miserable by the fundamental difference between them, yet they have little influence on their unsaved companions. "Be ye not unequally yoked together with unbelievers," says the plain Word of God (II Cor. 6:14). Such problems should be settled before marriage.

The marriage of a Catholic and Protestant is fraught with great danger. There is a great fundamental difference in the two religions, and the more devoted each is in his own faith the more intolerant he is toward the faith which contradicts his own in so many points. No home should be on such a divided basis as that the husband is a Catholic and the wife is a Protestant, or that the wife is a Catholic and the husband is a Protestant. They will not agree on where to go to church. They will not agree on the rearing of their children. They will not agree on the very fundamentals of the Christian faith; for example, on what it takes to become a Christian. Such a marriage is always likely to end in heartbreak. If two young people know that they love one another devotedly, know that they have so much in common that their love will ripen and last, and know that God has put His approval on the marriage, they may safely wait until this great problem is settled. Let them talk and pray together. Let them go to someone whom both trust, and let them earnestly seek to become of one mind.

Speaking from the Protestant viewpoint, I believe that a great many Catholics, however sincere, earnest and devout, do not really know what it is to trust Christ as a personal Saviour and be born again. For an earnest Christian who knows he has been converted, has been born again and is a child of God, to marry a Catholic, would usually, I fear, mean that he was marrying an unsaved one; and that would be an unequal yoke between a child of God and a child of Satan. I do not mean that one is a child of Satan because he is a Catholic. I only mean that those who are not converted are not saved. And from the Catholic viewpoint, if the Catholic religion were the true religion, if one could be saved only through the ministry of a priest instead of personal faith in

Christ, then it would still be an unequal yoke. There would still be many matters to quarrel about, many matters of heartbreak. Such a radical difference in religious convictions may mean the ruin of the marriage, or it may mean the ruin of the religious life of both parties. No one should marry until problems like this are carefully solved.

Some young woman may say, "If I wait till all such problems are solved, I may never get married. If I wait until I am loved and sought by a young man who does not drink, who is a devout Christian, who meets all my moral standards, then I may never have a husband and a home." Yes, that is true. To delay marriage may sometimes mean no marriage. But it would be infinitely happier and better for multitudes of people to go without marriage than to come to the heartbreak and misery that is inevitable when the fundamental rules for a happy marriage are violated. Any girl had better be a spinster, an "old maid," and never have a husband and home and children, than to be married to a drunkard or a libertine and whoremonger. And certainly any Christian girl had better never be married than to marry an unsaved man, a child of Satan. So, for a happy marriage, young people should wait until moral and spiritual problems which would hinder happiness and threaten disaster are settled for sure.

V.   Wait Until Health Justifies Marriage

A young woman, engaged to be married, is stricken down with tuberculosis. She goes to a sanitarium. Perhaps she improves in health, but there is the likelihood that she may spend several years in a sanitarium and that she may never be well. There is the likelihood that she could not safely have children and carry out the duties of wifehood and motherhood. Her young sweetheart loves her and feels that she needs him all the more since she is sick. He would be willing, he thinks, to care for her even though she might never be well. Should they marry? In most cases certainly not!

A normal, godly marriage means that two people take solemn vows for a lifetime partnership. Each has certain duties. I think that under ordinary circumstances no man should marry who is not well enough to make a living. I think that under ordinary circumstances no woman should marry who is not able to bear children and keep her home and be a comfort and blessing to her husband instead of a constant burden.

If there is venereal disease, then certainly marriage should be postponed until it has been entirely eradicated. No man has a right to marry until he knows himself to be free from contagious venereal disease. Even though he himself may not suffer physically from the latent disease, it is very probable that he will infect his wife, that the disease will prevent their ever having children. It is possible that the infected wife will infect babies, maybe blinding them at birth. More likely, drastic surgery will be necessary, making it impossible for the wife ever to bear children. Laws in progressive states provide that a man and woman must furnish physician's certificate of freedom from venereal disease before a marriage license is granted. No girl ought ever to marry any man who is not able and willing to fulfill this normal requirement. And it should not be a mere form. It is tragedy unspeakable for a marriage ever to take place where either party is a victim of this dread disease.

Sometimes hereditary insanity is so nearly certain to break out in a person that he should never marry. One who has epileptic fits, I think, should not marry. One who is not able to properly fulfill the duties of marriage ought not to marry.

So, before marriage, wait until health justifies marriage and gives prospect of a happy, normal union.

VI. Wait Until Financial Prospects Are Fairly Considered

Many a marriage has gone on the rocks when a young couple married rashly and then had to move in with the husband's family or with the wife's because there was no money for even a poor home. I have known of couples who married, when the wife must then return to her family and the husband live where he could with no chance to make a happy home. Hasty, ill-considered marriages are usually unhappy.

I would not say that marriages should wait until a man can own his own home, for many very happy couples have lived with great joy all their days in rented houses or apartments. But at least there ought to be a clear prospect that the young couple can have a cottage, or at least a tiny apartment where they can live to themselves, where the young husband can be the head of his home and the bride can be the queen of her husband's heart and the mistress of her own stove and dish pan!

I think it is usually wise for young people to finish college before they marry, if they plan to go to college. But professional training after college might delay marriage for several years, and often the young doctor or minister or lawyer is making his own way and ought to marry and let his wife share his hardships as well as his happiness during some years of training. Sometimes, when young people are serious, when they have long known each other, when their love is mature and sensible, parents should be willing to help on necessary living expenses of the young couple while they complete professional training.

My wife and I were engaged through my last three years of college, and through one year while I taught and paid up college debts and while she finished university. Then we married, borrowed $100.00, and went to theological seminary together. But we were sure of ourselves, we knew we loved one another, and we knew we were willing to sacrifice to be together. We lived in poverty but with great joy and very little real hardship. But I had earned my way through college and knew we could get by, and she had confidence in me and wanted to share those years of preparation rather than to wait alone for the time when I could support her in greater comfort. Our decision still seems to me to have been very sensible and the result very happy.

A young lady's parents should not require, or the young bridegroom expect, that he will from the beginning give his bride all that her parents could give her. No girl is fit to be a wife who is not willing to begin in the simplest kind of home where it will be necessary to scrimp and save and buy carefully and do without and make ends meet, for the sake of happiness. A daughter should be willing to begin where her mother began, and each daughter should remember that her father now, after twenty or thirty years of making a living, cares for his daughter much better than he could care for his wife in the beginning, in most cases. Decent poverty, frugality and some sacrifice should be expected of young people. It is far better for a young couple to marry at twenty-five on small salary than to wait five years more and marry at thirty with every comfort, but having missed five glorious years of doing without together and helping one another and enjoying one another.

But, while the prospective bridegroom need not reach the heights of financial success before he marries, there ought to be careful, sensible planning before marriage. It may be that the young wife, for a season, will need to work and add her pay check to that of her husband. If both understand this and it is planned out ahead of time, that may be a very sensible thing to do. But it must be borne in mind that sooner or later the husband will need to take the full responsibility for making a living, and that, in normal cases God will send little children to bless the home, and a mother will be needed to make homemaking itself her career in the home. Sometimes the bride should be willing to work to help make ends meet, but the plans should be that soon the husband will be able to make a sufficient income, though perhaps very moderate, for the support of his own home.

If the prospective husband has experience and training and character, and has for some years made his own way with success, usually he may be depended upon to provide for his wife. But there should be a decent prospect for a job, the young couple should know about what income they can expect to have for a start. The greatest happiness in marriage will be obtained by waiting until the young couple in love have very carefully weighed the financial prospects and find them favorable for a happy marriage.

VII. Wait for the Approval of the Girl's Parents

Usually a young couple to be married ought to have the approval of the bridegroom's parents. Almost without exception, they should have the approval and consent of the girl's parents.

Among honorable people of high ideals it has always been understood that every man owes a tremendous debt to the parents of the girl he marries. The mother brought her into the world with suffering. The father has provided for her needs at a cost of many thousands of dollars through the years. The father and mother have prayed, have planned, have hoped, and have toiled unceasingly to make their daughter into the fine woman that she is. They have paid a tremendous price for her happiness. Does the young sweetheart admire the loveliness of his dear one? How little he thinks that her beauty is accented by the clothes her father has bought and the mother planned. Is he fascinated

with her music, her beautifully trained voice or her skill at
the piano? That cost the father and mother much in planning, supervision and money. The very character of the
young lady so dear to him was built more largely by her father and mother than by anybody else in the world. He is an
ingrate indeed who would take a daughter from her father
and mother without a decent regard for their feelings and
happiness.

Let it be granted that the father and mother cannot select
the husband for their daughter, and they ought not to try.
But in most cases they certainly ought to have veto powers,
specially when the daughter is young and when the father
and mother are people of character and experience. Ordinarily the time to disapprove of the young man is when he first
comes courting, if there must be disapproval. Certainly every
mother and father have a right to disapprove their daughter's
association with people who are immoral or unchristian or
shiftless. The father is more likely to know what qualities in
the suitor's character would militate toward an unhappy marriage than the love-blinded daughter. The girl who goes
against the counsel of her loving and experienced father in
selecting a mate has two strikes against her in her marriage,
and there is very grave danger of unhappiness. So fathers and
mothers should plan ahead of time to see that their children
associate with the kind of people who are good enough for
them to marry if love should come out of the normal association of young people. The girl who never goes with a drunkard is not likely to marry a drunkard. The girl who associates
with only Christian people is very likely to marry a Christian.
Parents should be specially careful about the outer fringes
and the early stages of friendship both for their sons and
daughters. Naturally it is possible to protect their daughters
more than their sons.

I know that I feel the deepest responsibility for my six
daughters, and it seems to me unthinkable for a good father
or mother to allow their daughter's intimate friendship with a
young man to ripen into love without their careful investigation of his character and fitness. And this prerogative and
duty of fathers and mothers to watch over their daughter's
happiness is recognized by the best society everywhere. In
some cases engagements ought to be broken at the earnest
entreaty of the father and mother of the girl, provided their
objection is really based on what they know of the young

suitor's character and their appraisement of the chances of a
happy marriage. Marriages which are made hastily, without
the consent of the bride's parents, are very often unhappy
and often end disastrously.

I do not think that the old-fashioned formal way of having
the would-be suitor ask the father for permission to court his
daughter is necessary. But I do believe that every honest
young man of refined taste and appreciation ought to go to
the father of his sweetheart (or to the mother, if she has no
father), before the engagement is announced, to tell the parents of his love for their daughter and to plead for their consent to her marriage with him.

This plan has many advantages. First, common decency
and gratitude toward the father and mother of a girl demand
it. Every man should have a lifelong gratitude and devotion
to the father and mother of the woman they reared and educated at such cost to give her away to him. To expect a gift
of such value without a "by your leave" or thanks would not
be gentlemanly and would not be Christian.

In the second place, the young man who feels that he must
please the father and mother of the girl he loves will be
much more likely to adjust his life to a higher plane, and
both his manners and his morals will be the better for an
honest effort to satisfy the father and mother of the girl
whose hand he seeks. So every girl should accept a proposal
of marriage only with the understanding that it is to be approved by her father and mother, and no man should make a
proposal of marriage to a girl if he is not willing to face honestly her father and mother, tell them of his love and of his
life plans and seek their consent and approval.

Father and mother cannot foretell what young man may
arouse the ecstasy of love, the sweet allure of young passion
in their daughter's breast. But they can tell much better than
she whether he is likely to make her a good living, whether
he is likely to keep his marriage vows, and whether he will be
a man of whom their daughter would be proud after living
with him ten years! It is not sensible that the wisdom of father and mother in such matters should be ignored, and any
girl would so mistreat her father and mother only at her own
peril. Get the consent of the father and mother of the bride
before marriage!

In some cases, a girl of twenty-eight or thirty has lived
away from home for years, making her own way, and must

be expected to meet and love and marry a man not well known to her parents. But even then she will be wise if she takes her sweetheart to her father and mother for their approval, and he will be gentlemanly and Christian if he shows to them the grateful deference which is their honest due as her parents.

Some who wait will miss marriage, it is true. But in such cases, almost always, no marriage is to be preferred to a hasty marriage which will probably be unhappy.

VIII. A Christian Should Not Settle on Marriage Without Clear Leading From God

Every Christian should earnestly pray about the matter of marriage. Christian young people will do well if they solemnly determine, before love comes, that they will marry only in the will of God, as they are best able to know the will of God. That will mean that every Christian girl will know ahead of time the unconverted man is not to be her mate. She will guard the approaches to her heart against such an intruder who has no right to her love and to her hand. Every Christian young man will know ahead of time that a frivolous and vain and worldly-minded young woman whose life does not please God, is not fit to be his bride, his mate, his other self, and his partner in serving the Lord Jesus who died for him. Christians should plan ahead of time to love and marry only in the will of God. And that decision will save much heartbreak and trouble.

But suppose the young man who proposes is apparently a real Christian, a noble character and one to be greatly admired and loved. Suppose one's heart is stirred and there is no doubt in a young girl's mind that her affections reach out to the young suitor? Then she should make earnest prayer to God, pleading for the leading of the Holy Spirit, pleading that God will help her to know His will and not to make a mistake. And she should not marry until she has a sweet peace in her heart which is the indication that God is pleased. No Christian young man should ask a girl to be his wife until he has first talked the thing over with God and with earnest prayer and meditation has received in his heart a sweet assurance that this is God's will, that this love is a gift from God, that God's smile is upon his plans for marriage.

I remember a long unpaved country road that ran near the

college where I met my sweetheart (now my wife for many years). For long hours I walked that country road, back and forth, and looked now and then at the window where a light shone from my sweetheart's room, as I talked to God about my love and begged Him not to let me make a mistake, not to let me go against His will. Not until I felt assured that God had given me peace and that this love was from Him and would have His blessing did I press my suit and gain my dear one's consent to be my wife. I am certain that God in kindness put His blessings upon my plan. I am equally certain that He, in loving kindness, kept me from marrying the wrong girl. Before going ahead with marriage, every Christian should take this holy matter of marriage to God in prayer and should have the quiet leading of the Spirit of God and the peace that God gives when our ways please Him. God is interested in the welfare of His children. He is willing to lead us in the ways of peace and righteousness, and He longs to see us happy. How foolish it would be to think that we could not have His wisdom, His guidance and protection in a matter so delicate and where the future could not otherwise be well foreseen! Let no one, then, be in a hurry to marry. But let every Christian be content in whatsoever state he is. "Art thou loosed from a wife? seek not a wife" (I Cor. 7:27). If God sends true love, which is clearly according to His will, and gives a mate who is proper for a Christian, and puts His approval upon the marriage both by peace in the heart and by favorable outward circumstances, then Christians may marry and be happy. If God does not bring a loved one who is worthy, does not grow love in the heart, or does not give approval in a Christian's spirit, then let the Christian be content to be happy and single, rather than to marry out of the will of God.

CHAPTER V

Some Should Not Marry

"Now concerning the things whereof ye wrote unto me: It is good for a man not to touch a woman."—I Cor. 7:1.

"I say therefore to the unmarried and widows, It is good for them if they abide even as I. But if they cannot contain, let them marry: for it is better to marry than to burn."—I Cor. 7:8, 9.

"Art thou bound unto a wife? seek not to be loosed. Art thou loosed from a wife: seek not a wife. But and if thou marry, thou hast not sinned; and if a virgin marry, she hath not sinned. Nevertheless such shall have trouble in the flesh: but I spare you."—I Cor. 7:27, 28.

"But I would have you without carefulness. He that is unmarried careth for the things that belong to the Lord, how he may please the Lord: But he that is married careth for the things that are of the world, how he may please his wife. There is difference also between a wife and a virgin. The unmarried woman careth for the things of the Lord, that she may be holy both in body and in spirit: but she that is married careth only for the things of the world, how she may please her husband."—I Cor. 7:32-34.

"The wife is bound by the law as long as her husband liveth; but if her husband be dead, she is at liberty to be married to whom she will; only in the Lord. But she is happier if she so abide, after my judgment: and I think also that I have the Spirit of God."—I Cor. 7:39, 40.

Here in one chapter of the Bible, I Corinthians 7, are a number of solemn warnings that people ought to be in no hurry to marry. Some people fall in love, and who could blame them for that? Perhaps if they were more careful where they walked, they would not fall so easily. But some people hasten to *climb* in love. Some people are so anxious to be married that they are ready to love and marry nearly anybody who comes along who is available! This is not the part of wisdom, and is not the happy Christian attitude taught in the Bible.

Marriage is so beautiful and good and can help to make life such a taste of Heaven upon earth, if it is from God, and if people marry in God's will and under God's blessing, that no one should enter it lightly or irreverently. Only with the glad assurance that this plan is from God, that God has sent this mate, that God has planted and ripened this sweet love in the heart, that God has made these rosy plans for the future, that God has indicted these holy vows of love and self-surrender, should people, especially Christian people, enter marriage.

On the other hand, marriage can also be such an occasion of torment, such a dashing of hopes, such a frustration of tender dreams that people ought to enter marriage only after much deliberation and prayer and with full assurance that they are making no mistake.

The sentiment of the Scripture is that people do not have to be married to be happy. Many people are better off never to marry. "Art thou bound unto a wife? seek not to be loosed. Art thou loosed from a wife? seek not a wife," says I Corinthians 7:27. There are so many things that only God can completely work out for a happy marriage that a Christian should wait quietly on God and be content to have marriage only in His time or not at all. It is a great mistake to be in haste to marry. As I have said, "Marry in haste; repent at leisure," has the wisdom of countless tragedies summed up in it.

God laid down a general law that "it is not good that the man should be alone" (Gen. 2:18). It is true that "marriage is honourable in all" (Heb. 13:4). But that does not mean that God intends for everybody to marry. In I Corinthians 7:2 Paul says, "Nevertheless, to avoid fornication, let every man have his own wife, and let every woman have her own husband." Yet in the preceding verse Paul said, "It is good for a man not to touch a woman." And following that passage on husbands and wives, Paul says in I Corinthians 7:6-8, "But I speak this by permission, and not of commandment. For I would that all men were even as I myself. But every man hath his proper gift of God, one after this manner, and another after that. I say therefore to the unmarried and widows, It is good for them if they abide even as I."

Here we see then that it is better for some not to marry. Some have the "proper gift of God" to marry and others have the "proper gift of God" to remain single. Paul himself was single and wished that others might be so. Paul said, "It is good for them if they abide even as I." It is not best in every case that people marry. Some people are better and wiser and happier not to marry.

Many people can serve God better if they do not marry. In I Corinthians 7:32-34, mentioned above, the Holy Spirit led Paul to write, "But I would have you without carefulness. He that is unmarried careth for the things that belong to the Lord, how he may please the Lord: But he that is married careth for the things that are of the world, how he may please his wife. There is difference also between a wife and a virgin. The unmarried woman careth for the things of the Lord, that she may be holy both in body and in spirit: but she that is married careth for the things of the world, how she may please her husband."

A married man cares for the things of the world, how he may please his wife. A married man has a responsibility, a yoke, a burden which he can never fail to consider. There is an obligation to make his wife happy which every normal man feels. He feels the burden to provide for his own, and that is right. But this burden is often a snare, a temptation.

I know a great preacher who, after some years of pioneer work, winning many hundreds of souls, settled down as pastor in a beautiful college town. He built a good home. There his children grew up. Then, in answer to the pleadings of his wife, he promised never to move and give up that lovely home. His period of usefulness with the local church ended, a new pastor was called. And there he sat, year in and year out, rejecting calls that came for his ministry, because he had promised his wife never to leave the good home they had built and furnished and enjoyed together. In that case marriage was a snare.

I know of a great evangelist who must have won over a hundred thousand souls to Christ in his ministry. His children were growing up. His daughter needed to be in college. The wife pled that the children needed their daddy. So he accepted a pastorate and for one year stayed out of evangelistic work so that he would be with his family and home. He said to me later, "For that one year I never had the veil lifted from my eyes. I could never perfectly see the face of Christ until I surrendered the pastorate and went back into the work that God had called me to do."

Many a Christian girl has felt the call of God to soul winning. Many volunteered for foreign mission work or the work of daily vacation Bible schools, or child evangelism, or church visiting. Then when the call of love came, the call of God grew dim and they turned their backs upon plans and dreams and vows. They married and were absorbed in their homes and husbands and children, and all their days they felt guilty that they did not go ahead to do what they had once promised God they would do and felt was His will. Many a woman has been active in Sunday school and soul winning, has been a good pianist or soloist, a splendid Sunday school teacher. Then she has become so absorbed in her home and family and cooking and washing and family pleasures and duties that she has left off her efforts to win souls. So it is that the man who is married seeks to please his wife, and a woman who is married seeks to please her husband. No one ought ever to marry who does not first consider this natural temptation to put a mate before God.

In that tremendous book, *Goforth of China*, Mrs. Rosalind Goforth tells how the great Presbyterian missionary faced this problem. The following passage tells how Christians have to face the question of whether God or mate shall be first.

"So when, in that autumn he said, 'Will you join your life with mine for China?' my answer was, 'Yes,' without a moment's hesitation. But a few days later when he said, 'Will you give me your promise that *always* you will allow me to put my Lord and His work first, even before you?' I gave an inward gasp before replying, 'Yes, I will *always*,' for was not this the very kind of man I had prayed for? (Oh, kind Master; to hide from Thy servant what that promise could cost!)

"A few days after my promise was given, the first test in keeping it came. I had been (woman-like) indulging in dreams of the beautiful engagement ring that was soon to be mine. Then Jonathan came to me and said, 'You will not mind, will you, if I do not get an engagement ring?' He then went on to tell with great enthusiasm of the distributing of books and pamphlets on China from his room in Knox. Every cent was needed for this important work. As I listened and watched his glowing face, the visions I had indulged in of the beautiful engagement ring vanished. This was my first lesson in *real values*."

If a sweetheart must sometimes do without an engagement ring to put Christ first, if an evangelist must often be away from home most of the time for long years, as is commonly true, then some people ought not to marry at all.

C. T. Studd did mission work in China and India and later in the wilds of Africa. For some fourteen years he worked in Africa when it was necessary for his wife, practically an invalid, to remain in England. If long years of separation of husband and wife were necessary in their case, as both of them agreed it was, in order to do the best work for God, certainly sometimes Christians ought to give up the idea of marrying entirely in order to serve the Lord.

That was the case of Paul the apostle. The other apostles were married. Of all these leading preachers of the New Testament, it seems that Paul and Barnabas were unmarried. At least that is the implication of what the Holy Spirit had Paul write down in I Corinthians 9:5 , 6: "Have we not power to lead about a sister, a wife, as well as other apostles, and as the brethren of the Lord, and Cephas? Or I only and Barnabas, have not we power to forbear working?"

Paul had a right to marry, and so did Barnabas. Yet for the sake of getting out the Gospel Paul gave up the idea of a home, gave up any plan for marriage and for wife and children. He sought to serve the Lord first. So he was as a stranger and a pilgrim with no home, no certain dwelling place. He was in prison years on end. He traveled and toiled and was persecuted, stoned, beaten, hated. He had no money with which to support a family, no time to care for one. What woman would have been content to see Paul once in three or five years, perhaps, as he came back to Jerusalem or Antioch, and yet call him husband? Paul is an example that sometimes people serve the Lord better by not marrying.

We do not agree with Catholics, in their requiring of their priests and nuns that they never marry. It is not wrong to marry. Yet we must admit that many priests and nuns give up thoughts of home and marriage and family solely to please the Lord as they understand His will. Do you think that God never wants anyone to love Him that much, nor to give up that much for Him? By divine inspiration I Corinthians 7 tells us that many people should not marry and that many can serve God better by not marrying.

Paul and Barnabas were not married, we believe. There is no evidence that Elijah, Elisha, Jeremiah or Daniel were ever married.

Under modern conditions marriage does not change a

man's life as much as it changes a woman's life. There are many women who have been missionaries and have spent their lives in heathen lands telling others about the Lord. In many such cases they could not have done the missionary work they did had they been married. In the Union Gospel Press headquarters at Cleveland, Ohio, I saw many women who had given themselves to serve God. Some were young, some were old; but all were happy and devoted to a lifetime of getting out the Gospel. Many of them, I understand, had renounced all plans of marriage in order to serve the Lord more fully. Many nurses have not married but have given their lives in serving humanity day after day. I have no doubt that in many cases a man's unmarried secretary is more useful in his work than his wife. Many a preacher's ministry is doubled by loyal secretarial help by women who give themselves to a holy ministry and calling from God.

So each one must find himself the place God has for him to fill in life, and whether or not that place can best be filled and that work best be done with or without marriage. Some people should not marry because they can serve God best and do more good single.

CHAPTER VI

Man, God's Deputy as Head of the Home

"As for me and my house, we will serve the Lord."—Josh. 24:15.

"For a man indeed ought not to cover his head, forasmuch as he is the image and glory of God: but the woman is the glory of the man."—I Cor. 11:7.

"For the husband is the head of the wife, even as Christ is the head of the church: and he is the saviour of the body."—Eph. 5:23.

A man is *somebody*! We thank God for the glorious devotion and influence of good women. I have better reason than most men to appreciate the character, the virtue, the devotion and faithfulness of good women. My mother, who went to Heaven before I was six, was such a godly woman and such a remarkable character that her influence to this day is like a heavenly fragrance leading me toward God. My sweetheart waited for me four long years while we finished our college education and while I paid up college debts, and now for years her love has comforted me, served me and blessed me. I have six lovely daughters, my joy, my pride, for whom I devoutly thank God. My work is largely carried on by Christian young women, full-time workers, some of whom have been with me for long years, as well as by a number of other young women who are part-time workers. God is good, wonderfully good, to any man when He gives him a good wife or a lovely daughter. Fine Christian women do much of the singing and praying and serving in the churches. Yet it remains the clear teaching of the Word of God that a man is the highest work of God.

God's inspired Word tells us that the man "is the image and glory of God: but the woman is the glory of the man." A man is like God in a sense that a woman is not like God. For example, God is masculine. Mrs. Mary Baker Eddy, false prophetess of so-called Christian Science, calls God "Our Father-Mother God," but that is wholly unscriptural. God is always, in the Bible, called "He," never "Her." He is called "Father," not "Mother." Christ is called "the man

Christ Jesus," not "the woman." He is called "Bridegroom," not "bride," "King," not "queen," "Prophet," not "prophetess," "Son," not "daughter." Christ was a Man, a masculine Man. His body was a man's body. His work was a man's work. His temptations, a man's temptations. I do not mean that Christ is not the Saviour every woman needs, nor that He does not know her every longing, feel her every sorrow, meet her every need. But God would not have had the Bible so full of it if He did not want us to notice that Christ was a Man, not a woman, and that man is therefore made in the image of God in a sense that cannot be true of a woman. So, in the home, man is the deputy of God, and should lead the home for God.

Every man should realize that God has laid on him duties and responsibilities that women are not fitted to carry, and are not ordinarily required to carry. God commanded the man, Adam, not to eat of the forbidden fruit, before the woman was ever made (Gen. 2:17). Adam named all the animals also before Eve was created (Gen. 2:19, 20). When the two had sinned, it was Adam God sought and first reproached, though the woman had first sinned. It was to Adam that God said "cursed is the ground for thy sake; . . . . In the sweat of thy face shalt thou eat bread." It is not that the woman was not as guilty, nor also under the curse, for she was. But man clearly is held accountable for his wife, and is to earn bread for his wife.

Woe to the government that is not headed by a strong man or strong men. There have been some good rulers among women, notably Queen Victoria in England, but the actual administration was carried on by great prime ministers, including Disraeli and Gladstone. Queen Elizabeth was strong, but often capricious and sometimes vicious. The other famous women rulers in history have nearly always been wicked in character and disastrously incapable. We remember Jezebel in Israel, Athaliah of Judah, Cleopatra of Egypt, and Lucrezia Borgia of Italy. God evidently intended that rule should be by man.

Business owes much to women, but it is still true that strong executive leadership belongs to men.

So in the home God intends men to lead. Joshua said, "As for me and my house, we will serve the Lord" (Josh. 24:15).

In Home Relationship Man Is the Image of God

God intended each man to be the high priest in the home, to be God's chief representative there, to rule the home for God.

When Jesus taught His disciples to pray, and gave to all of us the model prayer, He said, "When ye pray, say: Our Father which art in heaven." Christians are always to think of God as their Father. The best illustration Jesus could give us of what God is like to the Christian, is the relation of a father to his child! This means that as God is all-wise and infinitely strong and infinitely good, every child is to look to his father as the wisest and best and strongest he knows. As we look to God for our food and our protection and the satisfaction of our heart's desires and for every breath we draw, so children in a home are to look to the father for provision, protection, guidance and joy! Oh, how great is the responsibility of a human father who is to his children the image of God.

I remember with joy the reverence I had for my own father and my unbounded trust in him. I felt he was about the bravest man who had ever lived. I asked him the most unheard-of questions, and I took, without a grain of doubt, his answers as being absolute truth. When my father sometimes said, "I do not know, Son," I had a feeling that if he would think awhile on the matter or give it a little attention he soon *would* know. If my father said a thing was right, I felt it was right; if he said it was wrong, then certainly for me it was wrong. I thank God that I have had few occasions even yet to believe my father was essentially wrong, now that he has been in Heaven a number of years. In his affection, in his providing, in his punishment of our sins, in his kindness, in his counsel, my father was to his eight children the best earthly image we ever saw of God.

What do you call your father? I revere the memory of my father now. Before he went to Heaven, in 1930, I always held him in profound respect. Yet the word "father" was a little too formal, and I never called him that. As a child I called him "Papa," and later that changed to "Daddy." Even in this feeling of intimate affection which a child normally has for his father, the father represents God. For in Romans 8:15 the Scripture says, "For ye have not received the spirit of bondage again to fear; but ye have received the Spirit of adoption, whereby we cry, Abba Father." The word "Abba" is a very intimate Aramaic term for father, and it would not be amiss to translate it "papa" or "daddy." It seems a little irreverent perhaps at first glance, but actually it would not be amiss for us to feel like calling our Heavenly Father "Our Daddy who is in Heaven." The better a father is, the better an image he is of God who is the Father of all those who are born again, born into His family as the children of God.

The Scripture also says that a husband is like Christ. A father, *to his children*, is the image of God the Father dealing with Christians. A husband in the home is to be *to his wife* as Christ is to the church. In Ephesians 5:22, 23 this beautiful symbolism is stated:

"Wives, submit yourselves unto your own husbands, as unto the Lord. For the husband is the head of the wife, even as Christ is the head of the church: and he is the saviour of the body."

Every wife is to be subject to her husband as if he were the Lord Jesus. Christ is the head of His mystical body, the church, and is the Saviour of that body. So the husband is the head of the wife, the Scripture says, and "he is the saviour of the body." The husband and wife are, in God's sight, "one flesh" (Matt. 19:5). The husband is the provider, the protector, the deliverer of his wife's body. Every man who marries takes the care of his wife as a sacred trust. Her body belongs to him, and he is the saviour, protector of her body.

Oh, what a good man I ought to be if I am to be the father of little children and if I am to be to them the image of God! How noble, how just, how morally clean, how spiritually wise a father ought to be, and how seriously every man ought to take marriage, since it means to his wife he is to be an image of Christ. She is to be subject to him "as unto the Lord." Surely, if a man is what he ought to be, representing God the Father to his children and representing Christ to his wife, he ought to have no trouble in winning his family to Christ.

Again, I say a man is *somebody!* It is a serious business to be a man. God expects great things of a man since he is made in the image and glory of God.

Man Is to Rule in the Home

God said to Eve after sin had come into the world, "Thy desire shall be to thy husband, and he shall rule over thee." And in Ephesians 5:23, we again remind you, the Scripture says, "For the husband is the head of the wife, even as Christ is the head of the church."

This does not mean slavery for the wife. Rule, government, authority, is of God. The only alternative to government and authority is anarchy and chaos. It is not slavery that we have a president and congress of the nation and governors for states, sheriffs in counties, mayors and councils and police forces in the cities. It is not slavery for a teacher to have authority in the schoolroom or a pastor in the church. So it is only law, order and government for God's man to be the head of the home, the head of the wife, and to rule over his wife.

Again, I Timothy 3:4, 5 says that a bishop or pastor of a church must be "one that ruleth well his own house, having his children in subjection with all gravity; (For if a man know not how to rule his own house, how shall he take care of the church of God?)"

Every preacher is to 'rule well his own house,' and to 'have his children in subjection.' How could a pastor represent God to his church if he did not represent God in his home? God's authority makes the husband ruler over his wife and the father ruler over his children. Of course, the Scriptures plainly teach that children are to obey mothers as well as fathers, but it could not be clearer than the Bible makes it that the man is to rule his home.

When any man marries, he should be ready to assume the holy responsibility, the labor, the obligations for the physical, moral and spiritual welfare of his home.

God Intends for Men to Be Examples of Moral Purity and Spiritual Devotion

Some people foolishly think that men, by nature, are necessarily more wicked than women. In many churches women are in the majority. Women, because they have more leisure and because they are more easily led, do more of routine church work, cook more pies, make more visits.

Hence some people believe that women are naturally more spiritually minded than men, but that is not true. The Bible, from one end to the other, clearly teaches that God demands as much, morally and spiritually, of a man as He does of a woman.

I heard a very silly preacher once say that there was not a man in the earth good enough to deserve to marry a clean, fine woman. That was a wicked slander. I know personally hundreds of men who are as clean in life, in language and in thought as any woman I know. Men, by nature, are more aggressive and less bound by convention. Women, by nature, are more anxious to please society, are more easily led, whether for right or wrong, than men. But man himself was made in the image and glory of God, while woman was made as "the glory of the man." Both are fallen, sinful creatures. The woman is by nature depraved exactly as the man is. An unconverted woman goes to the same Hell as an unconverted man, and just as quickly and as certainly. God has one moral standard for both.

Satan himself is the author of the idea that it is all right for men to smoke but not for women, that social purity is required of women but not of men, that cursing and swearing are masculine but not "ladylike."

It is true that cigarette smoking by women is a terrible evil. Women ought to be dainty, and cigarettes make them stink. Women ought to set good examples before their children, and cigarette smoking is certainly an evil thing for children. Cigarettes fray the nerves of mothers, poison nursing babies, spoil the sanctity of home. People who see a woman smoke think she is not a good Christian. Yes, obviously it is sinful and foolish for a woman to use tobacco—exactly as sinful and foolish as for a man to use it!

God intends men to set the pattern for the family. Husbands should be examples to their wives and to their children.

That is what Joshua meant to do when he made the holy and public vow, "As for me and my house, we will serve the Lord" (Josh. 24:15).

Any man who sets one standard for his wife and children and another for himself is a hypocrite. Any man who drinks when he would not have his wife and children drink, smokes when he would not have them smoke, curses when he would not have them curse, is dishonest and unfair. His family may

MAN, GOD'S DEPUTY AS HEAD OF THE HOME   99

love him, but they will not thoroughly respect him, because
he preaches what he does not practice. He is a hypocrite.

One day a father stopped his cultivator at the end of a
long cotton row to talk to two preachers, while his little son,
seven or eight years old, rode his stick horse nearby. The
stick horse that day was very fractious! But the little boy
conquered the stick horse in heroic and manly fashion, according to his rights. Beating on the broomstick, he threatened and cursed! The father was embarrassed and angry. He
seized the boy by the shoulder, shook him vigorously and
said, "If I ever hear you use a word like that again I will
wear out a cotton stalk on you! Don't you ever let me hear
you curse again!" But the preachers knew, just as the little
boy knew, exactly where he got his example. The father, too,
had cursed his horse, and the little son was simply following
the most powerful teaching a child ever receives, his father's
example.

Perhaps the child did not curse any more where his father
could hear him. Perhaps he gave it up for the time being, but
in his heart he said, "When I am a man like Dad then I can
curse as Dad does." Men, whether you like it or not, your example is molding your home, molding the lives and eternal
destinies of your children.

In matters of religion it is clearly intended that men should
take the lead for their families. Joshua said, "As for me and
my house, we will serve the Lord."

It is one of the sweet memories of my childhood that the
whole family always went to Sunday school together. All
went to Sunday morning services, all went to Sunday night
services, all went to prayer meetings, and all went to revival
campaigns together. No one ever asked at our home whether
someone else was going to Sunday school or church services.
Dad was in charge of that matter and it was a foregone conclusion that everyone would be in Sunday school on time. It
was already understood that everybody had his Sunday
school lesson ready, had his offering ready to give, had his
shoes shined and his hair combed and was dressed in his
"Sunday clothes." No one ever stayed at home to cook dinner,
company or no company. No one ever stayed at home with the
babies, for the babies were always carried to church. There was
never any farm emergency such as feeding livestock, harvest-
ing, butchering or canning that kept anybody at our house
away from the house of God at the appointed time. My fa-

ther saw to that. He was the head of the home spiritually as well as the material provider.

At Duke, Oklahoma, in 1930, I preached in a revival campaign in a big tabernacle closed in with canvas curtains in midwinter. One night a well-dressed farmer sat with his wife on the back seat; the next night they sat halfway down toward the front, the third night they sat on the second seat to my right. That Friday night I preached on "A Bible Kind of Home." In my enthusiasm I left the platform and stood on the front seat and said, "Any man who leaves it to his wife to return thanks at the table, leaves it to his wife to read the Bible to the children, leaves it to his wife to teach them to pray, leaves it to his wife to take the children to Sunday school and church, to set a godly example before them and try to win them to Christ, is a slacker, a shirker, a parasite! He is not fit to be a husband of a good wife nor the father of a family!" I looked down and saw the well-dressed farmer deeply concerned with what I was saying. Supposing him to be a Baptist deacon or a Methodist steward, I said to him before the whole large crowd, pointing my finger at him, "That's so, brother, isn't it?" He cleared his throat in embarrassment, his red face turning redder than it was already, and he said, "Well—er—I guess so."

"You needn't guess about it," I challenged, "*you know* it is so, don't you?"

"Yes," he said, "I *know* it is so!"

After the service was over one of the pastors cooperating in the meeting came to me is distress. "He will never come back any more," he said. "That man is an infidel. He has never attended any campaign in this town more than twice heretofore, but he had gotten so interested in this campaign I had hopes he would keep coming and maybe get saved. But now he will never come back!"

"Well, he got the buckshot from both barrels anyway," I said. "I had him where the wool was short and he had to admit what I said was true."

But the next night, Saturday night, the man was back again with his wife, on the second seat. When I gave the invitation I stepped onto the front seat, and while others were singing I said to him softly, "Aren't you ready to turn from your folly and unbelief? Aren't you tired of your sin?" He answered very frankly, "Yes, preacher, I am."

"Then do you believe that Christ is willing to save you now, that He died for you?" I asked. He said that he did.

"And are you willing to take my hand now in token between you and me and God that you here and now confess and forsake your sins and trust Him to save your soul?" I asked.

Deeply moved, he seized my hand and assured me that he would just then take Christ as his Saviour. I then asked him if he was willing to come out publicly and let it be known that he was accepting Christ as his Saviour. All this went on while the song continued and no one heard what we said to one another.

He replied, "Brother Rice, for twenty years my wife has gone up to the Christian Church alone. I didn't go with her. I didn't help her when she got the children ready for Sunday school. I have made fun of the Bible and scoffed at preachers and God. Would it be all right for me not to tell anybody until tomorrow morning and go with my wife to the church where she has gone for twenty years and claim Christ there tomorrow morning?"

For the first time in my life, and the last, I agreed that it seemed all right to postpone public confession of Christ. The next morning he aroused the whole household demanding that every child be ready for Sunday school. To the family's amazement, he dressed in his best and went to Sunday school and the preaching service. When the invitation was given he went forward to claim Christ, and was baptized at the close of that very service. He assumed his place, God-appointed, as the high priest, the spiritual head, the godly example in the home.

Man, are you acting as God's deputy in your home? Are you saved? Are you leading your family to Heaven?

Man's Responsibility to God

The responsibility that goes with man's position in the home is appalling. It is enough to scare any man when he realizes what God expects of him. In every home which is not a Bible kind of home the husband should be blamed first of all. He is accountable before God! If the home is not a success the husband and father is primarily and first of all responsible.

After the fall in the Garden of Eden, God made man responsible for the providing of food for his family. It was to Adam, not to Eve, that God said in Genesis 3:17-19: ". . . cursed is the ground for thy sake; in sorrow shalt thou eat of it all the days of thy life; Thorns also and thistles shall it bring forth to thee; and thou shalt eat the herb of the field; In the sweat of thy face shalt thou eat bread, till thou return unto the ground; for out of it wast thou taken; for dust thou art, and unto dust shalt thou return."

The husband is even called "the saviour of the body" of his wife in Ephesians 5:23. The wife and children should be all the help they can in earning daily bread and in the duties and labor of the home, as was the good woman of Proverbs 31:10-31. Yet God expects man to take on his broad shoulders the principal care of providing for his own. That applies even to the widows of his family as you see from I Timothy 5:4, 8.

Man Should Lead in Religious Matters

The husband and father should be the high priest of the home. That is clear from one end of the Bible to the other. When God came to the Garden of Eden in the cool of the day after man's sin, He called, 'Adam, Adam, where art thou?' The Lord properly held man accountable, though the woman took the lead in the sin. In Numbers, chapter 30, the Lord clearly teaches that even a woman's duty to God is controlled by her father or her husband. The father, or husband if she is married, has a right to set aside any vow of a woman to God or to establish it. Then the husband, not the wife, is accountable for any sin in the matter. Numbers 30:13-15 says:

"Every vow, and every binding oath to afflict the soul, her husband may establish it, or her husband may make it void. But if her husband altogether hold his peace at her from day to day; then he establisheth all her vows, or all her bonds, which are upon her: he confirmeth them, because he held his peace at her in the day that he heard them. But if he shall any ways make them void after that he hath heard them; then he shall bear her iniquity."

In I Peter 3:1 the Lord commands a wife to submit even to her unsaved husband, and in Ephesians 5:22, 24 wives are commanded to submit and to be subject to their own husbands "as unto the Lord" and "in every thing." Certainly that would include many religious matters. The Scripture plainly says that women even in the churches are commanded to be under obedience to their husbands and to ask their husbands about religious matters at home (I Cor. 14:34, 35). Hear what God says:

"Let your women keep silence in the churches: for it is not permitted unto them to speak; but they are commanded to be under obedience, as also saith the law. And if they will learn any thing, let them ask their husbands at home: for it is a shame for women to speak in the church."

God has plainly commanded men to lead in matters of religion.

A man is responsible for his family whether he wants it so or not. All the lying excuses will not change the fact that a man can rear his family and so teach them and lead them and discipline them that they will serve the Lord. In Proverbs 22:6 the Lord says, "Train up a child in the way he should go: and when he is old, he will not depart from it." The Lord did not say that a child properly reared would *come back* to his father's way and a righteous life; the Lord plainly says that *the child will never leave it* even "when he is old" or grown and out from under the father's care! Fathers are responsible for their children, even responsible for their eternal soul's welfare.

Children should obey and honor both father and mother, but God certainly holds the father first in responsibility as these Scriptures show.

This responsibility for teaching and rearing children to serve the Lord is so great that God commanded His people to be earnestly diligent about it. In Deuteronomy 6:6-9 we read:

"And these words which I command thee this day, shall be in thine heart: And thou shalt teach them diligently unto thy children, and shalt talk of them when thou sittest in thine house, and when thou walkest by the way, and when thou liest down, and when thou risest up. And thou shalt bind them for a sign upon thine hand, and they shall be as frontlets between thine eyes. And thou shalt write them upon the posts of thy house, and on thy gates."

A similar passage is found in Deuteronomy 11:18-21.

Joshua Chose the Religion for His Whole Household

We have a remarkable example of a godly man in the case of Joshua. You will be thrilled to read again his last charge to the men and officers of Israel as recorded in Joshua, chapter 24. Notice that his address was especially to the heads of families and officers, according to the first verse. "And Joshua gathered all the tribes of Israel to Shechem, and called for the elders of Israel, and for their heads, and for their judges, and for their officers; and they presented themselves before God."

To these Joshua gave a great address showing how God had brought them from Egypt, through the wilderness wanderings and into the land of Canaan, with a mighty hand and great blessings; and he urged them to serve the Lord. In verse 15 he came to the great climax of his address, as follows:

"And if it seem evil unto you to serve the Lord, choose you this day whom ye will serve; whether the gods which your fathers served that were on the other side of the flood, or the gods of the Amorites. in whose land ye dwell: BUT AS FOR ME AND MY HOUSE, WE WILL SERVE THE LORD."

Joshua spoke for himself, "I will serve the Lord."

For his wife he said, "She will serve the Lord!"

For his children he said, "They will serve the Lord!"

For his servants he said, "They will serve the Lord!"

If there were grandchildren living under his roof he said, "They will serve the Lord!"

Joshua said in effect: "You heads of families choose for yourselves and your families, and I will choose for all of mine. I will serve the Lord, and I will see that my family serves the Lord!"

God give us men like Joshua, men who will serve God themselves, and then will take on their shoulders and on their consciences the responsibility before God and man for the religious teaching and guidance of their families! This is what God requires of the head of a family.

Abraham Commanded His Household Even in Religion

Abraham was a friend of God, a man that God could trust. When the Lord was about to destroy Sodom and Gomorrah, He said:

"And the Lord said, Shall I hide from Abraham that thing which I do; Seeing that Abraham shall surely become a great and mighty nation and all the nations of the earth shall be blessed in him? FOR I KNOW HIM, THAT HE WILL COMMAND HIS CHILDREN AND HIS HOUSEHOLD AFTER HIM, AND THEY SHALL KEEP THE WAY OF THE LORD, to do justice and judgment; that the Lord may bring upon Abraham that which he hath spoken of him."— Gen. 18:17-19.

Abraham commanded his children and his household after him so that they kept the way of the Lord! And for that, God blessed him and told him what was in His heart. God give us heads of families like Abraham!

Eli, an Example of a Slacker Father

The sons of Eli, the priest of God, "knew not the Lord" (I Sam. 2:12). They were covetous and adulterers, and Eli knew all about it and rebuked them lightly (I Sam. 2:22-25). However, Eli did not put a stop to the iniquity of his sons as a father can and ought to do and so the Lord pronounced a curse against Eli and his family as follows:

"In that day I will perform against Eli all things which I have spoken concerning his house: when I begin, I will also make an end. For I have told him that I will judge his house for ever for the iniquity which he knoweth; because his sons made themselves vile, and he restrained them not."—I Sam. 3:12, 13.

Fathers to Have Rebellious Sons Stoned Under Mosaic Law

So rigid was God's requirement that fathers should rear their children in strict obedience and righteousness that He commanded that rebellious sons should be publicly stoned! The father himself, aided by the mother, was to seize the rebellious son who would not obey, bring him before the elders of the city, and have him stoned to death! God commanded in Deuteronomy 21:18-21:

> *"If a man have a stubborn and rebellious son, which will not obey the voice of his father, or the voice of his mother, and that, when they have chastened him, will not hearken unto them: Then shall his father and his mother lay hold on him, and bring him out unto the elders of his city, and unto the gate of his place; And they shall say unto the elders of his city, This our son is stubborn and rebellious, he will not obey our voice; he is a glutton, and a drunkard. And all the men of his city shall stone him with stones, that he die: so shalt thou put evil away from among you; and all Israel shall hear, and fear."*

We are not under the strict penalties of the Mosaic law now, but this should illustrate how seriously in earnest and conscientiously diligent a father must be in the rearing of his children! God holds the father accountable.

God Wants Strong Men, Not Weaklings, for Heads of Families

How much God expects of the head of a family! He is to be like God in his home, verily a high priest and a prophet of God. The blame for the broken homes, the untrained and undisciplined children, the immodestly dressed and fashion-mad wives, and the whole train of evils which curse our American civilization, must be placed upon degenerate, weakling men, slackers and shirkers and quitters, not willing to take the place of manhood and bear the burdens which God lays on men as heads of families. Man, if your home is wrong, you are wrong. If your daughter turns out to be an immoral woman and your son a highjacker, you are to blame in God's sight. If your family does not live within its income, if they do not serve the Lord in sincerity and in truth, the responsibility is yours. If they have missed the blessings of the family altar, prayer in the home, thanks at the table, old-fashioned Bible discipline, God holds you to account for it. If you have not won your wife and your children to know the Lord as Saviour and to follow Him in daily life, you have failed in your duty. How great is the honor of a husband and father and how heavy are his responsibilities! Any man who is not willing to take the place God assigned to the husband and father is not fit to marry a good woman nor to bring helpless children into this world. If a man reads this who is not truly born again and a successful, every-day Christian, then for the sake of your family and for Jesus' sake, get right with God today lest you should lead your family to utter ruin away from God! Only God can make a man what he must be to be a good husband and father. Seek His help today and every day, if that position is yours.

"Husbands, Love Your Wives, Even as Christ Also Loved the Church, and Gave Himself for It"

God's standards are high. In the same Scripture where He commanded women to be subject to their husbands in everything, He commanded husbands to love their wives, even as Christ loved the church! Notice the following verses in the fifth chapter of Ephesians:

"Husbands, love your wives, even as Christ also loved the church, and gave himself for it."—Verse 25.

"So ought men to love their wives as their own bodies. He that loveth his wife loveth himself."—Verse 28.

"Nevertheless let every one of you in particular so love his wife even as himself; and the wife see that she reverence her husband."—Verse 33.

Colossians 3:19 says the same thing, that husbands are to love their wives and adds, "and be not bitter against them." In I Peter 3:7 the husband is exhorted to treat the wife with that kindness and honor Christians should show to weaker ones. Notice the words:

"Likewise, ye husbands, dwell with them according to knowledge, giving honour unto the wife, as unto the weaker vessel, and as being heirs together of the grace of life; that your prayers be not hindered."

Husband, your wife is a part of yourself. You should love her as you love your own body. Love her with the unselfish compassion that Christ has for His church. That standard is so high that it should make every man very humble as he tries to be a good husband. If the man is stronger, he should be better. If the man has more authority, he should have more responsibility. As the salvation of a sinner and the security of His saints depend on Christ, not on us, so the Lord places more heavily on man the responsibility for a happy home.

Men Can Prevent Broken Homes

The man is to "cleave to his wife." Hear the Saviour quoting from Genesis in Matthew 19:5: "For this cause shall a man leave father and mother, and shall cleave to his wife: and they twain shall be one flesh." Husbands should have a pure and tender love for their wives; a love that passes over the wife's weaknesses without bitterness.

Husbands should love their wives as special gifts from God, helpmeets to make them happy, for "Whoso findeth a wife findeth a good thing, and obtaineth favour of the Lord" (Prov. 18:22) and "A prudent wife is from the Lord" (Prov. 19:14). A husband should love his wife as the mother of his children, being with him "heirs together of the grace of life" (I Pet. 3:7).

When a husband loves his wife even as himself, and as Christ loved the church, is not bitter against her and gives her honor as the weaker vessel, and leaving father and mother cleaves unto his wife, that home will very rarely be broken.

CHAPTER VII

Wives to Be Subject to Husbands

"Unto the woman he said, I will greatly multiply thy sorrow and thy conception; in sorrow thou shalt bring forth children; and thy desire shall be to thy husband, and he shall rule over thee."—Gen. 3:16.

"Wives, submit yourselves unto your own husbands, as unto the Lord. For the husband is the head of the wife, even as Christ is the head of the church: and he is the saviour of the body. Therefore as the church is subject unto Christ, so let the wives be to their own husbands in every thing."—Eph. 5:22-24.

". . . and the wife see that she reverence her husband."—Eph. 5:33.

"Likewise, ye wives, be in subjection to your own husbands; that, if any obey not the word, they also may without the word be won by the conversation of the wives; While they behold your chaste conversation coupled with fear."—I Pet. 3:1, 2.

Should a wife obey her husband? Should she be in subjection to him? Should she submit to him as if he were God, as a Christian should submit to Christ? Should a husband have authority over his wife as parents have over their children? Should women even reverence their husbands as good women sometimes have done, obeying them and calling them lord?

The Bible does command a woman to do all of this, as we will show from many Scriptures! But modern woman says, "No!" The modern feminist movement has insisted on woman's equality with man in every respect. Women have invaded fields of endeavor once given over entirely to men. I do not especially oppose woman suffrage, nor especially favor it, and I do not believe it materially changes the outcome of elections. But it is a significant fact that women, aided by preachers and reformers, have sought and secured the right to vote and hold office. Many religious denominations now have women preachers on the same basis as men. In almost every church, the church work from singing in the choir to financing the church and doing the Bible teaching, is done principally by women. Men sit passively in an occasional service, help pay the bills, and are politely indifferent as to whether the world goes to Hell or not!

Women Seek Equality With Husbands

In marriage the same spirit has come to prevail. Women expect a marriage in which they have as much say on nearly any question to be decided as their husbands, and when it comes to the rearing of the children, household problems, discipline, or expenses, they expect to have the deciding voice. The average modern woman would answer the questions at the beginning of this chapter with an emphatic NO! She would be seconded by the mass of educators, politicians and preachers.

Even the devout church woman these days does not know the Bible explicitly commands her to obey her husband, and she does not even pretend to do it. On this subject preachers have either remained silent, or have made it a theme of silly jesting from the pulpit, while they either do not believe in, or are afraid to preach the unmistakable command of God's Word concerning it. Preachers have usually by choice omitted the word obey from the marriage ceremony, with the general approval of women, men usually remaining silent.

After the authority of husband and father in the home has been taken away, the sense of responsibility which men had in other days toward the care of their families has rapidly decreased. If a woman does not expect to obey her husband, it is also true that her husband does not expect to support his wife. There are more cases of wife and child desertion than ever before. In modern homes men do not take authority over their wives nor women submit themselves to their husbands. In modern homes men, not being the head of the home, do not feel responsible to protect and provide for their families.

Failure of Modern Homes and Marriage

The modern world has boasted of its wisdom in forsaking the old standards of marriage and the home, yet the modern marriage has failed. In the United States last year there were approximately 250,000 divorces, or one divorce for every five marriages. Over one hundred thousand children, every year, are orphaned by divorce. Certainly these homes have failed! Thousands of other homes produce boys and girls who are turned into the world without any discipline, any moral or religious training that would make them even good citizens, much less devout and happy Christians. From these unsuccessful homes, whether broken by divorce or not, come the youthful derelicts who crowd our juvenile courts and reform schools and even our penitentiaries. Besides these, modern homes pour into society, year after year, a host of young people who are undisciplined, unruly, immoral, irreligious, rebels against law and convention. The marriage and home patterned after the modern standard has failed.

Why Marriages Fail

The Bible has definite and detailed instructions concerning marriage and the relations of husband and wife. God made man and then made woman to be a helpmeet for man. He performed the first marriage ceremony. He placed man as the head of the home then, and since that time no home has ever been successful and happy which has violated God's plain command. The failure of modern marriage is caused by failure to follow God's plan for the home. Where a man disobeys God's plain command about his duty as head of the home, and where a woman refuses to obey her husband as God commanded and usurps authority which God forbade her, sin reigns in that home, and sin always brings heartache and trouble.

Man to Be Head of Wife

When God created the world He put Adam in charge of it before woman was created. Eve was created not as an equal partner, but as a helpmeet, an assistant, under Adam's control. In Genesis 2:18, we read: "And the Lord God said, It is not good that the man should be alone; I will make him an help meet for him." In I Peter 3:7 the Holy Spirit calls the wife "the weaker vessel" though she is heir with the man of the "grace of life." It was Eve who was deceived by the Devil who took advantage of her weaker nature. The first sin for which God rebuked Adam in Genesis 3:17 was: "Because thou hast hearkened unto the voice of thy wife."

Concerning this very matter, Paul was inspired to write Timothy (I Tim. 2:11-14):

"Let the woman learn in silence with all subjection. But I suffer not a woman to teach, nor to usurp authority over the man, but to be in silence. For Adam was first formed, then Eve. And Adam was not deceived, but the woman being deceived was in the transgression."

God's plan is that the husband should be the head of the wife and He even likens that to the authority of Christ over the church. Ephesians 5:23 says:

"For the husband is the head of the wife, even as Christ is the head of the church: and he is the saviour of the body."

There could be no more positive or emphatic statement that the husband is the head of the wife, the head of the home.

The above Scripture illustrates the position of husband as head of the wife by the position of Christ as head of the church. The husband is head of the wife as Christ is the head of the church. But the Lord also says that the man is over his wife as Christ is over the man and as God is the head of Christ. First Corinthians 11:3 says:

"But I would have you know, that the head of every man is Christ; and the head of the woman is the man; and the head of Christ is God."

For this reason, the Scripture continues, the woman ought to wear long hair as a covering for her head, symbolizing that she is subject to her husband. Verse 15 then says that "if a woman have long hair, it is a glory to her," while man should not have long hair since there is no one between him and Christ. Verse 7 says:

"A man indeed ought not to cover his head, forasmuch as he is the image and glory of God: but the woman is the glory of the man."

Woman is the glory of the man, and verse 9 says that the woman was created for man. This is God's plan and it is good, good for the happiness and welfare of both men and women.

In the very nature of men and women, God has written the fact that men should be head of the home and wives secondary to them in authority and subject to them. God fitted man, body, mind and heart to have the chief authority and responsibility. He fitted woman, "the weaker vessel," to take a place as helpmeet. To change this order violates the laws of nature as well as the command of God. That is why modern homes are usually unhappy and cannot have the favor of God.

God Commands Wives First, Then Husbands

Every time God gives orders to husbands and wives about their treatment of each other in the Bible, He speaks to wives first, then husbands. When He commands fathers and children about their duties to each other, He commands children first and then fathers. He commands servants first, then masters; subjects first, then rulers. God wants no excuses left to subjects who do not want to obey their rulers, a servant who does not want to obey his master, a child who does not want to obey his father, or a wife who does not want to obey her husband. When God speaks to people about their duties to Him, He speaks first to men. When He speaks to people concerning their duties to others, He speaks first to wives, then to husbands. See how this works out in the passage beginning with Ephesians 5:22 and ending with Ephesians 6:9. See the same thing in the passage beginning in Colossians 3:18 and ending with Colossians 4:1, and likewise in I Timothy 6:1, 2.

That rule is followed every place in the Bible where duties of wives and husbands to each other are discussed. Read carefully Genesis 3:16, 17, Ephesians 5:22-25, Colossians 3:18, 19; and I Peter 3:1-7. God wants children to obey their parents even if the parents are wicked. Servants should obey their masters even if they are sometimes unkind. Citizens should obey the laws of their country even though they be administered by wicked and corrupt men. Likewise, God expects women to feel their duty to obey their husbands, good or bad, saved or unsaved. Nowhere in the Bible is a wife's duty to her husband conditioned on the kind of character he has or the way he treats her. This divine order in giving commands to men and women could not be an accident, but is evidently meant to leave those who should obey without any excuse for not doing so.

Wives Should "Submit to," "Be Subject to," "Be in Subjection to," "Be Obedient to" and Even "Reverence" Their Husbands

If women knew and cared about what God expects their attitude to be toward their husbands, they would be much more careful in accepting a husband, and marriage would last longer and be happier. God's Word on this question uses stronger language than any man would dare to use of his own choice on the same subject. In fact, God's language is so strong that most preachers in their cowardly submission to modern tendencies simply ignore it and do not preach it, or they explain it away as fit only for other times or only under ideal circumstances. Preachers must answer to God for the way they preach His Word. I will give you plainly what He says about a wife's duty toward her husband. I dare not do otherwise.

Wives, Submit "As Unto the Lord"

Study the Scriptures given carefully and remember that the words are God's words, not mine, nor any man's.

Ephesians 5:22-25, 28, 33 is one of the clearest passages on the duty of a wife:

"22 Wives, submit yourselves unto your own husbands, as unto the Lord. 23 For the husband is the head of the wife, even as Christ is the head of the church: and he is the saviour of the body. 24 Therefore as the church is subject unto Christ, so let the wives be to their own husbands in every thing. 25 Husbands, love your wives, even as Christ also loved the church, and gave himself for it: ... 28 So ought men to love their wives as their own bodies. He that loveth his wife loveth himself. ... 33 Nevertheless let every one of you in particular so love his wife even as himself; and the wife see that she reverence her husband."

Wives should submit themselves to their own husbands "as unto the Lord" (vs. 22). A woman should obey her husband as if it were the Lord she were obeying, for in truth it is. That means a cheerful obedience which comes from a loving and an obedient heart. To obey her husband should be a part of a Christian woman's religion. She submits to him "as unto the Lord."

Wives Should "Be Subject . . . in Every Thing"

Verse 24, quoted above, says that "as the church is subject unto Christ, so let the wives be to their own husbands IN EVERY THING." It is true that every man, woman and child, every servant and every citizen should put God first and obey Him first. But here the Scripture seems to take for granted that there will never be a case where God will call upon a wife to disobey her husband. Women are to be subject to their husbands just as the church is subject to Christ, even in everything! A woman is to be subject to her husband even in church, and in religious knowledge as we learn in I Corinthians 14:34, 35. Wives sometimes think they please God by spending time in routine church work when their husbands want them to attend to duties at home. I have known numerous cases where wives sought to give money to the Lord's cause without the husband's consent, sometimes stealing the money from his clothes to tithe. They did wrong according to Numbers 30:13-15. If the husband forbids it, he is responsible for any sin of withholding from God, not she. Wives should be subject to their own husbands in everything, says the Word of God. The wife is to be subject in her body to her husband, even as she is to have the freedom of his body (I Cor. 7:3-5). A wife should be subject to her husband in the way she directs the house, spends the money committed to her, controls the children, in the way she dresses, in the company she keeps—in everything.

A Wife Should "Reverence Her Husband"

Ephesians 5:33 even commands that "the wife see that she reverence her husband." The Bible does not say that men deserve reverence nor are worthy of it, but the Lord does teach that wives should give it. In this connection see I Peter 3:5-6:

"For after this manner in the old time the holy women also, who trusted in God, adorned themselves, being in subjection unto their own husbands: Even as Sara obeyed Abraham, calling him lord: whose daughters ye are, as long as ye do well, and are not afraid with any amazement."

Subjection of a wife to her husband is not a slavish cringing nor a sullen submission to what one cannot avoid.

Sarah loved Abraham so, admired him so thoroughly, that, queenly woman that she was, she was not ashamed to call him lord. She was in subjection to him with the kind of reverence which God commands Christian wives to have, and Sarah is here held up as a great example to wives who would please the Lord and have happy homes. A study of the Scriptures will reveal the companionship of Abraham and Sarah as about the most ideal and happy in the entire Bible. No other woman ever came between them, they never differed over their son, Isaac, they were sweethearts until death. Happy is the woman who feels toward her husband as Sarah did, who can obey her husband with happy reverence. If you, Mrs. Modern Wife, cannot feel so toward your husband, do not be surprised if you never have the love and fellowship which Sarah had with Abraham and the respect and reverence of your children which Sarah had from Isaac.

God Commands Husbands to "Rule," Wives "Be Obedient"

Other Bible commands about the wife's duty toward her husband are as follows:

"Wives, submit yourselves unto your husbands, as it is fit in the Lord."—Col. 3:18.

"That they may teach the young women to be sober, to love their husbands, to love their children, To be discreet, chaste, keepers at home, good, obedient to their own husbands, that the word of God be not blasphemed."—Titus 2: 4, 5.

"Unto the woman he said, I will greatly multiply thy sorrow and thy conception; in sorrow thou shalt bring forth children; and thy desire shall be to thy husband, and he shall rule over thee."—Gen. 3:16.

God uses strong terms here. He says to the wife, 'Your husband shall rule over you.' He says that older women should teach young wives to be obedient to their husbands, instead of encouraging frivolous and spendthrift wives to be rebellious and break the home. God's Word is explicit and plain, and women who want to be happy, to have the real love of their husbands lasting down to old age, and the respect of their children and neighbors, which are not accorded to modern, frivolous wives, should take to heart these commands from God's Word.

Excuses of Rebellious Wives

People always have plausible excuses for not doing right. Women give many reasons for not being subject to their husbands as God commands.

It is often insisted upon that in these modern days of liberty and equality no woman could keep her self-respect and live in a home and not be counted equal with her husband in authority. But the same woman who objects to being under the authority of her husband attends clubs of which she is not president. She works in a church of which she is not pastor. She is a citizen of a government where others rule over her. Even the policeman on the corner can command her to stop or go, turn left or right, or may hail her to court where she is as helpless as a child before the law. Men, too, cannot avoid authority over them. Other members of the club, the church, the citizens are often as good, or as wise, or as well-pleasing as the president of the club, the pastor of the church, or the judge of the court. Men who work for salaries or wages, and women, too, must take orders from those in authority. And sensible people can be happy in doing so.

The rebellion of a wife against her husband is exactly the same in spirit as the rebellion of a disobedient child against his father, of an incorrigible pupil against the teacher, or a criminal against the government; it is lawlessness pure and simple. In any government, business corporation, or home, there must be those in authority. Even if everybody wanted to do right; as long as people are frail, erring mortals there will be disagreements as to what is right. Someone must decide. God has appointed the husband and father in the home as the head, and the wife, the weaker vessel, as his helpmeet.

Wives Sometimes Wiser Than Husbands

Sometimes a wife has a better education than her husband. It frequently happens that she has natural abilities which her husband does not have. Sometimes a girl leaves a good job to marry a man who has a smaller salary than she had. Naturally she feels superior. Should such a woman take orders from her husband? Should she defer to his judgment? Should she "be subject" unto him? Should she "be in subjection"? God's Word says, "Yes"! A fourteen-year-old girl in home economics classes learns to sew beautifully and can make dresses which her mother could never make. She learns home decoration, can cook economical and attractive dishes and set a table in a way her mother never knew. She may be in high school while her mother never went beyond the fifth grade. Yet the daughter should obey the mother, not the mother the daughter. That is God's rule. A fifteen-year-old boy, with the help of a county demonstration agent, learns to select seed corn, break the ground, plant, replant, fertilize and cultivate corn so that he makes a hundred bushels to the acre. It has been done more than once when the father never made more than twenty or thirty bushels to the acre. The boy has advantages the father never had, reads books the father does not know the names of, has a better education; yet the boy should be subject to his father, not the father to the boy. That is God's way. So with the wife who thinks herself superior to her husband. She should not have married a man whom she did not love enough to obey. She should not marry any man if she does not love God enough to do right.

"Don't you think women are as good as men?" people sometimes ask. Certainly, they are usually as good, sometimes worse, but many times better than their husbands. But if one who reads this is a good woman, then she will want to do right, for good wives take a wife's proper place. If you are a better Christian than your husband, then the best way to prove it is to obey God's plain commands concerning your husband and home.

Christian Wives Should Obey Unsaved Husbands

The question constantly arises about a Christian wife with an unsaved husband, and the Lord plainly answers this question in I Peter 3:1, 2:

"Likewise, ye wives, be in subjection to your own husbands; that, if any obey not the word, they also may without the word be won by the conversation of the wives; While they behold your chaste conversation coupled with fear."

Here is the case of a husband who will not obey the Word, will not listen to the Gospel, and has not been saved. The Lord says for a wife to be in subjection to such a husband and that that is the way to win him to Christ. You wives who weep over your lost husbands and who plead and pray without success for their salvation, it may be that by your disobedient hearts you have blocked the answer to your own prayers and made it so that your husbands will not listen to your pleading. The kind of religion which will make a wife the modest, unselfish, lovely and obedient wife which God commands her to be, with that "ornament of a meek and quiet spirit, which is in the sight of God of great price," that Sarah had, who obeyed Abraham, calling him lord (I Pet. 3:4-6); that kind of home religion in a wife will have more to do with the salvation of many a lost man than any amount of public preaching of the Gospel.

People ask foolish, theoretical questions here. "What if a husband should command his wife to get drunk?" etc., etc. That is a supposition for which the Lord made no provision here. We may be sure the reason is that that will not occur to a truly Christian woman who loves and obeys her husband. Husbands respect such wives and respect their religion! That is the reason God says such a course should win the husband when the preaching of the Word fails. Wives should be in subjection to their husbands, even unsaved husbands.

Evils That Follow Wrong Home Life:

1. *Lost Happiness, Faith Gone, Love Fails*

If your home is not right, "be sure your sin will find you out"! Nothing is truer in God's Word than, "Whatsoever a man soweth, that shall he also reap." Disaster, trouble, heartache and ruin follow the home where the wife is rebellious and the husband a slacker, a shirker of responsibility. Such a home cannot be happy. There must be something more than a temporary sex attraction to make a happy home, and there cannot be any real peace and happiness until the question of authority and responsibility is settled and settled right.

For a wife to have her own way does not make her happy any more than it makes a rebellious child or a lawless citizen happy to have his own way. This is another case where the wages of sin is death, death to happiness and death to all the blessings which God meant should follow marriage and a home.

True happiness in marriage is based on faith. The woman who does not trust her husband's judgment and character enough to submit to his will, cannot have the happiness which comes from full confidence. Then the husband cannot trust completely such a wife who thinks first, not of what is right or best for the home, but of her own selfish will. The companionship of husband and wife is not worth the name when faith and confidence are gone.

When happiness is gone and faith is gone, love soon follows them away. A woman will not long continue to love the man for whom she has no respect. Here is a strange fact that though the Lord many times commands the wife to be subject to her husband, to submit to him, to be obedient to him, even to reverence him, yet in the Bible there is only a single command that a woman should love her husband! The reason must be that the highest and best love must always inevitably follow this path of duty. The woman who reveres and obeys her husband will find in her heart a deep-seated love which depends not on mere sex attraction, but instead blossoms out of her own character and her position and is a gift of God! The highest form of married love is possible only in a Bible kind of a home.

When a husband's love for his wife is based upon her youth, her charm, her beauty, these, alas, all too soon fade away, and such frivolous love cannot resist the effect of time, temper, poverty and age. But the woman who is adorned with that beauty of the heart, which does not fail with age, "even the ornament of a meek and quiet spirit, which is in the sight of God of great price," attracts and makes sure of her husband's unfailing love. A husband cannot but give such a wife, not only the thrill of young love, and the passion of maturity, but the steadfastness of real respect and admiration through the years. Men and women who take the places God assigned them may expect that reward of virtue, that blessing of God, a love which does not wither when hair turns white or when bodily passions pass away! But the rebellious wife and the slacker husband give wings to love and speed it away.

2. Disobedient Children in Discontented, Ungodly Homes

It cannot be an accident that a generation of rebellious wives and irresponsible husbands and a generation of disobedient, lawbreaking children should appear in the world at the same time. A government which cannot put down gangster rule in the United States may expect a continually growing wave of crime beginning with traffic violations and ending with murders and rape, year after year, throughout the United States. One citizen cannot violate the laws with impunity without cultivating a disrespect for law. So it is in the home. The man who cannot rule his wife as God commanded (Gen. 3:16), cannot long command his children. The man who takes a place as merely a money-maker for the home, a necessary evil with no authority, will find that his children laugh at his opinions, disregard his commands and scorn his white hairs when he is old! Where the wife is lawless, children will be lawless. No scheme man can devise for the home can secure the respect and obedience of children as God's plan for a man to be the head of his home, the head over his wife.

Modern woman wants to have her cake and eat it, too. One of the pitiful things about modern women is their failure with their children, their sense of helplessness. How many such women with their gray hair, bobbed and waved in the fashion, and faces painted and their dresses of sophisticated cut, assured of themselves, boasting of their independence and equality, are yet scorned and disobeyed by their children! Put this down as an axiom, that children do not obey and respect mothers who themselves are disobedient and disrespectful wives! People reap what they sow. There is something in the character of such a rebellious woman that will make her a thorn in the side of her children. She will interfere with their lives, break up their marriages, hinder the discipline of their children. They will love her and yet despise her. Let those who do not agree with God's plan weigh well before they break His plain commands about the home.

3. *Prayer Hindered by Wrong Home Life*

In I Peter, the third chapter, the Word of God warns us that the disobedient wife and the husband who does not love and honor his wife as he ought, have their prayers hindered. In the first verse we are told that wives will win their husbands to Christ by obeying them, and verse 7, closing the paragraph, says:

"Likewise, ye husbands, dwell with them according to knowledge, giving honour unto the wife, as unto the weaker vessel, and as being heirs together of the grace of life; that your prayers be not hindered."

You pray for lost children and they are not saved. Your prayers are hindered because of wrong home life. You pray for your husband to be saved, or the husband prays for his wife's health, but your prayers are blocked, are hindered, and an angry God does not listen because of your sins. If every other consideration fails to move the heart of the man and woman who reads this, then I beg you in Jesus' name to make your home right so God can answer your prayer. All of Christian happiness, the salvation of your children, the true prosperity of a Christian home, and the peace of a Christian life depend on keeping these plain commands of God.

Come Back to God's Way

If one reads this whose heart is heavy, whose home is unhappy, one whose dreams and plans concerning loved ones and home come toppling about your ears, then come back to God today, and let Him fix your heart. After all, a happy home is a matter of religion, a matter of being right with God. Why not make confession to each other in the home, start again with family altar, begin again those old-fashioned practices of our forefathers which made their happy homes and happy hearts?

Unsaved man, how can you have the kind of home that the Lord wants you to have until you let Christ come into your heart? How can you command over your children aright until first all of you love the Lord and serve Him? Why not say with Joshua, "As for me and my house, we will serve the Lord"? Trust Christ for forgiveness today, call on God for strength to be a real man, and have the Holy Spirit to guide you in your duties in the home today. May God help you to have all the joys of a happy home, the peace of a good conscience, and the favor of God who hears your prayers because you please Him in these matters.

CHAPTER VIII

Letter to a Young Husband

Dear Friend:

Your letter tells of your disappointment and grief over the first year of your marriage. You love the Lord, you want to serve Him, and yet you find that your own marriage is in some sense failing to give the happiness and peace it ought to give, and problems have arisen which you and your young bride do not know how to settle. Your case is typical of many, many others. Because of our most intimate friendship and because the problems that you face are faced by so many others, I think I should take time, heartily and lovingly and faithfully, to deal with the problems you are facing in your own life.

You asked me to pray and help share your burden. I will, but prayer is not primarily what you need. Young people like yourself and your good wife need first of all to learn to adjust themselves to one another and to the marriage relationship and to life in the light of God's Word. An earnest message from the Word of God will do you more good than prayer. And if you can come to your problems wholly surrendered to the will of God as we find it in the Word of God, then nothing will be too hard to settle happily.

You have it in your favor that both of you are Christians, that you truly love one another, that you honestly want your lives to count for God. You also have a loving Heavenly Father who knows all your burdens and problems and a Bible which has the answer to daily problems of duty and happiness. On the other side, it is fair to say that you are handicapped naturally by the inexperience of youth. There is hardly anywhere you could go to have Christian help on the problems, the intimate personal problems of marriage. There are no lectures you could attend. There are no books to read, Christian books, which are generally available, to help on many of the problems you mentioned. And for that reason I feel that I should write in some detail how God's Word applies to your problems.

I write to you primarily, and not primarily to your bride.

God has put the man as the head of the wife. You are stronger than your wife. You are the deputy of God in your home, God's high priest. Therefore the happiness of the home depends more on you than on your wife. "For the husband is the head of the wife, even as Christ is the head of the church" (Eph. 5:23). Again, "Likewise, ye husbands, dwell with them according to knowledge, giving honour unto the wife, as unto the weaker vessel, and as being heirs together of the grace of life" (I Pet. 3:7). Are you wiser than your wife? You ought to be, in many respects. Then that means that God will hold you more accountable for the happiness of your home than the wife. Are you stronger than your wife? Then God expects you to bear the principal load of maintaining a happy and successful home. Are you a better Christian than your wife? You ought to be. You are called to preach. You are older in years than she is. You naturally are expected to be a Christian leader under the circumstances. Then you ought to be a better Christian than your wife. You ought to be able to have grace enough to face the problems and get them settled. You ought to be able to influence your wife and lead her in the happy and good way. So I hope you will take on yourself a sense of the burden that God expects a husband to have for his own home. Do not blame the wife until first of all you make sure you have done all you ought to do.

From the Bible standpoint there is no getting out of this truth. So I write to you. I hope your good wife will read the letter and will pray with you about the solutions I suggest for some of your problems. But remember that God intends that you should take the lead in the home and that you should be accountable for having the home honor God daily. You are in some sense accountable for the wife. She left her home, changed her plans, changed her name, gave herself into your care. With a man, marriage is only a part of his life. If you were called to preach before you were married, you made no change when you were married. A man does not change his life work, usually does not change his residence, and does not change his name when he marries. But when a girl marries, that means a change of all of her life, her career, her plans. Marriage and home are a whole career for a good woman. So surely, when a woman has given herself so completely to a man as to marry him, and leave all for him, change her name for him and be his wife, then that man ought to feel accountable to God for her happiness and for the happiness of the home to which he brought her.

Now will you prayerfully consider the suggestions I make? I believe God will use them to help you to have a happy home.

I. I Fear You Have a Wrong Conception of How to Have a Happy Home

Young people generally feel that marriage itself brings happiness. A loving young couple thinks that just for these two themselves to be together will be Heaven on earth. It does not prove out that way. There are very definite limitations to the happiness that marriage itself can bring.

First of all, marriage increases trouble. That is necessarily true. First Corinthians 7:28 says, "But and if thou marry, thou hast not sinned; and if a virgin marry, she hath not sinned. Nevertheless such shall have trouble in the flesh: but I spare you." You see, the inspired apostle says of those who marry, "Nevertheless such shall have trouble in the flesh." It is harder to support two than to support one. It is harder to please yourself and please someone else than it is to please yourself alone. The husband has the added care of making the living, the care of making his family happy, the care of seeing that they follow in the steps of the Lord. All the burdens of the wife become the husband's burdens. All the responsibilities of children will devolve upon him. Likewise with a woman, it is much easier to live a single life than to be married, to bear children through the pain of childbirth; to wait on them, train them, and then after awhile lose them! There is trouble in the flesh, necessarily, connected with marriage.

Marriage is necessarily a yoke, an intimate and permanent one. That yoke can be a very galling and bitter yoke. Certainly marriage ties one for life to a companion.

No one ought to marry who does not face this simple truth of the burden and responsibility that is inevitable in marriage. If a man were marrying a perfect angel who had never sinned and could not bear in her blood the taint of sin, then he might well expect perfect happiness in marriage. He who marries under any such supposition, however, is blind indeed. Women are human beings. If children are often rebellious, then wives will be rebellious also because they have in them all the taint of sin that they had as children. If other women nag, or talk too much, or sulk, or fret, or want more attention, then every man who marries should expect that some of these traits will necessarily appear in his own beloved wife. She, too, is human just as he is. There is a burden to marriage, and no one ought to expect to miss it. There are great blessings in marriage, a Christian marriage, if two people really love one another and are willing to adjust themselves each to the other. But these blessings are counteracted somewhat by the necessarily inevitable burdens of marriage. You have trouble in the flesh. Do not think it strange. Every other man who ever married had trouble in the flesh, too. That is a part of God's bargain in marriage, and Christian people should believe the Bible and respect it.

I think you have the wrong conception of marriage in that you do not realize that happiness in marriage is an achievement. It does not necessarily come of itself. People are not happy just because they are married. They have to develop their happiness. They have to sow the seeds of happiness. They have to pay a price for happiness.

Even in the Christian life this is true. People are not happy Christians just because they have been converted. Unless they beware, Christians will soon lose their early joy and their first love. A Christian who does not take time to read the Bible, take time to pray, will not enjoy the Lord and will not feel His presence day by day. Happiness in Christian life does not come simply because one is converted, is a born-again Christian. It is a daily achievement. So happiness in marriage does not automatically follow when people who love one another marry. It takes daily care and duty to maintain a happy marriage.

I say, happiness is not just a natural result of marriage. It is a goal to be achieved day by day. One must sow the seeds of happiness day by day to reap the crop of happiness. And when you quit sowing, then you will quit reaping the happiness which God wants people to have in marriage. There are certain rules to follow, certain prices to pay for married happiness.

Then I feel that you have not realized that adjustment takes time. How wonderful it is that two people can become one flesh, as the Scripture says that they do. A man and wife may become so of one mind and heart, so wrapped up in the same thing that they do not have clashing personalities:

rather each one is a different part of one personality. Many people would feel that they were not all themselves if they should lose their dear companion. I have just talked to a couple who have been married forty-three years. They take their vacations together. They sleep in the same bed, even though it be an upper berth in a Pullman car! They never want to be away from each other. They never, even in joke, disparage one the other. They have really become one in their thinking, one in their desires and joys. Half apologetically, she mentioned one thing that she liked that he did not like. Each of them seemed a little troubled that they did not see alike on this one incidental matter of pleasure!

Do you think that this oneness just automatically happens when two young people stand before the minister in bridal dress and say, "I do"? If so, you are mistaken. The adjustment of marriage takes time.

When a new worker comes to Sword of the Lord Publishers and goes to work, we expect him to take weeks, perhaps months, before he learns to fit into the routine and fit into the personnel and ideals of this Christian publishing house. People who have been accustomed to doing things one way must learn to do them another way. People who have plans of their own must learn to defer to the plans of others. These new workers must learn all the literature published by Sword of the Lord Publishers, meditate on it, absorb it, learn to love it, before they can be wholly at one with the purpose of the organization. They must grow enthusiastic about *The Sword of the Lord*, the Christian weekly paper, that we publish. They must grow enthusiastic about the book on *Prayer* which has blessed so many thousands of hearts and homes. They must thank God for the millions of copies of the little book, *"What Must I Do to Be Saved?"* scattered all over the world to sinners; and they must be proud of those thousands who have trusted Christ as Saviour through the printed word which we distribute. I am saying it takes time for one to be really absorbed into the work of Sword of the Lord Publishers office.

And if that be true, how much truer it is that it takes time for a husband and wife to become adjusted to one another, for each one to fit his life plans and heart's desires to that of his or her beloved mate. It takes time for a home to grow and for a marriage to ripen and for thorough and happy adjustment to be made.

This is one reason why such a large percent of the divorces happen at about the end of the first year. People who thought that they would just automatically see everything alike and be happy, each with the other's will, come to see that it is not that easy. Disillusionment results. They sometimes think they could never be happy, that they are incurably "incompatible." However, that is not the case. It necessarily takes time for people to grow accustomed each to the other's ways and to make the concessions and give up the personal will that one must give up in order to please his companion in many, many matters.

Sex adjustment itself necessarily takes time. Among good Christian people it is the ideal that a girl should be sheltered and grow up without any special outward stimulus in sex matters. Of course, we believe that girls should learn to love and should become engaged and should marry at the proper age. But in the nature of the case, a girl who loves a Christian young man and marries him finds that the sex matters are still largely a mystery. Every young husband will find that it takes time in tenderness and petting and many caresses and much fondling, before his young wife comes to feel as he does about the marriage relationship. Investigations by physicians have found that the majority of young married women report that sex intercourse in the early weeks and months of marriage is very rarely satisfactory. Many women have been married a year before they learn to fully enjoy and appreciate the mating which is a part of marriage. God intended that a woman should enjoy her husband fully as much as a husband enjoys his wife. Love is just as dear to a woman as to a man and caresses are perhaps even more desired. God certainly made a woman as capable of full enjoyment of the privileges of marriage as a man. But God intended that a man should naturally be more aggressive in this matter than a woman, and He has provided that a woman needs to be taught and led and loved until she grows to the fullest response and the happiest experience in the love life of a married couple.

It is foolish, and I think even irreverent, to expect that the full joy of marriage should come at once. This is a matter of adjustment and achievement. It takes time for marriage to ripen into the complete mating of heart and mind and body which God intended. I say, the happiness of marriage is an achievement which takes time and thought and much love and unselfish devotion. Young couples are often impatient on this matter, particularly young husbands.

II. You Expect Too Much of Your Wife, I Think

Like many another husband, particularly preacher husbands, I think you expect too much of your young wife. Prayerfully consider what I have to say on this subject.

First, I think you expect too much of her spiritually. She is not called to preach as you are. It is true that she ought to be a good Christian, just as good a Christian in her own place as you are in yours, just as useful where God wants her to be useful as you are to be where God wants you to be useful. But it is nevertheless true that your wife is not called of God to preach. She does not have the burden on her soul that you have. Therefore, God will not give her the same preparation that He gives you. He will not give her the same burden about the Bible that He gives you. He will not give her the same insight into spiritual problems that He gives you. It would be a strange kind of God, don't you think? who would call a man to preach and then not give him any better preparation, any more heart passion, any more spiritual insight, than He would give to a girl who is never to preach. You see, you have rather felt that your bride ought to be as willing to spend long hours in studying the Bible as you are.

The truth is that your own study of the Bible is not altogether that of a simple Christian. It is the Bible study of a preacher. That is your profession. That is your life work. You must not expect any of the laity to feel exactly the same way about such matters as you feel, when to them it is not their full life's work.

You remember that the Scripture has a very clear teaching on this subject. First Corinthians 14:34, 35 says, "Let your women keep silence in the churches: for it is not permitted unto them to speak; but they are commanded to be under obedience, as also saith the law. And if they will learn any thing, let them ask their husbands at home: for it is a shame for women to speak in the church." Your wife does not know the Bible as well as you do. In fact, if you do right and she does right, she never will understand the Bible as well as you do. God's plan for her is, on many matters, that she should come to her husband and ask him the will of God and ask him what the Bible means. It is not fair for you to expect your wife to be the same kind of Bible student you are, nor to love Bible study as well, nor to be equipped as well for that study.

The same thing will be true about prayer. Of course, I believe in family devotions, thanks at the table, and such matters. But these should be the simple devotions and the simple Bible reading which Christians would have together, not a theological seminary. Your Bible reading and your prayer life will be one kind, and part of it you ought to do in the study and alone. The prayer and devotions which you have with your wife should be such simple and beautiful and brief devotions as any kind of a Christian can enjoy and appreciate and take part in.

It is not right for you to feel that your wife is uninterested because she does not have the same passion that God has put into your heart as a preacher. It is not right for you to accuse her nor to leave her to feel she is inferior, because she is not equal to you in this respect. I think you have expected too much of her about it.

And next, in her duties as a wife, it seems to me you have expected too much of your wife. You see, marriage is her career. Preaching is your career. You have not proved such a howling success in one year or so. I think God is using you. I think you are learning the business. I think you are growing in grace. Yet you yourself would quickly admit that you are only a beginner, only an inexperienced apprentice in the matter of the ministry. Then how could you expect your wife to be a finished and perfected wife and housekeeper and companion in this short time, You may be sure that there is as much to learn for your wife to be a good helpmeet and preacher's wife as there is for you to learn in being a preacher. So do not be impatient if your wife has not progressed any faster than you have. Her career is marriage. Your career is the ministry. Do not expect her to develop any faster than you do, each in his own life's sphere of service.

When a girl about twenty marries, it is only natural that she would still be young and have young ideas. She wants to be up late at night. She does not want to buckle down all the time to work. She wants to laugh and sing and play some as well as to work and be serious and sober and pray and read the Bible. It takes time for a girl to grow mature and into full wifehood.

Then I think that no woman has developed fully perhaps until she has borne a child or two. Nothing can take a woman out of herself as bearing a baby, nursing the little one, watching after him day and night and forgetting her own will and pleasure for the joy of serving the little one. You see, it takes time for a woman to become a successful wife and to become an expert at her life's career of marriage. It would be unfair to your dear girl, a sweet, good, loving and Christian wife as she is, to expect her to become suddenly mature and able to bear the loads which devolve upon a preacher's wife.

I lovingly urge that you do not forget that you have not yet reached such a place of eminence in your own profession that you can afford to be critical of her. She has had less time than you have to learn her profession, that of being a good wife. Patience here is not only right but is absolutely necessary if you would grow a happy marriage.

III. You Have Not Yet Fulfilled Your Duty to Your Wife

If your wife has somewhat failed in her place as a mate, that is not surprising. I hope you will prayerfully consider that you yourself have not yet been able to fulfill all your duty as a husband.

"Husbands, love your wives, even as Christ also loved the church, and gave himself for it; That he might sanctify and cleanse it with the washing of water by the word, That he might present it to himself a glorious church, not having spot, or wrinkle, or any such thing; but that it should be holy and without blemish. So ought men to love their wives as their own bodies. He that loveth his wife loveth himself. For no man ever yet hated his own flesh; but nourisheth and cherisheth it, even as the Lord the church."—Eph. 5:25-29.

Do you love your wife as Christ loved the church? That is the standard that the Holy Bible sets for Christian husbands. Remember how merciful is Christ to His church. What was His purpose in loving us whom He has bought with His own blood? "That he might sanctify and cleanse it [the church] with the washing of water by the word, That he might present it to himself a glorious church, not having spot, or wrinkle, or any such thing; but that it should be holy and without blemish." That is how men ought to love their wives. Christ in mercy loved us when we were wicked sinners. So a husband loves his imperfect wife and sets out to grow her into a holy and beautiful character without spot or blemish. Christ will never have His pay, never have His reward for His mercy and kindness to us Christians until we in Heaven are presented to Him without spot and blemish. So a husband must be willing to wait for the growing beauty of his wife's character and should set out to develop this character day by day.

How merciful is the Lord Jesus to us who have trusted Him! How long-suffering toward our weaknesses and our failures! He knows our frame and He remembers that we are dust. He loves us still. Every Christian husband is to feel that way toward the wife.

God has set the man to represent Jesus Christ in the home. I do not feel that I am worthy as to be called the Christ of our home as my wife is to be called the church or bride of our home. My love is not good enough to be called equal with Christ's or to be pictured by His love. But here is the holy demand of the Scripture that a husband is to so love his wife.

Of course the Bible commands wives to be subject to their husbands. Certainly wives should be obedient and should be meek and quiet in spirit. But the husband is to set out to develop this character in his wife. And by loving her, by devotion and long-suffering and forgiveness and constant goodness, he is to rule and win and train his wife until she can be presented to him as a complete and satisfying wife, even as Christ one day expects to receive the church without spot and without blemish.

Each of us must honestly confess that according to this passage in Ephesians, demanding that a husband love his wife as Christ loves the church, husbands should love wives more than wives are commanded to love husbands. Husbands have the larger duty, the more compelling responsibility in marriage. Do you feel that you have fully completed your duty in this matter? It would be good for all of our hearts if we husbands would confess our lack and our failure at this point.

The command of Colossians 3:19 is, "Husbands, love your wives, and be not bitter against them." The Holy Spirit who dictated this passage well knew how many husbands would be fretted by their wives. Many times every husband is fretted, I suppose, by the "trouble in the flesh" which the Scripture says goes with marriage.

Before you married, no doubt, your wife seemed to be a paragon of virtue and beauty. Remember that "love is blind." What a pity that it does not always stay blind after marriage! And so after you married her you found that she had faults and frailties as other women had. How surprised you were! But remember God's Word says, "Husbands, love your wives, and be not bitter against them."

No matter how much your wife has failed, be not bitter against her. You are to love your wife as Christ loved the church. You are to be long-suffering as He is long-suffering toward us. You are to be forgiving as He is forgiving. And even in matters where your wife is clearly wrong, which will sometimes be the case, you are not to be bitter against her. You are not to hold grudges, not to hold resentment, not to be bitter. For a husband to be bitter against his wife is a sin.

Here is a place for men to prove that they are stronger, are wiser, are better. Here is a place for every Christian man to prove that he is a good Christian. Part of a husband's duty is such a forgiving tenderness that he will never feel bitterness against his wife and never hold a grudge against her. Have you fulfilled your duty to your wife in this matter? Have you never been bitter against her? If you have sometimes failed, then let that be a reminder to be even more kindly toward her failings.

I fear you have failed your wife also in the matter of showing your affection, in taking time for caresses and kindness. You say that your wife wanted to stay up late at night, and then she felt bad that you were out of bed the first thing in the morning for your time of Bible study and prayer and devotions. No doubt, she feels cheated and feels that she does not get the loving attention that she expected.

You see, a woman wants caresses. A woman wants words of love. And she has a right to them, just as much right to them after she is married as before. And you will be accountable to God for her unhappiness if you do not take time to love her and pet her.

I am surprised and shocked to hear that any young married couple should have the mating experience only a dozen times in the first year of marriage. I am shocked because that indicates that something abnormal prevents what would be the natural and happy course for a young married couple. Perhaps there is some fear of pregnancy which interferes with her happiness and willingness, or you may have failed to caress her and love her enough to lead to the normal and happy surrender of a wife to her husband. Or it may be that you have been too critical so that neither of you had the devotion which is normally expressed in caresses and the marriage relationship. Remember that the Scripture says plainly, "Let the husband render unto the wife due benevolence: and likewise also the wife unto the husband. The wife hath not power of her own body, but the husband: and likewise also the husband hath not power of his own body, but the wife. Defraud ye not one the other, except it be with consent for a time, that ye may give yourselves to fasting and prayer, and come together again, that Satan tempt you not for your incontinency" (I Cor. 7:3-5).

That Scripture makes it clear, first, that God does not put any limit on the normal relationship of a husband and wife. Second, it clearly says that neither companion has a right to deprive the other of the expression of love and devotion which is normal in the marriage relationship. "The wife hath not power of her own body, but the husband: and likewise also the husband hath not power of his own body, but the wife." The word "power" there would better be translated "authority." As a wife does not have authority over her own body, but her body belongs to the husband, even so a husband does not have authority over his body. It belongs to the wife.

Then the Scripture plainly says, "Defraud ye not one the other." The only exception is when both are agreed to give themselves to fasting and prayer for a little season. Otherwise it is normal and right for husband and wife to use the same bed and for the wife to have her pleasure and the husband to have his pleasure. Both are to be satisfied. This is a clear teaching.

Your wife wanted you to give her attention in the morning, to lie abed and talk with her. She felt that her due and her right. Without being able to put it into words, no doubt, she felt cheated and felt that you did not love her as you should, when you had no time to love her and caress her, no time for sweet conversation in the beginning of the day. Remember that that was her right. Your body belongs to her. You do not have the say about it, but your wife does. I wonder, have you in this matter 'rendered unto the wife due benevolence' that is commanded in I Corinthians 7:3?

I know how important is the early morning watch, the

time of devotion to God when one reads His Word and prays and meditates. I hope you will keep it up all your days. But I am sure that you ought to adjust your plans so that you may have time for your wife and time to make her happy. I think that if you will spend enough time each day in the duties of a husband, in loving caresses and love-making, you will find that the husband-and-wife relationship will become normal and happy for both of you.

You should be proud of your wife. She wants you to think she is beautiful. She wants you to desire her affection. She naturally wants your hands upon her and your pride and love to be shown by the tender caresses and fondling which are the due of a wife. On this matter a husband who cheats or who falls short will find that he loses by it. And real devotion and unselfish care here by a patient husband who loves his wife and tries to make her happy as well as tries to obey the commands of the Bible, will bring wonderful rewards in the long run. He will find his wife will grow in understanding and devotion to him and she will feel that she was not cheated when she gave herself fully to him and that she is not unappreciated.

When a woman gives her heart and life to her husband, gives her body into his keeping, certainly she has a right to expect devotion and tenderness and some gentle love-making.

Happiness is to be achieved. And so love is to be fed day by day if it is to bear sweet and perfect fruit. I am sure that God wants you to seek Him early in the morning. But remember that you are to have the attitude toward your wife which Christ has towards the church. What if Christ should say to us Christians, "I have no time for you. I am so absorbed in My love for My Father that I have no time for you sinners who are members of My body, who are My bride"? That is *not* the way the Lord Jesus feels. That is not the way He acts. And that is not the way for a Christian husband to act. Your duty to God will not lead you away from your wife to such an extent as to leave her miserable and unhappy.

It is true that God must come first. It is true that sometimes a husband must leave his wife alone and lonely. But first let him make sure that he proves his love and devotion and has her assured that she has her rightful place as the queen of his heart! Give to your wife the proper due of devotion and love and caresses and fondling and appreciation, and you will find that she will be happy and so will make you happy, too.

Have you fulfilled your duty to your wife in these matters? A husband's part is not easy. The Scripture says in I Peter 3:7, "Likewise, ye husbands, dwell with them according to knowledge, giving honour unto the wife, as unto the weaker vessel and as being heirs together of the grace of life; that your prayers be not hindered." The wife is a weaker vessel, and so should have special honor. Though she be the weaker vessel, and though she be subject to her husband, she is still one of the two partners in the holy business of bringing life into this world. They are "heirs together of the grace of life." Any husband who does not dwell with his wife according to knowledge (that is knowledge of his responsibility and knowledge of the Scriptures on this point, knowledge of his wife's weaker nature and dependent need of him) will find his prayers hindered.

IV. And Now May I Humbly Suggest That Your Attitude Is Wrong in Some Details

First, I am sorry to say, you fear that your wife is not a Christian because she does not find the same joy in Bible study and Christian work that you do. The Scripture has plainly said, "Judge not, that ye be not judged" (Matt. 7:11). No one in the world has a right to judge whether others are converted or not, if they say that they have put their trust in Jesus Christ. And there is a certain plague, a certain curse, a certain punishment that follows this sin of judging others. Jesus said, "For with what judgment ye judge, ye shall be judged: and with what measure ye mete, it shall be measured to you again" (Matt. 7:2). You see, if you judge others you arouse a critical spirit, and this critical spirit is one of the great foes to married happiness. Again Jesus said on this same matter, "Thou hypocrite, first cast out the beam out of thine own eye; and then shalt thou see clearly to cast out the mote out of thy brother's eye" (Matt. 7:5). It is hard to be called hypocrite, but those who judge others are called that by the Lord Jesus. And this pharisaical attitude of judging others to be unsaved means that we certainly need to search our hearts and get a clear conception of our own needs and our own failures, and also of God's mercy.

Those who put their trust in Christ are saved. Many Chris-

tians do not have the theological understanding of all that
happened when they were converted. But if one came to
see himself a sinner and trusted in Christ for mercy, then he
is saved. And none of us knows the human heart, and we can
only, in fairness, believe the word of those who say they have
put themselves under the blood by trusting in the mercy of
Christ who died for them.

You think that your young wife does not have the devotion
to Christ that you have, and feel that she has never had the
spiritual experience of full surrender to Christ such as you
have had, because she does not enjoy such long seasons of Bible study and prayer as you enjoy. But I remind you again
that you are a preacher. This to you is not only Christian living but is a profession. It is your duty. God has laid burdens
on you that are not on all Christians. God has given you an
insight that not all Christians have. And you wrong your wife
in doubting her sincerity and in doubting her love for Christ
just because she does not yet enjoy the Scriptures, perhaps, as
much as you.

In the nature of the case, she is less mature spiritually than
you are. That is usually true about women. Women are more
fervent in their love for Christ, perhaps, and more easily led.
They have more leisure for church work than men have. But
well-developed Christian men are usually superior to well-developed Christian women in their understanding of the Bible,
and in their leadership. So you ought not to judge your wife's
heart in this matter. If she be weak, then lead her and teach
her, but believe sincerely in what she tells you about her love
for Christ.

To claim you have had experiences that she has not had
and to leave her with a feeling that you think her inferior
strike at the very root of her pride and happiness. How can
she be happy with a husband who is disappointed in her? She
could not feel as a wife wants to feel toward her husband
when she feels that she herself is a failure and that there is
little use of trying to please you. I only estimate her feelings
by what other women tell me of themselves. For every
woman longs to feel that she is the ideal of her husband in
that he loves and trusts her implicitly. So if she has fallen
short somewhat in her devotion to the Bible and in her seasons of prayer, then think of her kindly and remember that
God expects more of a man than of a woman and He ex-

pects infinitely more of a minister than of one who is not a minister.

But far more important than these is one matter in which I think you are grievously wrong. And that is you blame your young wife for your failure in the ministry. You say that in the year's time you have only won one or two souls as I recall. So you think because she did not pray with you, because she did not read the Bible with you, and perhaps because she was not willing to go continually from house to house in visitation, but rather wanted to stay and decorate the little apartment and enjoy it, that she is to be blamed that your ministry is a failure. But you are utterly mistaken. You yourself must take whatever blame there is for your failure. You have no right to put it upon your wife.

No wife in the world can keep her husband from winning souls if he stays right with God. Your wife cannot be blamed if the power of the Holy Spirit is not upon you. It is always the easy way out to blame others when we do not please God, and do not have His power and do not get results. May I speak frankly here and very kindly? It seems likely to me that the same superior attitude that has grieved your wife may have grieved others. Your self-righteous satisfaction with yourself and your critical attitude toward others would drive other people from you just as quickly as it has driven your wife away. Oh, how we do need, each of us, a humble and contrite heart! And how we do need to take the blame for our own failures and our own sins!

I remember that as a young minister I once felt I must lay the blame on others if I did not have a revival in my church. I have learned that that was wrong. Although we could have a greater revival and have more souls saved if every member of the church were right with God, I have learned that if I am right with God I can have many souls saved and I can have much blessing. Nobody in the world can keep God from blessing one man, one preacher, if he is wholly laid on the altar, if he is filled with the Holy Spirit, and if he really goes on to do what God tells him to do.

Your powerlessness must not be blamed on your wife.

The fact that your ministry is somewhat of a failure in your own eyes, and by your own confession, indicates that you may be to blame for the failure of happiness in your marriage, just as well as to blame for the failure in your ministry to have the success that you wanted to have. The people

to whom you preached were not blessed. They did not want
your ministry to continue. You did not have the persuasion,
the kindliness, the spiritual power to win them over. Of
course, some people would object to the Apostle Paul himself, but always he won some. Always he gained friends and
followers and got people converted. And so may you if you
have God's best blessing upon you.

Last of all may I say that in your letter you did not exhibit
any sense of your own lack. You had no confessions for your
own failure. You did not even confess to a sense of inexperience. It would be only normal for a young husband to make
mistakes, but I do not see how those mistakes can be reme-
died until one has a sense of his weakness and inexperience.
You asked me to pray, but you did not ask me for counsel
because you seem to feel that you did not need counsel, that
your end was already carried well enough, and that there was
nothing left undone by you. Forgive me if I grieve you, because I really want to help you and help your marriage. But
if you want God to help you to have a happy marriage, then
you must confess your own weakness and inexperience and
confess how you must have grieved your wife as you probably have grieved others. Surely you are human, as she is, and
you need mercy and forgiveness as she does.

Now I suggest that you set out to have a good time of
love-making with your wife. I think you ought to tell her that
she is lovely and beautiful, for she is. I think you should tell
her that you have sometimes failed her, have been impatient,
have not given her enough of your time and have not spent
enough time in caresses and love-making such as any young
wife wants and needs and has a right to. I think you might
admit that you have sometimes misunderstood her. I think
you should ask her to tell you frankly how she feels. I think
you should promise to try to make her happy. That is your
duty. And then I think you should set out to win her. Woo
her gently and kindly and pray much about it. Pray that God
will give her heart completely into your keeping and that you
may make her completely happy. Your own happiness will
necessarily follow.

And if you can have this victory, you will have victory in
your ministry also. You love the Word of God and I think
you know it well. I think you are willing to follow the Lord
Jesus if you can get pride and self-will out of the way and

somewhat conquer, by God's grace, this proud attitude which has stood in your way.

Now, do not take your troubles too seriously. They are a part of married life. You love your wife, and she loves you. Both of you are Christians. You are bound together for better or for worse. You will learn to solve your difficulties, and the Lord is ready to help you. There He is, just at your elbow. Then depend upon Him and be happy, and make your home what it ought to be.

CHAPTER IX

Normal Sex Life in Marriage

"And they were both naked, the man and his wife, and were not ashamed."—Gen. 2:25.

"Marriage is honourable in all, and the bed undefiled: but whoremongers and adulterers God will judge."—Heb. 13:4.

"Let the husband render unto the wife due benevolence: and likewise also the wife unto the husband. The wife hath not power of her own body, but the husband: and likewise also the husband hath not power of his own body, but the wife. Defraud ye not one the other, except it be with consent for a time, that ye may give yourselves to fasting and prayer; and come together again, that Satan tempt you not for your incontinency."—I Cor. 7:3-5.

The chapter heading says that sex life is normal in marriage, and that is true. Sex relations between husband and wife are normal, beautiful, good, and have not only the permission, but the blessing of God.

The Bible Provides Unhindered Freedom of Married Love

God made man and woman for each other in marriage. In the Garden of Eden, where there was no sin, God made a wife for Adam, and they were man and wife in every normal sense. There, "they were both naked, the man and his wife, and were not ashamed."

There God told them to "multiply, and replenish the earth" (Gen. 1:28). There in the Garden of Eden, had not sin caused them to be driven out, would have been born their children. The love-making and mating of husband and wife is as normal and blameless as eating and sleeping, working and playing.

Among the thousands of questions asked me seriously in letters, more than once is this one: "Was the first sin, the sin for which Adam and Eve were cast out of the Garden of Eden, that of sexual intercourse?" That question is silly, but at least one "Bible teacher," self-styled, who has published his ideas widely, answers that question in the affirmative. The same man had himself made a eunuch, though married, thinking thus to be a better Christian. But that is a perverted view. Adam and Eve mated by God's plan, and with His blessing. Their sin, in eating fruit of the tree of knowledge of good and evil, was a sin of direct disobedience in a wholly different matter. Not one word of Scripture hints that Adam and Eve were wrong to live as husband and wife, even in the Garden of Eden where there was no sin.

"Marriage is honourable in all, and the bed undefiled," says Hebrews 13:4. That Scripture says that marriage is intended to include the marriage bed, and that the mating of husband and wife is holy and blameless. In fact, God's Word takes it for granted that sex relations between husband and wife are always normal, not limited by any rules except their own happiness and choice. And what the Bible here states plainly, all the rest of the Bible implies. Not once in the Bible is there one word of reproach for any husband and wife because of their sex relations. Nowhere in the Book of God is there a hint or suggestion that such normal sex life should be limited to that intended to secure children, nor limited in any other way.

In fact, the Scripture, which is divinely inspired to give perfect instruction in all matters of duty, expressly says that the intercourse of husband and wife is a duty as well as a privilege, that it is a benevolence each mate owes the other, and a husband is to have authority over his wife's body, as she is to have authority over his, in this matter. It declares that they are not to defraud one the other of the normal joys of the marriage bed, nor to live without normal sex relations more than a short while at a time, and that only by mutual consent for such purposes as fasting and prayer. Read again the instructions of the inspired Apostle Paul in I Corinthians 7:3-5: "Let the husband render unto the wife due benevolence: and likewise also the wife unto the husband. The wife hath not power of her own body, but the husband: and likewise also the husband hath not power of his own body, but the wife. Defraud ye not one the other, except it be with consent for a time, that ye may give yourself to fasting and prayer; and come together again, that Satan tempt you not for your incontinency."

This plain Scripture ought to settle forever the truth that married love and partnership in sex life is normal, and has no restrictions in the Word of God. Christians ought to be temperate in all things, but what is temperate use of marriage must be decided by each husband and wife according to their own happiness and desire, just as each must decide what is temperate in eating according to the needs and hunger of his body.

A Christian once said he supposed that all sex life was sinful, even that of husband and wife, since David was inspired of God to say, "Behold, I was shapen in iniquity; and in sin did my mother conceive me" (Ps. 51:5). But he utterly misunderstood that Scripture. It simply says that David was a sinner because the whole race is sinful, and he inherited a sinful nature from his mother (and of course, from his father). David is confessing to God the depravity of his nature, and of all human nature. He did not mean that his mother sinned in his conception.

So married love should normally include sex enjoyment. Such sex life of husband and wife is holy and good and blessed of God.

Only Perversion of Sex Is Sinful

Most of us grew up, I suppose, with some feeling that sex is a guilty subject, an unclean subject. We were taught, if we grew up in decent Christian families, to maintain a modest reserve in sex matters. We were taught modesty about our bodies. That was well and good. But unhappily, most of what we saw or heard about sex matters was about their perversion. Dirty talk and perverted actions in the realm of sex left us with a sense of shame about it. What we heard about was not the normal use of sex. The relations of husbands and wives, the normal and beautiful and sacred begetting and planning for and bearing of loved and wanted children, was not taught as it ought to be taught, as God's plan for our happiness and good.

God has clearly taught in His Word that children should not see the nakedness of their fathers and mothers (Lev. 18:7). For gazing on the uncovered body of his father Noah, Ham earned a divine curse upon himself and his children. So, clearly, a proper reverence should be taught children toward the persons of their parents. Of course, there should be a sacred intimacy between husbands and wives that they should not share with their children or others. But the impersonal facts and beautiful mysteries and wonders of mating and reproduction, in which husband and wife are partners of God in creation, are "heirs together of the grace of life" as I Peter 3:7 says, should be taught to children. Let the details wait for personal experience. Let us not magnify sex unduly nor stir curiosity.

Let us teach every boy and girl that it is shameful to talk and think irreverently about sex as about other holy things. Any sensible person should be able to speak about God, or the soul's personal relation to God, or about Heaven, but only with reverence, and with natural modesty and respect. One would not want to discuss his most intimate heart's devotions to God with profane people, nor flippantly chat about Deity with blasphemers. So one with proper reverence will not joke about sex matters with lewd and lustful people. It is not wrong to talk or think about God or any of His works or plans if we be reverent before Him in our hearts and language. So it is not wrong to talk about sex matters nor think about sex matters if we be reverent and have in our minds only the proper and God-ordained use of sex.

Naturally, when two of us share a beautiful secret, which involves both, neither of us may discuss that secret freely with others, except by mutual consent. So husbands and wives, each with proper regard for the confidences and reserve of the other, do not usually discuss their own intimate love life. But each, with reverent heart and modest words, might feel free to discuss, in general and inoffensive terms, the impersonal facts of marriage, child-bearing and married happiness, with the proper persons as need may arise.

It is only the perversion of sex that is sinful. Its normal use is not sinful. It is not sinful to eat, nor to anticipate the pleasure of a good meal. It would be sinful to steal food or to scheme and plan to enjoy stolen food. So for a man and wife to enjoy each other is normal; as normal as enjoying their proper food. But for either to have intercourse with some other's mate than their own would be horrible adultery, for which the Old Testament law required the death penalty (Lev. 20:10). Even to plan or long for such a wicked thing would be committing adultery in the heart, our Lord Jesus said (Matt. 5:27, 28). You see, it is only a perversion of sex that is sinful. Normal sex life in marriage has God's blessing.

Women Normally Enjoy Sex Life as Much as Men

Some feminists, usually spinsters or frustrated divorcees, in propaganda for easy divorce, or companionate marriage, or for birth control, talk glibly about old-fashioned wives as living in "legalized adultery," as "slaves to man's beastly lust." Some would-be reformers have said a wife who is expected to submit to her husband in sex matters is treated as "a concubine." But all such talk is foolish and wicked, not even scientific, much less Christian. Actually women are by creation and physical nature as strongly sexual as men, and in normal marriage learn to enjoy the sex life as much as do men. Women have more nerve ends that are sexually excitable than men, have more areas of the body that are sensitive to love-making attention than men, and women are capable of as great enjoyment of sex relations as men are capable of, and of as frequent enjoyment. So all scientific authorities agree. The Bible often implies that women are to enjoy the marriage relation as well as their husbands. In the Song of Solomon the bride is heard saying, "His left hand is under my head, and his right hand doth embrace me" (Song of Sol. 2:6). And again she says of her bridegroom, "A bundle of myrrh is my wellbeloved unto me; he shall lie all night betwixt my breasts" (Song of Sol. 1:13). Genesis 30:16 tells us how Leah, not loved as well as her sister (both being wives of Jacob), hired her husband with sweet-smelling mandrakes to sleep with her. And God hearkened to Leah's love-hungry heart and gave her a son.

Three things need to be remembered about woman's sex nature. First, God has prepared a woman to be a wife, subject to her husband, loving him, obeying him, following him. For that reason God made woman less aggressive than man, not only in sex matters, but in other matters. As a woman is more easily led, so man is more masterful, more aggressive. Men ask for dates, men propose marriage. Yet women enjoy dates as much as men, and women want to marry, are probably more concerned about marriage than men, since with a woman marriage is usually her whole life's career. A woman does not naturally have as definite a biological pressure toward intercourse as a man, until or unless it is developed in marriage, but that does not mean that a woman does not enjoy intercourse as much.

Second, women are more or less undeveloped sexually at marriage, if reared in protected Christian homes. All decent men, I think, would prefer that their wives come to them as virgins, not only actually in a literal, physical sense, but also in a psychological and moral sense. Thus, God has made women so that, if not overstimulated by dancing, petting, or sex movies or stories, they come to marriage with a certain modest innocence, not fully realizing at first their own natural sex desires. They want affection, they want caresses, they want the devoted attention of their husbands. Normally, they also crave children. After marriage normal good women learn to desire and to enjoy sex intercourse with their husbands. They have as strong a climax of enjoyment as do their husbands. God made women for marriage just as He made men for marriage.

Third, women who live in protected homes have sometimes been so ignorant of normal marriage that they do not know what is expected of a wife, and sometimes come to marriage in such ignorance that they are shocked at what seems abnormal. Women sometimes have such a feeling of shame about sex matters that they harden their hearts against their husbands and become "frigid" wives without normal enjoyment of sex. But when that unnatural inhibition is removed by an understanding of God's plan for the mating of husband and wife, and when her normal sex nature is developed by the caresses and love play of an affectionate husband, such a wife almost always grows a happy and normal enjoyment of the sex relations of marriage. Women love as strongly as men. When they know that the marriage bed is a normal expression of married love, they grow to have the same normal enjoyment that their husbands have.

The Marriage Relation Is Not for Procreation Alone

Mating normally means the conception and bearing of children. So some prudish people have supposed that sex relations of husband and wife are intended only for the procreation of children, and that any intercourse not needed for the procreation of children should be avoided. "Legalized adultery" is a term used by fanatics who do not know what the Bible teaches on this subject, fanatics who think all sex is sinful and sex desire only a mark of depravity. But the clear teaching of the Word of God, borne out by the experience of the ages and the wisdom of good men, is that sex intercourse is intended to be for the comfort and joy of all married people, to develop their love one for another, and is not simply to be used to beget children. For married people frequent intercourse, like the caresses and endearments of which it should be the climax, is healthful and right and promotes happiness and morality.

In I Corinthians 7:3-5 we are plainly instructed that husband and wife should render to the other "due benevolence," that the wife has authority over her husband's body in this matter of mating, as the husband has authority over his wife's body; and that if either withholds himself or herself from the other it is defrauding and wrong. Nor are husbands and wives to stay apart, except by mutual consent, and then only briefly, so they will not be tempted with others. The clear meaning is that husbands and wives are to be careful each to satisfy the desire of the other, and that God puts no limit on intercourse between husbands and wives.

It is the teaching of experience that this kindness of one to the other leads to an increase of love, and the two grow more and more to feel that they are one, as indeed God says they are to become. "And they shall be one flesh," says Genesis 2:24. Kisses and embraces may leave husband and wife feeling unsatisfied, but the natural mating of a husband and wife not only satisfies the body but comforts the heart and tends to tenderness and mutual joy.

But this freedom, will it not lead to excess? Will it not undermine the health? No, the free way is God's way, and is best for health and happiness. As husband and wife grow older, their understanding grows, their mutual dependence on one another increases, and they enjoy the fellowship of mind more. But their desire for sex expression gradually subsides, just in proportion as the fires of youthful passion subside. Licentious people, whoremongers, for example, seeking to experience new thrills for jaded appetites by seeking new partners in the sex life, may indeed ruin their health. But with a happily married couple who would not think of perverting sex instincts by sinful union with outsiders, the sex stimulus is only normal, so there is no excess, no demand beyond that for which God has prepared the body. Actually, among people who are happily married and who live pure, good lives, without unusual stimulation of sex desire by sex pictures, plays, literature, dancing or petting with others besides the married mate, there is almost never any intemperance to hurt either spiritual welfare or bodily health.

Naturally sex desire and capacity decline somewhat after about the age of twenty-five, especially in men. Thus sex intercourse between husband and wife will be at its highest frequency right after marriage, ordinarily. Then the happiness of marriage will tend to become more and more mental and spiritual and somewhat less physical. However, strength and desire for occasional sex relations normally continue in well people who are happily married even into old age, long beyond the childbearing period of the wife. Married people who are well need feel no duty to limit their mating, except by their own choice. Marriage is for mutual love and comfort, and not only for the procreation of children. To this agree the best Christian leaders as well as practically all medical authorities.

Should husbands and wives have separate beds? I do not think so. It seems to me that one bed symbolizes the unity of husband and wife and that thus the fellowship tends to be more spiritual than simply physical. Certainly husbands and wives should get accustomed to caresses and mutual nearness without always thinking primarily of sex relations. And at any event there should not be separate beds except it seems best to both.

"Adjustment" in Marriage Takes Time and Patience

A silly idea has gotten abroad that happiness in marriage depends largely on a physical adjustment in marriage, that some men and women have sex peculiarities that make their intercourse normal and happy, while other men and women are so sexually dissimilar that they can never completely satisfy each other and so ought not to marry. On this silly and unscientific pretext, wicked and ignorant people have tried to justify intercourse before marriage, or trial marriages, or companionate marriages. The simple truth is twofold. First, happy sex adjustment, making the union of man and wife equally and fully satisfactory to both, almost never appears at once after marriage, but develops slowly. Second, any normal married couple who love one another and are patient and unselfish and kind can come to fullest happiness and perfect adjustment after a bit.

As I have said before, modest, protected, virtuous girls

come to marriage, just as sensible people would wish, not fully developed in sex desire, and not experienced in sex matters. Even if men be virtuous and without any sex experience, as is right, when they come to marriage the sex desire is already strong. So, after marriage women need a little time and love-making to develop them to normal wifehood, normal sex reaction and enjoyment. A scientific survey published a few years ago in a national magazine showed that the average woman who reported to a woman physician had not experienced a normal climax and completely satisfactory sex union with her husband for some months after marriage, a few not till after a year of married life. But these women were normal women who loved their husbands and who came, in due time, to the fullest enjoyment of the privileges of marriage.

Several causes may delay the maturity of a wife's sex life and the enjoyment God intended. The fear of pregnancy may make her unhappy and unable to give herself with happiness and willingness to her husband. Sometimes a state of mind born from thinking of sex as evil and the marriage relation shameful, may make the union less than happy, or even hateful to her. Or possibly some wives, not knowing what to expect, and having too little of caresses and love-making and fondling by the husband before sex intercourse, do not expect, do not definitely long for, and do not have, the enjoyment which is normal, and which other wives do have. There is good evidence, some physicians say, that a few happy, loving wives are kind to their husbands and make them happy, and bear children, without ever attaining a normal climax of sex enjoyment. We suppose they are few, and that that lack is caused by the failure of the husband, through ignorance or selfish haste, to pet their wives, caress them, and take time to insure the wife's full enjoyment.

Certain it is that patience, restraint and an unselfish effort to make the wife happy and please her, will pay any husband in happiness. Sex union should be the normal climax of endearing words, fondling, love-play and mutual devotion. Courtship should continue after marriage, and should be part of the preparation of heart, mind and body for sex union, always. A husband's gentleness and patience are well shown here, and contribute to the joy of both.

A wife will find that it is for her own happiness and normal development to yield herself freely to her husband, with a willing and obedient heart. So her marriage vows require, so the Word of God demands, and so her love prompts her. Wives who make their husbands happy will soon find themselves equally happy. A rebellious heart in the wife not only cheats her husband, but prevents her own adjustment and enjoyment. She must know that her husband has a natural urge, a biological necessity that she does not have, especially at first, and she must be patient and unselfish too. God will reward her with the fullest development of wifehood and with the greatest happiness as she takes the place God has given her for the happiness of her husband.

Above all, let me urge that men and women enter marriage and the married privileges with reverence and devotion for each other, and reverence for the marriage union as a holy and beautiful rite which has the blessing of God already, as a joy permitted and a duty He commanded husbands and wives. I think that if husbands and wives first give themselves to God, and then to each other, and if they count themselves in the presence of God and seek His blessings prayerfully, trustfully, humbly, their marriage will be a sacrament (in the sense of sacred), and the home a bit of Heaven. Wherever Christ is taken as Saviour and guide, where the blessing of God is asked by contrite and believing hearts, and where God's Word is followed, there marriage will truly be "holy matrimony" and the union of hearts and bodies be blessed.

CHAPTER X

The Blessing of Children

"And God blessed them, and God said unto them, Be fruitful, and multiply, and replenish the earth, and subdue it."— Gen. 1:28.

"And God blessed Noah and his sons, and said unto them, Be fruitful, and multiply, and replenish the earth."—Gen. 9:1.

"Lo, children are an heritage of the Lord: and the fruit of the womb is his reward. As arrows are in the hand of a mighty man; so are children of the youth. Happy is the man that hath his quiver full of them: they shall not be ashamed, but they shall speak with the enemies in the gate." —Ps. 127:3-5.

Everywhere in nature it is a truism that when creatures mate they should have offspring. Among animals, instinct has prepared them to expect little ones. Birds and animals seem to hunger for babies in the family and instinctively know what to do about feeding them and protecting them and training them. And with mankind, it is equally true that naturally people who marry expect children and long for children, except where selfish and immoral reasons cause people to plan to thwart nature.

Let every young couple who marries plan and pray that they may have their home blessed with children. This is the way of duty and the way of happiness.

To Have Children Is a Solemn Duty Commanded of God

The propagation of the race is obviously one of the principal reasons that God ordained marriage. In Genesis 1:27, 28 we are told, "So God created man in his own image, in the image of God created he him; male and female created he them. And God blessed them, and God said unto them, Be fruitful, and multiply, and replenish the earth, and subdue it: and have dominion over the fish of the sea, and over the fowl of the air, and over every living thing that moveth upon the earth."

Note the following facts in the Scripture. 1. God created man in His own image. This involves man in God's creative plan. Man, with God, should have part in the creation and propagation of the race. So in I Peter 3:7 we are told that husband and wife are "heirs together of the grace of life." 2. God made them "male and female." This means that the sex equipment of men and women, fitting them for marriage, for love, and the propagation of the race, is essential in God's plan. 3. We are told, "And God blessed them." God blessed them as a married couple. God put His blessing upon the union, and upon their mating. 4. And God commanded, "Be fruitful, and multiply, and replenish the earth." This married couple were plainly commanded to bear children. Not only were they commanded to have children, but the implication is that they were to have many. They were to "be fruitful," and when we speak of fruitfulness in a vine or tree, or of fertility in an animal, we certainly mean an abundant propagation. And we may properly infer that what God wanted Adam and Eve to do, He wants other married couples to do, and will put His blessings upon them likewise. 5. This man and woman, married, were to subdue the earth, and have dominion over it, largely by virtue of their children. Their destiny on the earth was wrapped up in the propagation of the race and in their having a large number of children.

In Hebrew the name Adam means man. So in some sense Adam and Eve represented all mankind and God's command to them is His command to us. Married people should have children, and God's blessing upon their home depends somewhat upon obedience to this command. Their place in society, their contribution to the world's good depends largely upon having children to do the work the father and mother may give them to do and train them to do.

After the flood had destroyed the millions of population resulting after many centuries from the creation of Adam and Eve down to Noah, God gave Noah the same command which He had given to Adam and Eve before. Genesis 9:1 says, "And God blessed Noah and his sons, and said unto them, Be fruitful, and multiply, and replenish the earth." Here again every element of God's command to Adam and Eve is repeated. Noah and his sons were commanded, "Be fruitful, and multiply, and replenish the earth." And then there followed the blessed promise that everything on earth was to be put under the care and command of mankind, and fish and fowl and beasts and herbs were given to mankind for meat. It was as if God said to Noah and his sons, "Do not be afraid to have children, many of them. I will provide food for them. I will give them work to do in subduing the earth."

It is important to notice that this command to Noah and to his sons was a command to the whole human race, for all the people on earth descended from the three branches of Noah's family. This is not a part of the Mosaic law. This is long before the time of Moses and the giving of the law and the separation of Israel as a nation. This is a command for all mankind. Married people should "multiply, and replenish the earth."

Some have thought that these commands to "multiply, and replenish the earth," first given to Adam and Eve in Genesis 1:28 and then given to Noah and his sons in Genesis 9:1, were emergency commands when the world had no population. They think that the command of God to multiply and replenish the earth would not be so applicable today when there are some two billions of people on the earth. But there is not a hint anywhere in the Bible that God does not want marriage to result in families of children now as at the beginning. God's plan for marriage then and His plan for marriage now are the same.

If there are more people in the earth today, more people are dying, and someone ought to fill up the ranks. If there were no more children born, then in one generation the whole human race would be wiped out. And, however many people there are in the world, to continue the race we must still follow the command to "multiply, and replenish the earth." God's command fits men today just the same as it fitted Adam and Eve and Noah and his sons and their wives. To have children is a duty of married people everywhere, by the plain command of God.

Let us consider certain reasons why God wants Christians to have families of children.

First, certainly God wants the population of the earth to be as largely Christian in character as possible. Children from Christian homes, taught to love and serve the Lord, ought to be the salt that saves society. Even if there were enough people in this world, if we had reached the limits of population so that the earth could not well bear an increase in population; then still there are not enough people who come out of Christian homes, with a Christian background, young people who are themselves Christian, won to God in their homes by godly parents. The Christian heritage ought to be spread over the whole world by the children who come out of Christian homes. So if any married couple in the world ought to have a large family of children, it ought to be a Christian couple whose children would be, if reared according to Bible standards, a benediction to the whole world.

Not only in Christian character and ideals can the children of Christian homes affect the civilization of the whole world, but God wants Christian workers, preachers and missionaries, great soul winners. Nearly all of these have to come from Christian homes. How happy and blessed is a Christian mother who has three or four sons to be ministers and missionaries! And how pleased God is with the children of such a home.

Then a Christian husband owes it to his wife to have children, and a Christian wife owes it to her husband. The selfish woman who does not bear children, or who has only one or two or three, cheats her husband and deprives him of the joy which should normally be a father's. The husband who does not willingly cooperate in the bringing into the world and rearing of a fine group of children, under normal circumstances, may think he is making his wife happy; but in the long run he is depriving her of the natural fulfillment of a woman's dreams, the desire of a mother heart which God put in every little girl. Actually, homes without children are likely to be unhappy homes, likely to end in divorce. And married people who have no children are likely to become self-centered, unhappy and querulous old people with little to live for and little opportunity to be a blessing to the world.

It is a solemn duty for married people to have children. Children are the normal fruitage of marriage. Those who marry owe a duty to God, a duty to civilization, a duty to their mates and to themselves to bring children into this world and to rear them for God.

Normal People Desire Children

No literature in all the world reveals the heart of mankind as the Bible does. The Bible gives us examples of evil men and women. But thank God it also contains a vast picture gallery of good men and women and shows us what were their hearts' desires, what were their joys and hopes and triumphs and fears. The good people in the Bible longed to have children, rejoiced exceedingly when God gave little ones to them to rear for Him.

The first woman who ever cradled a baby in her arms was Mother Eve, and she exclaimed with joy, "I have gotten a man from the Lord" (Gen. 4:1). I can almost see the face of that woman. She who had first felt the birth pangs of travail to bring a child into the world and whose eyes were first lighted with mother love and whose arms had first circled a little mite, a baby, was happy! And that is the way all the good women in the Bible felt about babies.

Hear Sarah, rejoicing over her son given her when she was ninety years old, "God hath made me to laugh, so that all that hear will laugh with me . . . Who would have said unto Abraham, that Sarah should have given children suck? for I have born him a son in his old age" (Gen. 21:6, 7). And she named the child Isaac, meaning laughter, so that everyone who ever called his name would remember how happy his mother and father were when the little one came after long years of prayer!

When Rebecca left her home in the East to travel by camel to marry a man she had never seen, to become the bride of Isaac, her loved ones sent after her this blessing: "Thou art our sister, be thou the mother of thousands of millions, and let thy seed possess the gate of those which hate them" (Gen. 24:60). Above everything else they wished Rebecca to have the great blessing of a large family. And that wish was half prayer and half prophecy inspired of God, for this same Rebecca became the mother of the whole race of Israel from which came the prophets of God through whom He gave the Scriptures and from which came the Saviour Himself.

How Leah rejoiced in her children! After the birth of her first son Reuben, she said, "Surely the Lord hath looked upon my afflictions; now therefore my husband will love me." After the birth of Simeon she was comforted and said, "Because the Lord hath heard that I was hated, he hath therefore given me this son also" (Gen. 29: 32, 33). Almost as good as having a husband's love was to have a son! And when her third son, Levi, was born, she said, "Now this time will my husband be joined unto me, because I have born him three sons" (Gen. 29:34). When Judah was born, she said, "Now will I praise the Lord" (Gen. 29:35).

And what about the beloved Rachel, favorite of Jacob? Was she happy that her husband loved her best of all? No, she envied her unloved sister who had children, and she sobbed to Jacob, "Give me children, or else I die" (Gen. 30:1). When God gave children to their handmaids, to be called their own sons, these two sisters, wives of Jacob, greatly rejoiced. When Rachel had a son of her own she said, "God hath taken away my reproach" (Gen. 30:23). But when the one son was born, she immediately said, "The Lord shall add to me another son." When Leah had her sixth son she rejoiced still and said, "God hath endued me with a good dowry; now will my husband dwell with me, because I have born him six sons" (Gen. 30:20). You see, these women measured their happiness by the number of their children. And they readily saw what so many women today fail to see, that married love depends very largely on the normal process of having children come into the home to bind husband and wife together and make the home what God intended it should be.

Let Hannah, the godly wife of Elkanah, become a model for Christian women everywhere. She had no son, though her husband loved her dearly. Poor Elkanah, troubled by a woman's tears, specially since they were from the eyes of his well-loved Hannah, said to her, "Hannah, why weepest thou? and why eatest thou not? and why is thy heart grieved? am not I better to thee than ten sons?" (I Sam. 1:8). A good husband and his loving care did not satisfy the heart of a woman which was made also to love little children. Such married love, she knew, ought naturally to culminate in offspring. And God noticed Hannah's fasting and tears and heard her heartbroken cry and gave her a child. She 'lent' that baby to the Lord to become a prophet, and he turned out to be Samuel, the great man of God. When children are so loved and longed for, they are likely to be specially blessed. When they come in answer to fervent prayer and when they are dedicated to God and reared for Him, how blessed are the results! More women should be like Hannah, who longed and prayed for a son.

When Elisha the prophet was given a prophet's chamber in the home of the great woman of Shunem, he tried to think what good thing he could do to reward her for her care of God's preacher. The very best thing he could think of to comfort her heart and reward her was to intercede with God for her that she might have a son. And God gave the son! No other happiness as great could have been given her. One who reads the narrative in II Kings, chapter 4, can sense how God feels about the blessing of children and how godly people also feel about the joy of the little ones that God sends to godly married couples.

In Luke, chapter 1, read how John the Baptist was given to aged Zacharias and his wife, Elisabeth. He could hardly believe it when the angel made to him the glad announcement, "Thy prayer is heard; and thy wife Elisabeth shall bear thee a son, and thou shalt call his name John. And thou shalt have joy and gladness, and many shall rejoice at his birth" (Luke 1:13, 14). When the little one was born and Elisabeth brought forth her son "her neighbours and her cousins heard how the Lord had shewed great mercy upon her; and they rejoiced with her" (Luke 1:58). Would it not be blessed if every woman who is pregnant, every woman who is privileged to join with God in the creation of a human being, could feel as Elisabeth did? We are told, "And after those days his wife Elisabeth conceived, and hid herself five months, saying, Thus hath the Lord dealt with me in the days wherein he looked on me, to take away my reproach among men" (Luke 1:24, 25). Such a blessing it is to have little children! How rich a mercy does God show on the man whom He allows to beget a child and on the woman whom He allows to conceive and bear a little one, her own baby, flesh of her flesh and bone of her bone!

Everywhere in the Bible it is implied that children are a great blessing sent from God. Psalm 127:3-5 states this expressly: "Lo, children are an heritage of the Lord: and the fruit of the womb is his reward. As arrows are in the hand of a mighty man; so are children of the youth. Happy is the man that hath his quiver full of them: they shall not be ashamed, but they shall speak with the enemies in the gate." Those who believe the Bible, those who feel about love and home and family as Bible Christians and saints did, will delight to have families and will pray that God will give them large families of sons and daughters, as the heritage of the Lord. "Happy is the man that hath his quiver full of them."

How Children Bring Joy

We have said that it is normal for people to want children, and have shown that the Bible saints regarded it the greatest honor when God gave them children. Bible Christians wanted many children. The Bible expressly says that children are an heritage of the Lord and are God's reward, and that "happy is the man that hath his quiver full of them," that is, has many children. Now I should like for you to consider some of the great joys and blessings that come to the man and woman who have little sons and daughters born to them.

1. *Children satisfy the inborn craving of a girl to be a mother and of a boy to be a father.*

Every little girl who cuddles her doll, gives it a name, a personality, sees it experience all the ills of little children, loves it, chastises it, talks to it and has it talk back to her with baby talk, is a proof that God made girls to become women and women to become mothers. It is as natural for a woman to want a baby as for the stomach to cry for food, or a tired body to cry for rest. The woman who never has children of her own will lavish her heart's devotion on a dog, on a cat, on a parrot or a canary; or she will become self-centered and neurotic and abnormal, a picture of dissatisfaction and frustration. God intended women to be mothers, and any wife who is not a mother has missed something of her God-appointed heritage. Sometimes God wants women to remain single, and sometimes God in His wisdom sees fit not to give a married woman children, even when she desires them. Such women, in the will of God, may turn their energy and devotion to other causes and lavish their hearts' love and devotion on other objects and be happy. One can always be happy in the will of God, and content with his lot, if he lives in trust and feels the presence of the Lord Jesus. But it is an obvious fact that women were made for motherhood, and there is a deep satisfaction, an abiding joy, a sense of the fulfillment of a woman's destiny, in having a child.

Any woman whose womb has not carried a child and who has not suffered in travail and felt the joy of creation, the feminine adulthood that comes with mothering a little one, has missed part of a woman's estate. Any woman whose breasts have never fed a little one, and whose arms have never held a tiny soft head against her bosom, and whose hands have never fondled the dimpled limbs of her own child, knows that she has missed part of that for which God made women. There is a fulfillment of natural instinct in mother-hood.

Likewise, every man who has no child realizes that he has never quite fulfilled his destiny, never quite come to man's es-tate, in the full experience of the privileges of man. Part of that is manifested in the elation, the joy and pride that a fa-ther feels in his first-born. He has, in some sense, become of age! He has taken part with Deity in the creating of a little soul and body! His marriage has culminated in fruit, and he is a father. There is a great sense of well-being, a sense of the fulfillment of destiny, a sense of having what one's heart has always desired, when one becomes a parent. Parenthood ful-fills instincts that are God-given, the deep-seated cravings and desires that are a part of human nature itself.

2. *Parents experience a growth in character that is impos-sible without having children.*

Dr. Hyman Appelman, fruitful and mighty evangelist, tells how he returned home from evangelistic services to see his baby son, a few weeks old, and in the night woke the baby up. He said that when the little one waved his hands and more or less accidentally caught his finger and held on, that he, the great evangelist that he is, with his tender heart, fell on his face and begged God to let him be the father to the child which he ought to be, and never to let him take one step that would cause the little fellow to believe his father was anything but the best man on earth! And Dr. Appelman said also, "I knew more about how God felt about sinners the day I had to whip my little boy than I had ever known before! I knew more about God's love and God's compassion and God's righteousness!" You see, there is a certain develop-ment of character, a certain appreciation of holy values, a certain understanding of deepest spiritual truth that comes in being a father or in being a mother.

It seems that the nine months pass so slowly while the prospective mother waits for the coming of the little one and while there are so many discomforts, so many unnamable fears, so many changes taking place in her own character; but God makes a woman out of a slip of a girl who never before felt very seriously about life. When a woman goes into the valley of the shadow, and knows that for her pain, for her fears, for her travail, she has brought back a little life into the world, that woman, I think, can never be quite the same again. How often I have seen a frivolous girl, obsessed with her desire for pleasure, with no thought higher than her fashionable clothes, her high-heeled shoes, her painted face or her hair-do, or a jazz band, suddenly become a mature woman, unselfish, thinking only of the little one! How often I have seen a woman who never before was fully unselfish about anything, become the soul of unselfishness as she washed little clothes and waited over a sick baby, and wept and hoped and prayed and trusted, and rejoiced then that the little one lived! God uses a baby to make a woman out of a girl, to make, sometimes, an ordinary woman into a saint! I know that there are other things needed in the development of a woman's character, but certainly the bearing and rearing of children do something to a woman that she can never get any other way.

And every man has a right to want to be the biggest man in the world to somebody. Every man has a right to want the utmost love and pride and admiration and confidence of somebody. Every man has a right to be the provider, the counselor of somebody. And who, pray, could that somebody be so well as his own little family, his children about him? What man ever felt his responsibility as much with others as he feels when his own little child thinks Daddy can fix anything? Whoever so much longed to be wise and good as a man does when his own child comes to believe that Daddy knows all about everything, and that whatever Daddy says is true?

No man can possibly feel as much need to live straight and clean before the birth of his children as he feels that need after they come to follow in his steps.

Children do something to make a husband and wife into mature people of character and responsibility and integrity. How blessed is the subtle effect of a little child upon his father and his mother!

3. *God gives someone to love when he gives a little child.*

The other day I saw a woman holding her little baby, kissing him, calling him pet names, over and over again saying, "I love you!" Her heart was running over with the most unselfish love of which woman's heart is capable. And with her love was happiness and joy. If she had the most expensive automobile in the world it could not bring joy as that little baby did. If she had a twenty-room mansion, with six or eight servants, she could not be as rejoiced as she is with that little one God has given her. When God gives a baby, He gives someone for a mother or for a father to love.

I saw in the daily press a few days ago an account of a father who killed himself. His sixteen-year-old son had died a few months before, and the father could never be reconciled. So he took his own life. His life had been wrapped up in his devotion to his son. The son had fulfilled all the needs of his love-hungry soul.

When a man has a baby, he loves his wife just as much, but he loves the baby in addition. That means that his joy is that much increased. When the second child comes along, strangely enough, the father can feel no diminution of his love for the first-born. But he simply enlarges his capacity to love, and with it his capacity for enjoyment and happiness. Blessed is the man who has many children because he loves much and has much reason for happiness.

4. *Children bind husband and wife together, make more sure the marriage tie.*

Investigations and surveys have repeatedly proven that homes without children are more likely to be broken by divorce than homes with children. In the first place, a husband and wife who have a mutual object of their love in a child or in several children, have good reason to forgive and overlook the failures that are certain to come, the differences of opinion that are inevitable with frail human beings. Instead of feeling perfectly free to throw the marriage vows to the wind and leave one another, a husband or wife with children feel that they must not leave the children, must not break the home, must not wreck other little lives. Then there is a sense of responsibility about doing right. One naturally has a more active conscience if he feels accountable for the little ones he has brought into this world.

But in addition to that, married love grows much through the birth and training of little children. A husband and wife do not necessarily come to understand one another very well or to love one another very well just because they are married. They may be so busy, so diverse in their interests, and spend so little time with one another that love does not properly develop, and the marriage does not have a safe background. But when God sends little children, their hearts are joined in the same love for this same little one. They plan together. They sacrifice together. They work in partnership.

Each is willing to give up his own way, partly, for the well-being of the little one. Little by little a man finds that he loves better the mother of his child than he loved the same woman when she was only his wife. A woman finds that she loves better the father of her child, the provider and protector and counselor of her child than she loved the same man when he was simply her husband. The birth of children binds the home together. It makes marriage sweeter. It makes the love of husband and wife grow richer. Oh, how great are the blessings brought to a home by little children!

CHAPTER XI

Birth Control

"And God blessed them, and God said unto them, Be fruitful, and multiply, and replenish the earth, and subdue it: and have dominion over the fish of the sea, and over the fowl of the air, and over every living thing that moveth upon the earth."—Gen. 1:28.

"And God blessed Noah and his sons, and said unto them, Be fruitful, and multiply, and replenish the earth."—Gen. 9:1.

"Lo, children are an heritage of the Lord: and the fruit of the womb is his reward. As arrows are in the hand of a mighty man; so are children of the youth. Happy is the man that hath his quiver full of them."—Ps. 127:3-5.

"Thy wife shall be as a fruitful vine by the sides of thine house; thy children like olive plants round about thy table. Behold, that thus shall the man be blessed that feareth the Lord."—Ps. 128:3, 4.

The use of artificial means, drugs and appliances to prevent conception has for centuries been regarded as immoral, wrong for the individual and dangerous to society as a whole. Those who would encourage widespread use of contraceptives, and other artificial methods of birth control or prevention, are in the minority and have always been opposed by most of the Christian and moral leadership of the world.

The Roman Catholic Church has steadfastly insisted that the use of contraceptives and the limiting of families, or preventing of conception, is a sin. Conservative Protestant leaders who believe the Bible and stand for historic Christianity have usually taken the same position. And common people everywhere have felt, unless sentiment has changed in the last few years, there was a great danger in the spread of information about birth control, or in the general practice of birth control. This sentiment of common, decent people, backed up by the intellectual leadership and the moral and Christian leadership of the world, used to be illustrated by the laws on the statute books of most countries, including the United

163

States (every state in the Union, except two), until recently, forbidding the general dissemination of information about birth control.

A radical minority, usually either anti-Christian or modernists who deny the authority of the Bible, carry on an insistent propaganda for birth control. Some of them, no doubt, are sincere and hope to do away with some of the handicaps and poverty which some large families undergo. But usually those who are outspoken advocates of birth control are either feminists, or the radical groups trying to make women more or less independent of men, or are social radicals who advocate companionate marriage, easy divorce, or free love. And the radicals who try to break down the Bible standard of permanent marriage between one man and one woman, try to break down the Bible standard for homes.

It is only fair to say that some good people who are earnest and sincere are followers of these radical groups. A certain element in the National Council of Churches leadership has openly advocated birth control. But the fact remains that through the centuries the general sentiment of Christian leaders and moral leaders has been that it is unwise and undesirable to spread widely information about methods of birth control.

It seems to me there ought to be a kindly presentation of this matter for married people, in the light of the Bible and of the best experience of Christian people. So in chaste language we here try to present the Christian viewpoint concerning birth control.

What Is Generally Meant by "Birth Control"?

First, let it be clear that the term birth control does not mean abortion. After a male sperm cell has united with a female ovum and the body of the child thus conceived begins to develop in the womb of the wife, to destroy that little life and so prevent a normal birth of a child is called abortion, not birth control. And abortion is murder. Until recent years, very few people in the world, we believe, would have justified this destruction of an unborn child after conception has taken place. At least they would not have justified it under normal circumstances. Abortion, that is the willful murder of the little one where conception has already taken place and life has already begun, was, until recently, a crime prohibited by the law and condemned by all decent people. Abortion is not what we mean by the term birth control.

Generally people who speak of birth control do not mean simply continence or preventing conception by abstaining from intercourse. I suppose that, if a husband and wife feel no special temptation, and desire for a season not to have intercourse, no one would accuse them of sin. Certainly if a husband and wife continued long without intercourse, for example a year or two, it would be no natural marriage and would be a violation of what God intended in marriage. But for a husband and wife to temporarily stay apart, by common consent, and when neither felt a need for intercourse, thus for a short time delaying the conception of children for some good reason, I do not know that anybody would condemn them. Certainly it must be left to husbands and wives when they choose to have intercourse. We do not refer to abstinence from intercourse when we use the term birth control.

However, it is only fair to say that the Bible does not teach that a husband and wife ought to abstain from intercourse. And there is a warning in I Corinthians 7:2-5 that one reason for each man's having his own wife and each woman's having her own husband is that they may avoid fornication, and that, therefore, the husband and wife are neither to defraud the other, "except it be with consent for a time, that ye may give yourselves to fasting and prayer; and come together again, that Satan tempt you not for your incontinency." It is not normal for husbands and wives to stay apart long, and they should never do so except by mutual consent and for a limited time, according to the Scriptures.

It is thought that each woman has a certain part of each month when she is not usually fertile, and that intercourse during these days is not likely to result in pregnancy. However, the medical authorities do not all agree as to what days of a woman's month she is relatively infertile, and it is likely that the monthly rhythm of women differs. Certainly there is no hard and fast rule by which people can thus prevent conception of children. But there is nothing against decency and morals, nothing against Christianity when husband and wife choose to have intercourse only in such periods that they think are less likely to result in the conception of children, provided they intend to obey God's command to multiply. Such a plan or such a restraint in the matter of the mating of husband and wife is not forbidden and is not what we generally mean by the term birth control.

What is generally called birth control is the use of drugs and appliances for the purpose of preventing conception when there is normal intercourse between the sexes. This use of contraceptive drugs or appliances is what is generally forbidden by Christian sentiment, and it is the dissemination of information about such contraceptive drugs and appliances which until recent years was generally forbidden by law.

In Most Cases Birth Control Is Obviously Unnecessary

Other consideration will show that for most normal people in the world there is certainly no crying need for birth control measures. Consider the following reasons why birth control is usually obviously unnecessary.

1. *Families in most of the world do not have more children than they want.* In most of the world it is still true that normal decent people rejoice over the birth of a child and expect congratulations. Fathers complain often of the added expense to families, just as they complain of the expense of wives. But men do not quit marrying nor quit desiring offspring for that reason. Mothers complain sometimes of the pain of childbearing, and sometimes they wish they did not have to stay at home to look after children but wish they could see more of the bright lights. Yet, generally, mothers want all the children they have, and would not part with any child for any amount of money. Among decent, honest, moral people, it is the exception to find people who have more children than they want. It is only among the irresponsible, the immoral, the unnatural, who want to give away their children, or who desert them and leave them as public charges to be cared for by society. Without the meddling of feminists and radical "reformers" there would be very few women and very few men who would wish to have fewer children or who would wish to prevent the normal conception of children.

2. *It is obvious that life comes from God.* Never a child is conceived but that God Himself gives the little spark of life. And when God withholds this gift, as He sometimes does, all the efforts of husbands and wives to have a child are in vain. It is obvious that God, who gives the little life at His pleasure, must know when it is wise and good to allow the con-

ception of children. How foolish it seems for people to set out to thwart God, to refuse the gift that God might give to them!

There is great weight in this argument, as you will see when you stop to consider that almost every mother and father who would have ever prevented the conception of a child or postponed it had that been possible, before it happened, are of an entirely different opinion after the child is born! The mother who didn't want a baby, later finds that the baby is exactly what she wanted. That wise Christian writer, Dr. B. H. Shadduck, in his pamphlet, *Stopping the Stork*, facetiously suggests that if people want to limit the size of their families they should wait until the child is two years old and then decide whether to kill it or not! There would be very little limiting of families, you may be sure, on that basis! Nearly every child is its own proof that it had a right to be born. The love and joy and pride that come from a child proves that God was giving an infinite blessing when the child was given, and that it would have been a foolish sin committed against their own happiness for the father and mother to have prevented the conception of that little one which later turns out to be so precious.

I remember when my wife and I first learned that our sixth daughter was on the way to our home. I was so busy that I thought, with a little vexation, that another child would be a burden. The mother was active in church work, taught a large class of young women in the Sunday school, had much visitation to do, besides her mothering of five daughters God had previously given. I thought that another child would be a burden, and I feared that there would be many problems in connection with rearing a sixth one coming six years after the fifth one. But how groundless were my fears! When the little one came, we named her Sarah Joy—Sarah for my beloved mother who has long been in Heaven and Joy because that is exactly what she was. Oh, how she lightened my burdens! I was carrying a load of work almost insupportable, yet I found myself growing young again playing with my baby! I have had more joy in teaching her, more delight in watching her grow, more fellowship with her, perhaps, than with any of the other five beloved daughters. The others I loved as much but this one I seemed to need more! How foolish I would have been if I had taken any means to prevent this gift which God so graciously gave to our home! There has never been a moment since she was born that I could have imagined it anything but a calamity if we did not have her. You see, little children have a way of proving to the fathers and mothers that God knew what He was doing when He gave them.

I was on a Bible conference program with a distinguished pastor, a widely known and well-loved Christian leader. He told me at the time with some concern that his wife was to have another baby. They already had eight children. Some of them were in college. His wife had now, thinking she was done with the burdens of childbearing and baby-tending, given herself largely to the work of the church. She taught a large class. She tried to enter into the social activities of her grown sons and daughters. And now another baby was coming! He said that surely God must know what He is doing, and that they had never felt it right or wise to try to prevent conception, but he was somewhat distressed as to how it would affect their home life. The young men in college, the grown daughters having suitors in the home, how would they feel about a new baby brother or sister? But later I was in that same home, after the baby had come and was a year or two old. The father and mother spent the evening recounting the remarkable and brilliant things the little one had done! The sons, college students and football players, vied with each other in taking care of the baby! The little one that God had sent was the joy of the whole household. More than that, the baby was the pride of the large church. The mother did not need to give up her class. Indeed, she was more popular than ever now that she had a baby! They had not tried to prevent the blessed little gift that God gave them. But how foolish they would have been to have done so! That father and mother and every member of the family would now tell you that nine children are much better than eight!

I am saying that, when you take a sensible view and let God prove His case through each child that He gives, it is obvious that birth control measures are not necessary. God certainly knows what He is doing when He gives a little life into the care of a husband and a wife who love one another and have made a home together.

3. *When mothers nurse their children, normally pregnancy is spaced about two years apart.* And during the childbearing period a woman may well find that it is best to have children

not farther apart than God would normally give them in such cases.

A woman who can do so ought to nurse her own babies. Breast-fed babies are generally more healthy. There is not so much danger of disease germs and of upset stomachs and of insufficient nourishment when a mother can nurse her own child. Usually normal women can breast-feed their babies. It is as normal for a mother to have milk for her baby as for a cow to have milk for her calf. It is true that if boys throw rocks at a Jersey cow and the milkman chases her about the cow lot with a stool, the Jersey cow will not give much milk. And if a woman lives an abnormal life, running about to night clubs, giving way to fits of temper, not taking adequate rest, not having peace of mind, she may find it difficult to have a normal supply of milk and the right kind of milk to take care of her little one. But a woman who lives a well-ordered, happy, peaceful life with plenty of rest, with a calm soul in fellowship with God, and in love with her husband and home, can usually nourish her own baby at her breast. It is better for the baby, but it is infinitely more important to the mother.

How precious is the mother's privilege of furnishing, from her own body, the food for her own baby. What tenderness! What heavenly peace! What love without bounds! These, God grows in the mother's heart as she nurses her own baby. No woman can ever be quite the same, can ever be quite as selfish and worldly-minded, I think, after she has for a ten- or eleven-months' period nursed her own precious baby at her breast. This is the normal culture of a mother's love. This is the normal delight of a mother.

I remember that in my masculine ignorance I supposed there would be great difficulty in weaning our first baby. I had, I am sure, heard people talk about how difficult it was to have a baby satisfied with other food and willing to be weaned. In fact, as a farmer and stockman, I had known how it is sometimes necessary to put mares and their colts in separate pastures for weaning and how difficult it was sometimes to wean a calf. Of course we, as a well-educated mother and father, gave our first baby orange juice and then some crushed vegetables and scraped banana and other such foods to supplement the mother's milk, as the months went by. One day I found my wife weeping. The baby, about ten months old, had normally turned to other foods and had weaned her mother! And every one of the six daughters since then, at the proper time weaned her mother, and I had to comfort a disconsolate woman who found it hard to give up the deep tenderness and joy in the stirrings of mother love that naturally go with the breast-feeding of a precious little child whom God has given as a reward of love.

There are always worldly doctors willing to advise a woman not to nurse her baby but to feed the little one with artificial formulas so that the mother will be free to gad about more, so a servant can care for the child. But actually the mother who listens to such a doctor will lose great joy. And actually her health is likely to be poorer.

It is a good thing for a mother to feel the need to be at home a certain amount of time, to feel the need to have rest and to eat good food, to abstain from cigarettes and cocktails for the sake of the little one she holds to her breast. The mother who nurses her child is more likely to have quiet nerves, to rest well at night. Certainly such a mother will have more joy from her baby, and the relationship between mother and child will be more normal. It is true that some mothers are unable to provide milk of the kind and quantity needed for their children. Some animals, likewise, cannot feed their own young. But such a case is abnormal and extremely unusual. Women who are willing to live normal lives of rest and restraint, to be careful in their diets and habits, and peaceful in mind and heart, will be able to nurse their babies and be extremely happy in doing so.

Now it happens that usually when a mother nurses her child, she is infertile. Ordinarily, the menses do not return while the breasts give milk. That means that, as a general rule, women who nurse their babies do not have pregnancies more often than about once in two years. All over the world normal women during the early childbearing period have children averaging not less than two years apart, sometimes more, when they nurse their children normally.

There is no need for birth control when in the early childbearing period a woman would normally have a child only every two years or more.

4. *Usually human fertility decreases with age.* A woman is not as likely to become pregnant at thirty-five as at twenty-five, nor as likely to become pregnant at forty-five as at thirty-five. Usually fertility ceases in the early forties. So about the time a husband and wife might begin to think they

have enough children to care for and educate, it becomes less likely that they will have children. Especially in this matter the radicals have been surprised to find that among decent people who want children, those who use contraceptive methods have about as many children as those who do not use contraceptive methods! Nature, or in other words God, arranges it so that people do not have more children than they need and can care for, more children than would be a blessing.

For illustration, I have six daughters. My impression is that their age ratio is perhaps typical. The fifth child was born when her mother was thirty-six. The sixth and last child was born when her mother was forty-two. Many other families where no artificial means have been used in preventing conception find that the likelihood of pregnancy decreases with age, and that fertility usually ceases in the early forties.

Since God takes care of diminishing the frequency of conception and thus limits the family by His own natural plan, in ordinary cases certainly there is no need for contraceptive measures. Birth control is not necessary, because God has already arranged that properly.

5. *In ordinary cases birth control is unnecessary because childbirth is normal and healthy, and the ordinary woman is equipped by nature to bear children as frequently as conception would ordinarily take place, and is equipped to nurse the babies, and all that without any undue strain upon her health.* It is as normal for a woman to bear children as for lower animals to bear young. In fact, it is customary for the larger animals, mammals, with gestation period as long as that for human beings, to breed and reproduce young with less rest period between pregnancies than a woman has who bears children about every two years during the most prolific period of her married life.

A woman's body is perfectly prepared for childbearing. The shape, the bodily capacity, the muscular development, the provision of mammary glands, are obvious equipment for childbearing and nursing. A woman's heart and lungs and digestive apparatus are adequately oversize to provide for the needs of the little developing body carried by the mother and for feeding the same little one after birth. The bearing of children should be regarded as natural and healthful and matter-of-fact. Certainly a pregnant woman should have good medical supervision, but pregnancy is not sickness. With proper supervision of diet, with proper rest and exercise, and with a happy heart, the mother of ten children may expect to live just as long as the mother of one or the mother of none.

Since most families actually want the babies that come, since God Himself gives life as He chooses and does not give babies except as He makes it possible to care for them, since normal nursing spaces children usually about two years apart, since fertility decreases as age increases, and since regular childbearing is healthful and natural (for which a woman's body is fully prepared), in most cases it is obvious that birth control is not necessary nor desirable.

Large Families Are Desirable

It is clearly the intention of the Scripture that people should want to have large families. "Be fruitful, and multiply, and replenish the earth," is what God commanded Adam and Eve (Gen. 1:28). Again, He gave a blessing to Noah and his sons, as He had done to Adam and Eve, and said, "Be fruitful, and multiply, and replenish the earth" (Gen. 9:1). Allowing for the possible early death of one child, every marriage would have to produce three children just to keep exactly the same population on the earth. But the command of God is to "multiply, and replenish the earth." To reproduce another generation of as many people as the present generation is not sufficient to fulfill this command. To "multiply" would indicate that parents ought to leave in the world more population than they found in the world. Families ought to be large enough to increase the population. That is the clear intent of the Scripture.

And the inference clearly is that large families are happy families and that a man is greatly blessed of God with every additional child he has. That is made clear specially in Psalm 127:3-5. "Lo, children are an heritage of the Lord: and the fruit of the womb is his reward. As arrows are in the hand of a mighty man; so are children of the youth. Happy is the man that hath his quiver full of them: they shall not be ashamed, but they shall speak with the enemies in the gate."

Here is the teaching God gives in these verses: 1. Children are from God, "an heritage of the Lord." 2. Children are "his reward," that is, a special blessing, given to those whom God loves and those who have pleased Him. 3. As a warrior would want many arrows, so would a man want many chil-

dren born in his young manhood. In other words, children
are a greatly desired addition to a man's usefulness and happiness. Whatever good thing a man wants to do for the world
and for God, his opportunity for doing it is greatly increased
by having many children. 4. "Happy is the man that hath his
quiver full of them"; that is, happy is the man who has all
the children he can have, or perhaps more literally, happy is
the man who has his house full of children. 5. The righteousness and integrity of such a man speak for themselves; and a
man's children will be his safety and happiness, to help him
overcome any enemy.

Any honest interpretation of that Scripture, Psalm 127:3-
5, means that large families of children are greatly to be desired, are a blessing from God, and result in greater happiness than small families.

Psalm 128, verses 1 to 4, tells us plainly that large families
are a special blessing from God, given to those who fear the
Lord and walk in His ways. These verses say:

*"Blessed is every one that feareth the Lord; that walketh
in his ways. For thou shalt eat the labour of thine hands;
happy shalt thou be, and it shall be well with thee. Thy wife
shall be as a fruitful vine by the sides of thine house: thy
children like olive plants round about thy table. Behold, that
thus shall the man be blessed that feareth the Lord."*

Now consider that Scripture. What will happen to the man
who fears the Lord and walks in his ways? He shall eat of
the labor of his hands, he shall be happy, and it shall be well
with him. In particular his wife will be a fruitful one and his
children will be "like olive plants round about thy table." A
fruitful wife and many children—these are the blessings that
come to the man who fears the Lord and walks in His ways.
"Behold, that thus shall the man be blessed that feareth the
Lord."

There are several very practical reasons for large families
which may help us to see why God has encouraged them in
the Bible and why large families are announced, by the Scriptures, to be such a blessing. Let us consider some of these
reasons for the wisdom of large families.

1. *Every reason for one child is a reason for other children.* Within the limits that God Himself has provided by His
own physical laws, every child that God gives brings his own
reason for being. If one child brings happiness, more chil-

dren bring more happiness. All parents of large families bear testimony to this. Nearly every argument against large families is a theoretical argument. When applied to a particular case, it does not stand up. There may be some theoretical argument for not having another baby, but when the baby comes, actually God provides for the tenth one as well as for the first one, and the tenth one is loved as much as the first one, and adds as much to the happiness of the home. Within the limits God has set in nature, more children mean more provision from God, more happiness.

2. *Large families are desirable because they care better for their parents in their old age.*

In I Timothy 5:4 God commands, "But if any widow have children or nephews, let them learn first to show piety at home, and to requite their parents: for that is good and acceptable before God." Children should requite their parents. This is a clear Bible doctrine.

The Townsend Plan people want the government to take care of all old people. The communists want the same thing. Socialists want the same thing. But actually, God's plan is that children should take care of their own parents. In fact, that is part of the meaning of the command, "Honour thy father and thy mother: that thy days may be long upon the land which the Lord thy God giveth thee," which is one of the Ten Commandments (Exod. 20:12).

When Jesus was on earth the Pharisees were accustomed to teaching young people that if they would give money to the support of the priesthood and the Temple, they need not care for their own fathers and mothers. But to such people Jesus said:

"Full well ye reject the commandment of God, that ye may keep your own tradition. For Moses said, Honour thy father and thy mother; and, Whoso curseth father or mother, let him die the death: But ye say, If a man shall say to his father or mother, It is Corban, that is to say, a gift, by whatsoever thou mightest be profited by me; he shall be free. And ye suffer him no more to do ought for his father or his mother; Making the word of God of none effect through your tradition, which ye have delivered: and many such like things do ye."—Mark 7:9-13.

You see, it is a duty for children to support their parents, to "requite their parents."

It is not wrong for parents to look happily forward to old age, knowing that if they have not been able to lay by the means for a comfortable old age, yet they have invested their time and money and love and toil in the rearing of godly children who will care for them in their old age. It is a poor kind of Christianity that does not accept the obligations God puts upon sons and daughters to care for their parents.

If there are only one or two or three children, they are not as likely to be able to take care of their parents. In the first place, the law of averages is against it. Suppose one of the children dies before reaching maturity. Suppose a daughter marries a man who does not like his father-in-law and mother-in-law. Suppose a son finds his health breaking down and finds it all he can do to provide for his own wife and children. There are fewer chances that there will be children able to take care of their parents out of two children than out of ten, for example, or out of six.

Or, to put it another way, it is easier for six or eight children to provide for their parents than for two children to provide for their parents.

And even more important is this truth, that children reared one or two to a family are selfish and undisciplined, and have difficulty having happy homes of their own without taking the responsibility of caring for their parents. Children out of big families have more sense of responsibility and are more likely to have the unselfish attitude and the sense of duty which will prompt them to care for their parents.

So parents, for their own happiness and welfare, should have large families when God makes that possible.

3. *Children of large families turn out to be better men and women, make better Christians.*

One day I saw a mother get on a train with her daughter who was perhaps ten years old. The father saw them into the car and left. The daughter promptly announced to the mother, "We are going to sit facing this way." Throughout the day she gave her mother orders, and the mother sometimes fretfully but usually meekly carried out the will of the child. One might think that that one child, having all the love and devotion of her father's and mother's hearts would be better cared for than the children in a large family. One would think that the man with a good income who could buy his daughter everything her heart desired because he had no other children to make demands upon him, would make her happier and make her into a better woman than would be possible if he had six or eight children. But actually, the fact that this girl was an only child was a definite handicap to her. She could not be as happy, she could not develop into as good a woman, she could not have as well-developed a sense of values, as mature a character, as if there had been other children in the family to share the attention she received, and to whom she must, necessarily, adjust her life.

I saw a woman get on the train some time before the above incident, with four children. They all wanted to sit on different seats. She could not please them all so she promptly piloted them to the seat she herself selected, plumped them down in their places, and told them what to do. The children were not dressed as nicely as the only daughter of her parents, mentioned above. No one child of the four could have his own way as much as if he were the only child. But out of a family of four little ones each of these children had a better chance to become good citizens, moral, upright, well-adjusted members of society, than if any one of them had been an only child.

An only child may get better clothes. An only child may get more attention. An only child may sometimes get better education, though rarely is that true. But the only child cannot get the discipline which necessarily comes by mutual association and contact and adjustment among a large family of children.

Any man should think very seriously before falling in love with, and marrying, a girl who is an only child. She will be spoiled and selfish, will want her own way, will not be a good risk. Any girl should think most seriously before falling in love with, and marrying, a young man who is an only child. He is very likely to be inconsiderate, self-centered, and spoiled. His mother is very likely to interfere in his life after he is married. Marriages of those who are the only children more often end in divorce than the marriages of those who come from large families. The man who had nobody with whom to share his skates, his ball and bat and his bicycle when he was a boy, will not be as well able to cooperate with business associates nor with his wife. On the other hand, the boy who had to learn that some property belonged to others, and had to respect the rights of his brothers and sisters when he was a child, will be much more fitted to live with other people when he is grown. There is a definite character development in being a member of a large family.

It is not often that an only child becomes great and famous. But very frequently the men of genius and of outstanding character and usefulness come from large families. John and Charles Wesley came from a family of nineteen, born to Samuel and Susannah Wesley. Note the example of Benjamin Franklin who was fifteenth in a family of seventeen.

I do not believe that native genius would be especially affected by large families, but character development and a humanitarian attitude would most certainly be developed in large families more than in small families. Children who have their own way, who never have to give up to others, do not make as good citizens, do not make as good husbands or wives, do not make as good Christians, as those who grow up in larger families. Lord Byron was a genius, but a very unhappy man and certainly not a great blessing to mankind. His rearing without the blessing of a large family could not keep Lord Byron from being a genius, but certainly it did not fit him for the humanitarian worth to bless society as John Wesley and Benjamin Franklin blessed it.

Consider the frugality, the forbearance, the largeness of heart, the humanitarian impulses of these men who came in poverty from large families and started in the world with the benediction of well-developed character grown in the home. Every child needs brothers and sisters. Every child needs someone with whom to play, someone with whom to share his toys, and perhaps someone with whom to fight! And every child needs enough brothers and sisters that mother will not have too much time to yield to every whim, or patience to put up with too much whining and crying. Overindulgence, the sin that ruins so many children in small families, becomes more or less impossible in large families.

The mother who has a half-dozen children is almost compelled to have some of them dry the dishes, some of them sweep the floor, some of them look after the baby. If she had only one child she could do these things herself. The child who learns to dry the dishes, to pick up his own toys, to mow the lawn and "help mother" is getting a kind of education that cannot be given in the schools. Large families turn out children of better character, better prepared for life, than do small families.

4. *Larger families are happier families.* Children who grow

up in a home with a number of other children live a happier, more normal life than children in small families.

In my father's family there were five of us boys and three girls. Our home was a gathering place for Christian young people for miles around. We always had a big time. My brothers and I rode horses together, went swimming together, worked together, and, of course, argued together. Life was not always smooth, but it was always interesting! If I did not work hard in school, my sister made better grades than I did, and that was a disgrace for a boy to let a girl beat him!

What big times we had! There was only one home in the community where we specially liked to visit—it was a home where they had more children than we had!

My brother, ten years older than I, and I often worked together. By the time I was fifteen I was as large as he was and felt that I ought to do as much work. He did not discourage that idea! It was a tremendous influence on my life that I had an older brother. When I was ten he caught me smoking a pipe and made me smoke it until I was sick!

There were always enough people at our house for a six-ball croquet game, enough to pitch horseshoes, enough to go swimming. There were always enough of us to have a sing-song and carry various parts. In the rough West Texas cattle and farming community there was competition in work, competition in study. I always took up for my younger sister, and my older sister always took up for my younger brother!

When my father got one of us sold on the value of a college education, he set a standard for the whole family. I think my brother George went to Decatur College and Baylor University largely because I did. I think that my two younger brothers, Joe and Bill, were largely influenced to preach the Gospel because I, the older brother, was a preacher. Our family was a little community all by itself and felt sufficient and happy that it was. We had our own traditions, our own standards. Our dad was the smartest man in the world. Our family had then the finest horses in the state. At least, so it seemed to us. "Remember whose boy you are, Son," said my father many a time when his boys rode away. It seems to me that there was an *espirit de corps* that would have been impossible in a family with fewer children.

Poor? Come to think of it, we were very poor. We did not think so at the time. It seemed to us that we were better off than most other people in the world. As I remember it now, we always felt a need to help other less fortunate people who did not have such nice families, such a happy home as we had. There was always plenty of food, plenty of work, plenty of study, plenty of singing, and plenty of churchgoing. I thank God I grew up in a happy, large family.

In my own home there have been eight of us to eat around the same table, eight of us to have family worship together. There was always somebody to play tennis with, or somebody to sing with, or somebody to play checkers or dominoes with. There were enough people present to start an argument, and enough other people present to see that it did not get too hot! At our home we had two pianos, two violins, an accordion, a guitar and a clarinet. Our children never much wanted to go to other people's homes to play or visit. Other people's children came to our home where there were so many people and where there was always something doing! My children never needed expensive toys to play with. People are more fun to play with than toys. And the most common food is always enjoyed when there are eight people around the table. I do not expect any of my six daughters to have a divorce nor an unhappy home. If these girls learned to get along in a little community of eight, it is most likely they can get along in a home of their own, and can be happy.

I am simply illustrating the fact that large families are happy families usually, and are much more likely to be happy than small families. It is people who make a home, and the more people there are who really belong, who are welded together in one well-controlled family, under the blessing of God, in a Christian atmosphere and with godly discipline and training, the more happiness there will be in the home. So, no wonder the Scripture says about children, "Happy is the man that hath his quiver full of them" (Ps. 127:5). No wonder that the Scripture says, "Happy shalt thou be, and it shall be well with thee. Thy wife shall be as a fruitful vine by the sides of thine house: thy children like olive plants round about thy table" (Ps. 128:2, 3). Large families make for happiness, if they be godly families, and if children be reared in the nurture and admonition of the Lord. It is a calamity for any child to be reared without brothers and sisters. It is a calamity for any man and woman to have only one child, so likely to grow up spoiled and self-centered and frustrated and unhappy.

5. Large families contribute much more to the welfare of the world.

Of course I speak now of the Christian home. Where children are reared for the Lord, reared according to Bible standards, reared with reverence for God and His Word, brought up to love and trust the Lord Jesus Christ, every child is a great contribution to the welfare and happiness of the world. I have no sons. But with six daughters I was more likely to have among them a wife of a great preacher than if I had only one. With six daughters I was more likely to give a daughter to help carry the Gospel to the ends of the world than if I had only one daughter. In fact, my earnest prayer was that God would take every one of the six and use them in some special way in a life of full-time service for God. Certainly six children can do more for the world than one.

Many a mother cannot reach multitudes for Christ. But she may rear a boy who can reach multitudes. And she is even more likely to be greatly useful if she has several sons.

Shall we leave it to the immigrant peoples from Europe and Asia to rear large families? Must we leave it only to Catholics to have large families and propagate their faith? Should illiterate people provide the big families of the world? Why should not those who are real Christians set out to obey the command of God in multiplying and replenishing the earth with large families? Why not rear sons and daughters who can make a multiplied impact upon the world for God? A large family, when they be reared in a Christian home and according to Bible standards, is the most important contribution any home can make to society. If Susannah Wesley had had a billion dollars to spend for the uplifting of the poor and fallen, for the support of orphan children and widows, for the endowment of halls of learning, she could not have made a contribution to the welfare of society to be compared for an instant with what she did in furnishing John and Charles Wesley to the world! The other Wesley children seem to have been fine men and women also. But if Susannah Wesley had had only two children, they would not have been John and Charles. Without the large family and the system of training inaugurated by that godly mother for her large family, John and Charles Wesley would not have been what they became, the leaders in a great evangelical revival.

Why Birth Control Is Positively Wrong

Is birth control, as it is ordinarily understood, positively wrong? I think it clearly is.

1. *The use of contraceptive devices to prevent the conception and birth of children is wrong because it goes against the clear tenor of Bible teaching.*

If it is a virtue to have large families, then it is lack of virtue to limit the family to less than what it would be if God had His way and gave the children that He wants to give to a home. Since married couples are commanded to "multiply and replenish the earth" (Gen. 1:28; Gen. 9:1), then not to multiply is a sin.

The lesson of Onan in the Scripture indicates that it is a sin to try to avoid having children. Genesis 38:7-10 says: "And Er, Judah's firstborn, was wicked in the sight of the Lord; and the Lord slew him. And Judah said unto Onan, Go in unto thy brother's wife, and marry her, and raise up seed to thy brother. And Onan knew that the seed should not be his; and it came to pass, when he went in unto his brother's wife, that he spilled it on the ground, lest that he should give seed to his brother. And the thing which he did displeased the Lord: wherefore he slew him also."

I think God was displeased with Onan partly because he was not willing to raise up seed to his dead brother, according to the teaching Onan had received, the teaching that was later given in the Mosaic law also (Deut. 25:5-10). Yet a withdrawal itself is not normal and leads to a sense of frustration and dissatisfaction, and medically is not recommended. Certainly Onan was wrong in not wanting a child. And God was angry with him and slew him.

May we not infer that any man who takes a wife and yet does not want children sins against God and angers God? It seems clear that people who marry and have normal mating and yet wish to frustrate the obvious intention of marriage, wish to avoid having children, sin against marriage and sin against the God who made them male and female and commanded them to multiply. From that viewpoint birth control is wrong. At least we must say that for men and women not to plan to have any children at all is a sin. It seems also that we may properly infer from the general tenor of the Scripture that to want less children than God would give without human rebellion and contraceptive devices is likewise a sin.

2. *Birth control advocates are usually anti-Christian in their attitude and propaganda.*

The first pamphlet on birth control in America was written by a freethinker, Robert Dale Owen. The first real book on the subject of birth control, advocating the use of contraceptives, was written by Dr. Charles Knowlton in 1832, also a freethinker, not a Christian, but definitely opposed to the Bible and rejecting Christ as the Son of God in his unbelief and infidelity. Those who advocate birth control usually do not believe the Bible, and often they sneer at the prudishness of old-fashioned people who do believe the Bible and try to live up to the moral standards established in the Word of God. Those who advocate birth control are usually in favor of trial marriages, companionate marriages, or free love. They usually do not accept the Bible standard for marriage that it is to be permanent. Down through the years those who have advocated birth control have been those who did not accept the authority of the Bible. Would anybody call Dr. Marie Stopes a contender for the Christian faith? Another most prominent writer on sex subjects, advocating birth control, was so notoriously immoral in teaching and practice that he was banished from one great tax-supported university after having been employed to lecture there. I say that the advocates of birth control are usually those who believe in easy divorce, or in trial marriages, or in open immorality and free love.

The communistic, atheistic regime in Russia openly advocated birth control and for years made even abortion legal. That government was deliberately and outrageously atheistic, was actively against the Christian religion and determined to stamp it out and to stamp out the moral standards which went with Christianity. Soviet Russia during the same period deliberately encouraged the easiest possible divorce, and the grossest immorality in sex matters was smiled upon. In recent years even Soviet Russia has seen the need to restore some earlier standards in the family and the home, to safeguard society. But birth control goes along with radical ideas about marriage, with an open attack on Christianity and a denial of the authority of the Bible. A very large percentage of those who advocate birth control (though not all of them) do not have the Christian attitude toward the sanctity of the home and marriage, and are against the Bible standard.

It is true that some leaders in the National Council of Churches have advocated birth control. But these leaders did not really represent Christianity nor the Christian feeling and conviction of the true churches of Christ in America. They were modernists, denying every fundamental of the Christian faith. Modernists (who specially advocate birth control) deny the inspiration and authority of the Bible, deny the historic Christian position on the deity of Christ and salvation through faith in His atoning blood, and certainly do not represent Christianity. One modernist, writing under Y.M.C.A. auspices, openly scoffs at the puritanical code of morals of the fundamentalists, the 'prudery' of those who are inhibited or restrained by the teachings of the Bible and of historic Christianity. Those who name the name of Christ but advocate birth control nearly always represent the radical or modernistic group who are not Christian in their concepts and deny the essentials of historic Christianity and the authority of the Bible. This goes to show that true Christians should beware of such teaching. Most birth control propaganda is linked up with immoral and unchristian teachings in other matters which certainly put birth control advocacy in a bad light and makes it unpalatable for those who are Christian and who follow the Bible standard of morals.

It is heartening to see how nearly unanimous Christian sentiment is against birth control and the dissemination of information about contraceptives. The Catholic position has been unyielding through the years. One pope after another has issued proclamations denouncing birth control by the use of contraceptives. The Catholic Church is solidly united on this question. The position of sound and orthodox Lutheran people (perhaps the second largest denomination in the world claiming to be Christian) is well stated, we believe, in the great book on marriage, *For Better Not for Worse*, by Dr. Walter A. Maier, the famous Lutheran Hour preacher. With great scholarship and Christian authority he shows the danger and harm of birth control devices and drugs. Since many, many letters come to me as an editor and Bible scholar regarding birth control, I took pains to find what was the sentiment of some of America's leading ministers and fundamentally sound Christian leaders. The editor of one of the strongest Christian magazines in America talked with me at length about the matter, and gave me notes he had from a distinguished Christian doctor, long the best known Christian scientist in America, now dead. I also consulted one who is, I think, the best known fundamental Bible teacher in America, a great preacher, a distinguished gentleman, a devoted Christian. I discussed the matter, also, with the most prominent leader in a denomination which makes much of its adherence to the Word of God. All these men agreed that the general use of contraceptives to prevent the conception of children (except in those rare cases where pregnancy would endanger the mother's life, as determined by a reputable physician with a Christian viewpoint), would be immoral and wrong and certainly is not to be practiced by Christians who follow the Bible.

3. *Birth control measures, if generally practiced, would be disastrous to public morals and public welfare.*

Birth control definitely strikes at the stability and happiness of marriage. Of course many a frivolous wife would rather not undertake the duties of childbearing. Many would be specially tempted to spend their time in the night clubs, the cocktail lounges and on the dance floor. A generation of young people, which marries hastily and without sufficient moral and spiritual background, has a tendency to shirk the moral responsibilities involved in the rearing of children. But is such a young couple happier to have no children? Is their home more likely to last and their marriage to be happy? The answer is, "No." Homes that have no children are not normal homes. They do not provide normal happiness. Marriage without children cannot provide the fullest and the greatest riches of love. Married couples who have no children are not as considerate of each other, do not have as much to bind them together. They do not have the same incentive to make their marriage a success. To encourage the widespread use of birth control information is to increase divorces and unhappiness and misery in the world. The breakdown of marriage strikes at the very heart of public morals and integrity and happiness. And it is certain that birth control measures would be used, and are being used, primarily as a way to escape responsibility, a way to avoid having a legitimate and normal number of children. Birth control advocates shed crocodile tears over the poor tenant-farm mothers or the wives of factory workers who live in slums and yet must expect great families because they do not have the "boon" of birth control information. But in actual practice it works out that birth control information does not result in the factory

worker having only six children instead of ten. Rather, it
works out that the fast living young couples, without moral
responsibility, without the steadying influence of the church
and faith in Christ, people who can afford children but do
not want the normal responsibility of fatherhood and motherhood, use contraceptives to prevent having a normal family.
The simple truth is that ordinary people do not have the
character and moral gravity and uprightness and spiritual
wisdom to decide how many children would be right and
proper and happy. The thing that only God Himself should
decide is often decided wrongly, you may be sure, when left
in frivolous and worldly hands.

If you think the common use of contraceptives would be
for the welfare of the nation, and for society, then consider
carefully what happened in France and in Russia when birth
control information was freely available, when the birth rate
fell, when the home disintegrated, and when morality de-
clined fearfully. The dissemination of widespread information
about birth control is certain to do great damage to marriage
and the home.

To put in the hands of people who are married and are
mates and who would normally be expected to carry out the
command of God to "multiply, and replenish the earth" the
choice as to whether or not they shall obey God's command;
to leave it to men and women to choose whether or not they
will let marriage have its proper fruit is to encourage selfishness and to discourage family virtues. Suppose a woman
chooses a new fur coat instead of a baby. Do you believe
that society is as much benefited by that woman's vanity as it
would be benefited by a baby, loved and longed for and
prayed for and reared in the nurture and admonition of the
Lord? Is a woman as much ennobled by the silky feel of fur
and the admiring glances of her theater-going friends as she
would be ennobled to bear a child, to love the little one,
croon to him, bathe and clothe him, and teach him in the
way of the Lord?

Suppose a young couple by preventing the conception of
children are able to live the night-club life and mingle with
the theater and restaurant throngs in the big cities. Suppose
that by not having children a woman can spend more time at
the hairdresser's and the beauty parlor, or that a man can
buy a finer car and have more money to spend on a month in

Canada in the summer or in Florida in the winter—is he a better man for that choice?

It is never a choice between actual starvation if one has a baby, and a bare subsistence without the baby. It was not that choice even in the most rigorous pioneer days. God always provides for the baby He sends if people trust Him and do right. Honest, hard-working, virtuous families always had room for another baby when God sent it. No one ever needs to use artificial devices and drugs to prevent the coming of a little one in order to have the common necessities of life. No, in these days when the day laborer has a refrigerator, a radio, and an automobile and works not more than forty hours a week and strikes to get a week of not over thirty-six hours, people do not prevent conception in order to have bare necessities or even the moderate comforts of life. People prevent conception because they do not want to take the normal duties, the normal responsibilities that should inevitably go with marriage. They want to cheat, having the pleasures of marriage without the normal responsibilities that God gave with marriage. The widespread use of contraceptives thus develops selfishness and immoral and irresponsible and unchristian attitudes toward life, while the normal bearing and rearing of children contribute to happiness, to the permanency of the family, and to the welfare of the nation.

Let us remember, too, that the dissemination of information on contraception reaches the unmarried as well as the married. And birth control information can be used as freely in cases of adultery and fornication as in proper marriage. In fact, those who commit adultery are more certain to wish to prevent pregnancy and the birth of children than a man and wife who are properly mated and where there would be no odium to the birth of a child, but rather congratulations on the part of all the loved ones and friends and of society in general.

Actual experience has proven beyond any shadow of doubt that when birth control information is spread, when contraceptive devices are sold publicly, when the moral conviction of a community is broken down on the matter of contraceptives, a great increase of immorality results. The fear of pregnancy, and hence of public exposure and shame, is the greatest deterrent to adultery and fornication. Even those who would be willing to commit sin do not wish to get caught in their sin. The Bible doctrine that "be sure your sin will find you out" (Num. 32:23) and that "whatsoever a man soweth, that shall he also reap" (Gal. 6:7) is true, and it is a deterrent to sin. But when people believe they can nullify the divine law and can get by with sin and that no one will ever know, and that they can escape the natural consequences of immorality, then immorality spreads rapidly. We are now in the midst of a generation that is finding out, they think, that they can get by with sin by the use of contraceptives and that they will not be brought to judgment for their crime against God and society in illicit intercourse.

All about us are young people, millions of them, who are reared without much teaching at home on moral matters, and particularly on sex matters. They attend the picture shows and have sex interest and passions stirred by the lewdness on the screen. They dance and neck, and hence are abnormally influenced to sex desire. Does anyone think that to put birth control information in the hands of millions of young people, irresponsible, unchristian, untrained in moral and spiritual matters, would be beneficial? Does anybody believe that a generation of sex-crazy young people would not be encouraged to sin if they thought they could sin and get by without any shame or suffering? Actually, Christians know that one never gets by with sin. God is not mocked, even if people think they are getting by. In the long run, sin never paid anybody, never made anybody happy. But those who have knowledge of contraceptives may think that they have now discovered a way to mock God, to go on with sin and avoid the results of sin. In actual practice when a generation of undisciplined girls and irresponsible young men have put in their hands birth control information, and the restraints are taken off in war time, as has happened in America in the last few years, a national orgy of prostitution and immorality takes place, as it has done here. I suppose no sensible person believes there would have been so much of the scarlet sin had there not been birth control information given to soldiers, and often to the khaki-wacky girls, the pick-up girls who walked the streets or waited around U.S.O.'s, railroad stations, and bus stations, to pick up soldiers, or sailors. If married people are generally taught birth control measures, it will result in widespread adultery, for unmarried people naturally get the same information. It will contribute to the breaking down of morals everywhere, as it has increasingly done within the last generation, wherever birth control devices and drugs and methods are publicized and popularized.

4. *Answers to the argument of birth control advocates.*

Those who wish to encourage widespread use of contraceptives make plausible arguments. But there is a sensible answer for every one of them, I believe.

(a) "By limiting the number of children, parents can give better training and education to the few children they choose to have." Actually there is no evidence at all that children from small families get along better in the world than the children from large families. The contrary is often the case. Children who are in a small family and never have to give up their own way, never have to work, never have to save, are less likely to succeed in life and to be happy than the children from a large family who had to live in economy, have to learn to work, have to adjust themselves to other members in the family and divide. Thus children from large families are better equipped for life in the large majority of cases. Public school education is available to the family of ten children just the same as to the spoiled darling who is the only child of his parents. The children from a large family will usually make better grades, make more friends, and get more out of their education, because they are more likely to have learned discipline and work and self-control. Even for that minority who seek a college education for their children, I would say that children from large families, even if they can have little financial aid from home, can go to college these days about as easily as the children of rich parents or those who have plenty of money to spend on an education for their offspring. In 1916 I went off to college with $9.35. With a rather intimate and long acquaintance with three Christian colleges, two great universities, a seminary, and a Bible institute, and a fair understanding of the educational field, I can say that normal young people who want to go to college and who are taught to work and study and who have good habits and character can go to college anywhere in the United States and work their own way. Many scholarships await students of ability, and jobs await on every campus and adjacent to every campus. Not only so, but the young men and women who work to earn part or all of their own expenses in college and university get the best education, in many cases. I doubt if many boys or girls miss college because they have brothers and sisters.

On the other hand, the child who does not have to work, who is the spoiled darling of his father and mother, often makes a poor student and later a poor citizen. My experience as a college student and a college teacher was that the poorest students in school were the children of rich parents, the students who had plenty of money to spend. With widespread acquaintance in college circles I find that the families where the father and mother have been to college and where there is a background that justifies a college education for the children, the children in large families are just as likely to go to college, if not more so, than the one or two children in very small families. Large families do not hinder education, do not hinder the correct rearing of children.

(b) "But the mother of two or three children can give them much more attention and more proper care than the mother of a large family of children," say birth control advocates. The actual truth is that Susannah Wesley with her great family of children (she bore nineteen children) had time to give one hour a week of the most serious religious instruction to each one of her children separately, while the selfish and worldly woman who does not desire another child, rarely takes time to teach her children about God. The extra time that women get for themselves by preventing the birth of children and thwarting God's plan for the home is more often used in frivolity, at the bridge table, the theater, the club, than in the care of her children. The selfish mothers of few children do not take as good care of their children as the mothers of large families of children.

Sometimes all the examples are cited from the slum and tenement sections of our cities, showing the dirt and misery of large families. But the dirt and ignorance and squalor usually are just the same with small families in the same neighborhood and with the same moral and educational standards. Families are not dirty because they are large families, and are not clean because they are small families. People are dirty, and the children are poorly raised, if the parents are that kind of people, whether the children be many or few.

(c) "But there is such a large infant mortality among big families," says the birth control advocate. It is true that there are more babies who die in slums than in better homes, more babies who die where there are flies, not because they are of large families but because parents do not have the culture or habits of cleanliness to avoid them. Relatively few people now live in slums. What are called slums now usually have sanitary plumbing and screens. Slums are rapidly passing out of the picture in America. It has only been a generation since people of fair income could have ice refrigeration, and it has been less than a generation that they could have electrical refrigeration. Public health is becoming more and more the concern of society and government. These days no woman need lose her baby because she cannot have medical advice or hospitalization if she needs it. Childbearing is normal and is not dangerous when people are healthy and when surroundings are clean. In a given strata of society it is probable that there is no higher death rate for large families than for small families. For that matter, the woman who bore six children and lost one, having five left, is certainly much happier and better off than the woman who only bore one and has one left.

(d) "But the mother who has children only when she wants them will love her children better and will be a better mother to them," we are told. No, the mothers who desert their children, a rather frequent crime these days, are nearly always the mothers of only one or two, or at most, three. Mothers of large families do not desert their children. Mother love is more apt to be sustained and normal in large families than in small families where the mother has willfully prevented the conception of children and does not value highly the gifts that God gives to marriage. The mother and the father, who take with joyful heart all the gifts that God sends as the fruit of their love, are better parents than the mother and father who want to have very few children, if any, and who begrudge the time and labor and pain that are involved in rearing a family. Any child is better off born into a family with several other children than born into a family and reared as an only child, or as one of only two or three.

(e) "To allow unlimited conception in marriage makes the wife the slave of her husband, a drudge," we are told. That viewpoint could only come from one who does not think that children are blessings, as God says they are, and who thinks that the greatest happiness can be had by avoiding the natural fruits of marriage. Those who do not want children ought not to marry. Those who expect to marry and have the joys of marriage should expect to take the responsibilities of marriage also. Any woman is a cheat who expects to have the joys of wifehood, the care of a husband, the security of a permanent home, and who is yet unwilling to bear children and take her place in society as a mother as well as a wife. Every harlot can understand the viewpoint of the woman who wants mating without children, but I do not see how decent Christian women can endorse such a viewpoint. Marriage is intended to result in children. Having children is one of the principal reasons for a home.

To all the objections of the birth control advocates it ought to be sufficient to say that no child is ever conceived except that God Himself does it and gives the immortal soul to the little body which is formed. Children are from God! And God knows what He is doing. If God gives the child, then the Christian parents who trust God will find out that God will provide also the means for the care and training and rearing of the little one.

Let me remind you again that every child proves his own value after he arrives in this world. Those who object to the birth of children are always objecting before the child comes and before they know what blessing God will bring with the little one. If every woman who longs to prevent conception would wait until the child should come and live with her two years, then no normal and good woman would be willing to do without the little one, such a blessing from Heaven it would prove to be.

(f) "But without contraceptive measures the birth of another child will sometimes kill the mother," says the birth control advocate. Remember that this is an exception, a most unusual case that is supposed here. It is true that some women cannot nurse their children, and such women sometimes would become pregnant within a month of the birth of a former child. I have known of a few such cases. But such frequent pregnancies are very unusual, and in the cases I have known, only took place once or twice. The children might be born within a year of each other, but usually the third and fourth children did not come so soon. In some cases, a prospective mother's health is so precarious that doctors advise that the birth of a child might be fatal. What should a Christian husband and wife do in such a contingency?

In the first place, let us remember that doctors are only human, and they do not know everything. They often form an opinion without God. I think that if a truly Christian doctor should come to a conclusion that a pregnancy would mean almost certain death to a woman, and if other doctors confirmed that opinion, then she would be justified in following the counsel of Christian doctors to delay pregnancy until her health could be somewhat regained, perhaps. But many of the most earnest Christians do not believe that contraceptives are legitimate even in such cases. I have known of a number of women who were told that to bear another child would mean their death, but who, after much prayer, asked God to take care of them, and then bore the child they desired without any undue strain and with no detriment to their health. Doctors have a way of advising according to people's desires. It is very rare that a doctor tells a woman who really desires a child that it is inadvisable and that the birth of a child would likely prove fatal. A Christian always has resources that most doctors do not know about. A Christian can pray to God, and God is not likely to give a child to one of His children who trusts Him and loves Him when it would be a calamity. God gives children out of His love and mercy and for the good of homes and the good of society. God can prevent the conception if it is not His will that a husband and wife, whose mating is normal and scriptural, have another child at that time. Or God can give strength to the mother and can take care of the little one who is loved and wanted, whether doctors believe it safe or not.

Certainly there is some hazard in childbirth. God in His infinite mercy intended that motherhood should be so serious that it should have a chastening effect, a sobering effect, on women, to make them good mothers. It is not likely that a woman would prove as good a mother to a baby left on her doorstep as to a child she had planned for and prayed for, had carried under her heart for nine months, and then bore with much pain, and nursed at her own breast. God's plan is the best plan. Whatever pain there is in childbirth is justified in the plan of God.

Is it dangerous to have children? Not as dangerous as to ride in an automobile! More women die in automobile wrecks than die in childbirth every year in America. That danger can be reduced if people are thoughtful and prayerful and righteous, whether about riding in automobiles or about having children. But women do not quit riding in automobiles because there is some danger involved, nor do women who want children and want to obey God try to prevent conception because there are some pain and some hazard necessarily involved in childbearing.

CHAPTER XII

Correction and Discipline of Children

"And, ye fathers, ... bring them up in the nurture [chastening] *and admonition of the Lord."*—Eph. 6:4.

"If ye endure chastening, God dealeth with you as with sons; for what son is he whom the father chasteneth not?"—Heb. 12:7.

"He that spareth his rod hateth his son: but he that loveth him chasteneth him betimes."—Prov. 13:24.

"Chasten thy son while there is hope, and let not thy soul spare for his crying."—Prov. 19:18.

"Withhold not correction from the child: for if thou beatest him with the rod, he shall not die. Thou shalt beat him with the rod, and shalt deliver his soul from hell."—Prov. 23:13, 14.

"The rod and reproof give wisdom: but a child left to himself bringeth his mother to shame."—Prov. 29:15.

"Correct thy son, and he shall give thee rest; yea, he shall give delight unto thy soul."—Prov. 29:17.

Most baby animals are entirely self-supporting within a few weeks or months at most, but it is normal for children to be in the home and somewhat dependent upon their parents for support for twenty years. A colt or calf can walk the day it is born, but a child normally takes ten or twelve months. Obviously God intended the child to be helpless and dependent long enough to stay in the home for training. God intended that the home should develop in children the moral qualities and principles and habits and adjustments essential to good character.

Animal parents take responsibility for training their little ones, and instinctively they are taught of God to chastise their young, to teach them obedience and safe habits. Hens and mother birds peck their baby chicks and nestlings. I have seen many a cow kick her calf to stop overboisterous attempts to get milk, painful to the cow. Mother bears cuff their cubs vigorously sometimes to stop a fight or to enforce

obedience. All horsemen and animal trainers know that punishment is sometimes necessary in handling animals. Certainly
children, more than animals, need discipline and correction.

Children Need Correction Because Naturally Wicked

There is a very definite reason why children also need punishment occasionally. That reason is that all children inherit
the fallen sinful nature which the human race has had since
the sin of Adam and Eve. Attractive, charming, lovable as
little children are, they are sinful in nature. It is true that

> Not in entire forgetfulness,
> And not in utter nakedness,
> But trailing clouds of glory do we come
> From God, who is our home.

Little children have something heavenly, something innocent, something wonderfully sweet about them. They are gifts
from God beyond price. But every such little child has a taint
of sin inborn. Every one has a nature that, if not curbed,
may lead to murder, to adultery, to blasphemy, to defiance of
God, to Hell itself!

God's Word teaches that little children are born with a
taint of sin. Psalm 58:3 says, "The wicked are estranged
from the womb: they go astray as soon as they be born,
speaking lies." David, in his heartbroken prayer after his
shameful sin with Bath-sheba, said, "Behold, I was shapen in
iniquity; and in sin did my mother conceive me" (Ps. 51:5).
He knew whence came his sin; it was the natural fruit of a
fallen, depraved nature which he had had from birth, even
from his conception! I do not mean that little children, unac-
countable infants who do not consciously sin, are lost.
Rather, the Bible teaches that they are kept, by God's merciful grace, until they come to the time of accountability to
God, to a personal consciousness of sin. No one goes to Hell
for the sinful nature he inherited. No one is punished in Hell
for Adam's sins of which he is the unconscious partaker by
inheritance. First Corinthians 15:22 says, "For as in Adam
all die, even so in Christ shall all be made alive." Whatever a
child lost by inheritance of the taint of Adam's sin, he has
gained back in Christ. The child is kept safe until he personally, himself, becomes a sinner. But we must remember in

dealing with children that we have a fallen, tainted, depraved nature to contend with, to restrain, and as far as possible, bring under control of a developed conscience, a moral character, and when the child is saved, under the mastery of a new nature, imparted at conversion.

A prominent man, speaking for the Atlanta Optimist Club one time, expressed a belief that every boy is good by nature and with a fair chance would be a noble, good man. Really, he expressed only a very dangerous half-truth, or less than a half-truth. Every child has capacities for good in the sense that God loves every child and wants to come into the heart and make the child good. And God has put certain capacities in the child which by careful discipline and restraint and nurture may develop into noble qualities. But left without discipline, without restraint, without punishment for sin and without definite influence for God and righteousness, every child in the world would turn out bad, wicked, unsocial, criminal! Every mother and father, viewing their precious baby, should remember that that little one is no better than Cain, the first child ever born, when he was cradled in the arms of his mother Eve. Your child and mine will turn out as Cain unless definitely restrained, controlled, disciplined, and influenced for righteousness and God.

The fallen nature inherited by every child demands that children should be brought up in the fear of God, with instruction and correction, as well as prayers and tears. When one realizes that the duty of parents is to take little ones with sinful, perverted natures and prepare them for Heaven, it is easy to see that punishment for sin and the restraint of strong authority is absolutely necessary in the home.

Parents, Like God, Must Punish Sin and Reward Righteousness

Parents stand in the place of God before their children, to a remarkable degree. Particularly does the father in the home have the authority of God over his children. He acts as God's deputy. The Bible often uses a human father to illustrate God's attitude toward His children. "Like as a father pitieth his children, so the Lord pitieth them that fear him" (Ps. 103:13). "When ye pray, say, Our Father which art in heaven," said Jesus (Luke 11:2). "If ye then, being evil, know how to give good gifts unto your children, how much more shall your Father which is in heaven given good things to them that ask him?" (Matt. 7:11). Parents, I say, stand before their children, clothed with the authority of God.

So in Colossians 3:20 we read, "Children, obey your parents in all things: for this is well pleasing unto the Lord." How striking is this statement, that the authority of parents over their children is to be unlimited, and that children are to obey their parents *in all things!*

The highest morality is summed up in the commandment, "Honour thy father and thy mother." That morality is to be rewarded thus: "that thy days may be long upon the land which the Lord thy God giveth thee" (Exod. 20:12). Parents have the authority of God over their children, and how serious, how all-important is this responsibility!

But God punishes people for sin. So the Bible declares from beginning to end. Even God's saints are subject to His chastisement for their own good. Since parents are to exercise the authority of God over their children to a very large degree, the Bible clearly teaches that parents should chastise their children for their own good, just as God punishes His children for their own good.

Hebrews 12:6-8 says, "For whom the Lord loveth he chasteneth, and scourgeth every son whom he receiveth. If ye endure chastening, God dealeth with you as with sons; for what son is he whom the father chasteneth not? But if ye be without chastisement, whereof all are partakers, then are ye bastards, and not sons." Here the simple rule is given that God chastises His children as all good fathers chastise their children.

"If ye endure chastening, God dealeth with you as with sons; for what son is he whom the father chasteneth not?" It is in the very nature of sonship to *receive* chastising when needed. It is in the very nature of fatherhood to *give* chastising when necessary. Any father who does not whip his children, treats them as if they were bastards (vs. 8). A man who as a whoremonger begets children outside of marriage, ignores his children, takes no responsibility for them, refuses to be a father to them. He does not support them, he does not teach them, he does not chastise them. He does not recognize the bastard boy as his son. So, God says that any man who does not whip his children to make them mind, treats them as bastards, as illegitimate children for whom he takes no responsibility! Nothing could show more plainly the truth that

God regards necessary chastisement of children as the inescapable duty of a father toward his children.

In these days when juvenile delinquents fill the jails, when homes for fallen girls are crowded, when teenage prostitutes throng every city and run after soldiers, when smoking, drinking, immoral, criminal youth has become the greatest moral problem in America, some educators frown on discipline of any kind. These silly, morally immature, impractical educators and theorists have utterly failed in turning out good men and women, citizens of character with Christian hearts and noble lives. Yet they scoff at corporal punishment which is so clearly taught in the Bible and so thoroughly vindicated by practical experience. The only answer to juvenile delinquency, the only answer to a generation which has grown up without faith in God, without self-control, without any steadfastness of moral character, is to come back to the Bible and find God's way of growing men and women with character. Prayerful, intelligent, Christian discipline in the home is absolutely essential to the growing of good men and women.

Another plain command of the Scripture on this subject is given in Ephesians 6:4: "And, ye fathers, provoke not your children to wrath: but bring them up in the nurture and admonition of the Lord."

Fathers are to bring their children up in the nurture and admonition of the Lord. I was startled to find that the word nurture in Ephesians 6:4 means chastisement or chastening. In fact, the word nurture is translated from the same Greek word *paideia*, which is translated chastening in Hebrews 12:5, in Hebrews 12:7, and Hebrews 12:11! It is the same word translated chastisement in Hebrews 12:8. The Greek verb, *paideuo*, on the same stem as this word, is used in Luke 23:16 and again in Luke 23:22 of the scourging of Jesus! Pilate said, "I will therefore chastise him, and let him go." The word nurture in Ephesians 6:4 means chastisement in the original Greek Scripture. So, fathers are really commanded to bring their children up in the discipline, or correction, or chastening, and admonition of the Lord!

For parents to chastise their children as necessary is explicitly commanded in the Word of God. Parents act for God in punishing sin, in rewarding righteousness, and in compelling the obedience of their children.

The responsibility of parenthood is almost overwhelming when viewed by the standard of Holy Scripture. Deuteronomy 21:18-21 shows us clearly that every father and mother had better have their son dead than for him to live in disobedience to their authority and teachings.

"If a man have a stubborn and rebellious son, which will not obey the voice of his father, or the voice of his mother, and that, when they have chastened him, will not hearken unto them: Then shall his father and his mother lay hold on him, and bring him out unto the elders of his city, and unto the gate of his place; And they shall say unto the elders of his city, This our son is stubborn and rebellious, he will not obey our voice; he is a glutton, and a drunkard. And all the men of his city shall stone him with stones, that he die: so shalt thou put evil away from among you; and all Israel shall hear, and fear."—Deut. 21:18-21.

It is understood from other Scriptures that a child properly brought up will not, when grown or near grown, be a rebel and a drunkard. But if parents under the Mosaic law had failed to train a son for God and righteousness to the extent that later the lad turned out to be a rebel, a stubborn and rebellious son, a glutton and a drunkard, they should first chasten him thoroughly and then "when they have chastened him," they find that he "will not hearken unto them," they are to bring him to the elders of the city to be stoned!

It is true that we do not have the same kind of civil government today. Instead of bringing such a son to be stoned, in these days he would have to be left to the officers of the law and the courts. Parents who do their duty, beginning from the babyhood of the little one, will never need to come to such an extremity. But this Scripture plainly shows that parents should feel the desperate importance of discipline. Disobedience to parental authority, long continued and deliberate on the part of a minor son, was thus punished, under the Mosaic law, with the death penalty!

Our modern, easy-going standards have let the very foundations of our society rot because we have not insisted on the authority of fathers and mothers being exercised in the home. The whipping of children to punish sin and compel obedience, as necessary, is absolutely essential to the proper development of character and the growing of moral, upright men and women. Fathers and mothers in this matter act for God Almighty and wield His authority in the home.

God Specially Holds Parents to Account for the Discipline and Control of Their Children

It is no small matter to be responsible to God for bringing a little life into this world. But every father and mother is responsible to God; and God holds parents strictly to account to enforce righteousness, to punish evil, to grow a character submissive to God and the right.

Abraham is an example greatly blessed because God could depend on him to control his children for the right. In Genesis 18:17-19 we are told why God took Abraham into His confidence about the planned destruction of Sodom and Gomorrah.

"And the Lord said, Shall I hide from Abraham that thing which I do; Seeing that Abraham shall surely become a great and mighty nation, and all the nations of the earth shall be blessed in him? For I know him, that he will command his children and his household after him, and they shall keep the way of the Lord, to do justice and judgment; that the Lord may bring upon Abraham that which he hath spoken of him."

Here we see that God decided to tell Abraham His plans, "For I know him, that he will command his children and his household after him, and they shall keep the way of the Lord, to do justice and judgment." This would make it so God would be able to fulfill His promise to Abraham: "that the Lord may bring upon Abraham that which he hath spoken of him."

How striking and impressive is the truth that God promised His blessings to Abraham, because He knew that Abraham would command his children and his household and make them serve God! The inference is obvious that if Abraham had not been one to make his household obey, God would not have confided in him His plans for the future and would not have made to him such exceeding great and precious promises. For a man to make his children obey, and so to bring them up in righteousness and judgment, is a fundamental matter of character, greatly honored by God!

Eli, the high priest of God in the days when Samuel was born, is a sad example of a man who failed God in this matter. Eli was a good man. As far as we know, God had no

complaint with the way he held the office of high priest, no
complaint about his moral life, no complaint about the way
he judged the people. By all human standards, save one, Eli
was a great and good man. But in the matter of commanding
his children, in restraining and correcting and disciplining
them, Eli was a failure!

When Eli was an old, old man and his sons were grown
and married with families of their own, God still held it
against him that he did not restrain his sons. Eli had rather
feebly protested against the adultery and the greed of his
sons (I Sam. 2:22-25). They did not obey their father, however, and Eli did not enforce his will upon them. For this
very reason, that is, because Eli did not vigorously take the
matter in hand and punish his own sons, grown, married men
that they were, God's curse came upon him! The prophet of
God came to Eli and warned him that Eli honored his sons
above God (I Sam. 2:29). This man of God prophesied that
Eli's two sons, Hophni and Phinehas, should both die in one
day, that Eli's family would be completely removed from the
priesthood. God said,

*"And I will raise me up a faithful priest, that shall do ac-
cording to that which is in mine heart and in my mind: and I
will build him a sure house; and he shall walk before mine
anointed for ever. And it shall come to pass, that every one
that is left in thine house shall come and crouch to him for a
piece of silver and a morsel of bread, and shall say, Put me,
I pray thee, into one of the priests' offices, that I may eat a
piece of bread."*—I Sam. 2:35, 36.

Then the little child Samuel grew up with a heart tender
toward the Word of God, and God gave him this message
against Eli:

*"In that day I will perform against Eli all things which I
have spoken concerning his house: when I begin, I will also
make an end. For I have told him that I will judge his house
for ever for the iniquity which he knoweth; because his sons
made themselves vile, and he restrained them not. And therefore I have sworn unto the house of Eli, that the iniquity of
Eli's house shall not be purged with sacrifice nor offering for
ever."*—I Sam. 3:12-14.

Read that again carefully and see the importance of it.
"Because his sons made themselves vile, and he restrained
them not," God said He would judge the house of Eli forever,

"that the iniquity of Eli's house shall not be purged with sacrifice nor offering for ever."

What was this terrible sin of Eli, this "iniquity" that would never be purged? What was this sin that should bring a curse upon all the unborn generations of Eli's house? It was simply this: Eli did not restrain his sons! He should have chastised them and made them obey, made them walk uprightly when they were children and young men. If he had done so then, they would not have disgraced him when he was old. But even after the sons were grown, mature men, God held Eli accountable when he did not restrain them. Eli, as a high priest, could have had his sons publicly whipped, could have put them out of the priesthood, could have had them stoned publicly, put to death for their crimes. He did not punish his sons, and so the curse of God came on his family forever!

I am simply saying that God holds mothers and fathers accountable for their children. There is no way to be a good Christian when you do not do right on this fundamental matter of the correction and discipline of your children.

"Do you mean to say that one cannot be a good Christian who does not rule well his children? Do you mean to say that this is a fundamental matter of Christian character, that parents must make their children obey, must punish them, restrain them, and discipline them?" So someone may ask. I answer, That is exactly what the Bible teaches. For example, in I Timothy, chapter 3, God gives the qualifications for a bishop or pastor of a church and likewise the qualifications for a deacon. About the bishop, I Timothy 3:4, 5 says that he must be, "One that ruleth well his own house, having his children in subjection with all gravity; (For if a man know not how to rule his own house, how shall he take care of the church of God?)"

Here it is clearly stated that no matter how sound in doctrine, how fervent in spirit, how clean in life, no man is fit to be pastor of a church who does not discipline his children and have his children in subjection with all gravity!

The same requirement is made for those who would be officers of a local church, the deacons. First Timothy 3:12 says, "Let the deacons be the husbands of one wife, ruling their children and their own houses well." A man who is not a good ruler over his own family, is not fit even to be a servant in the church of God (the word deacon means servant).

How many, many times the influence of one who longs to

serve Christ is utterly ruined because he has failed to rule well his own house! Disobedient, unruly children, undisciplined children bring to naught the influence of a godly father. Hence the Scripture commands, no man is to be elected pastor of a church or even deacon in a church, who does not follow the Bible commands about disciplining and ruling well and keeping in subjection his own children.

To rear godly children, to restrain them, to correct them, to bring them up in the chastening and admonition of the Lord, is one of the simple and basic Christian virtues without which Christian parents cannot please God.

Punishment a Necessity and Proper Molder of Character

Is corporal punishment actually necessary for a child? Are not other methods more modern and more effective? That is not what the Word of God teaches. Other punishment may be sometimes effective, and certainly there are other essentials to proper child rearing; but whipping has a distinct place, ordained of God, in the discipline and development of children.

Proverbs 20:30 says, "The blueness of a wound cleanseth away evil: so do stripes the inward parts of the belly." A blue bruise cleanses away evil from the character, when rightly given; stripes do the same for the inward life, says this Scripture.

Happy is the child who learns very early in life that sin brings trouble! One who gets soundly punished for sin will learn to fear sin and then to hate it. "The blueness of a wound cleanseth away evil: so do stripes the inward parts of the belly." This, God's Word says.

Certainly, then, sometimes punishment should be so vigorous as to leave stripes on a child. I remember poignantly the first time one of my little ones was so stubborn that I had to spank her two or three times about the same thing, and I was so vigorous about it that faint blue marks were left by my fingers. The beloved but stubborn child had surrendered to the inevitable, had given up her will in the matter and had quietly gone to sleep when I saw those marks. The sight cut me to the heart. I went alone to cry and pray. I knew of no other way besides the vigorous spanking to get the proper results, and I was sure I had done right. Yet the blue marks on the little body, so precious, left me stricken with grief. I remember well that I prayed something like this: "Heavenly Father, I do not pretend to know much about rearing children. I only know what You have said in Your Word, and I am going to try to do it. Now, oh, my Heavenly Father, You must see that it gets the blessed results You have promised. You must make my girls good girls!" And I bear the dear Lord record that He has fulfilled His Word in the matter of my beloved daughters. Blessed and holy results in character can come from a sound whipping given in Jesus' name and because it is right, in punishment for sin and to secure obedience.

This teaching that discipline, correction, punishment, whenever necessary, leads to morality and good character is taught further in Proverbs 29:15. There we are told, "The rod and reproof give wisdom: but a child left to himself bringeth his mother to shame." One who is restrained and held under control by his father and his mother will learn to control himself. One who is properly curbed and instructed as a child will learn to curb himself. One who has properly learned to appreciate and submit to the authority of the home will find it normal to submit to the authority of school and the authority of government and the authority of God. Real character is developed by strict and careful rearing by godly parents who believe what the Word of God says, that "The rod and reproof give wisdom."

In Proverbs 29:17 the same truth is restated. "Correct thy son, and he shall give thee rest; yea, he shall give delight unto thy soul." The father who corrects his son will later feel pride and joy in the grown son who will thus have learned to control himself.

These Scriptures agree that the correction of children, when done consistently and prayerfully, will curb the hot temper of youth, will train little feet in paths of morality and righteousness, and that the character thus developed will be a matter of pride and joy to the fathers and mothers who loved God and righteousness enough to rear their children according to the Scriptures.

Admiral Dewey, the hero of Manila in the Spanish-American War, tells us that a good whipping kept him from becoming a criminal. An Indiana farmer in 1898 published the following remarkable story, telling how the boy who later became Admiral Dewey, the hero of Manila in the Spanish-American War, was an unprincipled bully as a boy, headed for a life of crime, and was saved for society by a genuine whipping. The whipping was delivered by Z. K. Pangborn, major in the Civil War and later congressman. The article follows:

Major Z. K. Pangborn of Jersey City, the only man who ever whipped Admiral George Dewey, was nominated for congress a few days ago by the Republicans of the Hudson County District, New Jersey. Major Pangborn whipped Dewey while the latter was his pupil in a backwoods school near Montpelier, Vermont, half a century ago.

When Dewey was a boy, Pangborn, according to his story, being then fresh from college, undertook the management of a district school in Montpelier. The school had been in rebellion, and Dewey was the leader of the anti-teacher brigade. Several teachers had been removed, and one had been stood on his head in a snowbank. It was generally said in Montpelier that nobody could govern that school. When Pangborn appeared the first day he noticed Dewey up a tree throwing stones at small boys.

"You've got to stop that," said the teacher sharply.

"Go to blazes!" retorted Dewey from his perch.

Pangborn provided himself with a rawhide, which he tucked away over the schoolhouse door, and then placed several clubs of good hickory on top of the pile in the old wood box. The following day Pangborn was about to punish some unruly scholars when Dewey stepped up to his desk and said:

"Look here, Teacher, we're going to give you the best licking you ever had."

"Take your seats," ordered Pangborn.

Dewey shot out his right fist and it landed dangerously near Pangborn's jaw. Instantly the teacher seized his rawhide, and Dewey was writhing under the lash. When the other boys tried to go to Dewey's help, the teacher seized the hickory clubs and with one piece in each hand struck the boys about him with such vigor that they soon ran. He gave it to Dewey hot and heavy, and it was not long before the future conqueror of the Philippines was begging for mercy for the first and only time in his life. That put an end to the rebellion.

Dewey and Pangborn have been warm friends ever since. Dewey recently said to the Major: "I shall never cease to be grateful to you. You made a man of me. But for the thrashing you gave me, I would probably be a state prisoner."

Many another good man, as was Admiral Dewey, was saved from prison by a good whipping. Many others are in jail who could have been saved to society as good citizens by discipline.

Lack of Discipline in the Home Leads to Public Shame Later

Many a life of sin and shame is simply the outgrowth of a life without any discipline, without rebuke and without reproof. The child who was not punished for sin at home will naturally feel that he can get by with sin. And the same child will grow into a man without self-control, without a fear of sin, without a conscience well-developed. Proverbs 29:15 says that "the rod and reproof give wisdom: but a child left to himself bringeth his mother to shame." Do you leave your child to himself? Do you let him have his own way? Then, Mother, you might as well get ready to be brought to shame by the same boy or girl that you now refuse to punish!

There are a number of Bible illustrations of this truth, that undisciplined children turn out to be wicked adults.

Remember the wicked sons of Eli, the high priest of Israel, mentioned above. Though priests, they were never converted. First Samuel 2:12 tells us, "The sons of Eli were sons of Belial; they knew not the Lord." They were sacrilegious, despising the offerings of the Lord (I Sam. 2:17). They committed adultery with the women who came to the tabernacle to worship (I Sam. 2:22). Whence came all this wickedness of the sons of Eli? Why did these sons of a great man of God go so thoroughly wrong? It is simply that they were not disciplined and restrained and corrected by Eli. For I Samuel 3:13 gives us God's words about it: "For I have told him that I will judge his house for ever for the iniquity which he knoweth; because his sons made themselves vile, and he restrained them not."

What shame Eli and his wife must have had over these wicked, ungodly, unsaved, adulterous sons. But all that could have been saved with a few sound trashings at the proper time, and with careful direction and restraint along with teaching and prayer. "A child left to himself bringeth his mother to shame."

Another Bible example of a sinful manhood following an undisciplined childhood is that of Adonijah, the son of David by his wife Haggith. Adonijah rebelled against David and tried to seize the kingdom. First Kings 1:5, 6 says, "Then Adonijah the son of Haggith exalted himself, saying, I will be king; and he prepared him chariots and horsemen, and fifty men to run before him. And his father had not displeased him at any time in saying, Why hast thou done so? and he also was a very goodly man; and his mother bare him after Absalom."

David had never displeased Adonijah saying, "Why hast thou done so?" The lack of discipline and restraint, that lack of punishment, made Adonijah into the rebel who would have seized the kingdom. "A child left to himself bringeth his mother to shame."

Was that the way King David reared his boys? We suppose he was as lax with other sons as with Adonijah. Consider, then, that one son of David, Amnon, who raped his fair half sister, Tamar (II Sam. 13:1-19). "The rod and reproof give wisdom: but a child left to himself bringeth his mother to shame." How sad that David did not use the rod and reproof on Amnon and save the poor boy from becoming a rapist and being later murdered for his sin!

Absalom, too, was David's son. It is fair to suppose that David reared Absalom as carelessly as Adonijah. Absalom murdered his brother, Amnon, then set out systematically to steal the hearts of the people, and then rebelled against King David, seized the kingdom, committed adultery with David's wives, and that in public, and tried to kill King David, his father! Surely it is true that "the rod and reproof give wisdom: but a child left to himself bringeth his mother to shame."

Fathers and mothers who do not discipline their children may find that they turn out to be criminals.

Parents Should Begin Early, Continue Discipline Faithfully

How soon should the baby have his first spanking? A preacher friend of mine said, "I do not think you ought to whip a girl baby as early as a boy baby. I don't think anybody ought to whip a girl baby younger than three weeks old, but you might begin on a boy baby the day he is born!" That is an obvious exaggeration. Certainly no good could be accomplished by punishing a child before he knew what was wanted. The tiny baby needs no further spank, we suppose, than that administered by the doctor to make him cry and start him off breathing properly. But people are far more likely to do wrong by beginning too late about the discipline of children than by beginning too early.

Proverbs 19:18 says, "Chasten thy son while there is hope, and let not thy soul spare for his crying." Every parent should begin careful, strict control of his children with love and prayer and good example and teaching, and correction when necessary, "while there is hope." It will be too late some day to try to curb and control that proud and stubborn spirit of self-will which every child has by nature. Begin early!

As soon as the child can well understand the orders given by his mother or father, he should be expected to obey. Before the child is a year old, he certainly ought to lie still at sleep time, if well, ought to give up quietly things with which he might hurt himself or that he might damage. The child who walks certainly ought to come to his father or mother when told to come. It is far easier on both the child and on his parents if the child is clearly taught that mother and father must be obeyed. I remember with what surprise I learned that a couple of spanks can often settle a baby's mind about the dreaded nap, after he has kept the whole household in an uproar for half an hour.

"Chasten thy son while there is hope, and let not thy soul spare for his crying," says the Word of God. A consistent policy should be carried out by the mother and father. Discipline should be begun early, and father and mother should wisely and kindly follow out a simple, godly policy of maintaining obedience regularly, though justice be tempered with mercy and love.

"And let not thy soul spare for his crying," is the command to the father or mother who is to "chasten thy son while there is hope" (Prov. 19:18). Punishment will not often be necessary, perhaps, if obedience becomes the well-understood requirement, with no deviation. But when punishment must be given, it ought to be given thoroughly. Many parents whip a child only enough to anger him and arouse resentment. I have seen a mother spank a little boy or girl and then take a half hour of petting trying to win back the favor of the angry child. Surely that is wrong and contrary to this command of the Bible. If whipping must be done, then do it thoroughly, enough to get results; and it will save much trouble and heartache for both parent and child later on. When the child's will is surrendered, when there is an honest penitence for sin and the offender is willing to make right his wrong in loving obedience, there is no reason to continue the punishment. But until this attitude of submission is reached, "Let not thy soul spare for his crying." My father seemed to have a rule to whip until we cried and then whip until we stopped! And if my dad was doing the whipping, one would certainly find a way to stop crying, though one felt he would burst. My dear father did not whip often. I remember only twice, I think, that he whipped me. By the time I was nearly four, which is as far back as I can well remember, it was already established in my heart that "Papa" was to be obeyed instantly. And I cannot remember when I was not tremendously grieved, if I thought I had grieved him. Nor can I ever remember the slightest resentment toward him for the authority which he carried so simply and so grandly! When my father did whip, as was so rarely necessary, he did a thorough job that would always be remembered!

How long should a parent maintain strict discipline over his children? Part of that answer is certainly found in Deuteronomy 21:18-21 where even a grown son, if rebellious and disobedient, a glutton and drunkard, is to be brought by his own father and mother to the elders of the city to be publicly condemned and stoned. Part of the answer surely is found in the fact that Eli, the high priest, suffered an eternal curse on his household because he did not restrain his own grown sons! Certainly as long as a father and mother support their children, that long the children ought to be under the full authority of their parents. Any son or daughter who is young enough to eat at the father's table and to be provided for by the father's bounty is young enough to be whipped if necessary. Frankly, it would be very rare that a child properly reared would need a whipping after he were grown. But the authority of father and mother should be unquestioned, and whatever it takes to maintain that authority should be done. In my father's home when I was twenty years old I would not have thought of disobeying my father nor of speaking discourteously to him. If I had done so, it would have been no surprise to me had my father promptly slapped me down, husky horseman and football tackle that I was! The habit of obedience was so strong in me that I think it would not even have occurred to me to resist my father or even to run from him had he decided to chastise me when I was grown!

The other day a gracious southern lady, a most devoted Christian, told me with deep emotion of the last time her mother whipped her. She was about to be married and the mother was fitting the wedding dress on her daughter. The young bride-to-be was impatient and quarrelsome until the mother promptly removed the wedding gown and soundly whipped her daughter a few days before the daughter's wedding! Telling me about it, this southern gentlewoman told me with a catch in her voice over pride in her beloved mother, along with giggles over the ludicrous situation, how her mother had said, "You may be old enough to get married, but you are not old enough to sass your mother; and you are not too old to be whipped if you need it!" That godly mother of a departed generation won for herself a reverence and pride that will never die in the heart of her daughter, because she exercised a mother's authority in righteousness and whipped the daughter on the eve of her wedding!

In Cleveland, Ohio, I preached on "The Christian Home," and a man came to tell me of his blessed father now in Heaven. "I remember so well the last time he whipped me," said this Christian man of his father. "He whipped me with a buggy whip, and whipped me terribly hard. Then when it was done he threw down the whip and put both arms around me and cried and told me how he loved me." My Cleveland friend wept as he remembered it, and thanked God for the father who made him mind and whipped him when he needed it, even though he was a grown young man.

The Child Reared in Godly Discipline: "When He Is Old, He Will Not Depart From It"

Can we so rear our children as to guarantee that they will live godly lives? That is exactly what the Bible teaches! Proverbs 22:6 says: "Train up a child in the way he should go, and when he is old, he will not depart from it." The Revised Version is a little clearer, I think, and says, "Even when he is old he will not depart from it." Even when a child is grown, away from home, away from the restraints of father and mother, he will never depart from the training he had as a child, if he were really reared in the way he should go, says the Scripture.

I well know that there is more to good parenthood than whipping children. There ought to be godly example day by day. Children ought to be taught to work. There ought to be much Bible teaching. There ought to be much prayer. Chil-

dren ought to be won to Christ at an early age. But certainly
the very backbone of child-rearing is discipline, being taught
to obey, taught to do right, ruled lovingly in the ways of
righteousness by father and mother. Fathers are to bring children up "in the nurture [or chastening] and admonition of
the Lord," as Ephesians 6:4 says. If they follow the Bible
plan, the character of children will be so set for God and
righteousness and morality and subjection to authority that
when the children are grown, independent men and women,
they will never leave the godly ways taught them by their
parents.

I had this Scripture seriously challenged one day. I was a
young preacher attending the seminary and preaching on
Sundays to a country church. When I preached on the Christian home and used this Scripture in Proverbs 22:6 as a text,
a prominent man in the church, deeply distressed, asked me
to go to his home with him. There he told me, "Pastor, what
you preached this morning is not so. You said if we would
bring up a child in the way he should go he would never depart from it. I know that is not true. I know I did bring my
boy up right."

"But," I said, "that is not my statement. That is a statement from the Word of God. Here it is in the Scripture,
'Train up a child in the way he should go; and when he is
old, he will not depart from it.' You are challenging the
Word of God."

"Then, if the Bible says that, the Bible is wrong," he replied. "I know I did bring my boy up right. I am not to
blame that he went wrong."

I told him that no man had a right to maintain membership in a church of Jesus Christ and deny one verse in the Bible. And since he had made an issue of the matter and declared that the Bible teaching of Proverbs 22:6 was untrue I
demanded to know where his boy was. At first he refused to
tell me, out of embarrassment and shame. But when I insisted,
he said that the boy was in the Texas State Penitentiary at
Huntsville, Texas. "But I know I raised my boy right," he
said. "I am not to blame that my boy has gone wrong."

Since he had made God's Word out to be a lie, I determined to go to the heart of the matter, and I said,

"You say you raised your boy right. Then tell me this, did
you whip your boy and make him mind? Did you make him
get up the first time he was called? Did you require that he

say, 'Yes, Sir!' and, 'Yes, Ma'am!' to you and his mother? Did you whip the boy and make him obey?"

He replied, "You are young and you think such a rule will fit everybody. My boy was high-strung and nervous. We could not bear down on him sharply and demand strict obedience as can be done with some children. He wouldn't take it. He was too nervous!"

(Incidentally, I remember that I was very nervous and high-strung as a boy, too. But my father solved that difficulty very easily. He just got more nervous than I did!)

"So you did not make your boy mind. You did not believe the Scripture that says, 'The rod and reproof give wisdom; but a child left to himself bringeth his mother to shame.' You did not believe the Scripture that says, 'Correct thy son, and he shall give thee rest; yea, he shall give delight unto thy soul' (Prov. 29:15, 17). And your boy is in the penitentiary and you blame God! Tell me another thing. Did you have a family altar at your house? Deuteronomy 6:6-9 commands the father to teach the words of the Bible diligently to his children; to talk of them when he rises up and sits down, and to have them on the walls of his house. Did you have family worship? Did you have prayer and Bible reading in your home every day? Did your boy learn the Bible in the home and learn to pray?"

He replied, "You city people may have time for that, but we farmers have to get up early and work long hours. We didn't have time for any foolishness."

The boy who did not have time for fifteen minutes or thirty minutes daily of family worship had plenty of time to spend several years in the penitentiary! (And this man certainly misjudged me if he thought I was from the city!)

"So you didn't make your boy obey you, you never chastised him, you never taught him the Scriptures, you never had family worship. Let me ask one more question," I said. "Did you ever take the Bible and tell your boy that you wanted to show him how to be saved? Did you ever try to lead your boy to trust in Jesus as his Saviour and give his heart and life to God? Did you ever try to get your boy saved while he was at home with you?" I asked.

"I will have you to know that I am a Baptist," he said, "and we don't believe in dragging little children into the church before they know what it is all about."

It is a pity that he was such a good Baptist that he never talked to his child about being saved.

This father did not believe the Bible was true. He denied the truth of the Scripture, "Train up a child in the way he should go: and when he is old, he will not depart from it." Yet he himself had never whipped his son, never demanded and never gotten obedience. He had never taught the child the Word of God. He had never had a family altar with Bible reading and prayer in the home. He had never tried to show the lad that he was a sinner and needed a Saviour, never tried to bring him to trust in Jesus and to know Him as his own Saviour in the forgiveness of sins. And now that the boy was in a state penitentiary for his crimes against society, the father insisted that he had reared the boy aright! But you and I know that the father was to blame. You and I know that by any Bible standard, he had not reared his child for God, had not brought him up "in the nurture and admonition of the Lord."

Sometime ago a mother asked me to pray for her grown, married son. "He is a drunkard, a blasphemer, and living in terrible sin," said the mother. "I know he was reared right, and I believe he will come back to it when he is older," she said. But that is a misapplication of Proverbs 22:6. The Bible never promises that a child who goes off in outrageous sin will come back to the way of his godly parents. The Bible plainly teaches that such a child, brought up as he ought to have been in the fear of God and according to the Bible pattern, will never depart from that general course of an upright, moral, godly life.

Of course, the children who are led to Christ in the home, children who are taught the Scriptures, children who are disciplined carefully and nurtured under the authority of a godly father and mother, will make mistakes and will not be perfect. But the course of their lives will follow that which they learned at home. If the father and mother use the means at hand, follow the Bible plans of discipline and teaching and example and prayer, then the mother and father can safely lean on the promise of God's Word that the child will never forget his rearing and never leave that upright course he was taught in the home! And what a blessed, blessed promise is that on which every parent can lean. Here is a Scripture that can guarantee the happy, moral, upright future of our children if we believe it and act upon it in time.

Mrs. Susannah Wesley's Godly Way of Rearing Children

How were John Wesley and Charles Wesley, leaders in the great evangelical movement in England, founders of Methodism, reared? By what manner were such godly men, so well-controlled, so wholly given to the Lord, so brilliant in mind, so tender in conscience, so unswerving in principle, developed? Their mother, Susannah Wesley, taught them to fear the rod when they were a year old! So she herself says, and John Wesley himself published her statement. The holy lives of these saintly men, John and Charles Wesley, grew out of the godly discipline of the home. That the Wesleys themselves believed, and the Scriptures bear them out. Susannah Wesley believed the Scripture that "the rod and reproof give wisdom: but a child left to himself bringeth his mother to shame" (Prov. 29:15). She believed the Scripture that "the blueness of a wound cleanseth away evil: so do stripes the inward parts of the belly" (Prov. 20:30).

She believed the teaching of the Scriptures that one who is not chastised is treated as a bastard, not as a legitimate son (Heb. 12:7, 8).

In *The Heart of John Wesley's Journal* is published a letter from Mrs. Wesley to her son, part of which we give here:

"July 24, 1732

"Dear Son,—According to your desire, I have collected the principal rules I observed in educating my family; which I now send you as they occurred to my mind, and you may (if you think they can be of use to any) dispose of them in what order you please.

* * *

"When turned a year old (and some before), they were taught to fear the rod, and to cry softly; by which means they escaped abundance of correction they might otherwise have had; and that most odious noise of the crying of children was rarely heard in the house; but the family usually lived in as much quietness as if there had not been a child among them.

* * *

"Conquer the Child's Will
"In order to form the minds of children, the first thing to be done is to conquer their will, and bring them to an obedi-

ent temper. To inform the understanding is a work of time, and must with children proceed by slow degrees as they are able to bear it: but the subjecting the will is a thing which must be done at once; and the sooner the better. For by neglecting timely correction, they will contract a stubbornness and obstinacy which is hardly ever after conquered; and never, without using such severity as would be as painful to me as to the child. In the esteem of the world they pass for kind and indulgent, whom I call cruel, parents, who permit their children to get habits which they know must be afterwards broken. Nay, some are so stupidly fond, as in sport to teach their children to do things which, in a while after, they have severely beaten them for doing.

"Whenever a child is corrected, it must be conquered; and this will be no hard matter to do, if it be not grown headstrong by too much indulgence. And when the will of a child is totally subdued, and it is brought to revere and stand in awe of the parents, then a great many childish follies and inadvertences may be passed by. Some should be overlooked and taken no notice of, and others mildly reproved; but no willful transgression ought ever to be forgiven children, without chastisement, less or more, as the nature and circumstances of the offence require.

"I insist upon conquering the will of children betimes, because this is the only strong and rational foundation of a religious education; without which both precept and example will be ineffectual. But when this is thoroughly done, then a child is capable of being governed by the reason and piety of its parents, till its own understanding comes to maturity, and the principles of religion have taken root in the mind.

"I cannot yet dismiss this subject. As self-will is the root of all sin and misery, so whatever cherishes this in children insures their after-wretchedness and irreligion; whatever checks and mortifies it promotes their future happiness and piety. This is still more evident, if we farther consider, that religion is nothing else than the doing the will of God, and not our own: that the one grand impediment to our temporal and eternal happiness being this self-will, no indulgences of it can be trivial, no denial unprofitable. Heaven or hell depends on this alone. So that the parent who studies to subdue it in his child, works together with God in the renewing and saving a soul. The parent who indulges it does the Devil's work, makes religion impracticable, salvation unattainable; and does all that in him lies to damn his child, soul and body forever.

"They Had Nothing They Cried for

"The children of this family were taught, as soon as they could speak, the Lord's prayer, which they were made to say at rising and bed-time constantly; to which, as they grew bigger, were added a short prayer for their parents, and some collects; a short catechism, and some portion of Scripture, as their memories could bear.

"They were very early made to distinguish the Sabbath from other days; before they could well speak or go. They were as soon taught to be still at family prayers, and to ask a blessing immediately after, which they used to do by signs, before they could kneel or speak.

"They were quickly made to understand they might have nothing they cried for, and instructed to speak handsomely for what they wanted. They were not suffered to ask even the lowest servant for aught without saying, 'Pray give me such a thing'; and the servant was chid, if she ever let them omit that word."

Thus Susannah Wesley, saint of God, reared those great men whose influence kept millions out of Hell. Surely she proved well enough the truth of the Scripture that though "a child left to himself bringeth his mother to shame," the converse is also true, "The rod and reproof give wisdom," and "Correct thy son, and he shall give thee rest; yea, he shall give delight unto thy soul."

How Whipping Children Keeps Them Out of Hell!

There is a strange, strange statement in Proverbs 23:13, 14.

"Withhold not correction from the child; for if thou beatest him with the rod, he shall not die. Thou shalt beat him with the rod, and shalt deliver his soul from hell."

'If you beat your child with a rod, he shall not die,' says the Scripture. And the Scripture not only means that whipping does not kill a child, does not harm him; it also means that whipping is likely to save his life. The child who is properly disciplined is much more likely to live a long and useful life. He is not so likely to die of violence, since he will live an upright, godly life, and will not keep company with brawlers. He is not so likely to die of punishment for his crimes at the hands of the state. He is not so likely to die of disease brought on by sin. So the Scripture encourages parents with these words, "Withhold not correction from the child: for if thou beatest him with the rod, he shall not die. Thou shalt beat him with the rod, and shalt deliver his soul from hell."

The word for Hell here is the Hebrew word *Sheol* which generally means the place of departed spirits. But the usage in the Old Testament tends continually toward regarding *Sheol* as the place of torment of the unconverted. The New Testament word *Hades,* in the Greek, is equivalent to the Hebrew word *Sheol,* and when Jesus told about the rich man who "died, and was buried; And in hell he lift up his eyes, being in torments," He used the word *Hades.* So, although the Scripture says that good whippings at the proper time will keep a boy from a premature death, the Scripture also means what it says in the English, "Thou shalt beat him with the rod, and shalt deliver his soul from hell."

One of the saddest things I have learned in preaching in city missions, in jails, and in street services all over America is that often a criminal behind the bars, or a poor drunken bum on the street will say to me, "Sure, sure, I know all about that. I have read that Scripture many times. My father was a Methodist preacher," or "My father was a Baptist deacon." Many men have turned out to be criminals, many are outrageous sinners who grew up in the homes of devout Christians. Beyond any shadow of doubt, for a father and mother to be good Christians in the home is not enough. Good examples alone do not guarantee that the children will turn out moral and upright and religious. Even the reading of the Bible and prayer in the home are not enough to guarantee that the children will become good Christians. There must also be discipline, the reproof of sin and its punishment. Fathers are to bring their children up "in the nurture and admonition of the Lord," that is, in the chastening and teaching of the Lord.

To a mother who begged Dr. Bob Jones, Sr., to pray for her son, Dr. Jones said, "My praying won't take the place of your whipping." Children who are not taught to respect authority in the home will not respect it abroad. Children who rebel against fathers and mothers, and get by with it, will rebel against God. The child who is not made to heed his parents, may never heed the call of the Spirit of God to be converted.

Chastisement, done earnestly and with justice, yet tempered with mercy; chastisement done in the name of Jesus does two things for a child permanently. First, the child learns that sin does not pay. He comes to realize the fact so often expressed in the Bible that "Be sure your sin will find you out" (Num. 32:23); that "whatsoever a man soweth, that shall he also reap" (Gal. 6:7); that "the wages of sin is death" (Rom. 6:23). Any child properly reared, punished for his sins and rewarded for his obedience, compelled to defer to the divine authority as it has been entrusted to the hands of his father and mother—any child so reared, I say, will have a continual subconscious realization that sin is certain to come to judgment. And that conviction is the background of all true repentance. Such a child is the most fruitful kind of a gospel subject.

Second, the child properly punished for his sins develops a conscience that is hurt and grieved when he does wrong. Not only does the child properly reared feel instinctively that sin must come to judgment, but he comes to take the side of right in his own conscience and holds himself accountable for his sins. The child who is compelled to do right and is punished for sin, along with the proper teaching and the proper example, will want to do right.

Such children who have come to recognize the importance of right and wrong, who have come to have a conscience constantly alive and dealing with them about every action, are predisposed to hear the Gospel. It is easy to get them to have a sense of conviction for their sins and to have a sense of need for God and a desire to be saved. The easiest people in the world to win to Christ are those who have already a deep conscience on the question of right and wrong, those who have a reverence for God, a sense of responsibility to Him, and a fear of the results of sin.

In a town where I was pastor, there lived an unsaved man and wife with a large family of children. The man did not attend church, and I could not win him to Christ. But it happened that he was specially strict in rearing his children. He never allowed them out in bad company. They had to be home by a certain time each night. Even the boy twenty years old was held strictly to account, could only keep company with an approved list of friends, and must be in his own home by a set time each night. And the father whipped his children soundly when necessary to enforce his strict discipline. They loved their father, of course; but they also feared him in a reverential way.

It was my privilege to talk to these young people in the home of the unsaved father, and one by one I led them to trust in Christ. I never found people with more tender hearts. I never found lost sinners more quick to confess their sins and with tears of penitence to turn to Christ for mercy and salvation! Their father's example had not been good in the matter of serving God, but his strict rearing had made them fit subjects for the Gospel. The seed fell on good soil, soil that had been properly plowed, when it fell into their hearts.

Children properly reared can be easily won to Christ. But children who are reared in rebellion, reared to have their own way, reared with never a thought of punishment for their sins, are often calloused and rebellious and without any respect for God and His Word. They have no sense of shame for their sins, no fear of God nor of coming judgment.

The Bible is true, then, when it says, "Withhold not correction from the child: for if thou beatest him with the rod, he shall not die. Thou shalt beat him with the rod, and shalt deliver his soul from hell," as the wisest man who ever lived was inspired of God to write in Proverbs 23:13, 14. Any father and mother who do what they ought to do about discipline will find it easy to do what they ought to do about winning their children to Christ. Good whippings given in time, along with proper rearing otherwise, make it easy to win people to Christ and so keep their souls out of Hell.

Objections Answered

People have many objections to this Bible plan of whipping children to make them mind. We might safely take the Bible at face value and follow it implicitly, knowing that no objection will be valid against the Word of God. But a little consideration will show how foolish are the objections people offer against the Bible plan.

1. "Whipping is brutal, unfair." So some say. "For a great big man to whip a little boy or girl means that he is simply taking advantage of his size to oppress little people who cannot protect themselves," say some not very intelligent people.

Is an armed policeman unfair when with a gun and handcuffs at hand he arrests a burglar? Is a teacher unfair who takes authority over children in the school, decides what the lessons will be, how much written work will be required, and does not give a child an equal chance to decide about the lessons and work he is to do? That is silly on the face of it. If whipping is unfair, then any kind of punishment by any authority in the world would be unfair. That silly objection strikes at all authority in home and school and state and business. The truth is that God gives the father more strength and more wisdom along with his authority, just as the government gives the policeman a gun along with his badge. That strength and authority ought to be used to punish sin or prevent it.

It is true that a whipping inflicts pain. But does that make it wrong? So does filling or pulling a tooth by the dentist cause pain. So does a tonsil operation by a surgeon. The end in view justifies some pain. And the end in view in whipping children justifies some pain. By learning that fire burns, a child learns to keep out of the fire. By learning that sin brings punishment, children learn to keep from sin. In Hebrews 12:7 God says, "If ye endure chastening [whipping], God dealeth with you as with sons." Hebrews 12:11, in the same chapter, says, "Now no chastening for the present seemeth to be joyous, but grievous: nevertheless afterward it yieldeth the peaceable fruit of righteousness unto them which are exercised thereby." The results of whipping, done for righteousness' sake, are peaceable and happy, not brutal.

2. "I believe in ruling by love, and not by force." Many a person has said that. And all of us know that parents should love their children, bosses should love their workers, rulers should love their citizens, teachers should love their pupils. God loves His own creatures and pours upon us blessings unnumbered every day. Yet, God's great love does not make it unnecessary for Him to punish sin. He still punishes His own children, "scourgeth every son whom he receiveth," says the Scripture.

"I love my boy too much to whip him," said a mother. But that was really a dishonest evasion, as well as an untrue statement. Proverbs 13:24 says, "He that spareth his rod hateth his son: but he that loveth him chasteneth him betimes." If that woman had really loved her son, she would not have wanted him to grow up to be a criminal, as many undisciplined children do. She would not have wanted him to have a broken home because of his wild, undisciplined ways. Multiplied thousands of divorces come because of lack of discipline in youth. A child corrected and chastened in youth makes a much safer matrimonial risk. If she had loved her son, she would have wanted him to be happy; and a rebellious, self-willed youngster grows up unsatisfied and unhappy, unadjusted to society, unable to control his own passions and wants. So the mother who thought she loved her son too much to whip him, really loved her own ease too much. She had no integrity, no principle, no conviction which she loved enough to do right, and for which she would endure some pain to please God and for the good of her son. Certainly whipping is hard on the mother and father who love their children. But that is not as hard as later seeing them come to trouble and ruin because they were not disciplined in childhood. Intelligent parents had better do right and save later trouble by whipping in time and being happy later.

Do you think that all children would do right without any punishment if they were loved? Then, all of human authority is wrong. If that silly theory be right, then it is wrong to have policemen, wrong to have courts, wrong to have traffic rules and penalties, wrong to have laws against murder or theft or adultery. If that silly theory be right, then God is wrong to punish His own children, wrong to send punishment on sin, wrong to send sinners to Hell!

That foolish theory that love can rule adequately without any punishment for sin denies every fundamental doctrine of the Bible. It denies the fact of man's fallen nature, the taint of sin inherent in every child. It denies the inspiration of the Bible which so clearly commands us to whip children. That silly theory teaches that God is brutal and mean to have a Hell of torment or to bring sinners to judgment. Such an idea that love can rule adequately without punishment is wholly unchristian and antiscriptural. Bible Christians must accept it as a doctrine of God that sin needs to be punished and that when sin is unpunished men and women, boys and girls go further into sin. Real love in the hearts of parents for their children will help them to punish sin and grow good men and women who are afraid of sin and love righteousness.

3. "Whipping is likely to break their little wills." Surely the excuse was invented by somebody who never had a child of his own. When you have had six as I have, and have earnestly tried to bring them up in the nurture and admonition of the Lord, you will find out their "little wills" are not so

easily broken as you suppose. Self-will is the very heart of all sin. Isaiah 53:6 says, "All we like sheep have gone astray; we have turned every one to his own way." There is no danger of an honest whipping in a righteous cause breaking the will of a child. There is not even any danger of its breaking his self-respect if it be done honorably by godly parents for a good reason.

Break the child's will? Do you mean whipping would give a child an inferiority complex, make him indecisive, vacillating, without convictions? As Admiral Dewey was, I suppose? As John and Charles Wesley, as Benjamin Franklin, as George Washington? These great men, chastised when they needed it, reared to obey orders, seemed to have had plenty of will left! Actually, children who are taught obedience, made to give up rebellion; children who are chastised for sin really come to have more convictions, have more standards of right and wrong. A child who early in life develops great standards of right and wrong, justice and truth and discipline and self-control, by having parents who really exercise authority over him until he is well enough developed and grown up enough to control himself, has a far better basis of sound character, a better set of moral standards and convictions with which to meet life's problems. How I thank God that this overbearing will of my own, this flaming temper, this domineering spirit was curbed in youth and held in check by godly authority in the home until I developed conscience enough and habits sufficient and convictions strong enough to control it myself!

4. "But it is dangerous to thwart a child's desires," say some pseudo-psychologists. "Whipping may leave a child with repressed desires and inner rebellion that may ruin his life." That is a sample of the bosh taught in some universities, taught in child psychology courses, the piffle taught by lecturers to clubs of silly women who do not care about the Bible or God.

The simple truth is that the quickest way to straighten out the subconscious mind of a child and stop that inner rebellion, that sense of frustration, that spirit of "I'll get even," or "I'd like to kill my dad and my mother," is a good old-fashioned thrashing. That works even in the cradle. Many, many times I have seen a child scream and howl for his own way, fight his mother or father, and yell defiance for a half hour at a time. Then finally I have seen the mother or father with a few vigorous blows settle the whole matter. The spanked child would suddenly give up his rebellion, would cling in penitence to his mother or father, and when assured of forgiveness would peacefully go to sleep within a minute of time!

What is wrong with a lot of these criminals who are enemies of society, rebels against all authority, is simply that they never got whipped enough, never got really conquered, and so never learned to conquer themselves. The thing that is wrong with these wild, delinquent children, filling the jails, young people who are the burden of law-enforcement officers, of teachers and parents alike, is simply that they need some strong authority to take them in hand and make them do right. The best balanced, most complacent, happy personalities in the world are those who early learned to submit to authority, and by being exercised by chastisement found that it yielded "the peaceable fruit of righteousness," as the Scripture plainly promises (Heb. 12:11).

5. "But children who are whipped will hate their father or their mother," says some theorist who never tried it, who probably never had a child. A lady columnist wrote, "I am sure I should have hated my mother if she had whipped me." But the poor, ignorant lady would never have talked that way if she had had proper rearing. Do you mean that citizens hate a government which enforces its laws? All the evidence proves the contrary. A righteous government which vigorously enforces righteous laws and punishes crime, finds that crime decreases and the citizenship is loyal and patriotic. On the other hand, when law enforcement lags, then the whole moral fiber of the nation dissolves. Do you mean that John and Charles Wesley hated their mother, Susannah Wesley, because they were beaten when they needed it? Then you do not know the story of the Wesleys! All over America men and women have told me with tears how they revered the mother or father who reared them strictly, whipped them when necessary, and brought them up in the nurture and admonition of the Lord.

6. "But there are more effective ways of punishing children than by whipping," some people say. In answer, I will admit there are times when other punishments seem necessary. No doubt the child who scatters things on the floor should be made to pick them up, and sometimes if Sally pulls the hair out of Mary's doll baby, it may be she should give up her

own doll in exchange. Sometimes the boy who is not a good boy through the week should not be allowed to go to the picnic on Saturday. I say that sometimes the punishment should be directly connected with the offense, and other punishments sometimes ought to be given besides whipping.

But the fact remains that whipping has a place that nothing else can fill in rearing children.

For one thing, it is clearly commanded in the Bible. The Bible never commands fathers to make their children stand in the corner, or to get down from the table, or go to bed early, or to stay in the house when other boys play ball. The biggest argument for whipping children is that the Bible plainly commands it. And for a Christian who believes that the Bible is God's Word there is no answer to that argument.

But there are good reasons back of God's plan, as is true in every case. For one thing, whipping settles the matter quickly and definitely and can bring a child to penitence and confession at once. Suppose a child has to stay in after school for a week. No teacher knows for sure that the boy will be penitent at the end of a week, honestly sorry for his sins, and will resolve to do better. But a good, solid whipping could continue until the will were thoroughly subdued and until the boy penitently promised to do better. After all, no punishment does any good which does not affect the rebellious will of the child. And further punishment is not necessary, I believe, after there is a deep-seated resolve to do right and in the heart of the offender a genuine penitence for sin committed. As Proverbs 20:30 says, "The blueness of a wound cleanseth away evil: so do stripes the inward parts of the belly." Stripes do something for the rebellious, fallen nature of a child that cannot be done by other forms of punishment, it appears from the Scripture and from experience.

If little Sally pulled the hair from the head of Mary's doll, then having to give up her own doll might make her only more resentful, more determined to get even with Sally some other way. A sound spanking at the same time, with proper apologies and some genuine plan of restitution, would be much more likely to fix whatever was wrong in Sally's heart that made her want to pull out Mary's doll's hair. We can safely follow the plain commands of the Bible and know we are on the right track.

CHAPTER XIII

"Honour Thy Father and Thy Mother"

"Honour thy father and thy mother: that thy days may be long upon the land which the Lord thy God giveth thee."—Exod. 20:12.

"Children, obey your parents in the Lord: for this is right. Honour thy father and mother; which is the first commandment with promise; That it may be well with thee, and thou mayest live long on the earth."—Eph. 6:1-3.

"Children, obey your parents in all things: for this is well pleasing unto the Lord."—Col. 3:20.

"And he that curseth his father, or his mother, shall surely be put to death."—Exod. 21:17.

"He that smiteth his father, or his mother, shall be surely put to death."—Exod. 21:15.

I. God's Stress on Honoring Parents

The proper attitude of sons and daughters toward their parents is of vast importance, as will be seen by a careful study of the Scriptures on this subject.

1. *How striking that the command to honor father and mother is in the Ten Commandments!*

In this summary of God's laws there are only ten commandments. Four of them have to do with one's duty to God. Six of them have to do with one's duty to mankind. Only six commandments sum up all human duty toward mankind. And one of these six is the command, "Honour thy father and thy mother." Along with the basic commands against murder, against adultery, against covetousness, is this command, "Honour thy father and thy mother." How fundamental, how important in God's sight is the duty of children to honor their parents!

But wait! This command is not only one of the six commands regarding man's relationship to man. It is the *very first* of them. "Honour thy father and thy mother" comes before "Thou shalt not kill." It comes before "Thou shall not commit adultery." This is the very first of the commands about human relationships. After one is right with God and pleases God, the next most important thing in all the world is to be right with one's own father and mother.

This is also the first of the Ten Commandments with a promise of special blessing. In the command against bowing down to idols there is a solemn warning: "For I the Lord thy God am a jealous God, visiting the iniquity of the fathers upon the children unto the third and fourth generation of them that hate me" (Exod. 20:5). But there is no promise. The first command with a promise is this command, "Honour thy father and thy mother: that thy days may be long upon the land which the Lord thy God giveth thee." And when this same command is quoted by divine inspiration in Ephesians 6:2, the Holy Spirit calls attention to this solemn fact that this is the first command with a promise. In some sense God seems to have put this command about honoring parents at the very head of the list of human duties toward mankind. One's duty to God, his obligation to God, is greater than his duty to anybody else. Naturally so. But one's duty to his father and mother is greater than his duty to anybody else in the world. The duty of honoring father and mother is, if possible, even more important than the duties expressed in the other commandments following the fifth commandment. Surely God means to leave the impression that if one honors father and mother as he ought, other duties are likely to be observed and other commands obeyed.

2. *This command is carefully repeated in the New Testament.*

It is notable that one of the Ten Commandments, that regarding the Sabbath, is not repeated in the New Testament. In fact, Colossians 2:14-17 plainly lists the Sabbath along with other ceremonial laws which were nailed to the cross of Christ. They were "the shadow of things to come." The ceremonial law is not binding on New Testament Christians, and the Sabbath sums up, in some sense, the ceremonial law.

But it is not so about the fifth command, "Honour thy father and thy mother." In the magnificent Epistle to the Ephesians (Eph. 6:1-3) this command is quoted and re-enforced. It is as much a New Testament command as an Old Testament command. Throughout the New Testament it is clearly taken for granted that the morality involved in this fifth commandment is binding on Christians.

In Matthew 15:3-9 Jesus preached a brief sermon on this text, repeating and elaborating on the duty of honoring fathers and mothers. In Mark 7:6-13 the same story is told in detail. Jesus insisted that honoring father and mother is an essential part of honoring God.

3. *God plainly commanded the death penalty for incorrigible disobedience to this command.*

In Deuteronomy 21:18-21 is the following clear command that a rebellious son should be stoned on the testimony of his father and mother:

"If a man have a stubborn and rebellious son, which will not obey the voice of his father, or the voice of his mother, and that, when they have chastened him, will not hearken unto them: Then shall his father and his mother lay hold on him, and bring him out unto the elders of his city, and unto the gate of his place: And they shall say unto the elders of his city, This our son is stubborn and rebellious, he will not obey our voice; he is a glutton, and a drunkard. And all the men of his city shall stone him with stones, that he die: so shalt thou put evil away from among you; and all Israel shall hear, and fear."

Shocking, isn't it? Every father should be stung wide awake with this clear teaching which shows his responsibility to make his son obey. Disobedient and disrespectful sons and daughters ought to be convicted and alarmed to see how God hates their sin. As murder deserves the death penalty, so does incorrigible disobedience to father and mother deserve the death penalty!

In Exodus, chapter 21, God gives certain rules for organized society to follow. Under the Mosaic law certain sins were to be punished with death. Thus in Exodus 21:15 Jews were commanded, "He that smiteth his father, or his mother, shall be surely put to death." The death penalty just for striking father or mother!

But that is not all. Exodus 21:17 commands, "And he that curseth his father, or his mother, shall surely be put to death." The death penalty again, for disrespectful, reviling talk to father and mother! The same Scripture is quoted in the New Testament by the Saviour in Matthew 15:4, "He hath curseth father or mother, let him die the death." That is in the same verse where "Honour thy father and thy mother" is quoted by the dear Saviour.

Thus, every child must be taught that if he would please God he must honor his father and mother. To lift a hand against father or mother deserves death. To curse or revile father or mother deserves death! At the foundation of all Christian duty and decency and morality is this basic command, "Honour thy father and thy mother."

4. *The promise is "that thy days may be long upon the land which the Lord thy God giveth thee."*

I do not wonder that the Holy Spirit in the New Testament calls attention to this wonderful promise, and remarks that the fifth commandment is the first one with a promise. See how much is involved in this promise.

First, it promises a long life to the individual. Obedience to father and mother would involve temperate living, the restraint and character and self-control that would make for good health and a long life.

Second, such basic and fundamental morality and righteousness would naturally bring upon one the blessing of God and His protection against harm. God will see that righteousness is rewarded.

Third, "that thy days may be long *upon the land* which the Lord thy God giveth thee." Thus one's safe enjoyment of property and possessions is involved in honoring father and mother.

Fourth, and principally, the nation Israel itself was promised long, continued protection and prosperity in the land of Canaan if the nation would observe this command to honor parents. Honoring father and mother means respect for law and order, a good home government. But where government in the home succeeds, then government of the nation is revered and obeyed. And where God's blessing is on the individual home, it will be upon the nation. It is a well-known fact of history that when the home decays, the government and national integrity decay likewise. But when a nation teaches its children to revere father and mother, to obey them, that nation is blessed. Consider China. It has not been a Christian nation in the past. There have been many abuses, many sins and immoralities among the Chinese. But the one outstanding virtue of the Chinese is reverence for and obedience to parents. Sometimes Chinese have made an idol of this virtue, have even worshiped the spirits of their ancestors. But certainly God is pleased that Chinese people honor fathers and mothers. So for these five thousand years He has kept their country. There have been invasions. There have been wars. But China has remained, on the whole, blessed of God in the land that He gave them centuries ago.

Let us seek to earn for ourselves and covet for our children the wonderful promise that goes with this fifth commandment, "that thy days may be long upon the land which the Lord thy God giveth thee."

II. How to Honor Father and Mother Scripturally

The Bible is the most practical book in the world, and so we are not left to guess and wonder about how God means for sons and daughters to honor their parents. Let us see in the Scripture, then, how God wants us to honor fathers and mothers.

1. *Honoring parents involves respect for their persons.*

Every son or daughter from babyhood should have a genuine reverence and respect for the person of his father and of his mother.

To smite father or mother merited the death penalty (Exod. 21:15).

To curse father or mother meant also the death penalty under Mosaic law (Exod. 21:17; Lev. 20:9; Matt. 15:4).

Even a little baby should be taught never to raise a hand against father or mother. Even in play a child should not be allowed to strike father or mother, but should have a holy reverence for the person of his parents.

No son or daughter, from babyhood until old age, should ever revile or curse father or mother. A godly respect and reverence is required if one obeys this command, "Honour thy father and thy mother."

In Leviticus 18:7 the Scripture says, "The nakedness of thy father, or the nakedness of thy mother, shalt thou not uncover: she is thy mother; thou shalt not uncover her nakedness."

Parents should keep themselves properly clothed in the presence of their children. The proper respect and reverence which is commanded of a son or a daughter for his or her parents requires that one is not to uncover the nakedness of his father or mother.

Remember the tragic case of Ham, the son of Noah. Ham had a curse brought upon his children because he himself had dishonered his father, Noah, in looking upon him when he was unclothed. The story is given in Genesis 9:20-27:

"And Noah began to be an husbandman, and he planted a vineyard: And he drank of the wine, and was drunken; and he was uncovered within his tent. And Ham, the father of Canaan, saw the nakedness of his father, and told his two brethren without. And Shem and Japheth took a garment, and laid it upon both their shoulders, and went backward, and covered the nakedness of their father; and their faces were backward, and they saw not their father's nakedness. And Noah awoke from his wine, and knew what his younger son had done unto him. And he said, Cursed be Canaan; a servant of servants shall he be unto his brethren. And he said, Blessed be the Lord God of Shem; and Canaan shall be his servant. God shall enlarge Japheth, and he shall dwell in the tents of Shem; and Canaan shall be his servant."

It seems remarkable that God thought less of Noah's being drunk than He did of the sin of Ham in observing his father's nakedness! Some have thought that Noah did not know that the wine was fermented. That is possible. At any rate, a terrible curse was put upon Ham and his children because he had been an undutiful son, lacking in reverence and respect for his father's person. But Shem and Japheth were blessed because, without looking, they covered their father Noah.

A devoted Christian father sometime ago told me that he was troubled because modern psychologists and teachers on sex matters suggest that fathers and mothers go unclothed before their children, hoping thereby to avoid any particular consciousness on sex matters. He was anxious to do what was proper and right, but felt that decent modesty would keep every normal man from exposing himself before his little children. I soon showed him from the Scripture that such native modesty is God-given and that it would be sinful and wrong to break down the natural restraint and reverence which children should have for their parents.

If one visited the White House to see the President, any sense of decency would keep him from boldly striding into the presence of the President in his bath. Real respect and reverence of children toward their parents, as their superiors in age, in wisdom, and particularly in position, make it wrong for children to be familiar or disrespectful toward the persons of their parents.

In this connection let me say that the modern fashion of encouraging children to call their fathers and mothers by their first names seems to me not only silly but wicked and irreverent. The boy who calls his dad "Bill" or "Joe" certainly does not have the reverence and respect which is properly represented by the Scriptures mentioned above. Well-reared young people would certainly not call their high school teacher, the mayor of their city, their congressman, or their President by his first name. For exactly the same reason they ought not to call their father or their mother by their first names. For sons and daughters to speak disrespectfully to their fathers or mothers, or about them, is a grave sin. One who honors his father and his mother must hold for them a reverential respect.

2. *Honoring father and mother involves strict obedience.*

That is the very definite New Testament teaching. Read again Ephesians 6:1-3:

"Children, obey your parents in the Lord: for this is right. Honour thy father and mother; which is the first commandment with promise; That it may be well with thee, and thou mayest live long on the earth."

Honoring parents means to obey them.

Colossians 3:20 says, "Children, obey your parents in all things: for this is well pleasing unto the Lord."

Compare Ephesians 6:1 with Colossians 3:20. One says, "Children, obey your parents in the Lord." The other says, "Children, obey your parents in all things: for this is well pleasing unto the Lord."

I have known people who tried to use the command, "Obey your parents *in the Lord,*" as an excuse for not obeying parents who were not good Christians. Or sometimes rebellious sons and daughters have perverted this Scripture to make it an excuse for not obeying parents when they claimed to know better what would please the Lord than parents did. Any such interpretation is a misinterpretation, as one can easily see by comparing it with Colossians 3:20. Children are to obey their parents *"in all things:* for this is well pleasing unto the Lord."

In other words, there is no way for a minor child to be a good Christian without being a good, obedient child to his or her father and mother. Duty to God involves duty to father and mother. A child who is a rebel against his father or mother is a rebel against God.

It is true that sometimes a father may be wrong or a mother may be wrong. It is true that sometimes a father might command a child to do wrong, or a mother might command a child to do wrong. But very rarely would the child be a better judge about what is right or wrong than the father or mother. God simply does not leave it to the child to pass judgment on his father's or mother's command and decide what would be proper to obey and what would be proper to disobey. The plain Bible command is, "Children, obey your parents in all things."

A citizen had as well say that he would obey certain laws and that other laws of the land he felt led of the Holy Spirit to break. No, it ought to be a foregone conclusion that Christian children obey their parents, that Christian pupils obey their teachers, and that Christian citizens obey the laws of the land. When Peter said to the Jewish leaders, "We ought to obey God rather than men," he was not disobeying any law of the Roman governorship, or any of the Mosaic laws of which the Jewish rulers were guardians.

I am simply saying that children ought to obey their parents, and this fundamental meaning of this fifth commandment of the ten ought to be taken to heart as part of the basic morality commanded in the Bible. Every preacher and Bible teacher, every parent should stress obedience to parents as a fundamental of Christian living.

Suppose a child in some matters knows better than his father or mother; does that justify the child in refusing the obedience which God has commanded? Certainly not! I am sure that I have a better education, that I am a better Christian and a better citizen than many a traffic policeman; but that gives me no right to disobey his legal authority. Any son or daughter who is a Christian can best show his or her Christianity to an unsaved father or mother by the most devout and loving obedience. You may be sure that the more genuine and sincere the obedience from the heart that a child will render to his parent, the more the parent will be convinced of the Christianity of the child. "Children, obey your parents in all things: for this is well pleasing unto the Lord."

3. *Honoring parents involves financial support and provision for fathers and mothers by their children.*

Does the obligation of children to honor their parents

cease when the children are grown and perhaps married and gone from the parent's home? No, indeed! The devotion and respect due to parents must continue until death. Naturally, when children are grown and make their own support and perhaps have families of their own, the father and mother will not expect to dictate every detail of the lives of their grown children. But every child has a debt that he can never pay. Every grown son and daughter must feel that all the reverence and devotion and loyal submission to father and mother are little enough to pay for all the parents have done.

I well remember that when I was a grown man with a family of my own, I listened with profoundest respect to any opinion of my father. Though he did not try to maintain his authority over me, there was an unspoken authority, nevertheless. Had he felt it right to strictly command me on some matter, I hardly see how I could have disobeyed him. Certainly I would not have disobeyed him willingly, even then.

But the honor that mature men and women pay to their parents should often be expressed in financial support and provision. This was taught by the Saviour Himself, in expounding this very commandment.

Read Mark 7:6-13.

"He answered and said unto them, Well hath Esaias prophesied of you hypocrites, as it is written, This people honoureth me with their lips, but their heart is far from me. Howbeit in vain do they worship me, teaching for doctrines the commandments of men. For laying aside the commandment of God, ye hold the tradition of men, as the washing of pots and cups: and many other such like things ye do. And he said unto them, Full well ye reject the commandment of God, that ye may keep your own tradition. For Moses said, Honour thy father and thy mother; and, Whoso curseth father or mother, let him die the death: But ye say, If a man shall say to his father or mother, It is Corban, that is to say, a gift, by whatsoever thou mightest be profited by me; he shall be free. And ye suffer him no more to do ought for his father or his mother; Making the word of God of none effect through your tradition, which ye have delivered: and many such like things do ye."

The Jewish leaders had a rule of "Corban." If a man should say to his father or mother, "It is Corban," that is, to say that he was dedicating whatever he owed to his father or mother as a gift to God or to the religious leaders, then these leaders did not allow him to do anything in the way of financial support for his father or mother. Here religious duty was made a substitute for the financial care and support which is due a father and mother from their children. Jesus said that these religious leaders had thus dishonored God, had made the Word of God of none effect by their tradition. And the Scripture that Jesus quoted to them was this same fifth commandment, "Honour thy father and thy mother."

According to our Lord Jesus Christ, sons and daughters who honor their fathers and mothers support them in old age and provide for them as necessary. Jesus said that this is involved in the commandment, "Honour thy father and thy mother."

Some Christian men and women are proud of the money they give to their church or to missions or to some phase of the Lord's work. They ought to know that Jesus said they are making the Word of God of no effect by their tradition if they do not first see that father and mother are provided for. God does not want the offerings of a son whose father and mother are in want.

Certainly I believe in tithing, and I believe that any man or woman who does right in this matter of seeing that father and mother are provided for can afford to tithe, also. But Christian giving ought never to be made an excuse for not providing for father and mother.

This discussion by the Saviour, showing that those who do not support father and mother disobey the fifth commandment, is also given in Matthew 15:3-9.

Again in I Timothy 5:3, 4, this teaching is given that children should honor their parents by providing for them.

"Honour widows that are widows indeed. But if any widow have children or nephews, let them learn first to show piety at home, and to requite their parents: for that is good and acceptable before God."

How can children honor their widowed mothers? By supporting them! Children who want to show piety should "learn first to shew piety at home, and to requite their parents: for that is good and acceptable before God." Real Christianity requires children to support their widowed mothers, or even their widowed aunts.

It is a remarkable fact, not generally recognized, that I Timothy 5:8, in the same chapter, speaks of the support due a widowed mother. The Scripture says, "But if any provide not for his own, and specially for those of his own house, he hath denied the faith, and is worse than an infidel." This Scripture does not speak of a man's support for wife and children, but the support of parents, particularly of a widowed mother or aunt. Any man who does not see that the widows of his family connection are provided for, and specially for his own widowed mother, has denied the faith and is worse than an infidel.

How wicked, then, for Christian families to let mother or father go on relief rolls! Why should the government need to support the parents of Christian young people? Why should the church ever have to care for aged Christians who have reared children? Any man who wants the government to support his father and mother is, in that matter, worse than an infidel and has denied the faith, says I Timothy 5:8. God's plan is not old-age pensions nor relief nor a dole from the church for aged Christians. God's plan is that sons and daughters should provide for their parents. That is part of what it means to "honour thy father and thy mother."

Thus, we see that to keep the fifth commandment, sons and daughters who honor their father and mother must hold their persons in fervent respect, must obey them, must provide for them as necessary.

III. A Proper Honoring of Parents Is the Foundation of All Successful Human Society

So much of human duty and morality is involved in honoring parents in the Bible sense that there can be no successful and morally healthful society and civilization except in proportion as this command is obeyed. Those who honestly honor their fathers and mothers according to the scriptural command and its meaning will have a proper reverence for and devotion to God, will promote righteousness in obedience to law and government, will revere holy things and pass on the moral inheritance from one generation to the next.

Let us consider prayerfully how essential is honoring of parents as a foundation of moral and righteous human society.

1. Honoring parents naturally results in reverence for God.

The husband and wife are "heirs together of the grace of life," says the Word of God (I Pet. 3:7). Father and mother cooperate with Almighty God as joint creators of the little life that comes from their holy marriage. A human father is the nearest thing on earth to God that a little child can know. There is something essentially godlike in fatherhood and motherhood. The child who does not reverence his own father and mother will not reverence the Creator. One who has a proper reverence and godly respect for his parents will naturally respect the Creator. A man's inherent duty toward his parents is very much like his duty toward God. In fact, we are taught to call God "Our Father which art in heaven." It is intended that a human father should be the image and reminder of the Heavenly Father of a Christian.

There are some people who will not like the teaching of this article that children are to obey parents. There are some people who strenuously object to parents' whipping children. And who are these objectors? Why, they are the same people who do not believe the Bible, do not surrender and bow to the authority of Almighty God. Those who object to God's authority also object to the authority of father and mother.

Every sensible person knows that those who rebel against father and mother are also rebels against God. No wonder the Nazis in Germany taught children to spy upon their parents and report them to the Gestapo for any criticism of Hitler and his murderous policy! No wonder that in Russia, ruled by atheistic communists, parents were forbidden to teach their own children about God! Rebellion of children against parents goes with rebellion against God. That is the history of the whole human race.

In II Timothy 3:1-7 is a terrible catalog of the sins of men in the last days. Verses 2 to 4 say, "For men shall be lovers of their own selves, covetous, boasters, proud, blasphemers, *disobedient to parents*, unthankful, unholy, Without natural affection, truce-breakers, false accusers, incontinent, fierce, despisers of those that are good, traitors, heady, highminded, lovers of pleasures more than lovers of God."

Right in the middle of this catalog we learn that some will be "blasphemers, *disobedient to parents*, unthankful, unholy." Blasphemy and disobedience to parents go together. Disobedience to parents and unholiness go together. Disobedience to parents is naturally a sin of the ungrateful, the incontinent, the fierce, the despisers of them that are good, of traitors, of those who do not love God! The Scripture says that disobedience to parents is a part and parcel of these terrible sins of the last days. So those who do not honor parents do not honor God.

We can have a healthy and moral society only as we inculcate obedience and honor to parents.

2. Honoring parents promotes the right attitude toward law and government.

Every experienced and observant schoolteacher knows that disobedience to parents in the home results in disobedience to the teacher and to the rules of the school. Every juvenile court judge well knows that the homes where there is no honor for parents, and no obedience on the part of children, are the homes that turn out young criminals and hoodlums. Everybody knows that the report of the late Chief Edgar Hoover of the Federal Bureau of Investigation, saying that the breakdown in parental authority has resulted in a great increase in crime on the part of young people, is true. Sensible people should know that if children do not obey their parents they will not obey other people later, will not obey the authority of the government. We cannot expect a nation of good citizens to grow up from sons and daughters who do not honor their parents. If we expect our government to stand and legal human authority to be supported in a patriotic country, then we must sponsor and inculcate this fundamental virtue of obedience and honor to parents.

3. Honor to parents necessarily involves the right attitude of reverence toward sex and marriage.

Studies by psychologists have revealed that children who grow up in well-managed homes, who grow up in obedience to parents, are much less likely to have their own homes broken later by divorce. The closest that any man will ever come to the marriage problem, before he himself is married, will be as he observes the marriage of his father and mother. If, in his own home, a boy has been taught to observe the deepest reverence for the womanhood of his own mother, to regard her person sacredly, to respect her wishes and obey her commands, and if he feels an obligation to support her financially, he will naturally be a desirable husband with a proper reverence toward all good womanhood.

From long experience in dealing with troubled human hearts, with sinful human lives and entangled human relationships, I can say that the man who reveres his father and his mother is much more likely to have a normal attitude toward matters of sex and marriage. The man who reveres his mother will be more likely to revere his sister. One who reveres his mother and sisters will certainly be more likely to revere other women. The godly influence of a mother who has been greatly honored and strictly obeyed by her son has been illustrated many, many times within my own experience.

A great preacher whom I know well and love devotedly told in my hearing this story: He worked his way through high school while he lived at home on a southern farm and traveled some distance to school. But when the high school work was done, there came the time for him to leave the farm and go off to college. The family had gathered to tell him good-bye before his father should take him to the railroad station. His mother called him to one side and said something like this, "Joe, we have looked after you and counseled you and prayed for you. Now you are a man, and you are going off to college. You will have to be a man on your own, and you will often have to resist temptation without our help. But I want you to remember, Joe, that every night at nine o'clock in our family worship we will be praying for you. I want you to keep clean and straight, Joe, and I believe you will."

Joe went to college, was clean, worked hard and made good. He made the football team. On Thanksgiving Day of his fourth year in college, in the home-coming game, he was the halfback who carried the ball over the goal line for the winning touchdown. He was carried off the field on the shoulders of his teammates.

That night the coach said to the boys on the team, "You have worked hard, kept training and been in bed every night by ten o'clock. Tonight the rules are off. Have a good time."

When the big dinner was over and the other boys dressed for a late evening in the city, they told how they expected to visit the red-light district and urged Joe to go along. When he at first refused they said he was a sissy, tied to his mother's apron strings. At last Joe said, "All right, I'll go."

On the street together the boys laughed and talked. Suddenly the clock in a tower began to strike, one! two! three! the gong sounded on until finally it ended, eight! nine! Then the sound died away on the air. It was nine o'clock! Joe turned to his comrades and said, "Boys, I am not going. I don't care, you can call me anything you want to, but I'm not going!" Joe said he remembered that at nine o'clock his mother was at home praying for him. The reverence and respect he had for his mother, as well as his own Christian convictions, made it impossible for him to go on in the vile sin that was contemplated. And Joe was able to come later to his own marriage altar as pure and clean as was his bride.

I tell you that the proper honor and respect for father and mother guarantee a holy attitude toward sex and marriage.

I remember hearing Dr. Robert G. Lee tell how he went to South America to make money in order to finish his college work. His mother stood with her hands upon his shoulders, looked into his eyes and said to him something like this: "Bob, you will be a long way from home. But when you come back I am going to look into your eyes, and I can tell if you have dishonored your mother and your God." The now famous preacher went to South America. There were all the loneliness, the heart-hunger, the temptations of a far-off land as well as a ribald companionship. But he lived straight. When he came home he came to face his mother. She put her hands upon his shoulders again and he said to her, "Mother, look into my face. I have lived clean and straight. I never took a drink. I never gambled a dollar. I never laid a hand on a woman!" The mother looked into her son's eyes and was satisfied. I am saying that proper honoring of parents guarantees a moral and Christian attitude of reverence toward sex and marriage and home.

I have six lovely daughters. I would have never willingly given one of them into the arms and keeping of a young man who did not honor his own father and mother.

4. Honoring parents passes on all the moral and spiritual inheritance of one generation to the next, prevents the decay of civilization.

It is a tragedy unspeakable when godly parents find their children do not follow in their footsteps. It is unspeakably sad when temperate parents find their sons to be drunkards, their daughters to be licentious and impure. Why do these things happen? They happen because children do not honor their fathers and mothers.

A praying father and mother are important. A father and mother who demand and receive respect and honor are even more important! And that is because making children obedient is more important than asking God to do what we would not do. I believe in prayer when it is backed up by obedient action. I do not believe that God pays much attention to the prayers of a father and mother who will not do what God said about making their children obedient.

It is only by honoring parents that children can carry on to the next generation the spiritual and moral inheritance of their father's generation. This is part of the meaning of the promise connected with the fifth commandment. That promise says, "That thy days may be long upon the land which the Lord thy God giveth thee." A morally great civilization can only be continued where children honor their parents. Otherwise, nations decay, morality wanes, and a nation comes to ruin.

A striking example of this carry-over of the deep religious convictions and righteous principles of the father into succeeding generations is that furnished by the Rechabites during the reign of Jehoiakim, king of Judah. Jeremiah, chapter 35, tells us about it. Jeremiah was commanded, "Go unto the house of the Rechabites, and speak unto them, and bring them into the house of the Lord, into one of the chambers, and give them wine to drink" (Jer. 35:2). And did these sons of the Rechabites drink wine? They did not! "But they said, We will drink no wine: for Jonadab the son of Rechab our father commanded us saying, Ye shall drink no wine, neither ye, nor your sons for ever" (Jer. 35:6). Other commandments, likewise, did these men observe, given to them generations before by Jonadab, the son of Rechab. They passed on the moral and spiritual inheritance of one generation to the next. How great would be our country if children honored their fathers and mothers so that each generation should grow upon the foundation laid before it by their fathers and mothers!

Conclusion

In conclusion, I want to lay on your heart two great lessons.

First, parents themselves must see that children honor them. Children will not of their own accord do right without teaching and training. Parents must take it as the first Christian duty to their children to require obedience. There should be much prayer, much Bible teaching, day by day godly example. But more will be required, and whatever else is required, parents must do to insure the honor and obedience of children for parents. Parents should both earn and compel the obedience and respect and honor of their children. The greatest disservice the father and mother could ever do the beloved child is to allow him to grow up in his own way. All the virtues and all the blessings we hold dear are largely summed up in honoring father and mother.

And, second, I would lay on the heart of every one of you who reads this that the final and best way you can honor your parents is by turning to your mother's God and your father's God. Some of you who read this today had godly parents who are now in Heaven. With what longing and what concern they look upon you, left in this world! How grieved they must be over your sins, over your rejection of Jesus Christ! Nothing you could do in this world would so please them and so honor their memory as to turn to their God, accept their Saviour, the Lord Jesus Christ, as your own Saviour, and set out to meet them in Heaven.

And you whose parents are still alive, what matters the money you may spend on them if their hearts are broken over your sinful rejection of Christ? What matters the attention, the kindness shown father and mother, when your wicked heart goes against their dearest wishes in continuing in sin?

Some of you who read this today ought to go on your knees in humble confession of your sin before God, ought to sincerely repent of your sin and trust Christ to save you. Then when you have trusted your poor sinful soul into the hands of Christ Jesus, after you have depended on Christ to forgive you and save you as He promised to do, you should write your dear mother and say that her prayers are answered. Or you should write to your dear father and tell him that you have heeded his pleadings and followed his counsel and will meet him in Heaven.

"Honour thy father and thy mother: that thy days may be long upon the land which the Lord thy God giveth thee."

CHAPTER XIV

Family Worship

"As for me and my house, we will serve the Lord."—Josh. 24:15.

"Then Jacob said unto his household, and to all that were with him, Put away the strange gods that are among you, and be clean, and change your garments: And let us arise, and go up to Bethel; and I will make there an altar unto God, who answered me in the day of my distress, and was with me in the way which I went."—Gen. 35:2, 3.

"Aquila and Priscilla salute you much in the Lord, with the church that is in their house."—I Cor. 16:19.

". . . Nymphas, and the church which is in his house."—Col. 4:15.

". . . to the church in thy house."—Philem. 2.

There are fully as many reasons for family worship as there are for public services in a church building. The family is a more compact and permanent unit, more closely knit, than any church congregation. Public worship at church may be only a form, on public display on Sunday. But worship in the family tends to be more practical and real, participated in together by the people who know one another best and where Christianity must necessarily be a part of everyday life if the family worship be real and sincere.

Christians are encouraged to agree together in prayer. Matthew 18:19 says, "Again I say unto you, That if two of you shall agree on earth as touching any thing that they shall ask, it shall be done for them of my Father which is in heaven." And who could agree so well in prayer as the husband and wife who are one flesh?

The next verse, Matthew 18:20, says, "For where two or three are gathered together in my name, there am I in the midst of them," a blessed promise from the Lord Jesus Himself! Every family that bows in worship can include two or three that are gathered in Christ's name and so have as much

243

promise of His blessing as the largest congregation that ever meets together!

There is a grave responsibility of parents to children in religious matters. Fathers are commanded to diligently teach their children the Word of God (Deut. 6:7). Fathers are also commanded to bring children up "in the nurture and admonition of the Lord" (Eph. 6:4). If children are to be taught the Word of God, taught to pray, taught to live holy lives, and taught to put their trust in Christ as Saviour, then surely there ought to be regular worship in the home. There ought to be Bible reading and prayer and exhortation and singing in the home. And much of this should be at regular times and under the supervision of the father and mother of the home. How happy is the home that has regular daily family worship!

I. Examples of Family Religion and Worship in the Bible

Noah, a preacher of righteousness, preached 120 years without any converts except his own wife, his three sons, Shem, Ham and Japheth, and their three wives! There was one man whose religion was good at home! And there must have been family worship to augment and strengthen the message which Noah gave in public, else his own family would probably have been as unbelieving as were the rest of his hearers. In Genesis 7:1 we are told, "And the Lord said unto Noah, Come thou and all thy house into the ark; for thee have I seen righteous before me in this generation." It was one little family of God-fearers who went into the ark before God closed the door! It seems certain to me that they thanked God for their deliverance as they rode out the storm in the great ark. It seems certain that they must have had some fearful moments in which they, together, prayed and committed themselves to the mercy of the God they loved and served. When they went out of the ark after the flood, Noah builded an altar unto the Lord (Gen. 8:20). I am sure that the little family gathered around in meekest devotion while Noah offered the sacrifice and perhaps prayed. And when God blessed Noah, He blessed his sons also, commanding them to "be fruitful, and multiply, and replenish the earth" (Gen. 9:1). It was family religion which Noah and his wife and sons and daughters-in-law had. Each one surely trusted in the coming Saviour for himself or herself, but they must have united in their worship and teaching and prayers.

When the Lord appeared to Abraham to repeat His promise of a son who was to be called Isaac, the Lord said to Abraham, "Where is Sarah thy wife?" And to the two of them God made the blessed promise (Gen. 18:9-15). It is not hard to believe that with all of Abraham's altar-rearing and sacrifice-making Sarah was in heartiest agreement and that she joined him in holy conversation about God and in prayer and in faith in the promises of God.

Read how Jacob and his family had worship together.

"And God said unto Jacob, Arise, go up to Bethel, and dwell there: and make there an altar unto God, that appeared unto thee when thou fleddest from the face of Esau thy brother. Then Jacob said unto his household, and to all that were with him, Put away the strange gods that are among you, and be clean, and change your garments: And let us arise, and go up to Bethel; and I will make there an altar unto God, who answered me in the day of my distress, and was with me in the way which I went."—Gen. 35:1-3.

They brought their strange idols to Jacob and he buried them under an oak. They all went to Bethel and there Jacob built an altar and called upon the name of the Lord, with his family gathered around. There was no one there but Jacob and his own family and servants. It was really family worship. Jacob often talked about God to his sons. You cannot read his dying blessing on his twelve sons without realizing that worship and praise and faith were matters with Jacob and his sons.

Joshua, the great general who led the armies of Israel into the land of Canaan after the death of Moses, was a most devout man of God. He, too, had the worship of God in his home, and his whole family was led by this godly man to serve the Lord. In Joshua 24:15 he said to other men of the tribes of Israel, "And if it seem evil unto you to serve the Lord, choose you this day whom ye will serve ... but as for me and my house, we will serve the Lord." Not only would Joshua serve the Lord, not only would he pray and learn the commandments of God, but his family, his whole household, should serve the Lord, too, Joshua promised. Such a family religion necessarily involves Christian teaching and some family worship.

If we had come one dark night about A.D. 53 to the town of Philippi in Macedonia, and could have peeped into a certain home hard by the jail, after the midnight hour, we should have seen a strange scene. Here was preaching of the Word, here were tender exhortations. Here was a real revival scene. Paul and Silas were preaching the Word with only one family as hearers. First the father, the burly jailer, was converted, and then his wife and children and servants. And then after they adjourned to some pool for a family baptizing, they had a meal to take the place of the supper that Paul and Silas had missed in jail; and the family, now all converted, sat about the table rejoicing. Acts 16:33, 34 says, "And he took them the same hour of the night, and washed their stripes; and was baptized, he and all his, straightway. And when he had brought them into his house, he set meat before them, and rejoiced, believing in God with all his house." That, I say, was family worship, a family scene. And do not believe that Paul and Silas had all the leadership in it. It seems evident that the jailer himself, after trusting in Christ, led his family also to follow his footsteps. What joy he had when they all, like himself, were trusting in the Saviour and happy in the forgiveness of their sins! I have no doubt that the same kind of a scene was repeated many, many times, even when Paul and Silas had gone on their way. You see, the Christian religion is a family matter. I do not mean that people are saved by families. But God intends that fathers and mothers shall win their own children, shall teach their children, shall worship with their children. Worship in a home is normal Christianity.

In fact, the New Testament churches seem to have first gathered in homes, and the family was the first congregation in many cities. There were no regularly prepared church buildings at first. The apostles preached in synagogues until they were cast out by the unbelieving Jews, and then they preached in open streets, by the riverside, and particularly in private homes. Acts 18:7 tells how Paul, when opposed by the Jews in the synagogue at Corinth, "departed thence, and entered into a certain man's house, named Justus, one that worshipped God, whose house joined hard to the synagogue." There he preached, and Crispus himself, the chief ruler of the synagogue, attended these services in the home next door, and was converted along with many other Corinthians.

So many churches met in private homes that three times such churches are mentioned by the Apostle Paul in his epistles. In I Corinthians 16:19 Paul says, "Aquila and Priscilla salute you much in the Lord, with the church that is in their house." In Colossians 4:15 Paul said, "Salute the brethren which are in Laodicea, and Nymphas, and the church which is in his house." And writing unto Philemon, Paul sends greetings to "our beloved Apphia, and Archippus our fellowsoldier, and to the church in thy house" (Philem. 2).

"The church in thy house"! What a simple picture of worship in a home! It seems likely that in each of these cases Paul or one of the other preachers had come, had won the husband and father to Christ and then the family, and there the preacher stayed, preaching every day and teaching the family and others that would drop in. And soon a regular congregation gathered in the patio, or in the living room, or perhaps in the cool of the day upon the broad, flat housetop. Do you have a church at your house? My own heart is searched with tender feeling as I meditate on the fact that God intends me to have a church in my own home! Sometimes neighbors will be there to hear the Word of God and to join in prayer. But always I have my own family for which I am accountable to God. And we must have worship in the home.

II. Some Essentials of Adequate Family Worship

Many fine families have a hurried but devout word of thanks before each meal that the family eats together. That is good, but that is not enough. Godly mothers or fathers often pray with their children before they go to bed. That is precious, and I cannot believe that any child will ever have any memory sweeter than praying with mother or with dad before being tucked in for the night. But still I believe that is not enough. Let me suggest some of the necessary elements, as I see them, to a successful and a proper family worship.

1. *The whole family should worship together.* For mother to pray with her children is not enough. For a husband and wife to have their prayer at bedtime, just those two alone, is very sweet; but that does not fill the need. Surely the whole family should be together in worship and should take part. They should unite their prayers. Each should contribute his part toward the success of family worship, and should obtain his part of the blessing that comes from united prayer and praise and hearing of the Word of God. If there is a reason for the family eating together (and there certainly is a very good reason for it), then there is reason for the family to

worship together. If there is a reason for the family to be together at Christmas or Thanksgiving, there is reason for the family to gather regularly for family worship. The family is a unit before God. The father is to take a particular responsibility for his whole household. They ought to have worship together. Even in the homes where the father works at odd hours or where different members of the family work at different hours, and where it is difficult to have meals together, yet some plan should be worked out so that the whole family can have worship together regularly.

2. *All in the family should take part.* It is fine for a father to lead in prayer, or for a father or mother to read the Scriptures. But some plan should be worked out so that each member of the family may take part in the worship daily. Even if there is a little baby, if he is old enough to talk, he should be taught to memorize some little verses, or he should be taught a simple sentence of prayer. And the baby should be present in the family circle and taught to listen with reverence. He should learn to bow his head when others pray. That is not hard for the little one to learn, and it will make a profound impression upon his life. Then as soon as he is able to read, he should take part in the reading of the Scriptures. Let all take part in family worship. One of the most serious drawbacks to the family worship of many pioneer homes was that the children of the family endured, but did not enjoy and did not participate in, the worship. Many a father, devout and sincere, has taught his family to kneel while he prayed. That was good, but how much better it would have been if each of the children had had part in the reading and had had part in the praying, and perhaps in singing. But every member of the family should worship. Every member of the family should feel that it is his duty to be present and to take part.

3. *Family worship should certainly include the reading of the Bible.* Personally, I like best the reading of the Word of God chapter by chapter. Many families have a custom of reading one page from a devotional book, like *Streams in the Desert* by Mrs. Cowman, or *Morning and Evening,* by C. H. Spurgeon. These are rich and blessed, and I believe their comments are very helpful. But I do not think that one verse of Scripture is enough for a time of worship. There ought to be enough Scripture given and carefully attended to, to bless the whole day and to teach something of the will of God and

of His dealings with His people. Many thousands of families have been blessed by the book of selected Scriptures called *Daily Light*. It is very fine. But, however good these Scripture verses may be, I believe that there is a greater value in using Scriptures consecutively, in their order. Children ought to read Scriptures and be able to find them in the Bible. They ought to find what God is talking about in the context. There is great virtue in using the Word of God in its own proper order, and with the context and connotation that God has given to it. I do not believe that any way is as good as having the Bible itself, and reading from the Bible.

Many homes have a very simple and delightful but not a very profound way of having family worship. With a little box of cards, each one containing a Scripture promise, each person present draws at random a card and reads the verse of Scripture thereupon. God is merciful and often makes such promises a great blessing to those who read. But again I do not feel that this haphazard and accidental way of getting a few selected Scripture texts is as valuable as setting out to read the whole Word of God and absorb it and learn it and love it, in the family worship period. Use the Scripture, use it honestly, have everybody read it in the family worship.

4. *Certainly the family worship should include prayer.* I think that all those in the home who are Christians ought to pray. Little children ought to learn to pray in the presence of their fathers and mothers, and in the presence of their brothers and sisters. It ought not to be flamboyant nor artificial. But in simple words, children should be taught to call on God for what their hearts desire and for what they need. Their prayers will need some suggestion and guidance. When company comes, the children's prayers should not be shown off as if they were some play or some exhibition of mental brilliance. But each one should have a simple part in the worship when the time for prayer comes.

I believe that little children, even before they are converted, ought to be taught to pray. I know that when I was a very small boy I learned to pray,

> Now I lay me down to sleep,
>   I pray the Lord my soul to keep.
> If I should die before I wake,
>   I pray the Lord my soul to take.

Even before I was conscious that I was a sinner, my heart was turned to love God and trust Him and to ask for His daily care. I remember when I was in the first and second grades in school I was taught to bow my head upon my desk and sing a little prayer of praise,

> **"Father we thank Thee for the night,**
> **And for the precious morning light."**

I believe that my heart prayed and gave thanks in those times of prayer and praise, in those simple words. I believe it had a profound influence upon my heart's attitude toward God. Little children can be taught the Lord's Prayer, and can be taught other simple prayers, and the matter can be discussed until the words may become their own sentiments and their own simple petition, very dear and sweet to our Father in Heaven, no doubt.

After a child has reached the age of accountability and becomes an open rebel against God, after he has been taught the way of salvation and earnestly entreated to trust Christ and will not do it, I do not see how he can pray an acceptable prayer, unless he prays for mercy and forgiveness. In such matters, of course, sincerity must always prevail. We are not to teach children that they are the children of God until they have been converted. We are not to let them think that the outward forms and ceremonies of religion are enough when the heart has not come to know and trust Jesus Christ. I know that prayers out of false lips are an abomination to God. But at the same time I feel that in every godly home where children are reared as they ought to be reared, they can be taught to love and trust the Saviour while very, very young, and that there need not be any very long period after a child becomes conscious of his sins until he comes to deliberately and lovingly surrender himself to Christ and trust our Saviour for the forgiveness of his sins and the saving of his soul. So I say, teach the little children to pray and have all those at the family worship join in prayer, in a suitable manner, if they can do so honestly.

5. *Family worship should be daily.* The blessings of God come every day. Why would any family be content to thank Him together as a body less than once a day? The strength that we receive from the study of God's Word is certainly needed every day. The family is together every day about

other matters in any normal home. Why, then, should there
not be a special season of worship, as a family, held every
day?

God has divided our time into day units. The body is so
constituted as to need one period of rest in each twenty-four
hours. The Saviour commanded us to pray daily for our daily
bread. Daily we are to forgive our enemies, and we are never
to let the sun go down on our wrath (Eph. 4:26). Once a
day men make a new start at labor. Every day good Christians must make a new dedication of themselves to God and
call on God for new strength for the day, new forgiveness for
sins, new help in temptations. And thus it is normal and right
that a family should meet daily for worship.

6. *Family worship should be early in the day.* The Lord
says, "Those that seek me early shall find me" (Prov. 8:17).
We are told of Jesus that, "in the morning, rising up a great
while before day, he went out, and departed into a solitary
place, and there prayed" (Mark 1:35). The Lord Jesus
prayed in the early morning. Saints down through the ages
have found the early morning prayer watch an indispensable
part of a happy and useful day. The family is at its freshest
and best in the early morning. Each one will have burdens
and cares enough. Each one will be drawn away by his or
her diverse interests. Surely the Lord who wants people to
seek Him early would be pleased to have a special season of
worship set aside in each family early in the day, where that
is possible.

7. *The mealtime is probably best for the worship period.*
First Timothy 4:4, 5 says that "every creature of God is
good, and nothing to be refused, if it be received with
thanksgiving: For it is sanctified by the word of God and
prayer." That indicates that every meal ought to have prayer.
It also hints, at least, that the Word of God should be used at
mealtime.

At any rate, the average family will find it easier to get together at a mealtime than at other times. And the whole
meal itself is sanctified and the family life is better knit together, if the worship can be put in connection with one of
the meals of the day, and preferably the early meal, the
breakfast. It seems to me that after breakfast is the ideal
time, in most homes.

III. Our Plan for Family Worship

It may be helpful if I give here the plan for family worship which we have used in our home for many years. Others may have plans better fitted to their needs, but many young couples, I am sure, and perhaps some families long established, may find here suggestions as to the best way to have a happy and blessed family worship period every day.

When Mrs. Rice and I were first married, we read the Bible and had prayer together at bedtime. That was sweet, and I suppose I inherited that thought of family worship at bedtime from my own childhood. Yet there were a good many objections to that time. In the first place, the day was already done, and there was very little reason to ask God's blessing on the day when it had already been spent without calling upon Him. There could be confessions of sin, and making requests for the morrow, but the tag end of the day is not the best time to invoke the blessing of God upon the day's labors and ask Him to fill the heart and mind with His goodness and lead one by His Spirit. Then as God gave the little children to us, we soon found that bedtime was sleep time. It was hard to keep little eyes open and little minds attentive. I was often out late preaching, and if the family was with me it was late to try to get the peace and calm and the happy attention which is needed for the best worship and for learning the Word of God. And if I came in alone, the little ones were already in bed and asleep. So obviously, some other plan had to be found if our family was to have a happy period of worship together.

After some experiments, we found that the breakfast time was for us the best time. We tried having family worship before breakfast. But that would not do if every member of the family were to take part in the worship. No one could be cooking the hotcakes or poaching the eggs, or making the cocoa while we had worship. And then after gathering at the table for our Bible reading and prayer, the rest of us would have to wait while part of the family got breakfast ready. That was not an economical use of time, nor was it happy. And it interfered in the preparation of breakfast. So we came to the custom of having family worship immediately after breakfast.

Now Bibles are at hand, one for every member of the

family, and when the breakfast meal is over, all sit at their places, ready for the worship. Each one has a Bible of his own, and we reverently open our Bibles and look on. I start the reading of the Scriptures, reading two verses. Then the girl on my left reads two verses, and so on all around the table, and around the second time and third time, if necessary. We usually read an entire chapter at the sitting. If we are reading in the Psalms, we read two or three usually, because they are shorter.

We found the best place to start was in the New Testament. So we read through Matthew, a chapter each morning, around and around the table, each one reading two verses as his or her turn came. The next morning we would read the next chapter. And so we went through the New Testament. Then we began in the Old Testament. We have read through the New Testament perhaps eight or ten times, and through most of the Old Testament perhaps five times. Ezekiel, we have read less frequently than some of the other books. We have read the Psalms more often than other Old Testament books. Genesis we find is fascinating to the children and easily understood. The Gospels are always rich, even to the smallest children. And a little comment and explanation make the epistles both interesting and wonderfully helpful.

It has always been a big event in our family when a child learned to read and so could take part in the reading of the Word. Joy, when she became eight, had been reading for several months and over only a few of the largest and hardest words did she stumble. Incidentally, I think the family worship period is one of the strongest reasons why my children love to read and read well and intelligently and read mature and helpful books. At first we would pick out an easy verse for "the baby" (We used to have a baby at our house so much of the time!). Before the baby could read, in each case, we have taken time at the morning worship period to teach part of a verse of Scripture or to review one that the child had learned before. We feel that even a little child needs to take part in the family worship.

Sometimes I would say, "Elizabeth, what do you think verse 23 means?" Or sometimes I would say, "Suppose each of us pick out the verse we like the best in this chapter." Sometimes before our season of prayer, we would ask anyone in the family to mention what she thought we ought to pray for. Sometimes we sang a chorus or two. Sometimes we had each one name one thing for which we ought to be especially thankful. And then we had our prayer.

At the head of the table, when I was at home, I lead in prayer first. Then each one around the table in order lead in prayer. And then when all the rest had prayed, I prayed again, asking God's blessing on us for the day. What a sweet and blessed time we had in this family worship together!

I believe that this plan or some modification of it will prove wonderfully rich and sweet to every home that can use it.

Sometimes it may be that the family can be together only at noon, or at night. But usually morning is better than evening, and almost always it is easier to get the family together at mealtime than at other times.

IV. Some Problems of Family Worship

Do not think that it will be easy to maintain daily family worship. For that matter it is hard enough, in a modern family, an urban family with diverse interests, jobs, friends and amusements, to get people together even for meals. Yet it is important to get people together for meals. Much of the happiness of a home is lost when the family does not meet together frequently as a unit. And it is more important that the family meet together for worship than for meals.

Yet Satan will make a special attempt to break down the family altar and stop the daily season of worship in the home. Those who set out to have family worship should know ahead of time that it will take earnest thought and care and that there will be obstacles to overcome. But anyone who tries to please the Lord and looks to Him humbly for help can find the help he needs. Those who want to have a family altar will find some way and some time when the family can be assembled for the family worship, I believe. One mother told me that it had seemed so difficult to have family worship, but she was determined to do it. So now part of the family has worship at one time, and part at another, and she said with delight, "And now I get in on the worship at both times!" Where there are unusual hours of labor, a special problem is involved, but God will help Christians to make the home worship regular and helpful if the father and mother are determined and resourceful and faithful.

I think the head of the home must lead out in family worship. No family worship is the success that it ought to be if the husband and father is only a noncommittal spectator. God intends that a father should lead his family. Each father, however timidly, should take an active part in the family worship and be responsible for it, in some sense. He may feel that he must rush off to his work. He had better remember that any child he has is worth more than his job, worth more than his business. He had better remember that the eternal welfare of one of these little ones committed to him is worth more than all the money he will make, and that he should value the family worship above any ordinary duty in life.

The wife and mother in the home has a serious obligation in regard to the family worship. She is responsible for the daily housekeeping program. Necessarily, if her meals are not on schedule, or if she allows other things to interfere so that there is not sufficient time for the worship before the children go to school or before the husband must leave for his work, the family worship period cannot be a success. It is of great importance, then, that she do her part by having everybody up on time, having the children's faces washed, having the meal prepared and out of the way in time, if the worship period follows a meal.

Schools are very exacting. In some matters certainly they ought to be. Promptness must be required of pupils. But every home must decide that the family worship is fully as important as being at school on time. In our own home occasionally my daughters were late getting down to breakfast, or others were late in their tasks about the home, or the meal was not on time, and so the young people were impatient and fearful that they would be late to school. Sometimes a girl would say, "But I just *must* press my dress before I go to school," or "If I don't get that theme ready today, I will lose ten percent off my grade." But I insisted firmly, "Family worship is more important than school, more important than your job or your pleasure. We will take plenty of time for family worship, time for the Word of God, time for prayer. Then if you want to be at school on time tomorrow, just be sure that you get other things out of the way so you can be ready for family worship on time." If you plan to serve God, you must put God first. God will not have the second best. The family altar that becomes secondary to the other interests of the father or mother or children will not last long but will be abandoned. So put the family altar early in the day, set aside plenty of time for it, and insist on giving it the place of honor in the day's schedule. And then how sweet and precious is the meeting around the Book of God and the meeting of the hearts of a family in prayer and praise!

Someone must see that the Bibles are ready, placed conveniently at hand, perhaps on the buffet, or on the dining table. The worship period should not be too long, not long enough to become a tiresome bore. It should not be long enough to lose the interest and attention. But if it be given its proper place of importance and if people come to it with earnest, prayerful hearts, determined to make it a blessing, there will be time every day for at least a chapter of God's Word and for a complete circle of prayer on all ordinary occasions.

I am an evangelist. That means that most of the days of the year I was away from home. Then my good wife had to lead out in the family worship. My daughters often had to read their Bibles and pray without me. I thank God that each morning I feel that they were praying, "God bless Daddy today. Help him to win souls." When I was away from home, I often read the same chapter for my own devotion as the family was reading at home. And always there was a tug indescribable, a longing to be there with my loved ones gathered around the breakfast table with the Word of God and prayer.

Do you know the meaning of that familiar song, "Home, Sweet Home"? Do you ever say to yourself as did John Howard Payne,

> 'Mid pleasures and palaces,
>   though we may roam,
> Be it ever so humble, there's
>   no place like home!
> A charm from the skies seems to
>   hallow us there,
> Which, seek thro' the world, is
>   ne'er met with elsewhere?

If you know what it is to have a family altar; if you know what it is to have united prayers of the family rise up to God every day; if you know what it is to join in the singing of sweet songs and hymns and spiritual songs with your own family; if you know what it is to study the Word of God and let the sweet Holy Spirit guide the hearts of all the family to-

MARRIAGE AND HOME 257

gether in praise and prayer and holy resolution, then you will be able to sing from the heart the old song, "Home, Sweet Home." For any home is sweet where God dwells. Wherever there is true worship, there must be love and fellowship and understanding and a daily benediction from God.

CHAPTER XV

Prayer in the Home

In a funeral parlor in Dallas, Texas, a young man about nineteen or twenty stood by the casket of his father. He said, "Brother Rice, I think my father was a Christian. He said he was. He lived a good life. But, oh, how much happier I would be if I had only heard him pray at least once!" That son felt, as most other sons and daughters would, that if a father and mother were very good Christians they would pray in the home, would pray with and for their children.

In Luke 9:18 is a strange verse. About the Saviour it says, "And it came to pass, as he was alone praying, his disciples were with him: and he asked them, saying, Whom say the people that I am?" When Jesus was *alone*, that is, away from the multitude, and in secret prayer, His disciples were with Him. The relationship of the Saviour and His disciples was so intimate that He could count Himself alone while they were with Him. And in some sense other members of a family ought to be able to enter into the prayer life of the father and mother. Prayer at home is not like prayer in a public church service. It is more intimate, more personal, and is more easily shared by the other members of the family than by outsiders.

Obviously, if a Christian is going to pray anywhere he must pray at home. Few of us would have any confidence in the kind of Christianity which makes much of public prayers and does no real praying at home.

We have given another chapter entirely to the subject of *Family Worship in the Home*. There ought to be, surely, one public time of Bible reading and prayer and worship daily, with all the family taking part. But there certainly ought to be much prayer in the home besides that at the family worship. We here make some suggestions about the kinds of prayer there should be in the home, including that at the family worship, and at other times and occasions.

I. Private Devotions by Individual Members of the Family

Jesus said, "And when thou prayest, thou shalt not be as the hypocrites are: for they love to pray standing in the synagogues and in the corners of the streets, that they may be seen of men. Verily I say unto you, They have their reward. But thou, when thou prayest, enter into thy closet, and when thou hast shut thy door, pray to thy Father which is in secret; and thy Father which seeth in secret shall reward thee openly. But when ye pray, use not vain repetitions, as the heathen do: for they think that they shall be heard for their much speaking" (Matt. 6:5-7).

Here is a clear doctrine of prayer. Prayer must not be done for public show, must not be intended primarily for the ears of others. Prayers must not be vain repetitions, as the heathen have. But prayer ought to be the honest heart cry of a soul, particularly of a Christian, asking his Heavenly Father for what he needs and desires. So, Jesus teaches that prayer ought often, nay usually, to be secret prayer. Only the man who prays much in secret can be trusted to pray honestly in public, without special regard to what others think of his prayer. Secret prayer is absolutely essential to the happiest and most prosperous Christian life.

This does not mean that it is wrong to pray in public, or wrong to join with others in prayer. We are given precious promises about where two or three shall agree in prayer. We have many Bible examples of where Jesus and others prayed in public. But prayer can be kept on a spiritually honest basis only as one prays much in secret.

If the father and mother are to lead their children aright in their devotions, then they must have special strength and grace, and they ought to talk to God in private before they lead their children in the public family worship. Necessarily the father and mother have problems that are too intimate and too deep for the understanding of little children. Every Christian, whether young or old, needs a time of waiting upon God, a time with his Bible and in prayer.

The ideal time for this morning watch, this time of secret devotion, is on first arising. The evangelist, D. L. Moody, had a custom of arising at four o'clock in the morning for a time of Bible study and prayer alone before anyone else in the family was stirring. For those who find it hard to take time for secret devotion, a missionary some years ago suggested a simple motto of four words which will settle that matter for any Christian if he takes them as a solemn vow to God. "No Bible, no breakfast!" was that motto. Those who do not have time to read the Bible and pray do not have time to eat. A Christian needs a time alone with God for his prayer, for his confession, for a little memory work, or for sweet meditation on the Word of God in claiming promises.

Ralph Cushman has said:

I MET GOD IN THE MORNING

I met God in the morning
    When the day was at its best,
And His presence came like glory
    Of the sunrise in my breast.

All day long the Presence lingered,
    All day long He stayed with me,
And we sailed in perfect calmness
    O'er a very troubled sea.

Other ships were blown and battered,
    Other ships were sore distressed.
But the winds that seemed to drive them,
    Brought to us a peace and rest.

Then I thought of other mornings,
    With a keen remorse of mind,
When I, too, had loosed the moorings
    With the Presence left behind.

And I think I know the secret,
    Learned from many a troubled way:
You must seek God in the morning
    If you want Him through the day.

Only this morning my private Bible study in the first two chapters in John yielded two remarkable lessons that I had never seen before, and how sweet they were to my heart! And one who prays alone will pray about things that he dare not ask for in the presence of others, no matter how close and dear they are.

Even the children of the family who are Christians ought to be taught to have private devotions. Perhaps they ought to have suggestions about it. A mother may set her children to learning the Twenty-Third Psalm, the Beatitudes, the Lord's Prayer, or the Ten Commandments. Or she may give a list of verses and have one verse learned each morning, and have it repeated to her later in the day or at the family worship period. Perhaps some of the children will find especially precious the little book called *Daily Light*, with a collection of Scriptures for every day on special topics. Some members of the family will like Mrs. Cowman's book, *Streams in the Desert*. It gives for each day in the year a verse of Scripture, comment by some famous preacher and a sweet poem that comforts and blesses. But each individual who is a Christian ought to be encouraged to have his little quiet time alone with the Bible and God. It will take some supervision from father and mother for younger children. But it will be the forming of a beautiful habit, one of the most essential habits that will almost guarantee a happy and useful Christian life for one who has trusted in Christ.

II.   The Prayers at Family Worship

In another chapter we have suggested the reasons and time and method of family worship, but now a word ought to be said about the prayers at family worship.

First, let every member of the family who is a Christian pray. Preferably, the prayers ought to come in order. Some person, probably the father, ought to pray first, and then if each one prays in a regular order around the table, no one will be left out and each one will feel that he has a regular and usual part in the worship.

Let the prayers be simple and direct and such that every member of the family can understand and in which all can join. Prayer should always be very honest and openhearted, asking for what the heart craves and needs. The more simple and direct the prayers, the more likely they are honest prayers and the more likely God will be pleased with them.

The family worship ought always to include praise. Children ought to be taught to thank God for the rest of the night, to thank God for the meals, to thank God for mother and father, brothers and sisters, and other blessings.

Often the father and mother will be called upon to suggest

what the children should pray for. Perhaps the children themselves should think about it ahead of time and suggest, before the prayer, some things for which they should ask. And they should suggest matters for thanksgiving too.

The prayers ought to be practical, and certainly the children should learn to pray for one another. Often at our breakfast table one of my girls has prayed, "Lord, help me to remember what I have learned and be able to express myself on the test today and make a good grade." And often my girls have prayed for one of the sisters who was to take an examination or who needed help in a job, or who was to take part on a Christian program. "Lord, help Daddy to preach tonight and let souls be saved," has been a frequent prayer of little girls at our family altar many, many times through the years.

A month before Mary Lloys, my second daughter, was married, nearly all her sisters prayed repeatedly, "Lord, help us in the plans for the wedding that it may be beautiful, that Mary Lloys and Chuck will be happy, and that the ceremony may be a help and inspiration to others." Then when the happy young couple were gone on their honeymoon, Mary Lloys' sisters prayed for her happiness and safe return and prayed that the marriage might be all that we had hoped it would be.

If Mother has lost her check book, then the breakfast table worship is a good time to pray that the Lord might help her find it.

If one member of the family has a cold or any illness, all those around the table frequently pray for the dear one, whether present or absent. How sweet to bear one another's burdens, and find the family's hearts knit together in prayer to God at the family worship!

Of course, the parents will need to set the example about the unselfish praying and bearing of one another's burdens in prayer. Surely the mother and father should call the children by name and pray God to bless them. If one has done wrong, then with loving heart the mother and father should specially remember that one and plead with the Lord that he may be kept from any sin and that he may overcome any special temptation. I do not know of anything that is more likely to help a boy or girl to be good and honor his father and mother than to hear that father's or mother's loving voice lifted in prayer for him. That is a sweet heritage that every child ought to be able to remember always. Parents ought to pray for their children. They ought to pray for them at the family worship.

This example has a blessed effect on the children who join in the family worship. They enter into the burdens, the joys, the problems, the needs of the home. They join in prayer. When our girls were at home, they use to pray for money to pay the college bills. They joined in thanking God when He sent the money for necessary expenses. A spirit of unselfish prayer can be developed by the example of father and mother at the family altar.

Little pumps need priming. Little children need suggestions about how to pray. Often the prayer ought to grow out of the Scripture that is read. A good promise might be quoted and memorized and its meaning explained. Then it ought to be applied to some personal need, and children feel free to pray for that need, on the authority of the Word of God. Often mother or father should simply suggest, "Let us pray for So-and-so." Or the father might ask, "What shall we pray for today?" And then there is a general agreement about the prayer that must be pleasing to God.

I suggest that the fathers and mothers be particularly careful that the language of their prayers be simple and direct. The ponderous and theological praying is very rarely in order. Elegant but obscure language with long words and high-sounding phrases have little place in prayer at any time, even public prayer in the church. They are utterly out of place at the family altar. Let prayer be simple and childlike and direct and sincere. Let the fathers and mothers pray such prayers as the children may emulate, at least in spirit. They certainly ought to be able to understand the words and join their hearts in the petitions that are uttered by father and mother.

III. Thanks at Meals

Perhaps there ought not to be many inflexible rules about a home. But certainly there ought to be a custom never broken of thanking God for meals.

Ten times in the New Testament we are told that Jesus gave thanks to God for food. Six times more we are told that He blessed the food before He ate or before He broke bread for others. If the dear Lord Jesus, our Saviour, the Maker of

Heaven and earth, when in human form, felt a gratitude welling up in His heart to His Heavenly Father, then how wicked are we if we do not likewise gratefully thank God! And if He, so busy, so crowded, so often in public, felt He must always give thanks for food, always ask the Father's blessing upon it or bless it Himself, then surely we, too, ought never to taste food except with a prayer that God will bless it and with grateful hearts to the bountiful Creator who gave it.

This custom of the Saviour in blessing bread was poignantly remembered among His disciples. When Jesus had risen from the dead and walked one day on the road to Emmaus and drew near to two disciples, their grieved hearts were inattentive to the Stranger who walked beside them. And their eyes were temporarily blinded that they should not know the risen Saviour. Their hearts burned within them as He opened to them the Scriptures, but they did not recognize Him until they sat together for their supper at some little inn or home in Emmaus. Then, "it came to pass, as he sat at meat with them, he took bread, and blessed it, and brake, and gave to them. And their eyes were opened, and they knew him; and he vanished out of their sight" (Luke 24:30, 31). You see, the blessing of the bread was such a custom with Jesus that the disciples instantly recognized Him by this action. Oh, that we were as careful to give God the praise and to ask His blessing as was the Lord Jesus Himself!

The twenty-seventh chapter of Acts gives us the graphic story of the shipwreck in the Mediterranean when Paul and his 275 companions were driven for fourteen days in the doomed ship before a tempest and then were cast upon an island. Read the following thrilling words and see how Paul thanked God for food in the midst of terror on every side.

"And while the day was coming on, Paul besought them all to take meat, saying, This day is the fourteenth day that ye have tarried and continued fasting, having taken nothing. Wherefore I pray you to take some meat: for this is for your health: for there shall not an hair fall from the head of any of you. And when he had thus spoken, he took bread, and gave thanks to God in presence of them all; and when he had broken it, he began to eat. Then were they all of good cheer, and they also took some meat. And we were in all in the ship two hundred threescore and sixteen souls."—Acts 27:33-37.

It must have been poor, cold, stale bread that Paul ate and had others eat that day in the midst of the tempest as the day came on. Paul gave devout thanks to God! In such trouble, with their lives evidently in jeopardy, Paul might have been excused if he had held onto the ship's rigging with one hand and eaten with the other and had forgotten the formality of thanking God. He might have thought, "I am thankful in my heart, but this is no time for the niceties of an orderly meal." Or Paul might have thought that he, a prisoner, was in poor position to be leading in a prayer of thanksgiving among those 275 others, some of them officers, some soldiers, some passengers, and some prisoners like himself. But that did not deter Paul. God had provided the food. Paul wanted to eat it with a grateful heart. So there on the lurching ship Paul "took bread, and gave thanks to God in presence of them all." Thanksgiving at meals was an unbreakable custom with Paul and grew out of a heart of gratitude to God for His never-failing mercies.

There is a special promise for those who give thanks to God for food. In I Timothy 4:1-5 we read:

"Now the Spirit speaketh expressly, that in the latter times some shall depart from the faith, giving heed to seducing spirits, and doctrines of devils; Speaking lies in hypocrisy; having their conscience seared with a hot iron; Forbidding to marry, and commanding to abstain from meats, which God hath created to be received with thanksgiving of them which believe and know the truth. For every creature of God is good, and nothing to be refused, if it be received with thanksgiving: For it is sanctified by the word of God and prayer."

Several facts are stated in this Scripture about thanksgiving for food. (1) God created meat "to be received with thanksgiving of them which believe and know the truth." It is a fundamental plan of God who made food that it should be received with thanksgiving by all those who know God. (2) Any kind of meat is good for food, whether pork which Jews under the ceremonial law refused or the beef and lamb which they accepted. The important thing is not whether it is beef or pork but whether one thanks God for it. There are now no ceremonial restrictions on the kind of food people eat, just so they thank God for it. (3) The food itself is blessed by the Word of God and prayer.

I believe that the family in which the people always thank God for food, in which the children are taught to be reverent and grateful, and in which Scripture is used in family worship ought to expect better health than families which do not so thank God. God has sanctified the food in such a home. It will be blessed to better health and to more enjoyment by the kindly, loving God who gave it, if it be received with thanksgiving.

Christian people should always thank God for meals even in a public place. If you are in a restaurant alone you need not pray aloud, perhaps, but you can bow your head and thank God. If two Christians or more are in a public eating place, nothing could be more proper than that they should bow their heads and one of them should modestly thank God for the food and ask His blessing upon it. Someone may feel it is a show of Christianity and that it might leave a bad impression upon the onlookers. On the contrary, no one in the world, I think, would say that it is out of place to thank God, and no one would feel that thanks for food was improper. Rather, if one has any sense of decency, he will say that the man who believes in God ought to be grateful to Him. Certainly one who did not appear to be grateful would be giving a poor testimony of his Saviour in the public place. I have made the simple resolution that anywhere I could not feel free to thank God for food, I ought not to eat. Anywhere I cannot take my Lord with me and give Him due credit, I ought not to go.

If I eat in a home of others who do not ask me to pray or give thanks and who do not themselves give thanks, perhaps I would not always speak up boldly and ask that we all bow our heads. Paul did that on the ship where he was a prisoner. I think usually if a Christian wanted to thank God for food nearly anywhere people would respect him for it. But if one eats at the table with others who are not Christians and does not feel like asking them to join him in thanks to God, at least he can himself bow his head and silently give thanks to God who is the Maker of every good and perfect gift, and who in unchanging providence blesses us with fresh provision every day.

Who should return thanks at the family table? I think ordinarily the father. If the father is not present, perhaps the mother should do so. Since the father is the head of the home and is to speak for his family as God's deputy in many matters, it seems fitting that the father should speak to God and express the thanks of all hearts for the food. At our home I have usually led in thanks at the table.

However, there is no rule for that. I often have asked at the table, "Who would like to thank God for our food to-day?" And some one of the family volunteered. Sometimes I have called on one or another by name.

I think it is all right for little children to thank God for food. For that purpose perhaps they ought to be taught some little prayer and taught the meaning of it. Then in that prayer they may express the gratitude of their hearts until they are able more freely to frame the words from their own hearts. But it is my judgment that usually forms are not best and that each one ought to thank God from his heart. Surely the prayer of thanks should be genuine and every heart around the table ought to be taught to praise God earnestly for the food which He has given.

Sometimes the baby of the family is taught to return thanks for food. But too often this is only play to the child, and mother and father proudly show him off to visitors and have him repeat his cute words of thanks. But they are thinking more of how bright the child is than of how good God is to give the food, I fear. Let the thanksgiving be sincere and genuine. If little children give thanks, let them be taught to do it earnestly and simply and not to be heard by men, and certainly not to show off before company. And while the children are taught to thank God, the father, or some other member of the family, should earnestly express the thanks of the family assembled.

IV. The Children's Bedtime Prayers

> Now I lay me down to sleep,
> I pray the Lord my soul to keep;
> If I should die before I wake,
> I pray the Lord my soul to take;
> And this I ask for Jesus' sake. Amen.

How many thousands of little children have sleepily said the words of this little bedtime prayer as mothers knelt beside them by the bed or as they knelt by mothers' rockers with their heads perhaps upon their mothers' knees!

There are many reasons why it is wise to have prayer with the little ones before they go to bed. It is a time of good-bye.

Little children hate to go to bed and go to sleep. They sometimes dread the dark. More often they do not want to leave the excitement of company and the fascinating things that grown people do after little children go to bed! At any rate, there ought to be a little ceremony and a solemn prayer to God, to make bedtime holy and give a restful peace to children's hearts.

After a little memorized prayer, the child should be taught to add some honest petitions of his own, like "God bless Daddy, and God bless Mama, and God bless Grandmother," and should remember to ask God to bless his brothers and sisters by name. When my youngest daughter was taught to pray, sometimes the Lord's prayer and sometimes "Now I lay me," she was taught always to follow with simple words of her own. She came to trust Christ as her Saviour when she was five years old, so most of the time she had a right to call God her Father. We taught her to say, "Help me to be a good girl and mind Mother and Daddy." Often she prayed for people who have been in the home during the day, or for her schoolmates, or for her teacher. It is perfectly proper for mother or daddy to suggest to the little one the things for which he or she ought to pray.

The childhood prayer ought not to be raced off without attention and as a mere form. The child should feel that he is in the presence of God and that he is honestly making petition to a loving Heavenly Father who is willing to hear and who longs to bless him.

Take time for the prayers at bedtime. Sometimes the child kneels by mother or daddy. We have found it nice that mother or daddy should kneel by the bedside and pray and then have the little one pray. Then the child can be tucked into bed and given the good-night kiss. Sometimes it is necessary for an older sister to pray with the child. But always it ought to be a time very sweet and precious, and it certainly will be that to the child if the father or mother takes time and takes it seriously.

When my older daughters were very small I thought perhaps there was too much form and ceremony about the bedtime prayers. Although we taught them to pray, we did not make a ritual of the bedtime prayer. I wish now that we had. It has been very precious with our younger children and I am sure has been as sweet to the father and mother as it has been helpful to the little ones.

V. Prayers for Special Occasions as Needed

There is good reason to have regular times of prayer. But certainly there are many reasons also for having special prayers on special occasions.

Blessed is the Christian who forms the habit of turning naturally to God in prayer every time a special need arises. Since the members of a Christian family should be very intimate and near to one another, of course there will be many occasions through the day to pray or to thank God.

After we moved from Dallas, Texas, to Wheaton, Illinois, in 1940, I took the entire family back to Texas on a brief visit. While there I preached in the home church where I had been pastor for years. On our return we followed a very common custom. At the start of a journey we pray for guidance and for safety and for happiness on the road. On this particular day of which I speak we asked God to keep us on the right road, to make us happy together on our vacation trip, and particularly we asked God to help us find some precious soul that we could win that day.

In Oklahoma we got on the wrong highway. There had been a detour and perhaps I did not watch the signs as closely as I might. At any rate, we found ourselves some thirty miles off the road. We stopped at a filling station to inquire the road. I felt a little strange that God had allowed us to miss the road after we had so definitely prayed for His guidance. But there I found an openhearted man who needed the Gospel. He was hungry for forgiveness and salvation. He was glad to pray with me and asked the Lord Jesus to come into his heart and forgive his sins. Earnestly he thanked me for talking to him about his soul. I left some tracts with him, urged him to make his conversion known to the public and to get in a church with God's people, and we went on our way. A chorus arose from the car, my daughters reminding me that we had prayed just an hour or two before that God would guide us on the journey and that He would help us to win a soul that day! God led us out of our way to the soul we prayed for. They were happy that they had joined with me in the prayer and that they had seen the answer too.

Always when we start on a journey we ask God for His protection. No doubt that is one reason why we have never had any serious accident in many tens of thousands of miles of driving.

Nearly every child is at some time or other afraid of storms, afraid of lightning and thunder. So we have found it wise with each of our children when they become frightened simply to stop and pray. We teach the child that God watches over His children and that we are perfectly safe to trust in Him. When there is the example of a father and mother who are cheerful and unmoved by the lightning and thunder and wind, and of older children likewise unafraid, and the sweet comfort that comes from the Word of God that He watches over His own and a definite prayer that God will take care of us, most little children are then no longer afraid. All of our children very soon became happily accustomed to trusting the Lord in such matters and are now unaffected by any weather conditions or normal hazards.

In the junior high school, in the room with one of my daughters, a little boy was taken suddenly sick with polio, and died within two days. My daughter came home deeply distressed partly from grief and I think partly from fear. Mrs. Rice promptly sat down and read with her the marvelous ninety-first Psalm. "He that dwelleth in the secret place of the most High shall abide under the shadow of the Almighty. I will say of the Lord, He is my refuge and my fortress: my God; in him will I trust. Surely he shall deliver thee from the snare of the fowler, and from the noisome pestilence. He shall cover thee with his feathers, and under his wings shalt thou trust: his truth shall be thy shield and buckler. Thou shalt not be afraid for the terror by night; nor for the arrow that flieth by day; Nor for the pestilence that walketh in darkness; nor for the destruction that wasteth at noonday. . . . Because thou hast made the Lord which is my refuge, even the most High, thy habitation; There shall no evil befall thee, neither shall any plague come nigh thy dwelling. For he shall give his angels charge over thee, to keep thee in all thy ways" (Ps. 91:1-6, 9-11). After such Scriptures and a quiet prayer of committal to the Lord, my daughter's fears were gone and her heart was comforted and she could eat again and be happy.

It is obvious that many occasions will arise when two of the family or all of the family ought to have prayer together over some special need or for comfort in some trouble or for forgiveness for some sin.

Sometimes when it has been necessary to punish one of the children we have talked it over and the child has been willing to confess with tears her sin. And then we went together to God in prayer asking Him to forgive the little one and to help her do right in the future.

I believe that the prayers of little children need not be just a form. I believe that God hears the prayer of a child who is taught to pray in faith, taught to pray in the will of God, and on the basis of promises in the Scripture. Prayer, if resorted to continually about commonplace needs, can become the most real and precious thing in the life of a child who has been taught to trust Christ and love the Lord.

Years ago my daughter, who was then seven, lost a report card from school. After looking far and near, high and low, she and her mother decided to pray about it. When the little girl, kneeling by her bed, had prayed for God to help her find the lost card, she opened her eyes, and, lo, they fell upon the lost article at once! She praised God for it, laughed for joy, and wrote her daddy how God had answered her prayer.

One time we got into the car to go to the office. Several of the daughters in the summertime were working full time in the Sword of the Lord Publishers office. I should be there at eight-thirty for the period of devotion and prayer. The car would not start. There was gas in the gas tank. Nothing that I knew of was wrong, and yet the car did not start. After stepping on the starter several times I sat rather nonplused. Joy, then seven years old, who sat beside me, said, "Daddy, I know what we should do!" Rather facetiously and with not much good humor, I answered, "Yes, I suppose we could push the car down the street."

"No, that was not what I meant," she said.

"Then what could we do, dear?" I asked.

"We could pray!" she said, very quietly.

Rebuked in my heart, I bowed my head and there aloud asked God to help us start the car, since I had already done all I knew to do and we would be late for the office time of worship which began at eight-thirty unless we could go at once. After the prayer I stepped on the starter, the motor caught at once, and we went on our way. My heart was greatly blessed. I believe God cared about our prayers and that it is proper and right to pray about such matters. He has started my car for me many a time when I could not.

These are only illustrations of the fact that there ought to be many times of special prayer in a Christian home and family.

My good wife and I have had some precious times of prayer in the night when each of us was awake. We often pray together at bedtime and some days we pray several times during the day about various problems that arise.

About the Temple at Jerusalem, Jesus said, "It is written, My house shall be called the house of prayer." But every home ought also to be a house of prayer. Blessed is a family that remembers to pray, not only at the regular appointed seasons of prayer but on special occasions as need arises or as the heart feels the call to pray.

CHAPTER XVI

Teaching the Bible in the Home

"And these words, which I command thee this day, shall be in thine heart: And thou shalt teach them diligently unto thy children, and shalt talk of them when thou sittest in thine house, and when thou walkest by the way, and when thou liest down, and when thou risest up. And thou shalt bind them for a sign upon thine hand, and they shall be as frontlets between thine eyes. And thou shalt write them upon the posts of thy house, and on thy gates."—Deut. 6:6-9.

"Therefore shall ye lay up these my words in your heart and in your soul, and bind them for a sign upon your hand, that they may be as frontlets between your eyes. And ye shall teach them your children, speaking of them when thou sittest in thine house, and when thou walkest by the way, when thou liest down, and when thou risest up. And thou shalt write them upon the door posts of thine house, and upon thy gates: That your days may be multiplied, and the days of your children, in the land which the Lord sware unto your fathers to give them, as the days of heaven upon the earth."—Deut. 11:19-21.

"And that from a child thou hast known the holy scriptures, which are able to make thee wise unto salvation through faith which is in Christ Jesus. All scripture is given by inspiration of God, and is profitable for doctrine, for reproof, for correction, for instruction in righteousness."—II Tim. 3:15, 16.

Where it is revered and taught and believed and followed, the Bible is certainly the most potent civilizing influence in the world. It is the most powerful influence both for morals and happiness. It is not simply the church which is uplifting and blessed in its influence on human society; but it is the church as it teaches and preaches and practices the Bible, as it knows the Christ of the Bible, as it has the salvation and life offered in the Bible, and as it promotes the righteousness of God revealed there.

Christianity is the religion of a Book, the Bible. The Christ

275

of Christianity is the Christ of the Bible, the Messiah, foretold in the Old Testament, the Jesus of the Gospels, the Lord Jesus Christ of the epistles, the virgin-born Son of God. There is no authentic Christianity which does not accept the infallible authority of the Bible.

Hence, the home where the husband and father says with Joshua (Josh. 24:15), "As for me and my house, we will serve the Lord," must be a home where the Bible is believed and loved and taught and lived.

The home-taught Bible is the greatest source of moral character. Homes where the Bible is diligently taught to the children and where the Lord Jesus becomes their own Saviour and Lord will have no child delinquency problem. Sound habits, a social conscience, and moral responsibility follow the light of the Word of God into the minds of children.

Do you want your children educated? The beloved Dr. William Lyon Phelps, I believe, said that a knowledge of the Bible was worth more than a college education in value both for happiness and usefulness. "The fear of the Lord is the beginning of wisdom" (Prov. 9:10), and the Bible is the foundation of all true education, the best of all teaching on literature, ethics, philosophy, history, humanity and religion.

But it is imperative that your child know the Bible for the most important reason in the world, that he may be led to know Christ as his own Saviour. "That from a child thou hast known the holy scriptures, which are able to make thee wise unto salvation" (II Tim. 3:15), wrote the Apostle Paul, and he continued, "All scripture is given by inspiration of God, and is profitable for doctrine, for reproof, for correction, for instruction in righteousness" (II Tim. 3:16). God's holy Word is given by divine inspiration and is therefore most profitable for doctrine (teaching), for correction, for instruction in righteousness. By careful, spiritual teaching of the Bible, parents can win their children to Christ and correct their faults and instruct them in right living.

God Commands His Word Be Taught in the Home

The home is the best place in the world to teach the Bible. *That is where God puts the responsibility.* Deuteronomy 6:6, 7 says, "And these words, which I command thee this day, shall be in thine heart: And thou shalt teach them diligently unto thy children, and shalt talk of them when thou sittest in thine house, and when thou walkest by the way, and when thou liest down, and when thou risest up." Note the divine language says, "Thy children." The teaching is to be done "when thou sittest in thine house, and when thou walkest by the way, and when thou liest down, and when thou risest up." That is a clear picture of parents teaching the Word of God to their children in the home. And it is a picture of such diligent, earnest, line-upon-line, precept-upon-precept teaching, woven through all the fabric of home life as could not be adequately done anywhere else but in the home.

"And thou shalt bind them for a sign upon thine hand, and they shall be as frontlets between thine eyes. And thou shalt write them upon the posts of thy house, and on thy gates" (Deut. 6:8, 9), says the Word of God. This pictures Scripture texts always on the heart and on the tongue of father and mother, Scripture mottoes on the wall and on the gate, Scriptures always before the eyes and consciousness of the children.

A similar passage in Deuteronomy 11:18-20, after which verse 21 says, "That your days may be multiplied, and the days of your children, in the land which the Lord sware unto your fathers to give them, as the days of heaven upon the earth." Here we are told that a home may be a place of "heaven upon the earth," if there the commands of God are so loved and taught; and that a nation of such Bible-teaching homes will be one of long and untroubled lives.

You see, God clearly commands that His Word be taught to children in the home. Again, Ephesians 6:4 says, "And, ye fathers, provoke not your children to wrath: but bring them up in the nurture and admonition of the Lord." "Nurture" is translated from a word usually translated "chastening," but "the admonition of the Lord" must mean the teachings and commands of the Bible. Fathers are to bring up their children in the teachings of the Word of God.

It must be observed that God addresses "ye fathers" about the Bible teachings in the home. Fathers and husbands are first accountable for the Christian life in the home, and so are responsible for seeing that the children are taught the Word of God. In I Corinthians 14:35 women are commanded to be in silence at church, as far as speaking in public before mixed crowds is concerned; and "if they will learn any thing, let them ask their husbands at home." You see, husbands are to know the Bible, are to be at the head of the

Bible teaching in the home, authorities to whom their wives
may safely go for spiritual help and scriptural wisdom. Honest Christian husbands and fathers must accept the responsibility for the Bible teaching in the home.

That does not mean that men will do all the Bible teaching
to the children, nor even most of it, necessarily. Mothers are
usually with the children more than fathers, they have more
leisure, often, than fathers; and women are ideally fitted by
God's goodness for teaching little ones, particularly in storytelling, the method so useful with little children. As women
often spend most of the money of the family, under the direction and authority of their husbands, they certainly may and
should do much of the Bible teaching. But there is a serious
responsibility that men are given from God of teaching their
children of heavenly things.

Outside Agencies Can Never Do Adequate Bible Teaching

The Bible teaching which parents are commanded to give
their children simply cannot be adequately done outside the
home.

1. *The Sunday school does not have time enough.* The Sunday school, at best, in a session of one hour or sometimes
slightly more, gives not more than thirty minutes of time
each week to the actual teaching of the Bible. How much
arithmetic, or reading, or English, would a child learn in half
an hour a week? No child will adequately learn the Bible in
such limited time. But notice, I said the Sunday school *at best*
gives not over thirty minutes to Bible teaching, the rest of the
period being given to singing, records, preliminaries, etc. But
the average Sunday school does far less than the best in Bible
teaching, for a number of reasons: (a) The lesson is usually
taught from a quarterly which may or may not actually ex-
pound the Scripture and make it plain. (b) Much of Sunday
school literature is worse than useless, actually teaching that
the Bible is not inspired of God, is not reliable in history or
science and that its teachings about Hell, atonement, regeneration and judgment are not true. (c) Often Sunday school
teachers are worldly or even unconverted, and so are woefully
unfit to understand or teach the child about God. Spiritual
truths are spiritually discerned, and one who is not taught
by the Holy Spirit of God cannot understand and cannot suc-

cessfully or even safely teach others to understand Bible truth. (d) Most Sunday school teachers are only volunteer teachers, not trained to teach, and not real students of the Bible. With the best of intentions, converted and sincere teachers often waste much of the Sunday school hour. Planning parties, making nature study notebooks, drawing pictures, and reading aloud from the quarterly often take up the lesson period.

I think it surely must be obvious to the thoughtful reader that Sunday schools, while certainly good when teachers are true to the Bible, are utterly unable to teach as much of the Bible as God says needs to be taught to children. And through many years of experience I have learned that most people who have attended Sunday school regularly for years have never even read the Bible through once, do not understand the great doctrines of the Bible, and cannot quote from memory correctly a single chapter of the Bible (usually excepting the Twenty-third Psalm) nor even twenty-five precious promises of the Bible!

2. *Other church activities are also inadequate in Bible teaching to children.*

The preaching services of a church ought to be, and often are in Bible-believing churches, really profitable in Bible teaching. But often younger children do not attend the preaching services, the sermons are usually not planned to hold the attention of children and in many cases have little Bible content. Only at its best is preaching exposition of Scripture, practical, spiritual and easily understood. The "lecture" method, even then, is not enough for children.

The daily vacation Bible schools, when in the hands of well-trained, spiritually capable workers, majoring on actually teaching the Bible, as they often do in fundamental Christian circles, are amazingly successful in teaching God's Word to children. I have seen again and again where such schools, meeting several hours daily for two or three weeks, using object lessons, flannelgraph board technique, gospel choruses, and teaching both small classes and mass groups, have given a child more interest in and knowledge of the Bible than long years of Sunday school had given. In one such two-weeks' session a child may learn dozens of Scripture verses and their meaning, learn the choicest Bible stories, and learn the plan of salvation clearly enough to trust Christ for salvation himself and show others how to be saved.

But the daily vacation Bible school is an intensive course that can last only a few days in the year, and its lessons may not be ingrained into character as daily, year-round teaching will be. It is good but not enough.

3. *The public school cannot adequately teach the Bible.*

It would be good for the Word of God to be read in public schools daily. But how many teachers are adequately prepared, either in knowledge or spirit, to teach the Bible? And Catholics would not have Protestants teaching their children the Bible, with any spiritual application, nor would Protestants have Catholic teachers, nor would Jews be pleased with either Catholic or Protestant teaching. Certainly Bible-believers would not consent to have modernistic infidels or atheists teaching their children. The public school cannot do it.

Even the religious instruction given for credit in some schools or in nearby churches in compatible groups by well-trained instructors is not adequate. Usually the teaching is so watered down to offend no denomination or shade of opinion that it is poorer than the average of Sunday school teaching. Dallas, Texas, has a good textbook on the outline of Bible history and narrative with little offensive doctrine taught by approved teachers in churches. Chattanooga, Tennessee, largely Protestant and Bible-believing, has the best Bible teaching in schools I have ever seen, inaugurated under the supervision of a Christian gentleman who is headmaster of a fine military academy with well-trained, orthodox volunteer teachers. But even at best, no Bible teaching can take the place of that which should be done at home. There is not enough of it, it is not doctrinal enough nor definite enough nor practical enough. At worst, "Bible teaching," so-called, in public schools or even in universities, is damning with infidelity, is cursed with unbelief, is poisoned with anti-Christian sentiment of wicked teachers.

4. *Teaching outside the home cannot meet the home problems, the moral and spiritual problems of the child, adequately.*

One of my daughters when she was little, was afraid of the thunder and lightning at night. Awakened by the storm, trembling and weeping, she groped to her mother's and father's bed. That was the time to teach her the verse of Scripture, "What time I am afraid, I will trust in thee" (Ps. 56:3), and "The angel of the Lord encampeth round about them that fear him, and delivereth them" (Ps. 34:7). Taught that God was everywhere watching, loving and keeping His own, and fortified by the Word of God straight from His Book, she was never much frightened by storms afterward. That was Bible teaching fitted to the daily need, impossible to be done so aptly at any other place or time as at home at the time needed.

As a small boy of five, dressed up for church, I told my mother a lie. With tears and trembling lips, my mother dropped on her knees beside me and told me how God hates a lie, told me about the commandment, "Thou shalt not bear false witness" (Exod. 20:16), and that Satan "is a liar, and the father of it" (John 8:44). I was so convicted that I felt myself a guilty sinner in the sight of God. I believe I became accountable to God as a conscious sinner that day. I have hated a lie ever since then as something horrible.

So the Scripture needs to be applied to moral problems as they arise, and by those who know the child's needs most in the home life, his own father and mother. The child on public behavior in church or schoolroom is not known as his parents know him. He must have the instruction or correction of Scripture applied to his heart by his parents if it is to master his life.

How the Home Bible Teaching Should Be Done

I can only suggest here some ways that Bible teaching should be done in the home.

1. *In the family worship period.*

I have elsewhere suggested that at the family worship period daily, at least one chapter of the Bible (unless of unusual length and difficulty) be read. I suggested that the reading be consecutive, chapter by chapter, through one book of the Bible, then through another, and then all, or nearly all, of the Bible be read so through the years. The actual reading of the Scriptures themselves with all the family looking on and taking part, to insure careful attention, will result in a wonderful store of Scripture knowledge and an understanding of spiritual truths.

To make this worship period more effective in teaching the Bible to all, the father (or mother when necessary) should do the following:

(a) Prepare ahead of time by looking over the Scriptures

to be used, giving thought to doubtful questions and looking up the necessary answers if he or she does not know.

(b) Call special attention to especially helpful verses, explaining some of them. Do not go into boresome detail, but arouse interest and satisfy it with honest explanations as far as possible.

(c) Suggest some verses to memorize. Interrupt the reading, or omit occasionally, to drill on verses memorized.

(d) Stop and apply the Scriptures occasionally to daily life, to gently rebuke a failure, to warn of a temptation.

(e) Stop and pray over failures and faults which are brought to mind by the Scriptures read.

The daily reading with such prayerful attention will prove very heplful in learning the Word of God and in applying the spirit of its teachings to the heart and daily life.

2. *Bible teaching by storytelling is easy.*

"Daddy, tell me a story," has been the plea of all my six daughters, often repeated before they could talk plainly. Children love stories. They love Bible stories best of all because they are "truly, truly stories." Children are always disappointed when they learn that they have been lied to about Santa Claus, that dogs and cats do not talk as they were supposed to do in fairy tales, and that this sad world really has no fairies with magic wands, no Aladdin's lamp, no magic carpets. Thank God we can tell them Bible stories that are fully as interesting, with the assurance that they will never prove a disillusionment but will be a joy all their lives.

The Bible is the most interesting book in the world. There are some uninterested people, but there are no uninteresting parts of the Bible. Every home that has children should make much of the golden stories of the Word of God. Here is an inexhaustible storehouse. We suggest that you try the following:

Adam and Eve in the Garden of Eden and the first sin

Cain and Abel.

Noah, the ark, and the flood.

Abraham, the friend of God, and Sarah, and how Isaac was born in answer to prayer when they were old.

Lot, the man who put money first, and the story of Sodom.

How Isaac got a bride.

The story of Jacob and Esau.

The story of Joseph.

The baby Moses.

Israel coming out of Egypt, the plagues and the Red Sea miracles.

The manna from Heaven, the grumbling Israelites, and the fiery serpents.

Crossing the Jordan and the capture of Jericho.

David and Goliath.

David and Jonathan.

Samson, the strongest man who ever lived.

The love story of Ruth.

Esther, the Jewish girl who became queen.

The story of Elijah.

How Sennacherib's army was slain by God's angel.

The story of Daniel in the lions' den.

Three Hebrew boys in the fiery furnace.

The handwriting on the wall and the fall of Babylon.

The story of John the Baptist.

The birth of Jesus.

The prodigal son.

The raising of Lazarus.

The crucifixion of Jesus.

The conversion of Saul.

Paul's shipwreck.

The above are only samples. The Bible is full of fascinating stories.

There are several ways that Bible stories may be used.

(a) Parents may read from Bible story books to the children. Hurlbut's *Story of the Bible* is an old favorite. The stories are well told, interesting, and generally true to the Bible. However, there is not much doctrinal content.

Egermeier's Bible Story Book by Elsie Egermeier is better, I think, than Hurlbut's.

Very often one many find smaller books of Bible stories. We suggest that you write to the publishers of this book or to other orthodox Christian publishing houses.

Parents who do not feel able to tell stories of the Bible without help may read these stories to their children. It is probable that soon they will be able to tell the same stories. It is a wonderful fact that children like to hear the same stories over and over again. Then as the children grow old enough to read they will like to read the same stories for themselves.

(b) Parents may tell the stories from the Bible to the children. That is really not at all hard. If mothers or fathers will sit down and read the story of Joseph through two or three times, they will find that they get enough of the story to tell it happily to the children. The children will be uncritical and delighted. Then read the story over again a time or two to freshen your mind, and tell it again. Do not be surprised if the children ask lots of interesting questions about what certain words mean and what happened next. A big part of the Bible is fitted to tell to children and is most interesting and profitable. By all means, apply the moral of the story. The Bible is a book of instruction from Almighty God and no one need be ashamed to let the Bible speak for itself and teach what it wants to teach. Bible stories used as intended will have a tremendous effect on character development. And, incidentally, by learning to tell the stories to the children the father and mother become familiar with the precious Book themselves and grow in grace wonderfully. It is really much more simple than it sounds.

(c) Read the stories directly out of the Bible. The King James authorized version of the Bible has a stately and beautiful, but generally very simple, language. Try the story of Joseph as a continued story, reading one chapter a night, before the children's bedtime, as an example. Jonah makes a good continued story and so do the Gospels of Matthew, Mark and Luke and the book of Acts. Children will understand the parable of the ten virgins in Matthew 25, the story of the prodigal son, and the story of the lost sheep, even if they do not get all of the meaning.

For little tiny tots Bible stories in mother's simple language, or daddy's, may be best but as a usual thing the language of the Scriptures, God's inspired language translated into English, is preferable to all other. The Word of God itself "is quick, and powerful" (Heb. 4:12). God said, "Is not my word like as a fire . . . and like a hammer that breaketh the rock in pieces?" (Jer. 23:29). And Jesus said, "Heaven and earth shall pass away, but my words shall not pass away" (Matt. 24:35). There is life in the very words of the Bible, and often the wonderful words of life should be read out of God's own Book to the children. They will not understand all of it, but they will understand much of it and will grow in holy reverence for the Word of God. They will ask lots of questions. And the same Scriptures may be read frequently. Take time to explain hard words if necessary, read slowly and with interest, and God will bless the story.

In 1930 I was in Akron, Ohio, in a revival campaign, and

my wife was reading through the book of Matthew with the children, a chapter each night, in our home in Fort Worth. Three little tots gathered on their tiny chairs and stools about her knees while she read. Grace was seven, Mary Lloys five, Elizabeth about three, I think. Night after night they listened with deep interest to a chapter or two or three. One night Mrs. Rice came to the story of the crucifixion in Matthew 27. Tenderhearted little Mary Lloys suddenly began to weep and said, "Mother, I want to be saved!" She was accustomed to prayer in the home, the talk about people being saved, and the need for a Saviour. As she heard the story of our Saviour's death at the hand of sinners, dying in our stead, her heart could delay no longer her personal surrender to Him. She probably does not remember all the details of that Bible reading now, but the effect upon her heart and character is indelibly engraved. Oh, mothers, fathers, read the Word of God to your children!

MY MOTHER'S BIBLE

There's a dear and precious book, though it's worn
    and faded now,
  Which recalls those happy days of long ago;
When I stood at mother's knee, with her hand upon my brow,
  And I heard her voice in gentle tones and low.

As she read the stories o'er, of those mighty men of old,
  Of Joseph and of Daniel and their trials;
Of little David bold, who became a King at last;
  Of Satan with his many wicked wiles.

Then she read of Jesus' love, as He blest the children dear,
  How He suffered, bled and died upon the tree;
Of His heavy load of care, then she dried my flowing tears
  With her kisses as she said it was for me.

Well those days are past and gone, but their mem'ry
    lingers still,
  And the dear old Book each day has been my guide;
And I seek to do His will, as my mother taught me then,
  And ever in my heart His words abide.

The Bible can become very precious to little children, almost in their infancy. Mothers and fathers who read the Bible to their children may find it said of their sons and daughters, as it was said to Timothy, "From a child thou hast known the holy scriptures, which are able to make thee wise unto salvation" (II Tim. 3:15).

3. *Teaching the Bible in memory work.*

"Thy word have I hid in mine heart, that I might not sin against thee" (Ps. 119:11). It is important that every child, and every adult, too, learn much of the Bible by memory. But it is easier to memorize in childhood at the ages from eight to twelve or thirteen, which is properly called "the golden age of memory." Children are not only able to memorize but like to do so when it is made attractive, and they like the element of contest and rivalry often introduced in learning and practicing memory work.

In our home we have memorized, parents and children, the following Psalms: the first, the eighth, the fifteenth, the nineteenth, the twenty-third, the twenty-fourth, the thirty-fourth, the thirty-seventh, the fifty-first, the one hundredth, the one hundred third, the one hundred twenty-first, the one hundred twenty-sixth. As I remember we also learned part of the twenty-seventh and part of the ninety-first Psalms. Some of the Psalms we have quoted often and fixed in memory well. Perhaps the children could not now quote fully a number of them without looking on the Bible. I could not quote all of them from memory. From the New Testament we have memorized the Beatitudes and the Lord's Prayer, and from the Old Testament the Ten Commandments. We memorized the third chapter of John, the fourteenth chapter of John, the eighth chapter of Romans, the twelfth chapter of Romans, the fifteenth chapter of Luke, the twenty-eighth chapter of Matthew, and the thirteenth chapter of I Corinthians. Hundreds of other verses through the Bible we have memorized.

Some of this memory work was done at the family worship period at the breakfast table. Some was done as we drove in the car on vacation trips. Some was done by individual studying, as prizes were offered for the memorizing of entire chapters. They would learn so many verses and recite them and then go back to learn more and recite them. Mrs. Rice and I always tried to learn as much as the children did, though it really seemed much harder for us, particularly for me in late years with many, many burdens. Sometimes I challenged the children that I would learn a Psalm as quickly as they did. I think nearly all of them learned the thirty-fourth Psalm before I could learn it, and I never got it perfectly. We encouraged the learning of memory verses in connection with Sunday school lessons and with daily vacation Bible school. How happy and blessed is the child who has his mind filled with the wonderful Word of God, learned in days when the truth can become so absorbed as never to be forgotten!

It will take hard work on the part of the father and mother, but the Word of God will bring as much blessing to them as to the children. Memory work should be encouraged, the proper Scriptures selected, the proper encouragement given, sometimes prizes given and sometimes praise which can certainly help at hard times and places. Then the truth learned in memory verses should be applied to the hearts of the children.

4. *Scripture should be particularly used to teach needed lessons as occasions for them arise.*

This truth is taught in Deuteronomy 6:6, 7, in these words: "And these words, which I command thee this day, shall be in thine heart: And thou shalt teach them diligently unto thy children, and shalt talk of them when thou sittest in thine house, and when thou walkest by the way, and when thou liest down, and when thou risest up." Since fathers and mothers are to talk about the words of Scripture "when thou sittest in thine house, and when thou walkest by the way, and when thou liest down, and when thou risest up," it is obvious that Bible teaching must be interspersed with all the conversation and the living in the home.

I was a strong, rather impatient and hot-tempered boy of about seventeen, though a Christian, when my father taught me a great lesson from Scripture. I had been rough to my team on the farm, and he simply said, "Son, the Bible says, 'A righteous man regardeth the life of his beast: but the tender mercies of the wicked are cruel'" (Prov. 12:10). That simple word went to my heart with such force that that one hearing of the verse printed it indelibly on my mind. I never consciously memorized it, but from that time on I remembered it. And I saw that true mercy and kindness in the heart would be reflected in the way I treated the dumb brutes God had given into my care. How powerful those few words from God's Scripture!

We children wanted to go too often to visit in the home of a neighbor, a family greatly loved, and my father said, "No, the Bible says, 'Withdraw thy foot from thy neighbor's house; lest he be weary of thee, and so hate thee'" (Prov. 25:17). When applied to such a personal and practical problem, the Word of God became unforgettable.

All my children were quieted in their fear of storms by verses of Scripture like, "What time I am afraid, I will trust in thee." A member of my office staff tells me that when she was afraid in an electrical storm, the Scripture, "His lightnings enlightened the world: the earth saw, and trembled" (Ps. 97:4), was a great help to her with other Scriptures which show that God controls all these elements and that nothing can hurt His dear ones without His consent. I have already told how the ninety-first Psalm took away the fear of polio in my daughter's heart when one of her schoolmates was suddenly stricken and died. Those verses, "Because thou hast made the Lord, which is my refuge, even the most High, thy habitation; There shall no evil befall thee, neither shall any plague come nigh thy dwelling," have been used to comfort and assure many of God's children. Parents need not let their children grow up afraid when there are so many Scriptures that can apply and will comfort the heart.

A very special example of the blessing of using Scripture and teaching it to the children as occasion demands is in teaching the little ones to trust in Christ as Saviour. Scripture may be used to show that all are sinners and then to show that Christ died to pay for our sins, and that one may have everlasting life by trusting in Him.

If fathers and mothers really talk about words of the Bible when they sit in the house, when they walk by the way, when they lie down and when they rise up, as Deuteronomy 6:7 commands, the Word of God will find lodgment, like seed in good soil, and watered by God's blessed Holy Spirit, will bring forth eternal fruit in the hearts and lives of the children.

5. *Scripture mottoes on the walls unconsciously become part of the lives of those who see them.*

Deuteronomy 6:8, 9 commands concerning the words of God's commandments and His promise that "thou shalt bind them for a sign upon thine hand, and they shall be as frontlets between thine eyes. And thou shalt write them upon the posts of thy house, and on thy gates." It is not difficult thus to keep the Word of God before the whole household by means of little plaques and mottoes available at Bible supply houses and book stores. Some are cast from beautiful aluminum, some are molded from plastic wood or in plaster of Paris and then painted beautiful colors. In my early ministry I was greatly blessed by a picture given to me by a young woman. Upon a beautiful mountain scene she had written in careful and exquisite script Psalm 121:1, "I will lift up mine eyes unto the hills, from whence cometh my help." How often it led me to pray! How often it led me to trust the Saviour when there was no one else to whom I could go for help! The home of Christian people ought to look like the home of Christians. Mottoes and plaques on the walls ought to indicate that this is a house in which people worship God, where God's Word is revered, loved and followed. By all means, have Scripture mottoes and plaques in the home with memory verses from the Bible.

CHAPTER XVII

Winning Children to Christ in the Home

"From a child thou hast known the holy scriptures, which are able to make thee wise unto salvation. . . ."—II Tim. 3:15.

". . . the unfeigned faith that is in thee, which dwelt first in thy grandmother Lois, and thy mother Eunice. . . ."—II Tim. 1:5.

"But Jesus said, Suffer little children, and forbid them not, to come unto me: for of such is the kingdom of heaven."—Matt. 19:14.

". . . and rejoiced, believing in God with all his house."—Acts 16:34.

"As for me and my house, we will serve the Lord."—Josh. 24:15.

It is planned here to show: (1) That children need saving; (2) that parents should show children how to be saved and win them to Christ; (3) that there is real danger in delay and that to discourage or hinder a child from accepting Christ as his own Saviour is a wicked sin; (4) that Christian influence in the home makes children want to be saved and makes it easy to win them; and (5) how actually to win your children to Christ.

I. All Children Old Enough to Be Accountable Need Saving

Many people suppose that if a child be reared in a Christian home, be taught to pray and live right and love God, he will never need definitely to accept Christ for himself and be converted, or saved. That is an idea clearly contrary to the Bible. Children, no matter how well reared, by nature are sinful in heart as are all the human race. If left to natural tendencies they may turn out to be criminals, drunkards, harlots, blasphemers—enemies of God and man. Cain, the first child ever born, in a world with no taverns, no street gangs, no bad literature, no bad companions, turned out to be a murderer. David said of his inherited sinful nature, "I was shapen in iniquity; and in sin did my mother conceive me" (Ps. 51:5). Of all humankind we are told in Scripture that "they go astray as soon as they be born, speaking lies" (Ps. 58:3). So all children are sinful by nature and need a new heart and forgiveness.

Until little children reach the time when they know right from wrong, and so become accountable sinners, of course they are kept safe. After they know themselves to be sinners, after they are sinners by choice as they were before sinners by nature, children are lost sinners, aliens from God, and need to be saved the same as any other unconverted, lost sinner.

Good environment cannot change a bad heart. Only a miracle of God can do that in regeneration. Suppose one took a rattlesnake into the home, fed it on food from the family table, trained it as a pet, let it hear songs and prayers and good advice, and let it be treated only with kindness; still the snake would be a poisonous, dangerous reptile. Training and environment will not take the poison sacs out of its jaws, the rattles from its tail, nor the snake nature out of its reptile heart! So good environment does not make men good nor make children Christians (except as they are taught to come to Christ in their hearts, to trust Him for forgiveness, and thus have a supernatural birth which is wrought by God's Spirit). Christians are made, not by growth and good environment, but by a definite transaction whereby God makes a lost sinner into a Christian, a child of God, when that sinner trusts in Christ as his atoning Substitute and Saviour.

So the Scriptures teach repeatedly. Jesus told Nicodemus, "Verily, verily, I say unto thee, Except a man be born again, he cannot see the kingdom of God" (John 3:3); and, "Verily, verily, I say unto thee, Except a man be born of water and of the Spirit, he cannot enter into the kingdom of God" (John 3:5); and again, "Marvel not that I said unto thee, Ye must be born again" (John 3:7). Nicodemus was a member of the Jewish Sanhedrin, a rabbi, a Pharisee, and therefore a particularly moral and devoted religious leader. But he could not be a Christian without being born again. Neither can you. Neither can your child. There is no substitute for a personal acceptance of Christ as Saviour, a personal decision to trust Him and receive Him.

"He that believeth on him is not condemned: but he that believeth not is condemned already, because he hath not believed in the name of the only begotten Son of God."—John 3:18.

"He that believeth on the Son hath everlasting life: and he that believeth not the Son shall not see life; but the wrath of God abideth on him."—John 3:36.

"He that believeth and is baptized shall be saved; but he that believeth not shall be damned."—Mark 16:16.

You see from an honest interpretation of these Scriptures and many others, that God makes no distinction. One who trusts Christ for salvation is saved; one who has not trusted Christ for salvation, after becoming accountable, is lost. Romans 3:22, 23 states plainly that there are no exceptions. ". . . for there is no difference: For all have sinned, and come short of the glory of God." All alike have sinned. All alike must be saved or remain forever lost. So children need to be saved the same as anybody else.

Many Scriptures indicate that God wants children to come to know Him early. Jesus said, "Suffer little children, and forbid them not, to come unto me: for of such is the kingdom of heaven" (Matt. 19:14). Jesus wants little children to come to Him. Certainly He wants them to come consciously to Him in their hearts in personal trust and surrender.

Ecclesiastes 12:1 says, "Remember now thy Creator in the days of thy youth, while the evil days come not, nor the years draw nigh, when thou shalt say, I have no pleasure in them." Children should turn to God in childhood. So that means they should be won in the homes to know and trust Christ as their own personal Saviour.

II.   Parents, of Course, Are First Responsible to Win Their Children to Christ

Fathers and mothers can never wash their hands of their children nor be excused from their responsibility for the souls of the children God commits to their care.

"And, ye fathers, provoke not your children to wrath; but bring them up in the nurture and admonition of the Lord," says Ephesians 6:4. That command is not addressed to the Sunday school, the church, nor the day school.

"And these words, which I command thee this day, shall

be in thine heart: And thou shalt teach them diligently unto thy children, and shalt talk of them when thou sittest in thine house, and when thou walkest by the way, and when thou liest down, and when thou risest up," says Deuteronomy 6:6, 7. This teaching of the Word of God certainly involves showing the children how to trust Christ as Saviour.

"Train up a child in the way he should go: and when he is old, he will not depart from it," says Proverbs 22:6. That duty of parents certainly involves getting the child right with his Maker. The child thus won to Christ in the home and taught to live for Him, because he is converted and established in Christ, will never leave the Christian way of life.

All of the above Scriptures, and many others, show that the home is the place where children should be led to Christ.

When Paul the apostle came to Derbe and Lystra he found there a young man, Timothy, whom he did not need to win to Christ. Timothy was already saved. Acts 16:1 tells us, "Then came he to Derbe and Lystra: and, behold, a certain disciple was there, named Timotheus, the son of a certain woman, which was a Jewess, and believed; but his father was a Greek." Timothy was already a disciple, a Christian, one who had believed or trusted in Christ.

Who had won Timothy? I think there is no doubt he was won by his mother and his grandmother. His father was a Greek, not a Jew, and I suppose had not known the Old Testament Scriptures which foretold the coming of Christ, the Messiah. But his mother and grandmother were saved and, teaching him the Scriptures, showed Timothy how to be saved. That, I think, is the clear inference of two Scriptures on the subject: "That from a child thou hast known the holy scriptures, which are able to make thee wise unto salvation through faith which is in Christ Jesus" (II Tim. 3:15), and, "When I call to remembrance the unfeigned faith that is in thee, which dwelt first in thy grandmother Lois, and thy mother Eunice" (II Tim. 1:5). Surely it was in the home and by his mother and grandmother that Timothy was taught the Scriptures and taught how to have faith in Christ. And other mothers and fathers as well as grandparents should win their children to Christ also.

III. The Danger of Delay in the Salvation of Children

"How shall we escape, if we neglect so great salvation," says Hebrews 2:3. To delay salvation is dangerous and wicked for anybody. I have carefully counted those who were converted to Christ by certain ages, as publicly acknowledged in large audiences all over America; and I have found that a majority of all Christians become Christians before they are fourteen years old! There are more children saved by the time they are ten years old than there are adults saved after they are twenty-five! So for one to reach the age of fifteen unconverted, not having come to know Christ as a personal Saviour, means that he has already thrown away more than half the opportunities he will ever have to be saved. Unless boys and girls are won to Christ in childhood, usually they are never saved. Most people who do not accept Christ as their Saviour while they still are children go to meet God unprepared, doomed to eternal punishment.

How earnestly, therefore, should parents strive to win their children! The best time to turn the child's heart to Christ is while he is still under the strong influence of the home, before he becomes enamored of the sins of the world. You had better win him before the temptations that come with developing sex consciousness, the temptations of drink, of worldliness, and bad company, and the atheistic teachings in high schools and colleges are pressed upon him.

Children may be led away from the truth by wicked teachers or companions or bad literature. The heart that is not given to Christ early will naturally harden with sin as the days go by. Unsaved children will come to feel their Christian parents are out of date and fanatical about religion if these same sons and daughters are allowed to go on unsaved. Or, children may die. The chance to win your children to Christ will slip through your fingers, dear father or mother, if long neglected.

A beautiful fourteen-year-old girl with lovely blond hair came often to our home in Shamrock, Texas, when I was pastor of the First Baptist Church there. Though she was a member of another church, Goldie often attended our services and sang the alto part in duets with a girl of our congregation. But Goldie died after two days of sudden pneumonia. Since the family were near neighbors and Goldie had been often in our home, I went to comfort them.

Goldie's mother lay across the bed, inconsolable. She did not appear to listen to family or friends who tried to comfort her. Goldie's body lay in state in the parlor, and an hysterical older sister patted the cold cheek and talked to the cold and lifeless form.

"You can see Goldie again," I said to the mother. "She had given herself to Christ, had trusted Him to save her. She was a born-again Christian. You must not weep as if you would never see Goldie again."

As I talked, suddenly the mother sat bolt upright and said to me,

"How do you know Goldie was a Christian? How do you know she was saved?"

"Because I asked her," I said. "She was at my home with Olita Bryan for a meeting of intermediate young people. I asked her if she were saved, and she told me she had trusted Christ in a young people's meeting at the First Methodist Church during a revival campaign. She said she felt assured that her sins were forgiven and she had peace in her heart."

"Oh, thank God!" the mother cried. "Thank God! Thank God! I did not know she was saved. I had never talked to her about it. I had thought there was plenty of time, and now, after she is dead, I have been thinking I had let my girl go to Hell and that I would never see her again!"

How greatly was the mother comforted to know that the little girl, before her sudden death, had been won by others. But how many others who also neglect winning their children lose them without ever having the comfort of knowing they were saved. Parents should know that delay and neglect in winning their children to Christ are tragically dangerous and wrong.

Sometimes parents feel they might well wait until their children decide for themselves that question of faith in Christ. I have even heard foolish talk about leaving the child "freedom of conscience" in his choice about whether or not he would be a Christian. But this question is one of right and wrong, a decision for God or Satan. Questions of moral right and wrong should have all the weight of parents' influence placed squarely on the side of the right.

A mother said to me, "But Brother Rice, my ten-year-old girl thinks everything I do is right. I have such a profound influence over her that I hesitate to tell her she should put her trust in Jesus."

"Would you hesitate to use your influence over her to keep her from stealing? Would you think it unwise to influence her against drinking or immorality?" I asked. "Well, to accept or reject Christ, repenting or not repenting of sin, are as clearly matters of right and wrong as are stealing or honesty, virtue or harlotry. Why do you suppose God ever gave a mother influence over her child, if not to win her to Christ?"

She saw the point, and that day talked to her ten-year-old daughter. That night the child came, glad to acknowledge publicly her acceptance of Christ and her dependence on Him for salvation.

Sometimes I have known a father and mother to hinder their children who wanted to accept Christ. Sometimes it was for fear the child, after becoming a Christian, would join some other church than that of the parents. Sometimes parents were unsaved and so were definitely on the side of Satan and against Christ and God and the Bible. Sometimes such parents feel that the child is too young to make an intelligent decision. But to hinder a decision or to delay it, when a child knows he is a sinner and needs forgiveness and wants to come to Christ and trust Him in the heart, is always wrong. Jesus said, "Suffer little children, and forbid them not, to come unto me: for of such is the kingdom of heaven." He says, 'Allow them to come to Me. Do not forbid them. Little children need to come, and of such children who come to Me is the kingdom of Heaven largely made up.'

When children are honestly taught the Gospel, not simply taught denominational dogma and urged to go through church ceremonies, they may be safely encouraged to decide once and for all to take Christ as a personal Saviour. Christ is ready to receive all such little ones, to put God's Spirit into their hearts and make them into real Christians. It is never wrong to allow and even to encourage a child to accept Christ and to love and trust Him.

Satan never moves a child to want to be a Christian. That, if sincere, is always from the Holy Spirit of God. Even if the child does not fully understand all that is involved in becoming a Christian, yet who would say there is any harm for him to decide to confess his sins to Christ and in his heart to trust the dear Lord Jesus as his own Saviour and so live forever?

It is sometimes wise for a child to delay church membership, to talk with father and mother, to be taught more perfectly by the pastor before going through baptism and church membership and the communion service. But it is never wise to delay or hinder any child from the heart decision to accept Christ as Saviour and to trust and love and follow Him. You had better let the little one's heart get on the right side, consciously, as soon as he feels the need to do so. Then the more complete comprehension of the mind can well follow.

How young may a child know he is a sinner and turn to Christ in penitent faith? Some have supposed that all children become accountable at twelve because Jesus entered the Temple at the age of twelve and confounded the doctors of the law. But such an idea is not even hinted in the Scriptures. Jesus Himself was perfect and sinless and never needed to repent and be converted. His example had nothing to do with the age of accountability. And certainly, if properly taught, most intelligent children will come to be conscious of their sin and their need of a Saviour long before they are twelve.

I was led to Christ when near my ninth birthday. But I had long been conscious of my sinful heart and my need for forgiveness, and if someone I trusted had shown me how, I would have come to Christ for salvation earlier. My six daughters were all led to trust in Christ by the time they were six years old.

For one to be saved so young is unusual, I know. But my children were taught to sing little gospel choruses as soon as they could carry a tune, which was by the time they could talk plainly. They were accustomed to prayer in the home every day. They heard talk about sin and salvation and Jesus. They learned memory verses from the time they were three years old. Each of the six was carried to church services in a basket by the time she was five or six weeks old. All through babyhood and young childhood, most of them were in revival services and heard plain and simple gospel preaching many, many times. Thus, they came to think about spiritual matters when very young. I taught them strictly to obey and that punishment follows sin. Children so reared will early come to be conscious of their sin and their need of a Saviour. Where the Bible is taught in the home children come to the age of accountability much earlier than they otherwise might, I believe.

IV.   Christian Example and Environment Make it Easy to Win Children

It is easy for parents to win their children to Christ if they begin in time and follow God's plan.

First, family discipline prepares the heart of the child to become a Christian. Proverbs 23:14 says, "Thou shalt beat him with the rod, and shalt deliver his soul from hell." God intends the father and mother to represent Him in the home. That is particularly true of fathers. If the father and mother conquer the child's will, inculcate in him a fear of sin and a hate for wrongdoing, a conscience has been established which will take sides with the right, will move the child to want to be a Christian. A child who is spoiled and undisciplined and who does not obey his parents will not want to obey God nor give up his way to trust and love and serve Christ.

Then the example of the father and mother becoming Christians and living the Christian life will have great weight in leading the children to Christ. A beautiful Bible example of that is the case of the Philippian jailer whose conversion is described in Acts 16. "Believe on the Lord Jesus Christ, and thou shalt be saved, and thy house" (Acts 16:31), he was told. He must have taken that word to heart. For not only did he trust in Christ for himself, but with his permission, and we suppose on his invitation, Paul and Silas "spake unto him the word of the Lord, and to all that were in his house." All his household were converted together, and he rejoiced, we are told, "believing in God with all his house."

The jailer believed in Christ, was baptized, and set out to make any restitution possible by washing the stripes on the bloody backs of Paul and Silas and by setting meat before them. The jailer was so wholehearted in his repentance and his acceptance of Christ and in setting out to live openly for God that his whole family followed him in turning to God! When parents set the right example in being saved and in living an open and happy Christian life, it is easy to win children to Christ.

The family altar or worship period, the reading of the Bible, prayer, and Christian conversation help the child to see that to be a Christian is both proper and happy, both profitable and desirable, and these things prepare the child to accept Christ.

If the child is taken to church services where there is evangelistic preaching, if he is kept in a good Sunday school where the truth is taught, these things will all mean that he will expect to be saved, will be called by the Spirit of God, and will want to be saved. Then leading him to trust Christ will be an easy matter which any parent who understands God's simple plan of salvation can do happily. Every father and mother who begin in time and are themselves right with

God can win their children to Christ without the loss of one. Oh, parents, win your children in the home!

V.   How to Do It

Parents should watch closely and pray often for the time when each child becomes conscious of his sin and feels a need to trust in Christ. In Wheaton, Illinois, lived a family who had a little daughter five years old. The mother carefully taught her not to be mean to the baby sister, to be quick to obey and to control her temper. Yet one day the child, when reproved for some wrong, burst into weeping and said, "Mamma, I *can't* be good! I try to, but I *can't!*" The mother showed her that all of us have sinful hearts and need to let Jesus come in, through His Holy Spirit, to make us want to be good, to give us Christian hearts and to help us do right all the time. Eagerly the little girl agreed to pray for Jesus to come into her heart, to forgive her sins, and to help her to be good! The child was ready to be saved, and she showed good evidence that she did take Christ as her Saviour and that He did help her to be good!

My wife and my baby, Joy, then less than five years old, came to be with me a week where I was preaching in a revival campaign in an Illinois town. On a Sunday afternoon there was a baptizing of new converts, and Joy was greatly impressed. She understood that all these had given themselves to Jesus and were converted and should now live for Him. We returned to our room, and as I lay on the bed to rest before the evening service, my little one was solemn. Referring to a little boy eight years old who had been baptized, she said, "Daddy, was that little boy old enough to be saved?"

I told her that I thought so, that he said he knew he was a sinner and then turned his heart to trust in Christ. I saw the deep concern on her face, and I said, "Were you wanting to know whether you were old enough to be saved?"

She said yes, that was what she was thinking. Was she old enough?

"I will tell you how you can know," I said. "There is no set age for people to be saved. But the Bible says, 'For if our heart condemn us, God is greater than our heart, and knoweth all things.' If you know you do wrong and your conscience tells you you need forgiveness, then God knows all about it, and He counts you a sinner, too, and you need to be saved."

As she sat on the bed beside me, my little girl who seemed little more than a baby to me, said she wanted to give her heart to Christ. We went over John 3:16 together. She understood that Jesus died for her, and that if she would trust Him and depend upon Him, He would give her everlasting life and she would never perish. Then I suggested that we pray. I told her that I would pray aloud and asked her to pray in her heart and to tell Jesus, who knew all she was thinking, that she wanted Him to forgive her sins, and to tell Him that she would right then and there accept Him, trust Him and count Him her own Saviour.

I have never had any reason to doubt that she was genuinely saved, born again. Her talk is Christian, her acts are Christian, and I believe she is saved. She has often said to me, "Daddy, I surely am glad I am saved, aren't you?"

How earnestly we should watch for the evidence that our little ones are taking in the truth and can understand the plan of salvation.

I did not insist that Joy be baptized at once. We taught her what baptism meant, and later, when she was seven years old, she was happily baptized.

Let every father and mother learn some simple verses from the Bible on how to be saved. I like specially John 1:12; John 3:16 and John 6:37 for showing a child how to be saved. Do not be afraid they cannot understand the plan of salvation. They can. It is as simple as trusting a doctor when one is sick, as simple as believing mother or daddy forgives a wrongdoing when a child confesses it and they say they will forgive it.

In Fort Worth, Texas, I drove my car up in front of a home, and the family, who had been on the porch and lawn, gathered around the car. A ten-year-old girl came to my side of the car and I put my arm around her and asked her if she were a Christian.

"No," she said. "I wanted to join the church, but Daddy wouldn't let me."

I assured her that no doubt her father simply meant that she was not to join the church until she had really trusted Christ in her heart, that no one could be saved by merely joining a church, and that her father was right that she should not join until she had been converted. Then I asked her if she ever got angry, ever failed to obey or ever did things selfish and wrong. With grave face she said she did, and she knew she was a sinner.

I quoted her John 3:16, "For God so loved the world, that he gave his only begotten Son, that whosoever believeth in him should not perish, but have everlasting life." I asked her if she did not believe Jesus would be glad to save her, if we should bow our heads there and ask Him to do it.

"Yes, I know He would," she said, and said she was willing to do it.

About that time the father, I believe, spoke up and said, "Brother Rice, that is a joy that I wanted to have for myself."

"You have waited until she is ten years old. She wanted to be saved before, but did not know how to tell you. You simply refused her request to join the church but did nothing to show her how to trust in Christ. Now I feel you had your chance, and this matter must be delayed no longer." So we bowed our heads, the dear girl put her trust in Christ and seemed happily assured that her sins were all forgiven.

Sometimes it is well to say to a child after he has said he is conscious of his sins and asks forgiveness and then definitely commits his heart to the dear Lord Jesus, "Now shall we tell the pastor about it?" (or the father, or someone else dear). Help the child to know how to say it, and great joy and sweet assurance usually follow that open confession of Christ as his Saviour.

Do not expect that a child who is saved will never do wrong. He is still human, still subject to the same temptations that assail others. He may have sincerely trusted Christ, but he will still need help to grow into a strong Christian.

Nor should you expect a child to be able in theological language to tell about his salvation. Babies do not know much, but that is no sign they are not really born. Being saved does not involve a college education. There may be real spiritual life in a child, but he will still need training and daily help to do right and to develop the habits of a Christian.

VI.   The Sin of Causing Little Believers to Stumble

When I was about nine years of age I gave my heart to the Lord Jesus and went forward in the First Baptist Church in Gainesville, Texas, to let it be known publicly that Christ was mine. Returning home happily that Sunday noon, I asked my father if I might join the church and be baptized. (He had not been to the services.) He said, "Well, Son, when you are old enough to repent of your sins and be regenerated, you may join the church." He was right in what he said, but he said it in words I did not understand. I only understood that he thought I was too young to be saved, and I did not know what he meant by the words "repent" and "regenerated."

As a result of that discouragement, I thought I must have been mistaken. My father was not only the smartest man in the world and the best, but he was a preacher, so he must know whether or not I was too young to be saved. For three years I went on trying to get saved, but making no outward move. At last I began reading the Bible and found the precious promises in John 3:18, John 3:36 and John 5:24. I found that one who believes or trusts in Christ as his Saviour "hath everlasting life, and shall not come into condemnation." Then I was saved! I did not remember how I had felt; I did not know whether I had met other requirements; but I knew I had, as far as I knew how, believed in Christ, depended upon Him to save me. And now I discovered the Bible said I had received "everlasting life"! Thank God, I never have had any more doubts that I am a saved, born-again child of God!

That illustration from my own childhood shows how serious it is to discourage children who trust in Christ. We dare not neglect to teach them God's way of salvation, to encourage them to come to Christ the best they know how, even if their understanding is imperfect. God is always pleased when a child's heart gropes for Him. And when one comes, ever so hesitantly and ignorantly, Jesus promises him, "Him that cometh to me I will in no wise cast out" (John 6:37).

A solemn warning is given by the Saviour on this matter. "But whoso shall offend one of these little ones which believe in me, it were better for him that a millstone were hanged about his neck, and that he were drowned in the depth of the sea" (Matt. 18:6). To cause a little one who believes in Christ to stumble is a fearful sin, to be so severely punished that one had better die than commit it, Jesus said.

Fathers, mothers, you have immortal souls in your hands. Take care how you let them slip through your fingers into everlasting ruin! When my first baby girl was laid in my arms, a precious bundle of six and three-quarters pounds, I thought she was the prettiest baby I had ever seen. And then and there I felt that God had given me not only a little body to clothe and feed and a little mind to train, but an immortal soul to bring to Christ! I have never gotten away from that feeling. Satan shall never have a child of mine, so help me, God! And thank God, already I have seen each of my six come to Christ and trust Him as Saviour.

Better leave undone all else, if need be, until you win your children to Christ and see that they are safe in God's fold. Salvation is first. Then you may think of lesser things: education, food and clothing. Father, mother, have you gotten your children in?

CHAPTER XVIII

Character Building in the Home

"Train up a child in the way he should go: and when he is old, he will not depart from it."—Prov. 22:6.

"And, ye fathers, provoke not your children to wrath: but bring them up in the nurture and admonition of the Lord."—Eph. 6:4.

"But they said, We will drink no wine: for Jonadab the son of Rechab our father commanded us, saying, Ye shall drink no wine, neither ye, nor your sons for ever."—Jer. 35:6.

It takes years to grow a strong, good character. A child is not a mature Christian even after he has been taught to trust in Christ as his Saviour; by a miracle of God's grace he has received a new attitude of heart, a disposition to want to do right, and by the regenerating work of the Holy Spirit of God in his heart and life has been made into a Christian by what we call conversion, or being born again. He is not a strong, well-developed character. For people to be converted, to mean well, for people to want to do right is not enough. There must be a developed strength and wisdom, a custom of doing things right when meeting situations on great moral principles. This custom of doing right, this habit of fulfilling one's duty, this righteousness that has become part of one's nature and ingrained into the reflexes and acquired tendencies of a well-developed Christian character—these take time to grow.

When God provided that children would take nearly twenty years to grow up, He clearly intended that parents should use those long years in growing Christian character in the child to make him a godly man, strong, happy, moral, adequate to do the work, to master the difficulties, to meet the problems and decide the choices that he must face.

Wicked or dissolute men or women have sometimes turned to Christ and have been converted after years in sin, and in some instances they have been changed in character and made into noble men and women. God's grace is able to

305

change old and hardened criminals into law-abiding citizens, to change drunkenness into sober, self-controlled morality. But the whole world bears witness that the usual plan of God is that character should be developed in childhood and while sons or daughters remain in the homes of their fathers and mothers.

Daniel, a lad of high school age, perhaps, carried into far away Babylon, tempted with the enticing meat and drink from the king's table, had courage and judgment to purpose in his heart that he would not defile himself with the king's meat nor with the wine which he drank (Dan. 1:8). That strong character was developed in his youth and doubtless in the home of his father and mother. Daniel lived a life of high principle and self-control and godliness, with no essential change, from the time of his youth until he was an aged man, the counselor and prime minister of kings.

Young Joseph was put over the affairs of Potiphar's household down in Egypt. When tempted by Potiphar's wife, though he was but a lad, he had the strength of character to refuse her and the good sense to flee from the temptress. The integrity of the lad had already matured. Joseph could be trusted in later life because he was already trustworthy by the time he reached maturity. Who can doubt but that his character was developed in the home of his father Jacob?

Young Timothy, already a Christian when Paul first met him (Acts 16:1-3), had been taught from a child by his godly mother and his grandmother the Holy Scriptures which were able to make him wise unto salvation (II Tim. 3:15; II Tim. 1:5). Later Paul was able to send Timothy to Ephesus, and to put him in charge as the bishop over many elders and preachers in that great wicked city, and to find Timothy trustworthy. He could write to Timothy, "Let no man despise thy youth; but be thou an example" (I Tim. 4:12). Timothy was already a strong, well-developed character when he reached maturity. He may have needed to learn further judgment and to grow in experience, but his character was already well formed when he left his mother's and father's home.

The sons of Jonadab were put to a severe test, as described in Jeremiah, chapter 35. God had Jeremiah to call the sons of Jonadab the son of Rechab and to set pots of wine before them and say, "Drink ye wine." But they said, "We will drink no wine: for Jonadab the son of Rechab our father commanded us, saying, Ye shall drink no wine, neither ye, nor your sons for ever" (Jer. 35:6). How happy the young man who has been so reared in his own home that certain codes of conduct have become ingrained in his character and consciousness so that it is already determined that he will not do some things, and that he will do some other things, because he has learned—not by sad experience but by godly teaching—the way of a righteous and holy life!

The greatest single influence on character, of course, is conversion, that is, coming to repent of one's sins and taking Christ as Saviour and Lord of one's life. With the Holy Spirit's dwelling in the body of a born-again child of God, and with a heart that has turned consciously and deliberately from the course of sin to a course of righteousness, by choice, one has the best foundation of true character. Then after one is a child of God, naturally the constant use of the Word of God, learning the precepts of the Bible and becoming accustomed to following them, is a great source of molding godly character. The habit of regular prayer cannot be overestimated as a molder of character. I think that we may safely say that conversion, that is, coming to trust in Christ as Saviour, and then learning the Word of God and coming to God daily for one's cleansing and for the guidance and help and provision needed are the greatest influences on Christian character. These we have discussed in other chapters.

However, there are a number of other factors in character building which have been dealt with only in passing in other chapters and which ought to be discussed in some detail here.

A strong, godly, happy character is the very best thing any father and mother can leave for their child. Would you leave your child money, property? Help him build a strong and godly character and he can make money and acquire property. In the time of the greatest financial depression, when men walked the streets looking for jobs, there was always a shortage of young men and women of proven character, of proven devotion to duty, of acquired skill in work. I have been proud that when I was only a private in the army in World War I, I was put in charge of the dental supplies in Camp McArthur, Texas, because, the major said frankly, that none of the nineteen commissioned officers and none of the noncommissioned officers could be trusted not to drink up the alcohol in the storehouse nor could they be trusted not to sell the gold which was stored there for dental work. He straitly charged me not to allow anybody else to have the key. No one was to get any part of the fifty thousand dollars' worth of dental equipment without my being present with them in the storerooms. There is always work and always responsibility for those of proven character.

Would you leave your child fame and position? He will earn it for himself if you can make sure that he has the kind of godly character that Daniel had, that Joseph had, that the Rechabites had, and that Timothy had.

Do you long for your children to be happy? Nothing will so guarantee happy marriages, loyal friends, and the other elements that make up for joy in this world, as will your seeing that they go out to face the world with a well-developed and trustworthy Christian character.

I should like to mention here some necessary elements of character building in the home, aside from winning the child to Christ and teaching him the Word of God and teaching him to pray.

I.   Obedience, the Foundation of Character

Obedience to authority is the very foundation of character. Obedience to father and mother makes a good son or daughter. Obedience to the laws of the land and the appointed authorities in government makes a good citizen. Obedience to her husband makes a good wife. Obedience to his boss or foreman makes a good workman. Obedience to God makes a good Christian. Rebellion against authority is the heart of all sin. How important it is then to teach and to train children to obey in the home! I suggest the following truths:

1. *Children should be taught to obey without question, and when necessary, without waiting for any explanation.* Some would-be advisers of parents say that parents should always take time to explain to children why they should do this or that, and that a father or mother should never command a child to do something on the unsupported authority of his parents without the child's knowing why. But that teaching is silly. Such "obedience" is not obedience at all. The father and mother in such cases exercise salesmanship perhaps, but certainly they do not exercise authority. Suppose that every young man or young woman starts out in life with the thought, "I will obey only the laws that my own judgment

tells me are necessary and good. I will break any law that does not seem to me to be necessary." Any citizen living on such a basis would be a criminal and not a good citizen. Good citizens obey the speed laws because they are good citizens and because laws are to be obeyed, not because they have weighed out every problem involved. Good citizens stop at stop signs because they obey the law, not because they have considered intelligently the problem involved at every street intersection and have decided that there ought to be a stop sign at this corner, and no stop sign at another corner.

How could any Christian claim to serve God if he obeyed only those commands that he had been thoroughly convinced were applicable to his own case? No one really obeys God who does not obey Him blindly, obey Him whether he knows why certain commands are given or not.

And likewise no child is obedient who does not obey his father or his mother because they are in authority and because obedience itself is a virtue. A child who does not give blind obedience, unquestioning obedience, is really not giving any obedience at all. So parents should insist on obedience, and often should insist on obedience without any explanation.

2. *Obedience must be instant obedience, without argument.* If a father says to his son, "Do it now," and the son does it an hour later instead of now, then of course the son is a rebel, is disobedient. Any real obedience accepts it as fundamentally true that the one in authority knows best what to do, and so the one under authority submits and obeys, not in his own time, but in the time and way he is ordered to obey.

This is simply an amplification of the statement above, that obedience must be required even when there is no clear understanding on the part of the child of the necessity of the order given. What child is wise enough to weigh whether a drink of beer would do him any harm or not? What teenage girl is wise enough to judge as to whether she ought to be home at a certain hour at night? Real obedience is unquestioning and instant obedience.

3. *For character building parents should allow no exceptions to the rule of instant obedience.* If a child obeys four times because he wants to and the fifth time disobeys because he wants to disobey, then actually there is no heart obedience. Heart obedience recognizes the authority of the one who gives commands, and sets out to obey those commands whether they are always easy or not; whether they are al-

ways pleasant or not. Real obedience, necessarily, means a heart-submission to do the will of the one in authority, and not to please one's self.

Any child who gets his way one time out of ten will always, in the back of his mind, plan to rebel again when he finds obedience distasteful and when he particularly and strongly wants his own way, or when he thinks he can "get by." Only by insisting that children obey without exception can a father and mother inculcate that sense of respect for authority which is necessary for a great character. Only by being taught to obey all commands from legitimate authority can a child come to be governed by the principle that he will always do what is right instead of what he wants to do. Only by coming to observe such a principle of action can one rule his own heart and resist his own temptations and be what his best and highest self longs to be.

Be sure of this, that no child's will is submissive, until it is a settled matter that he is to obey all commands, whether he understands the reason for them or not, whether he thinks them wise or not, or whether they go contrary to his own pleasure or not. Parents should require instant and implicit obedience and that without any exceptions.

4. *Teaching obedience requires real character on the part of parents.* The parent who would teach his child to be steadfast must himself be steadfast in his requirement. And along with justice there must be mercy. Children are only human beings. Often they fail to obey, without any intentional rebellion. Johnny did not come home at four o'clock from playing ball with a neighbor boy as he was commanded to do, simply because he got so interested in the game that he forgot to look at the clock or inquire the time! Or Mary was left to do the dishes and fully intended to do them promptly and get through on time, but when she fed the table scraps to the puppy he was so cute that she wasted half an hour playing with him, forgetting the dishes! Fathers and mothers must distinguish between willful disobedience and the natural frailty which must be overcome by a combination of firmness and kindness. And more important still, parents who are to act for God in the home, with an authority that is tremendous, must see to it that they are never capricious, that they always have reasons for their demands, and that love and good sense and reasonableness are back of every order given. Children do not need to know just why a particular com-

mand is given, but they have a right to know that father and mother always try to do right, that they love their children, that they give their orders with the best interests of the child in mind, and with a holy sense of responsibility to God. It takes much prayer and development of real character to be a good father or mother and to teach one's children obedience.

II. Children Should Be Taught to Work

It is said that a snobbish British nobleman once said to an American businessman, "I say, old chap, don't they have any gentlemen in America?"

Rather indignantly the American questioned, "What do you mean, 'any gentlemen in America'?"

"I mean men that don't work."

"Oh, yes," said the American, "we have lots of that kind of people in America, only we don't call them gentlemen; we call them bums!"

Perhaps such a conversation never really occurred. If it did, any such nobleman would poorly represent the best aristocracy of England. But be that as it may, certain it is that everybody ought to work. People who have money ought to work the same as those who do not have money. People who need to earn their living ought to work, and people who do not need to earn their living ought to work. Anybody who is able to work and does not work in some fashion is a parasite in this world and lacks the fundamentals of good character. Work is a blessing, not a curse. God said, after Adam and Eve had sinned and were cast out of the Garden of Eden, "Cursed is the ground for thy sake" (Gen. 3:17). That is, all for man's good, God cursed the ground, made it grow weeds that men would have to cut down, made the ground hard so that men would have to plow it, made animal-kind wild so men would have to domesticate beasts of burden and pursue animals for food. Nothing much worse could happen to mankind than not to have to work.

How wise was Henry Ford when he taught his son Edsel to work and took him into the enormous Ford business! And what a good example it is to America that the grandson, Henry Ford, III, succeeded to the management of the great Ford manufacturing interests. John D. Rockefeller carefully trained his son to be able to manage the vast estate that that multimillionaire left. If John D. Rockefeller, Jr., did not need to spend his time and energy in making more money, it was well that his father had him carefully trained to work at intelligently giving away where it would do the most good the money that he inherited and managing the benevolences begun by his illustrious father. The Fords and the Rockefellers give a good example to America. What a folly and shame it is when rich men raise sons that are profligate and drunken and useless parasites on society, simply because they never learned to work!

How I thank God that I grew up in a poor family, in a home where it was a principle that work was right. When I was ten years old I was driving a six-mule team to a big disc-breaking plow day after day on a big ranch in West Texas. The hired man would put the bridles and collars on the big mules because they were too tall for me to do that, but I learned to put on the rest of the harness, to drive my big team to the field and there to hitch them to the plow. I learned to tell when it was noon by the sun straight overhead which cast no shadow, to take my team to water, to feed them in the wagon bed, eat my lunch, and then again to hitch them to the plow and proceed with the day's work until sundown. My work was needed, and it was taken for granted that a boy ought to earn his keep and learn to do a man's work. How I thank God for the resourcefulness, the self-respect, the sense of responsibility that I got as a child by daily hard work!

From the time I was fifteen I largely earned my own way so that when it was time to go to college it never entered my mind that I should lament the fact that my father had no money to send me. It never occurred to me to doubt that there would be honest work for me to do and that I could earn my way. And so it was. Thank God for the blessing of work!

It was a tradition in our family that our women folks were not to work in the field as did most of the women in our farm and ranch community. Yet it was an unwritten law of my father's that every girl had to learn to hitch a horse to the buggy or to saddle her own horse, and every girl had to learn to milk the cows. The milking was my job, and with a feeling of superiority mingled with impatience, I watched my sister learning to milk the cows. She frightened the Jersey cows, she spilled the milk, she cried in vexation, but she learned to do the chore that someday she might have to do. And then I went on with my regular job of milking.

The girls at my father's house learned to cook, to bathe and dress a baby, to keep a house.

Years ago I had the mingled joy and sadness of giving my second daughter in marriage to the missionary student with whom she planned to go to the other side of the world to carry the Gospel. When the wedding and the reception were over, the wedding pictures taken, when the bride had changed to her traveling suit and the bride's bouquet had been thrown and the good-byes were said and the car rattled away with noisemakers tied to it, my wife burst out weeping. At first it seemed hard to console her as she put away the beautiful wedding dress which had been committed to her care. But after a bit she dried her tears and said, "I ought not to weep. Mary Lloys will be happy. She can cook as well as I can, and she loves to cook. She can sew as well as I can. She loves to keep house. She will have a happy home. She has been taught to work and taught to love work."

So see that every child has work to do. The mother may feel that she would rather dry the dishes herself than to watch the children mishandle her precious china or crystal ware. Never mind, that boy or girl is more important than the china or crystal ware! Perhaps the mother can make the beds and sweep the floors in less time than her daughter can do it under her mother's supervision. But happy is the mother who takes the hard way, temporarily, and supervises the work carefully and teaches her daughter to do the work. Let every child have appointed tasks and let him do those tasks regularly, do them according to strict standards, do them on time. Let there be no argument about it, but let it simply be understood that on certain days the lawn is mowed, that after each meal the dishes are promptly washed and put away, that at a certain hour dinner preparation begins, that nice people always straighten their rooms and make the beds, and that work is not only a necessary, but a very happy part of life.

Much of the time Mrs. Rice and I could not afford a maid in the home to lighten the housework. But after some of our six daughters were about grown we felt that it was not right nor wise to have a maid to do work that the children could do and ought to do. It is never wise for children to have others do their work and to feel that play is more important than work. So I counsel that every boy and girl should be given regular tasks and be taught to work as a matter of honesty and integrity.

Remember that the Word of God says, "That if any would not work, neither should he eat" (II Thess. 3:10). A good habit and conscience about work is an essential part of Christian character.

III.   Children Must Be Taught Regular Habits for Happiness and Usefulness

One who does not have well-developed habits for the routine of daily living will have a miserable time trying to get in all his duties. I remember very painfully the trouble I had about shaving before I came to the regular custom of shaving every day. At first once a week was enough. As my beard grew heavier, I needed to shave more often. Every day I would anxiously examine my face and hope I could get through till the next morning without too conspicuously needing a shave. My face was tender, my beard was tough, shaving was never easy, and I was always torn between a distaste for shaving and the fear that I would not be presentable. I spent far more time considering the matter than if I had shaved every day. At long last I came to the point where I began to make shaving a matter of daily routine. In the morning shaving became a regular part of my toilet, and when once that habit was established I had no more distress about shaving. Shaving is necessary, it has its place in the day, and I never have any argument with myself about whether I shall shave or not shave. I have lost all the distress which came from the daily argument with myself and the guilty feeling I often had that I had not shaved when I needed to. So the happy, well-ordered life must be made up very largely of a group of well-established habits.

What a foolish way to live when one must stop and give new consideration and argue the pros and cons every day as to whether he will wash his teeth, whether he shall go to bed at ten or eleven, whether he shall bathe morning or evening or dare wait until tomorrow! Happiness, success, character—all these depend very largely upon a good set of habits developed in childhood. Therefore I suggest that parents take particular pains in having regularity in the home and that children be taught to do regular things at regular times and without many exceptions. I suggest the following matters that need regular attention.

1. To go to bed at a regular time without complaint. With little children of pre-school age there ought also, perhaps, to be time for an afternoon nap.

2. There should be good habits of personal cleanliness. Regular baths, washing hands and face before meals, brushing the teeth morning and evening should become regular matters carefully supervised until a habit is formed. To give careful attention at this time will save much trouble later on.

3. Children should especially be trained in orderliness and neatness about their clothes and belongings. When clothing is removed it should be hung up, or put in the laundry according to careful instructions. Pajamas and nightgowns should be put in their regular places. Toys, dolls, paints and brushes and books should be returned to their proper place. It is important to provide regular spaces for children's playthings. It is easy to provide a drawer or a box. A habit of putting away one's own toys and playthings is very important training in orderliness and in taking responsibility. The boy who leaves his tricycle on the walk and his skates on the stairway will leave his employer in the lurch later. The girl who leaves her clothes on the floor for her mother to hang up will fail later to carry her part of the responsibility for the home. The mother who is wise in helping her children form good habits is not simply teaching them to put away toys and clothes but is teaching them to be responsible for their acts, to carry their part of the burden of Christian living in a home and in society.

IV. Training in the Right Use of Money

Every normal person will have to use money. To waste money is to waste life by misusing the hours of labor that it took to earn the money. Money represents toil and planning and investment, therefore money should be very carefully used. Children should learn to earn money, to spend money, to save money, and to give money.

1. *Children should earn some money*. A word of warning is needed here. Children should certainly *not* be paid for everything they do about the home. Every child should grow up to feel a deep sense of gratitude to father and mother for all the blessings of the home: for food and shelter and clothes and

loving care. Every child should know that he can never repay all he owes his father and mother, and that it is only normal and decent and right for him to bear his share of the labor in the home. So every child should have some regular daily tasks for which he is not paid, but which he does, of course, as a member of the family, because work is good, because it helps mother or dad, and because decent people do all they can to pay their own way. But children should have some way of earning money. My daughters earned money by watching babies. After they were older, they worked in the Sword of the Lord office and worked side by side with older people and did comparable work, and were paid according to their value to the work. Sometimes an unusually hard task around the home seemed to be more than the normal share of the work for one child, and that child was paid for the extra work.

Some parents give children an allowance. I do not say that that is unwise. Sometimes children should have a little money to spend even when there is no way to work outside the home. The normal, decent things that nice people are supposed to do anyway should be done without pay, of course. Sometimes fathers and mothers will reward children for unusual faithfulness by a special gift, a picnic or a trip or a much desired toy or article of clothing. But keep two principles distinct: one principle is that children should earn some money, and another principle is that they should have certain duties around the home to help their father and mother and because that is right and work is itself proper and honest for all people able to work. No one is capable of spending money wisely who has never earned money.

2. *Children should learn to spend money wisely.* The spending will need some supervision by the parents, but not too much. Let there be no prodigal and senseless spending. Money, and the toil it takes to earn it, are too precious to be wasted. But let children learn to buy. Every girl should learn to shop for groceries, with her mother along. If the child is helped to plan the menu for a meal before she goes shopping with mother, and if the mother specifies about how much the meal may cost, and the number of pounds of this or that that will be needed, daughter will learn from the shopping expedition and will greatly enjoy it. Every well-reared girl will be immensely proud when she has planned a meal and bought the ingredients, and finds that it comes within a certain lim-

ited budget of so much per person per meal. Children should, as soon as possible, begin to realize how much their clothes cost. We have found it very wise to let girls in their teens begin to select the material for their school and play dresses and pajamas and to learn to sew.

Little children should sometimes buy presents for others. They should have counsel and suggestions. And you may be sure that the boy who earned fifty cents by hours with the lawn mower, or carrying a paper route, will not so likely spend it foolishly as the boy who was given fifty cents without doing anything to earn it.

3. *Children should be taught to save.* Thrift is scriptural and right. Proverbs 6:6-8 says, "Go to the ant, thou sluggard; consider her ways, and be wise: Which having no guide, overseer, or ruler, provideth her meat in the summer, and gathereth her food in the harvest." To earn money and save it for a time when it will be needed is proper and wise and is commended in the Scriptures. There are many good purposes for which a child might save money. He might save for a pair of skates or a wagon or a bicycle. He might save money for his own clothes. In many families it has been found that the help financially is greater because a boy will take better care of his clothes when he helps to buy them. Children should save money for their Christmas shopping. Some children start bank accounts or buy war saving stamps or bonds to save for a college education. Some save money for two weeks in a summer camp or for a visit on the train to grandmother's. Many children have been taught to save money to give to the Red Cross, or the Community Chest, or to give to the church. Saving money to support foreign missions is usually exciting for children in Christian homes, and all the virtues of work and thrift and generosity and devotion to Christ are encouraged.

4. *Children should be taught to give money.* There will be community projects in which children ought to be taught to share, such as the Red Cross, or Community Chest, or such as buying lunches for poor children at school. These matters must each be judged on its own merit. But Christian people should certainly teach their children to give regularly, week by week, to the support of the local church and to missions and to other Christian enterprises that deserve the support of God's people. Instead of the man of the house giving the money for all the family, each child should be taught to give

for himself. At first the father will need to supply the money for the gifts, but even if the same amount of money is given it is better that five or six people should have the joy and the character development that comes from giving, than that the father alone should give the money. Then later each child will be taught to give out of the money he earns. Sooner or later every person of good character must learn self-denial, must learn to give up some pleasures in order to do right and to serve holy causes. How good it is for a child to learn to save back some of his money instead of spending it for ice cream or playthings, and regularly to acknowledge his love for God and his devotion to the cause of Christ and the church of Christ and the ministry of the church, by supporting God's work with tithes and offerings, Sunday by Sunday.

V. Children Must Be Taught Courtesy in the Home

Manners and morals are so closely related that no man can be a good man who is not courteous. He may not know some accepted outward forms of gentlemanly behavior, but he will be a gentleman in his heart, will earnestly seek to please people and to make them happy, if he is a good man. So the teaching of courtesy is actually a part of character development, a matter of moral development and godliness. First Peter 3:8 says, "Love as brethren, be pitiful, be courteous." One is not a good Christian who is not courteous.

Courtesy begins for the child in "Please" and "Thank you!" The child who says, "Please," thereby acknowledges his place as a subordinate to his father or mother, and as a gentleman or lady he requests what he has no right to demand. Saying, "Thank you!" inculcates a real sense of gratitude in the heart of a child for favors he cannot pay. It ought to be a well-established rule that the child who does not say, "Please," does not get the food he wants. Rebellion at this point should be punished as quickly and drastically as any other overt and deliberate sin against father and mother and the household. I like very much the southern custom in good families of teaching children to say "Yes, Sir!" or "No, Sir!" to father or other adult men instead of a simple "Yes" or "No." And I like the old-fashioned "Yes, Ma'am" to mother instead of a simple "Yes." Respect and courtesy, thus expressed, become a part of the child's normal attitude toward others. Young people should be taught deference for old people. Boys and young men should be taught deference toward ladies. Yesterday in the hotel in Spokane, Washington, I heard a man, who came into the elevator with his wife and son and daughter, say to the lad, "Do you remember who I said should go into the elevator first?" So when the elevator stopped, the boy, about eight, stood back carefully until his mother and sister left the elevator, and then he proudly followed. The boy will have a finer respect for womanhood, a sense of a need to protect and defend women, I trust, because his father taught him a little custom of courtesy.

And children should learn to be courteous to one another, each to respect the rights of the other. Each should be glad to wait until the other is served at the table. Children should be taught to "love as brethren, be pitiful, be courteous." That is a part of Christian character.

VI.   The Art of Living Peaceably With Others Should Be Taught at Home

Much of what might be said here has already been discussed in the chapter on "Correction and Discipline of Children." Children who are taught a reverent and godly fear of their parents, in the sense that they long to please them and fear to make them unhappy, are more easily taught to get along with others. The greatest relationship of a child is with his own father and mother. Other relationships are secondary. The child who is taught obedience and courtesy as we have advocated above, will not find it so hard to learn to get along with others.

I well realize that to get along with others covers the whole field of human character and life and happiness. No one ever perfectly learns this lesson as long as he is in the flesh. But children can be taught in general certain rules and habits of conduct about getting along with others.

1. *No fighting should be allowed.* No child should set out to punish another child. That should be left in the hands of father and mother. No child should be allowed to force his own way upon a younger child or a weaker one. Of course, there will be arguments and good-natured scuffles, but children should be taught to keep the peace.

2. *Children must be taught to respect one another's possessions and not to take what is not their own.* This lesson must start when the child is first able to creep about and mother

has to say, "No, no, don't touch!" and enforce her command by taking from the little one the thing he is not to be allowed to handle, and if necessary, rapping his hand. or spanking him. It is an unhappy home where everything of value has to be moved out of reach of children because they are not taught the difference between mine and thine, are not taught what they have a right to touch and handle and what they must leave alone. Some children are a terror to every home in which they visit because they have never been taught to leave alone what does not belong to them, or what they have not been given permission to see and handle. No child should be allowed to take what does not belong to him.

3. *Children should be taught to share their property.* Big sister must let little sister play with her doll for a little time, carefully watched by mother or by herself to see that little sister does not pull the dolly's hair off her head, or punch the little eyes out. Mercy must be taught as well as justice, and charity as well as honesty.

4. *Children must be taught to forgive and to ask forgiveness for a wrong.* "I am sorry"—those are about the hardest words in the language to say. Proverbs 28:13 says, "He that covereth his sins shall not prosper: but whoso confesseth and forsaketh them shall have mercy." So one of the greatest essentials of Christian character is a heart that is penitent over sin or mistake or error and wants forgiveness. A child must be taught to be sorry for mistakes or sins, or for wrongdoing toward anyone, and to try to make it right by an honest confession.

Children likewise must be taught to forgive. Jesus said, "But if ye forgive not men their trespasses, neither will your Father forgive your trespasses" (Matt. 6:15). Little children who kneel by their beds at night to pray ought to be reminded that they must be sure to forgive everybody else before they ask God for forgiveness for the mistakes and sins of the day. Little children ought to be taught that solemn warning, "Let not the sun go down upon your wrath" (Eph. 4:26). Let no little child go to bed with a known and deliberate sin unconfessed, and make sure that no child goes to bed with a black grudge in his heart against anyone.

Oh, how tender and forgiving mothers and fathers ought to be at this point! Little feet stumble so easily! Little tongues wander so naturally from the truth! Little hands drop so many things and break them, and take so many things they ought not to touch! Godlike mercy and kindness in forgiving and teaching forgiveness ought to be the part of every mother and father.

The problem of teaching character in the home is enough for a whole volume. It cannot be covered in one chapter, but I can only make some suggestions that I am sure will be helpful if taken to heart. But let every father and mother bear well in mind that character must be built in the home, day by day, line upon line, precept upon precept, here a little and there a little.

CHAPTER XIX

Home Cooperation With Church, School and Community

The home must fit the child for the world and a life outside the sheltered precincts of his father's and mother's immediate influence. The child will have his friends from outside the home, will find a mate outside the home. The business of making a living or a career of usefulness must be carried on outside the home. The home cannot ignore the outside world, but must cooperate with agencies, institutions and people outside.

The school can do for the child that which cannot be easily done in the home. The church has a contribution to make to the child's spiritual welfare and training without which the child would be poor indeed. A child's work or play will throw him in constant contact with outsiders. The home, therefore, must cooperate with the church, the school, and the community.

I. Cooperation With the Church

The church is a divine unit of society. However good the home, it cannot take the place nor do the work of the church. In Genesis 35:2, 3 we are told that "Jacob said unto his household, and to all that were with him, Put away the strange gods that are among you, and be clean, and change your garments: And let us arise. and go up to Bethel; and I will make there an altar unto God, who answered me in the day of my distress, and was with me in the way which I went." Jacob took his family to church! He remembered that when he had gone away from home, and his life was endangered by the anger of his wronged brother, there at Bethel he had met God. There in a dream he had seen the angels of God ascending and descending. There God had given to him the covenant originally made with his father Isaac and with his grandfather Abraham. So in a time of distress and trouble Jacob heard the voice of God and went back to Bethel, "the house of God." He took his family with him to worship God. Every family needs to attend the house of God.

323

When Jesus was born, Mary, the mother of the baby Jesus, along with Joseph her husband, was anxious to bring Jesus to the Temple. Luke 2:22 says, "And when the days of her purification according to the law of Moses were accomplished, they brought him to Jerusalem, to present him to the Lord." That was not baptism, but it was certainly a dedication. Every godly mother ought to feel a hunger to take her child to the house of God and there with solemn prayer beg God to help her rear the little one to His glory. And every father, of course, ought to do the same.

Joseph and Mary had an annual custom of going to Jerusalem for the feast of the Passover and they took the young Jesus with them. When Jesus was twelve years old He went up to Jerusalem with Mary and Joseph "after the custom of the feast," Luke 2:42-49 tells us. Jesus remained in the Temple. "And it came to pass, that after three days they found him in the temple, sitting in the midst of the doctors, both hearing them, and asking them questions. And all that heard him were astonished at his understanding and answers" (Luke 2:46, 47). In this annual visit the religious teachers at Jerusalem contributed to the training of this Son of God and Son of Mary.

But Jesus went to the synagogue every week besides this annual pilgrimage to Jerusalem for the passover week. Luke 4:16 speaks of Jesus after He was thirty years old, after He was baptized and began His public ministry, and says, "He came to Nazareth, where he had been brought up: and, as his custom was, he went into the synagogue on the sabbath day, and stood up for to read." Fathers and mothers do well to follow the example of Mary and Joseph, and every child would do well to follow the example of Jesus who regularly went to the house of God and read the Word of God and took part in public worship.

1. *Take the children to church early.*

Blessed is the child who from earliest infancy has the impact and influence of the church, of the gospel ministry, of the Sunday school teaching upon his heart and life. I remember when I was four years old I attended the Sunday school in a little country Baptist church near Gainesville, Texas. Sweet is my memory of the beautiful little picture cards we had in the "Card Class," the Christmas lesson we were taught a few days after my fourth birthday when the golden text was, "There was no room for them in the inn" (Luke 2:7), and the godly deacon who taught that lesson to us. I was deeply impressed with the birth of the baby Jesus, our dear Saviour for whom this wicked world had no room!

I remember the preaching services, which, of course, I attended with the family. Although I do not recall any of the sermons that I heard that young, yet there was a sense of happiness and awe that I had about the services. Some of the songs that were sung I do remember: "Turned Away From the Beautiful Gate," "In the Sweet Bye and Bye," "No, Not One," and "When the Roll Is Called up Yonder." I know that I was carried in my mother's arms as a baby, and when I was old enough to sit alone, I sat on a folded quilt on the floor and learned to be quiet in church. Thank God for the heritage that in my earliest recollections there is the fragrance of godliness, a memory of singing and praying and preaching of the Word of God and sweet fellowship with God's people.

My wife and I, both university graduates, naturally were taught that little babies must never be taken into crowds and that little ones must be at home asleep by eight. We did not heed such talk, but all of our six daughters were taken to church in a basket when they were four or five weeks old. Usually there was no money to pay a maid to stay at home and keep the children. And if there had been money to hire a maid, we would not have wanted the kind of maid who was willing to stay away from church. And we would not be guilty of keeping someone else from the house of God that we might worship with more freedom. So the little ones were taught to lie quietly or to sit up and play with a rubber toy or nibble a graham cracker. There was no crying, no jabbering, no confusion to disturb the public service. Others were forbidden to disturb the baby. The mother heard the sermon, took part in the song service, and otherwise lived a normal life. Babies have to learn to behave in church sometime if they are ever to be decent citizens. It is much easier to learn under one year of age than after that time. Parents who have no discipline, who do not train their children to obey, may find difficulty in taking little ones to church. But those who follow God's plans can rear happy children who will sit quietly in church from babyhood on.

Certainly a baby will sometimes need to be given a drink. Sometimes he will have to be taken out of the auditorium to avoid disturbing others. If necessary, a proper spanking outside may quickly settle the disturbance. Some churches have very convenient soundproof rooms for mothers and babies. But no mother should ever stay away from the house of God and from public worship because she has a baby. I know that there is infinite value in having the idea of churchgoing instilled into little minds and hearts from infancy. Begin taking the child to church as early as possible!

It is my own conviction that not even the junior church, as good as it is, can take the place of the public preaching service in which little children sit by mothers and fathers and learn to become cooperating members of society while they hear sweet songs and understand what they can of the services.

Little children cannot understand all the table talk of their elders, yet in enlightened homes children learn to sit nicely at the table, learn to eat quietly, and to be cheerful and happy in the fellowship of older people without disturbing the happiness of the family or embarrassing guests. Certainly the same principle obtains in the matter of public worship. Do not wait until the child understands all about theology, or can understand the discourse of the pastor before you take him to church.

If your church does not welcome little children, if the service is so formal and impractical and unspiritual that a little child will not be blessed by it, you should pray for your pastor and church leaders that the form of service will be changed; or you should go to another church where the Gospel in its simplicity is preached, where the hymns and gospel songs can bless the hearts of common people and of little children, and where the services more nearly approximate that of New Testament churches. No church is right in the form of service and in its spirit and leadership which does not make room for little children and where little children cannot be blessed. Remember that Jesus said, "Suffer little children, and forbid them not, to come unto me: for of such is the kingdom of heaven" (Matt. 19:14). Little children did not interfere with the teaching and preaching of the Lord Jesus. He was glad to have them come to Him. He took children up in His arms and blessed them. He did this in the midst of a great congregation gathered to hear His parables and teachings. The church must make room for little children, and fathers and mothers must take children to church.

In many Sunday schools babies, as soon as they are born,

can be enrolled in the cradle roll. Then as soon as mother is able to go to Sunday school, the little one may be kept in the nursery so mother can be in Sunday school class and learn the Word of God without distraction. By the time the little fellow is four years old he can begin to feel at home in the Sunday school, after a tactful introduction with the mother near at hand. He can be taught some verses, will like Bible stories, and can learn little songs and pantomimes.

2. *Some methods of cooperation.*

First, see that children, as well as parents, are regular in attendance. The aim of the parents and of the Sunday school ought to be to establish such a habit of regular Sunday school and church attendance that the child will never be willing to miss the Christian fellowship, the spiritual refreshing, and the worship of God each Sunday in his church, or wherever he may be. And it is equally important that the child should feel that the church comes before the school, comes before play, comes before visiting. Even in vacation time a child should be taught very carefully to maintain a custom of attending church, even if it must be away from the home church.

Then children should be taught to give regularly in the Sunday school and church. When the child gives money to the church, he grows to feel his responsibility to God for his income and all God's good gifts. When a child gives a dime out of a dollar, he can easily be taught to feel that the whole dollar was received from the Lord and must be used to His glory. For the child to have a coin to give in the Sunday school, and also in the preaching service, adds greatly to his happiness, his sense of "belonging," his sense of cooperation with others who love God. Later when he has an income of his own it will add greatly to his self-respect as well as to the worship in his heart to be taught to give one-tenth of his income and freewill offerings beyond, as he feels a desire to do. Systematic giving is not needed nearly so much by the church as it is needed by Christians themselves. Teach your boy or girl to give regularly to the church and its ministry.

Parents should not send the children to Sunday school or church alone. A child may go to church and feel that the Sunday school and church service are all right for a child, but the boy will think, "When I get big like Dad, I will stay at home as he does, or play golf, or go fishing on Sunday." The father and mother must set the example in worshipful attendance, in happy fellowship at the church, in liberal giving.

Make sure that the church is always "talked up" at home. How many parents have ruined the influence of the church over their own children by their careless criticism of the minister, of some church official, or of Christians who attend the services! Let it always be understood that the church, while not perfect, is God's own institution, and that a certain reverence is due to any true house of God and any true minister of God. Let it be understood that ministers are human, but that as a class they are the cleanest and most unselfish set of men on earth, and that ministers ought to be defended by godly people everywhere. It is true, as has been said a million times, no doubt, that "there are too many hypocrites in the church." Since the church is full of human beings, naturally that is true. There are also too many hypocrites in the lodges, too many hypocrites in business, too many hypocrites in the schools. Judas Iscariot was a hypocrite among the first twelve apostles. And there are no doubt many insincere people in churches today, many unconverted people. But the fact yet remains that any child will be better in the church than in the tavern, and any child will be better influenced on the whole by a church where the Gospel is preached and the Bible is believed than he will be in the public school or by his playmates. It is wicked and foolish and disastrous to criticize and break down the confidence of the child in God's institution, the church, which ought to be to him such a blessing and comfort and strength, such a medium of Christian cooperation and fellowship and service. Stand by the church. Do not criticize it before the children!

Put the church before the school. Instead of leaving the children at home to do their lessons on Sunday night, or on week nights when revival services or Bible conferences or prayer services are on at the church, let the children postpone their lessons and come to the house of God. What they will get by the gospel preaching, the sweet singing, and by seeing souls saved in the church will be worth more to them than anything they would learn in school. That their souls may be saved if they are not already Christians, and that their hearts may be revived if they are Christians, it is important that young people regularly attend the house of God, that they attend revival services and Bible conference programs. Let the church, after the home, be first in the heart and mind of the child. It is rare that children cannot do their necessary school work and yet have time for the services at the church. But let amusement and social affairs and even the necessary work of the schools come second to that of the church. Let the children be taught, "But seek ye first the kingdom of God, and his righteousness; and all these things shall be added unto you" (Matt. 6:33).

3. *When the child has been converted, he ought to be encouraged to join a church.*

The Bible does not indicate that anybody ever ought to join any church, or be baptized, or be known as a Christian until he has personally trusted in Christ as his Saviour and so become a born-again child of God. But as soon as a child has been saved, whether at home or in the services of the church, he ought to be taught that he has a right to church membership. He should be prepared for it with reverent talk and counsel. Then, of his own choice and with holy resolutions to please God and serve Him, he should be allowed to join the church, and to take on himself the public responsibilities of a Christian.

4. *Do not allow your child to attend a modernistic church which would break down his faith in the Bible and in Christ.*

There are "churches" in cities and towns all over America that are not worthy of the name. They call themselves churches, they claim to be Christian institutions, yet they do not believe any of the fundamental doctrines of the Bible, they do not have any of the essential characteristics of Christianity. A man who does not believe that Jesus is the virgin-born Son of God, does not trust in the atoning death of Christ for his salvation, is not a Christian even though he may wear priestly garb and stand behind a sacred pulpit and pretend to preach the Gospel. All modernist preachers, who deny the inspiration of the Bible, deny the essential deity of Jesus Christ, deny His miracles, deny His virgin birth, deny His bodily resurrection, deny the need for a new birth, deny the fact of Heaven and Hell, are, in the words of Jesus Christ Himself, "blind leaders of the blind." They are "false prophets, which come to you in sheep's clothing, but inwardly they are ravening wolves" (Matt. 7:15). To sit under the influence and teaching of such men in the pulpit is a sin. It is painful and wrong for an adult who is already truly converted. It is utterly disastrous and inexcusable to leave a child to be influenced by such an ungodly pretender to Christianity. Christians should not attend churches that deny the deity of Christ, that deny the inspiration and integrity of the Bible, that deny the essential tenets of historic Christianity. And if you bring your children up in such an atmosphere, in such a modernistic church, you may be responsible for the eternal damnation of their souls, and you are almost certain to have a part thus in the wreck of their faith. Do not take your children to a modernistic church and do not allow them to go. In II John, verses 10 and 11, is this plain command: "If there come any unto you and bring not this doctrine, receive him not into your house, neither bid him God speed: for he that biddeth him God speed is partaker of his evil deeds." It is wrong to support infidels deniers of the deity of Christ, with your money or with your presence. How wicked then to allow your children's faith to be wrecked by these unbelievers, these hypocrites "who privily shall bring in damnable heresies, even denying the Lord that bought them" (II Pet. 2:1). Of such false teachers it is said that "through covetousness shall they with feigned words make merchandise of you" (II Pet. 2:3). Modernist preachers want the standing, the honor, the security, the income of the gospel minister, while they deny every essential obligation that is involved in the ministry. Do not let them damn and blight the faith of your children and perhaps their immortal souls as well.

Some mothers and fathers love to go to the church where they have attended twenty years, perhaps the church where they were converted. They well remember when their own mothers and fathers attended this same church. They well remember when some loved pastor preached the Word of truth there in the power of God and when souls were converted. They put money and loving care and service into that church. Now they are loathe to leave it although it has become an entirely different kind of church. The man of God who preached the Gospel has been followed by an infidel speaking smooth but deceitful phrases, subtly breaking down the faith of the people in the Word of God. Perhaps the Spirit of Christ has departed from the services. Perhaps no sinners are ever saved at her altars. The church has become perhaps only a moral-uplift society, or less than that, a social club. Let not sentiment cause you to sin here. Break the ties of sentiment! If you cannot bring the church back to God, then do not teach your children to follow the infidels who reign there now. See that your children attend a church where they hear the Word of God. See that they attend a church where Jesus is spoken of as the Saviour, the Son of

God, and where sinners are taught to love and trust Him. See that your children are brought up in a church where Christianity is a real and living thing. Take them with you to services where hearts are blessed, where prayer is made to God in Jesus' name, where Christians listen with joy to the preaching of God's Word.

II.   Home Cooperation With the School

Briefly let us summarize some of the duties of the home as regards the education of the children.

1. *Cooperate in seeing that children study.*

The school is for education. The school is, or ought to be, for the promulgation of the truth. Since all truth comes from God and "the fear of the Lord is the beginning of knowledge" (Prov. 1:7), Christian people and good citizens are for education. So the home should cooperate with the school in seeing that children study their lessons. Themes should be turned in on time. Homework, when required, should be done carefully, and children should be encouraged to meet the high standards of the school. Particularly should children from Christian homes set out to lead their classes and prove that good Christians are good students.

2. *The home should cooperate with the school in maintaining proper discipline.*

Regulations of the school, as long as they are proper ones, should be held sacred by the home. Children who obey their parents will naturally be expected to obey their teachers.

3. *The schools will lead in many good community enterprises.*

Schools will encourage children to give to the Red Cross and to relief purposes, to attend good lectures, to see exhibits in the museum, to read good literature. Whenever the causes advocated by the schools are proper causes, they should be heartily approved by the home.

4. *Extra-curricular activities in the school, when they are harmless and good, should usually have the approval of parents.*

May the Christian boy play basketball or football on the high school teams? I think that if proper safeguards are provided for morals and if these athletic activities do not put the boy in bad company and hinder his Christian life it is wise for the boy to be allowed to take part, when time and strength permit, in such athletic activities. I played college football, with very great help to myself and I think to the improvement of my character. In some local situations the athletics will be under poor coaches, men of low moral standards, and drinking and profanity and gambling will be so much linked up with athletic activity that Christians will want to shun them. It is my judgment that that is not ordinarily the case. Should the Christian girl or boy play in the high school band? Yes, if acceptable standards are maintained. But they should certainly not play for dances. One of my daughters, very enthusiastic in the social life of her high school, wanted to be a cheerleader, and after long practice and training was elected as one of the cheerleaders. Might she be allowed to be a cheerleader at the high school basketball and football games? No, not if it involved wearing shorts or a tiny ballet skirt! Otherwise there would be nothing wrong in helping cheer at the basketball and football games. But she must dress as does a Christian, look as a Christian should, and act as a Christian. Other cheerleaders respected her convictions and the convictions of her father. It was arranged that all the girl cheerleaders would dress in uniforms with nice skirts at the basketball games and my daughter would help them. At the football games where others wore slacks she did not appear as cheerleader. She had a part in high school life, she did not compromise, and she had the respect of everybody involved, and a good conscience.

5. *Christian homes must definitely take a stand against unchristian activities and teaching in the schools.*

Should Christian boys and girls attend the high school prom or dance? Certainly not! Dances are not for Christians. Christian young people must be taught that there is a price to pay for a happy Christian life. It is not too heavy a price, and later they will be glad that they gave up sinful pleasures in order to keep a happy heart, a pure conscience, and a good influence over others. The homes and churches should see to it that when the high school graduating class is entertained in a dance, the Christian members of the class have a social affair of their own with a happy time and innocent amusement together, with some devotion and prayer and praise.

Some schools have ballroom dancing in the curriculum. This is often an honest effort to encourage friendship and to overcome shyness and awkwardness in the teenage group.

Nevertheless ballroom dancing is in itself so lust-provoking, so evil in its influence, that Christian people must object. Let a Christian student frankly say that his conscience does not allow him to dance. Let parents take the matter at once to the principal and insist that they will not permit their children to dance. It will be a comfort for you to know that this matter has come to be an issue in many communities, and in every case an enlightened public sentiment will back up Christian parents who are not willing for their children to be perverted and wrongly influenced by ballroom dancing in the school. If necessary, the matter can be taken to the school board. A Christian young person had better lose credit in a course and lose popularity with fellow students than to be guilty of conduct unbecoming a Christian and conduct hurtful to his own spiritual life and moral welfare.

It is unfortunate that in science departments of schools all over America the theories of science (not scientific facts) are taught which discredit the Bible. Children, with uninformed minds and without sufficient educational background to refute the theories, are taught that man is descended from brute beasts, that the Bible is not true, that everything living came into being by evolution, that if there be any God at all He is so far away that He cannot be reached by prayer, that He never works miracles, that He never answers. Christian homes must set themselves solidly against such teaching. Better that a child never have a high school education than that his faith in God should be wrecked, or that his reverence for the Bible as the Word of God should be broken down. Boys and girls from Christian homes should be warned ahead of time of this infidel propaganda carried on by those who are practically atheists. They should be warned that it is only a propaganda, that it is not true science. They should be given books that show the fallacy of such so-called "scientific teaching."

When my first daughter was ready for high school, I had taught her carefully through the Bible and particularly had taught through the book of Genesis in the church of which I was pastor, and had shown her what is God's teaching about the creation of all things by direct act of God. I had shown her the teaching in the first chapter of Genesis, ten times repeated, that each species was created to reproduce "after his kind." I got her Dr. Harry Rimmer's book, *The Theory of Evolution and the Facts of Science,* and went over it with her very carefully, showing that the evolutionists were only guessing, that there was no scientific evidence for evolution, that no one had ever observed one animal crossing from one species to another, or the origin of a new species. I showed her the fallacies which had been discarded by evolutionists as one by one their points were disproven. I told her, "No high school teacher in the world knows any more about this matter than your daddy. If he did, he wouldn't be just a high school teacher. So if any question comes up that you do not understand, you and I can find the answer to it, and we can prove that the evolutionary teaching of those who do not love God and do not believe the Bible is false." I armed my daughter with other books, written in popular vein and for young people, that showed how wonderful was God's creation in the human body. *God and You*, or *Wonders of the Human Body* by Arthur I. Brown was very stimulating and helpful to her. So when her high school teacher began to make remarks about evolution, my daughter was ready to ask questions that he could not answer and to say, "Well, what about this?" She found it easy to pick flaws in any argument for evolution. The truth is that most high school teachers are many years behind the times in scientific knowledge. Many still teach the nebular hypothesis which is now long discarded, and many teach evolution by the method of "natural selection," which scientists do not now believe. The science teacher was first a little irritated, and then became cautious, and finally asked my daughter to bring a book on the subject. He read it with real interest. Thereafter my daughter was not embarrassed before others, and concession was made by the teacher to Christian belief in any discussion.

I do not say that my way is the best or only way. I simply insist that parents must safeguard their children and must see that their faith in the Bible is not broken down. There is not any real reason to discredit the Bible, either in matters of science or history or religion. It is the infallible Word of God. Not one known fact of science discredits the Bible. Christian people should not allow high school teachers to ruin the faith of their children. It is not necessary. Children properly prepared in Bible study and willing to stand up for their faith will come out not only with a good education, but with a stronger faith in God than before.

I do not mean that children shall be disrespectful toward their teachers, even when they disagree with them. I do not mean that parents shall encourage children to be arrogant. Christian students must act as Christians should toward their teachers. They must not pretend to know more than they know. But any Christian boy or girl has a right to say, "I believe the Bible. Anything that is against the Bible I will not believe."

The child does not belong to the school. He belongs to the home. The home must have the first say and the last say as long as the child is sheltered under its roof. And the authority of father and mother must be used, along with prayer and godly example, to see that the child's faith in God is maintained and that education is not a damning blight instead of the benediction it should be.

6. *When children of Christian homes are sent to college, their moral and spiritual welfare should be safeguarded.*

Parents like to send their children to their own alma mater. So despite the communism taught in the classes or the sneering at God's Word, children are often sent to a college where their faith is wrecked. Or it may be parents are thinking about the prestige of a degree from some great university. So into a modern Babylon of wickedness and unbelief they send an immature and unsuspecting high school graduate to get a college degree. The boy or girl cannot answer the sophistries of their teachers. Oftentimes they cannot stand alone amid the temptations of modern college life. How much better it would have been had they never gone to college rather than that their moral standards should be lowered, their faith in God broken down, their belief in the Bible shattered!

If a child must leave home to go to college, why not send him to a Christian college? There are a number of good Christian colleges in America where the Bible is revered, where Christian standards of conduct are encouraged. Before parents or guardians entrust to a college the precious life of the young man or woman for whom they are responsible, they would do well to inquire diligently whether the school teaches that the Bible is the inspired Word of God, whether it teaches that Christ is the Son of God and Saviour, whether it holds to the Christian standards of conduct. Parents must remember that God comes before the schools, and character and Christianity are the most important parts of an education.

III. The Home and Community Life

We can only touch briefly certain duties of the home in regard to community life not involved in the cooperation with church and school.

1. *Worldly amusements.*

The Christian home will have to set its own standards about amusements. It will be fortunate if other Christian families of like ideals live nearby. But anywhere one is in the will of God one can have God's help to rear his family aright. There are many innocent forms of amusement. I see nothing wrong with tennis, badminton, croquet, checkers, chess, Ping-Pong, etc. I do not think Christians should play with cards usually used for gambling. Christian young people can have music, conversation, take pictures, give their Christian testimonies. Christian young people who have high standards are really happier than worldly people who compromise and give themselves over to hurtful and worldly amusements. Dancing is definitely wrong because of the sex stimulation that is inherent in the close bodily contact. Petting and necking are wrong, of course. It is my deep conviction that Christian people ought not to attend commercial picture shows which are so largely given to themes of sex and crime, and whose standards are set by immoral Hollywood people. (See my book, *What Is Wrong With the Movies?*) Basketball games, football games, skating (only in proper surroundings and circumstances) are permissible, with proper chaperonage. Ice skating where the climate permits is popular. Roller skating rinks sometimes sell beer, have many rough customers, and sometimes have dancing on skates. Christians will want their young people to avoid such places. But there is always plenty for Christian young people to do if they put Christ first. I know that I was very happy in my boyhood without ever attending a dance, without ever a drink of beer, or a cigarette, and under rigorously enforced rules of good company and proper chaperonage. And I am glad to say that my own daughters have been both happy and popular, living under the strictest standards, and have a full and joyous life.

2. *Dates.*

Naturally young people, boys and girls, want to be together. In the early teens it seems wise that boys and girls should be allowed to be together some in mixed groups, where they play together at a party, where they go together in a group to some amusement or game or picnic, without having formal dates. In the early teens, of course, young people should be required to be at home at certain early hours, should have proper chaperonage when they are on dates. This old-fashioned custom will safeguard both the morals and reputations of the young people, and Christians ought to more or less make their own standards in such matters, instead of giving way to the careless and loose standards of the world. Even older young people should be in at respectable times, and fathers and mothers should, by earnest teaching and some supervision, see that their daughters are not over-tempted into petting and necking and indiscretions which may lead to more serious sin. Let daughter be taught that her young man friend is to come to the house for her. Let the young man be introduced to father and mother and be treated with respect and kindness and made to feel at home. Invite him for a meal, and let the natural fellowship of young people, a boy and girl, develop around the piano, the radio, or the Ping-Pong table or the tennis court.

I have a most happy memory of one home where I was often a guest as a young man. I went to see a girl in the home, but soon found myself the guest of the whole family. The mother, an English woman of distinguished manner and genuine culture, was a fascinating conversationalist. On a sheep ranch in West Texas they had an Edison phonograph with about a hundred classic records. The sprightliest conversation with the whole family, the courtesies that poverty and the rural atmosphere could not diminish, made every visit a happy one as well as a wholesome one. There I learned to know and love the best music, and I spent many happy hours there. The boy and girl friendship was never very serious, yet a pleasure that is almost homesickness comes to mind as I remember this country boy's visits to the home of his girl friend.

3. *Christian parents must keep control.*

"Everybody else goes" will be the cry of young people in Christian homes, perhaps, but the father and mother must determine for themselves whether everybody else is right in going to some place of amusement. Christians must set their standards in the home and not be governed by the community standards, which are often very worldly and are usually set by unchristian people.

The home is a light in the darkness, a haven in the storm, a place where the days are "as the days of heaven upon the earth," if God's commands are there known and loved and followed.

CHAPTER XX

Adultery, the Ruin of Marriage and Morals

"Thou shalt not commit adultery."—Exod. 20:14.

Men and women cannot have an adequate conception of the sanctity of marriage and the absolute necessity of making marriage a lifelong partnership of one man and one woman without a discussion of the scarlet sin, adultery. Sex sin before marriage tends to break down character and ideals and greatly jeopardizes the marriage, while adultery after marriage is the ruin of everything holy and good in marriage, the ruin of marriage itself.

The only references to marriage in the Ten Commandments are "Thou shalt not commit adultery" (Exod. 20:14), and "Thou shalt not covet thy neighbour's wife" (Exod. 20:17).

Only by seeing how God hates adultery can we see the sanctity of marriage in the home.

Any Bible preacher can preach on the scarlet sin, adultery, without apology, since the Bible deals so frankly and so repeatedly with the subject. In Genesis we have the story of the Sodomites, the incest of Lot with his two daughters, Judah's sin with his daughter-in-law, the attempted seduction of Joseph by Potiphar's wife, the ruin of Dinah by the young prince of Shechem and the curse on Reuben because he went up to his father's bed. The Mosaic law in Exodus, Leviticus, Numbers, Deuteronomy has repeated instructions about the punishment of the scarlet sin. It is placed in the Ten Commandments, both in Exodus and in Deuteronomy.

Throughout the Bible God's Holy Spirit deals plainly with this sin. In Joshua we have the story of Rahab the harlot. Judges tells how Samson, a judge of Israel, went to see a fallen woman. Second Samuel gives the sad story of David's sin with Bathsheba, and the Scripture tells how there followed the rape of his daughter Tamar.

In the New Testament Jesus repeatedly discussed the scarlet sin. Again and again He preached to "this adulterous generation." He gave fornication as the only legitimate reason for a divorce.

Romans tells of the degeneration by which much of the race became savages, enduring the curse of God, because of sex perversion. The epistles give warning after warning against fornication, adultery, chambering and wantonness. The book of Revelation tells of the horrible plagues of the tribulation, partly in judgment on great Babylon for her fornications and adulteries. And then finally, after a glorious picture of Heaven, we are plainly warned that whoremongers and adulterers are outside.

It is manifest, then, that honest preachers who profess to preach what is in the Bible or to follow the example of prophets and apostles and of Jesus Christ Himself, must preach on this scarlet sin.

There are abundant reasons why such preaching is needed. First, millions of people have no idea how horrible the sin is in God's sight. If they knew how God regards it, and if their consciences were enlightened, many of them would never go into this sin. Second, if preachers preached the horrible judgments of God upon this sin, many would fear it and avoid it, even though they did not love God. And, third, and more important yet, honest Bible preaching on sin creates an acute consciousness of God, leads to conviction for sin and to repentance. Every great revival must have honest dealing with the sin question. There is no use of preaching grace to people who do not know that they have ever sinned. God's commands about adultery may be called a part of the law, but "the law was our schoolmaster to bring us unto Christ" (Gal. 3:24).

Some will object that the language is too plain. But we are exhorted to "utter by the tongue words easy to be understood" (I Cor. 14:9). In the revival in Ezra's day we are told: "So they read in the book in the law of God distinctly, and gave the sense, and caused them to understand the reading" (Neh. 8:8). If Bible preachers like Jesus and John the Baptist and Paul and Stephen and Peter used sharp, plain words that cut people to the heart, why should not honest preachers today be as plain and direct in dealing with the Word of God and sin?

And besides, I remind you that all these matters are dealt with in the secular press. A recent newspaper told of the closing of the red-light district in Evansville, Indiana, by army order, of the rounding up of prostitutes, of tests for venereal disease. Picture shows deal with the problem and glorify sex. Cheap "pulp" magazines revel in "true confession" in sex crimes, and love triangles. There are some good books read by many intelligent people, written by doctors and scientists, on sex questions. Sociologists study the evils connected with sex very frankly and seek remedies. Laws are passed, censorship imposed on filthy pictures and filthy literature. If sex matters are common talk everywhere, then why should there not be somebody who could speak with a voice of authority—the authority of God's Word—on these questions? And so, by God's grace, I seek to enlighten, to warn, to show the way to victory. the way to mercy and peace, and the way of salvation for sinners.

I give this message in print in response to the request of many, many people who have heard me preach upon the subject. As God has blessed such plain preaching before to the warning of the innocent and the convicting of the guilty, and the leading of many to repentance and salvation, so, I pray, He may use this message.

Sex Is God-Given; Marriage Is Holy and Clean

"Marriage is honourable in all, and the bed undefiled: but whoremongers and adulterers God will judge."—Heb. 13:4.

Marriage is properly called "holy matrimony." God Himself made man and woman, male and female, made them one for the other, and gave them the mating instinct. When God first put Adam in the Garden of Eden, God made him with a need for a wife. Genesis 2:18, 21-25 tells us of the first marriage, where God Himself performed the only ceremony there was, and the angels of God were the only witnesses!

"And the Lord God said, It is not good that the man should be alone; I will make him an help meet for him ... And the Lord God caused a deep sleep to fall upon Adam, and he slept: and he took one of his ribs, and closed up the flesh instead thereof; And the rib, which the Lord God had taken from man, made he a woman, and brought her unto the man. And Adam said, This is now bone of my bones, and flesh of my flesh: she shall be called Woman, because she was taken out of Man. Therefore shall a man leave his father and his mother, and shall cleave unto his wife and they shall be one flesh. And they were both naked, the man and his wife, and were not ashamed."

We were plainly told that God said, "It is not good that the man should be alone," and God Himself presented Adam with his bride. It was God who made them one, not only one in spirit and mind, but one in flesh. Their bodies were made the one for the other, just as their natures were made each to supplement the other. And then the Lord tells us, "And they were both naked, the man and his wife, and were not ashamed."

These holy creatures that knew nothing of sin, and were as pure as the angels of God, were mated. And even while they were in the Garden of Eden we are told, "And God blessed them, and God said unto them, Be fruitful, and multiply, and replenish the earth, and subdue it" (Gen. 1:28). Mating with these perfect creatures was not only permitted, it was plainly commanded. So marriage is a divine institution. Sex is as natural and right and as holy as any physical or mental or spiritual quality of man.

Satan has tried to defile the thoughts of the whole race about marriage and mating. Whispered dirty comments, chalked vulgar words on back fences, the snickers of lewd people over dirty jokes, the embarrassed silence of good people—these have all left the impression that sex matters are all vile, that mating is naturally and inevitably wicked. There is the foolish theory that the sin by which Adam and Eve fell was the marriage relationship, despite the fact that the Lord expressly commanded Adam and Eve to mate and multiply, and despite the fact that the particular sin by which they fell is mentioned, and it could not possibly be a sex matter. Not long ago, I read a tract, published by the leader of a modern cult, demanding sex abstinence altogether on the part of married Christians. That is unscriptural, foolish, sinful.

In Hebrews 13:4 is this plain statement: "Marriage is honourable in all, and the bed undefiled: but whoremongers and adulterers God will judge." There is nothing wrong with marriage. There is nothing unclean or sinful about the marriage bed and the marriage relationship. There is nothing innately sinful about sex. But a *perversion*, a *misuse* of sex relationship is wicked, so that "whoremongers and adulterers God will judge."

The loving mating of a husband and wife is as normal, as proper and as guiltless as eating, drinking, sleeping, or any other normal bodily function. One can sin by eating, but eating is not a sin. One could eat stolen food, and that would be wicked. And it is likewise wicked for a man to take another man's wife or another man's future wife. In the Ten Commandments God puts coveting your neighbor's wife along with the sin of coveting your neighbor's ox (Exod. 20:17). It is not wrong to have your own wife, nor is it wrong to have your own ox. It is sinful to have or covet either that does not belong rightfully to you.

God puts no restraint on the marriage relationship. First Corinthians 7:3-5 says, "Let the husband render unto the wife due benevolence: and likewise also the wife unto the husband. The wife hath not power of her own body, but the husband; and likewise also the husband hath not power of his own body, but the wife. Defraud ye not one the other, except it be with consent for a time, that ye may give yourselves to fasting and prayer; and come together again, that Satan tempt you not for your incontinency." And then the next verse says that this separation for a short time of the husband and wife by consent that they might give themselves to fasting and prayer is permitted, but is not commanded.

Nothing could be clearer from this Scripture than that the marriage relationship is intended to be an act of love in which the husband seeks to please the wife and the wife seeks to please the husband, and neither counts the body his or her own. The only proper restraint on the marriage relationship implied here would be such moderation and temperance as would make for happiness and health and spiritual prosperity.

There is not even a hint in the Bible that the marriage relationship was given only for procreation. Marriage is for the procreation of the race, but it is also for mutual love and comfort and happiness.

Therefore, as we enter into a study of the scarlet sin, adultery, let no one feel that his or her sex instincts are naturally wicked. They are not. And it is proper for earnest Christian people and other decent and intelligent people to study this matter with a wholesome interest, trying to find the will of God and the way of happiness. Any perversion and misuse of sex is sin, but the sex equipment and sex instincts of men and women are a part of God's good creation. We should think about such matters reverently and prayerfully, and we should take these gifts from God as holy gifts to be properly enjoyed and used, and to be reverently protected from defilement and sin.

God's Measure of the Terrible Wickedness of Adultery

The scarlet sin is not a trivial sin. It is one of the most horrible sins against God. It is one of the most shocking crimes against mankind.

By considering some Bible statements we will see how God regards this sin of adultery. Five Bible evidences show it to be a most wicked sin deserving the severest punishment of an angry God and outraged society.

1. *Adultery is forbidden in the Ten Commandments.* Remember there were only ten of these commandments which summed up all the law of God. Four of them dealt with one's duty to God. Only six of them were required to sum up all a human being's duty to his fellow men. And one of these six commandments is the command in Exodus 20:14, "Thou shalt not commit adultery."

This command is immediately preceded by the command, "Thou shalt not kill." In God's sight adultery ranks along with murder, is one of the most horrible sins, and is one which is as strictly forbidden as murder.

2. *God commanded the death penalty for adultery.* In Leviticus 20:10 the Lord commands, "And the man that committeth adultery with another man's wife, even he that committeth adultery with his neighbour's wife, the adulterer and the adulteress shall surely be put to death." Again in Deuteronomy 22:22 we are told, "If a man be found lying with a woman married to an husband, then they shall both of them die, both the man that lay with the woman, and the woman: so shalt thou put away evil from Israel." And the following verses demand the death penalty for the scarlet sin, if the woman involved is engaged to another man. Other Scriptures command the death penalty for sodomy and for sex sins with beasts.

Remember that the death penalty, under God's law, was only given for the most horrible crimes. The death penalty until recent years was given only for murder, for treason, and in a few cases for rape or kidnapping and such crimes. But God commanded, and often had His command enforced, that the adulterer and adulteress should surely be put to death. That is part of God's measure of the wickedness of adultery. Adultery is wicked as murder and treason are wicked!

3. *The scarlet sin is the only scriptural ground for a divorce.* Everywhere in the New Testament divorce is discouraged. Jesus named only one sin that permitted the breaking of the marriage by divorce. In Matthew 19:9 He said, "And I say unto you, Whosoever shall put away his wife, except it be for fornication, and shall marry another, committeth adultery: and whoso marrieth her which is put away, doth commit adultery." The word "fornication" here comes from the same root in the Greek, as the words for "harlot" and "whoremonger." The only difference between fornication and adultery is that fornication, that is harlotry or whoremongering, seems a more deliberate or repeated indulgence in the sin. It is the same scarlet sin, and a divorce is not allowed "except it be for fornication," said Jesus.

Drunkenness is not a sufficient reason for divorce. If a husband comes home drunk, beats his wife, wastes the money so that there is no food and insufficient clothes, and makes a Hell of the home, still that wife does not have a right, according to the Bible, to a divorce.

Or if either mate shall desert the other, without rhyme or reason, yet God does not permit a divorce.

If a man's wife commits murder, still he does not have a right to divorce her. If a husband is sentenced to the penitentiary, state laws may allow a divorce, but God's law does not.

Even insanity is not mentioned in the Bible as a proper ground for divorce.

Any divorce that is granted for any reason "except it be for fornication," is an unscriptural divorce in God's sight; and if either party marries after any divorce except for fornication, that party commits adultery.

So horrible is this sin in God's sight that it is the only one for which He allows a marriage to be broken.

4. *Venereal disease, the physical plague God puts on those who commit the scarlet sin, is a loathsome and dreaded disease.* Syphilis is almost never caught except in the sex relationship. It is spread almost entirely by the social sin. Syphilis often results in death. It may lurk in the body for years after the victim thinks he has recovered and later cause locomotor ataxia, paralysis, or insanity. It may affect the heart, cause brain lesions, and many other troubles which can never be traced. It often requires major operations on women, causes sterility, has made multiplied thousands of children blind from birth, and is blamed for the birth of afflicted and sub-

normal children. Gonorrhea, too, is a treacherous and dangerous and loathsome disease. These venereal diseases are said by historians to have caused the downfall of empires. Scientists say that the bones of the mummified Pharaohs discovered in Egypt show the marks of syphilis and thus explain the decay of the race and the downfall of Egypt. But these venereal diseases, which God has put as a plague upon the scarlet sin, show His holy indignation at this perversion of sex.

Alcoholic drink causes cirrhosis of the liver (hobnailed liver), enlarges the capillaries of the skin, inflames the lining of the stomach, weakens the lungs. Tobacco and dope habits have serious physical results. Overeating may seriously shorten the life. Every kind of sin has some effect upon the body. But there is no kind of sin that has such a horrible physical curse upon it as the venereal disease curse God has set to show His displeasure with sex sin.

5. *Many Scriptures expressly say that adultery, fornication, the scarlet sin, leads to Hell.* Proverbs 7:27, speaking of the harlot, says, "Her house is the way to hell, going down to the chambers of death." The house of the prostitute is the way to Hell!

Again in Proverbs 9:13-17, we are told how a foolish, sinful woman sits at the door of her house and calls to men, enticing them to come to her. But the next verse says, "But he knoweth not that the dead are there; and that her guests are in the depths of hell." The guests of the harlot woman go to Hell!

In I Corinthians 6:9, 10 is another such plain word. Those verses say: "Know ye not that the unrighteous shall not inherit the kingdom of God? Be not deceived: neither fornicators, nor idolaters, nor adulterers, nor effeminate, nor abusers of themselves with mankind, Nor thieves, nor covetous, nor drunkards, nor revilers, nor extortioners, shall inherit the kingdom of God."

Notice that "neither fornicators ... nor adulterers ... nor abusers of themselves with mankind ... shall inherit the kingdom of God." If fornicators and adulterers and sodomites cannot inherit the kingdom of God then that means that their souls are lost forever.

Ephesians 5:5 says, "For this ye know, that no whoremonger, nor unclean person, nor covetous man, who is an idolater, hath any inheritance in the kingdom of Christ and of

God." This is simply another statement that the whoremonger shall not inherit the kingdom of God.

Again, in the book of Revelation we are told of the wonderful city of God, where "there shall be no more death, neither sorrow, nor crying, neither shall there be any more pain" (Rev. 21:4). But in the same chapter we are told, "But the fearful, and unbelieving, and the abominable, and murderers, and whoremongers, and sorcerers, and idolaters, and all liars, shall have their part in the lake which burneth with fire and brimstone: which is the second death" (Rev. 21:8).

"Whoremongers," says the Scripture, "shall have their part in the lake which burneth with fire and brimstone: which is the second death."

And then after a further description of the beautiful city, of the river of life and of the tree of life which bare twelve manner of fruits and of the throne of God and of the Lamb that shall be in it so that there is no need of candle nor sun in that blessed city, then we are told in Revelation 22:15, "For without are dogs, and sorcerers, and whoremongers, and murderers, and idolaters, and whosoever loveth and maketh a lie." Whoremongers, says the Word of God, are left outside the beautiful city of Heaven!

These Scriptures above, in six different places in the Bible, teach that the scarlet sin leads to Hell. There is a way of forgiveness, but evidently there are millions of people in Hell who went there because of the scarlet sin. And that shows how wicked is this sin, and how God hates it!

Summarizing, note these five things that show how horrible is the scarlet sin: adultery is forbidden in the Ten Commandments along with murder; adultery received the death penalty under Mosaic law; the scarlet sin is the only reason for which Jesus permits divorce in the New Testament; venereal disease is God's loathsome punishment in the bodies of those who commit this sin; many Scriptures say that the scarlet sin leads to Hell, that the whoremonger has no part in the kingdom of God!

Dear friend, in view of the horrible nature of this sin in God's pure eyes, how can you risk His wrath by committing it?

CHAPTER XXI

Divorce, the Wreck of Marriage

"The Pharisees also came unto him, tempting him, and saying unto him, Is it lawful for a man to put away his wife for every cause? And he answered and said unto them, Have ye not read, that he which made them at the beginning made them male and female, And said, For this cause shall a man leave father and mother, and shall cleave to his wife: and they twain shall be one flesh? Wherefore they are no more twain, but one flesh. What therefore God hath joined together; let not man put asunder. They say unto him, Why did Moses then command to give a writing of divorcement, and to put her away? He saith unto them, Moses because of the hardness of your hearts suffered you to put away your wives: but from the beginning it was not so. And I say unto you, Whosoever shall put away his wife, except it be for fornication, and shall marry another, committeth adultery: and whoso marrieth her which is put away doth commit adultery."—Matt. 19:3-9.

"And unto the married I command, yet not I, but the Lord, Let not the wife depart from her husband: But and if she depart, let her remain unmarried, or be reconciled to her husband: and let not the husband put away his wife. But to the rest speak I, not the Lord: If any brother hath a wife that believeth not, and she be pleased to dwell with him, let him not put her away. And the woman which hath an husband that believeth not, and if he be pleased to dwell with her, let her not leave him. For the unbelieving husband is sanctified by the wife, and the unbelieving wife is sanctified by the husband: else were your children unclean; but now are they holy. But if the unbelieving depart, let him depart. A brother or a sister is not under bondage in such cases: but God hath called us to peace. For what knowest thou, O wife, whether thou shalt save thy husband? or how knowest thou, O man, whether thou shalt save thy wife?"—I Cor. 7:10-16.

Divorce has rapidly increased in America until now approximately one marriage out of two ends in divorce. The return of the service men will greatly increase that rate.

Among the reasons for this increase of divorces are a decrease of the influence of the Bible and Bible standards of living, a decrease in sex morality, the feminist movement with its emphasis on the independence of women, and the increase in percentage of people who come to adulthood and marriage without any discipline in the home, without inculcated respect for authority.

Because of the strict position of the Catholic church, in areas which are largely Catholic the percentage of divorces is less. In areas where Protestants predominate, the percentage of divorces is higher. New York State, until recently, recognized only one legitimate cause for divorce, adultery; other states allow divorce for varying causes, some of them for drunkenness, non-support, desertion, mental cruelty, and even "incompatibility."

But when people are converted and set out to live according to the standards of the Bible, divorces decrease. The Scriptures above, the one from Matthew 19:3-9 in the words of our Saviour Himself, the other divine inspiration given to the Apostle Paul, sum up the Bible position on divorce. The Bible teaches that marriage should never be broken except by death, that the only legitimate reason for divorce is continued adultery, that is, fornication, and that Christian people can readjust wrecked happiness, regrow marital love. The home where there is disagreement, quarreling, broken vows, abuse, and even hatred, can be made into a happy home by the grace of God.

I.   Marriage Is a Lifetime Contract; Should Never Be Broken

In the teaching of the Lord Jesus on the question of marriage and divorce, several plain facts stand out, facts that should never be forgotten.

1. *One comes to marriage leaving father and mother and all else. The husband is to "cleave to his wife."* In Bible times the only divorces were on the initiative of husbands. There is no record of women divorcing their husbands. Women had little or no place in the commercial world, no way to make a living, and naturally clung to their homes. The Saviour in Matthew 19:5 quotes from Genesis 2:24 which says, "Therefore shall a man leave his father and his mother, and shall cleave unto his wife: and they shall be one flesh." Hence

marriage means the honest forsaking of all others, that a man may cleave to his wife. Any such marriage is necessarily lifelong in its import.

2. *Of man and wife it is said, "They twain shall be one flesh."* A man and wife actually become one. Genesis 2:21, 22 tells us that God caused a deep sleep to fall upon Adam, that He took one of Adam's ribs, closed up the flesh, and made Eve to be Adam's wife. Adam said, "This is now bone of my bones, and flesh of my flesh" (Gen. 2:23). God could have made a woman without Adam's rib, but God thus chose to symbolize the fact that a man and wife are of one flesh. Literally, a husband and wife become one in the bodies of their children. In normal and happy marriage, man and wife become a part of each other in a spiritual sense so that breaking the marriage is like rending the body apart. In their thoughts, customs, aims, enjoyment, hopes, and interests a man and wife become one. This necessarily means that the mating should be for a lifetime.

3. *God Himself seals every marriage, makes it official and binding.* People are not always wise in their marriage choices. They do not always do right in marrying. Some people marry who have no right to marry because one or both had divorces that God did not sanction, or because one is a Christian and the other is not, or because the motives back of the marriage are not honest motives and the vows are not sincerely taken. I say, not every marriage is a proper marriage. But whether the marriage be good or bad, God Himself seals it and joins the husband and wife together. God makes every marriage binding, and in that sense all marriages are made in Heaven, at least are made binding in Heaven. So the Lord Jesus says, "What therefore God hath joined together, let not man put asunder."

A woman seeking a divorce sometimes says, "I do not believe I was ever really married in God's sight. I did not love my husband. We were not fitted one for the other." But that is a silly and wicked excuse which God will not accept. He says that always the marriage is binding, and that God Himself joins husband and wife together. Marriage should be permanent.

Other Scriptures bear out the same teaching that marriage is binding until death. First Corinthians 7:39 says, "The wife is bound by the law as long as her husband liveth; but if her husband be dead, she is at liberty to be married to whom she will; only in the Lord." Marriage is binding until death. After one's mate dies, God gives the privilege of marrying again. But all marriage is intended to be a lifetime contract broken only by death.

II. Divorce for Drunkenness, Desertion, Non-Support, Cruelty, or Incompatibility Is Wicked, Forbidden in the Bible

In Old Testament times, Moses, because of the hardness of the people's hearts, allowed a man to give his wife a writing of divorcement and send her away. But from the beginning God did not intend this. God made man and woman male and female, and made them to cleave one to the other until death should part them. In the plain words of the Lord Jesus, God never sanctions divorce except for the cause of fornication. A man may be a drunkard, may waste his money, beat his wife, leave his children in direst poverty, yet his wife has no right to a divorce. A woman may be a shrew, her home may be disorderly and dirty, yet her husband has no right to a divorce on any such ground. Mankind is a race of sinners. Every man must know that the woman he marries has faults. Every woman who marries must realize that she is marrying a frail human being like herself. Any woman who marries a drinking man is likely to find herself tied to a drunkard. Any home in which Christ is not taken as Saviour and Lord and in which He is not followed lovingly and loyally is likely to be made into a hell on earth. But no one should ever marry who does not accept the hazards involved and plan to keep the vows that he makes at the marriage altar to love and cherish and honor his mate "until death do us part."

If people will accept the honest position that marriage is to be dissolved only by death, they will be slower to marry. They will also be slower to go into sin that might ruin the happiness of marriage. But marriage is not to be broken for any reason but fornication.

In fact, the Scripture indicates that no divorce is recognized by the Lord unless one of the mates has been guilty of fornication. A couple, divorced on unscriptural grounds, is still regarded as married in God's sight. For Jesus said, "Whosoever shall put away his wife, except it be for fornication, and shall marry another, committeth adultery" (Matt. 19:9). A married person in taking another wife or husband commits adultery, because he is already married. And Jesus said, "Whoso marrieth her which is put away doth commit adultery." When a man takes a divorced woman whose marriage was not broken by fornication, he is taking a married woman; in other words, he is taking another man's wife. God still counts the marriage binding until it is broken by fornication. So no one should ever plan to get a divorce for drunkenness, non-support, cruelty, desertion, incompatibility, or for any reason other than for persistent adultery, called fornication.

III. Fornication Breaks the Marriage, Allows Divorce

When Jesus said there should be no divorce "except it be for fornication," the word for fornication is the Greek word *porneia,* the term for whoredom. This word, in the Greek, has the same root as does the word for whoremonger and the word for harlot. So what Jesus meant to say was that unless the wife played the harlot, or unless the husband were a whoremonger, divorce should not be sought nor granted.

Adultery and fornication are the same act. Some people have thought that adultery was a sin of married people, and fornication the sin of single or unmarried people. But that is not an accurate classification. Adultery, to be sure, is a term usually used about married people, but not always. For example, in the Ten Commandments, "Thou shalt not commit adultery" covers all sexual sins. No intelligent person would say that the Ten Commandments forbid immorality on the part of married people, but do not rebuke the same sin by unmarried people. In the Bible the word adultery is used for a single act of illegitimate intercourse, while the word fornication is used for a course of whoredom or harlotry. Hence, it seems to me that the Saviour means that if a wife has gone into a course of harlotry and cannot be reclaimed to purity and fidelity to her husband, the husband has a right to divorce. Naturally, I believe that the same principle would hold about a wife's divorcing her husband who is a fornicator, that is, a whoremonger, a habitual sinner in this matter.

I believe the inference is that if a woman fell into adultery, the husband should, if he can, forgive and reclaim his wife. The inference is, I think, that if a husband fell into one act of adultery, a temptation, the wife ought to forgive him, win back his love and devotion, if possible, and his fidelity to the marriage vows, and keep him as a husband.

In fact, though the Lord Jesus permits a divorce for fornication, He does not require it. The Lord Jesus never commanded, nor is there any statement in the Bible, that a marriage necessarily ought to be broken for any sin or any cause. The Lord *permits* divorce for fornication, that is, whoredom, by one of the mates, but He does not demand it.

I think it is obvious that a persistent course of harlotry on the part of a wife and of whoremongering on the part of a husband robs marriage of its essential meaning and beauty. Sad and tragic as a divorce always is, a child of God is permitted to seek a divorce if the mate is definitely committed to a course of immorality and sexual sin.

But what is a Christian to do if his mate departs and will not live with him? That is answered in I Corinthians 7:10, 11: "And unto the married I command, yet not I, but the Lord, Let not the wife depart from her husband: But and if she depart, let her remain unmarried, or be reconciled to her husband: and let not the husband put away his wife." Let a wife not leave her husband. Let the husband not leave his wife. But if the two are estranged for other reasons than fornication, the Christian should remain unmarried, hoping to restore the home with the mate.

Sometimes when one mate is converted and becomes an ardent Christian, the ungodly companion rebels. The Christian finds his marriage threatened by his ungodly companion's leaving. What should the Christian do in such a case? The answer is given that he should remain unmarried, or the wife who has an unsaved husband should remain unmarried, hoping to have the marriage restored. First Corinthians 7:12-16 says, "But to the rest speak I, not the Lord: If any brother hath a wife that believeth not, and she be pleased to dwell with him, let him not put her away. And the woman which hath a husband that believeth not, and if he be pleased to dwell with her. let her not leave him. For the unbelieving husband is sanctified by the wife, and the unbelieving wife is sanctified by the husband: else were your children unclean; but now are they holy. But if the unbelieving depart, let him depart. A brother or a sister is not under bondage in such cases: but God hath called us to peace. For what knowest thou, O wife, whether thou shalt save thy husband? or how knowest thou, O man, whether thou shalt save thy wife?"

Thus it is clear that while a Christian ought not to marry an unsaved person, if they are already married, the marriage ought not to be broken. The Christian wife ought to remain with her unsaved husband, or the Christian husband ought to remain with his unsaved wife, "For what knowest thou, O wife, whether thou shalt save thy husband? or how knowest thou, O man, whether thou shalt save thy wife?" One must not break his marriage because the companion is not a Christian. And as long as there is hope, the Christian must remain ready to be reconciled. The children of such a marriage are legitimate children. God's blessing is upon the home in which a Christian stays with his unsaved mate for Jesus' sake.

But what if the parted mate marries someone else? Often this question arises when a marriage has been broken and when the divorce was not based upon fornication. Suppose a husband has left his wife. Or suppose that years ago they quarreled, with either or both to blame, and broke up their home. They got a divorce, though it was not on scriptural grounds. Now suppose the husband has married another woman. What should his former wife do? Is she free? Should she count herself divorced?

The answer is yes. When a man marries again, and lives with another woman, that in itself is adultery, is fornication, enough to break the former marriage. In such a case the wife should count herself divorced and count her marriage broken by fornication, since he who was her husband is now the husband of another. And Jesus said, "Whosoever shall put away his wife, except it be for fornication, and shall marry another, committeth adultery" (Matt. 19:9). So the husband, on taking a second wife when the first marriage was not broken by fornication, committed adultery. That, of course, would break the former marriage. If the first marriage was not broken before one mate remarried, it would be broken as soon as one mate remarried and started living with another companion. Fornication is the only Bible ground for divorce, but one has a right to a divorce on Bible grounds.

IV. Do Not Break a Second Marriage

Divorced people who have married again should not break the second marriage. The second marriage has broken the first marriage. God Himself holds the second marriage binding. To break it would do no good, but would do great harm.

Many people, even Christians, have the tragedy of divorce in their past. Many people, like a Christian woman who wrote to me recently, either married a divorced person, or were themselves divorced and married again, before their conversion. Should the second home be broken? Is it a sin for a wife or husband to be true to a second marriage? Can God be pleased as long as the second marriage is maintained?

These are serious questions. The answer, according to God's Word is this: DO NOT BREAK THE SECOND MARRIAGE! Two wrongs never made a right. It would usually be impossible to restore the first marriage, and the Bible does not command it, even if it were possible. Confess the sins of the past, but do not sin again by another divorce or separation!

Here is a letter I wrote in answer to the inquiry of a troubled Christian woman:

"You married a divorced man, you say, seventeen years ago. Five years ago you were saved and have been earnestly living for Christ ever since. Now some preachers say that if you continue as the wife of this man you should not take the Lord's Supper. You ask my counsel.

"I will answer your problem prayerfully, the best I can. It is the same problem many others have.

"My conclusion, backed up by the Bible, is this: you should continue as the wife of your husband. The past is gone and cannot be undone. It would be an additional sin for you to quit your husband, or to refuse to live with him as his wife. Your husband likewise is married to you and has no other wife. The past is gone. He cannot change it. His former wife is not now his wife. To break the present marriage would be a sin. If you are now living for God the best you know, then you have a perfect right to go on and serve the Lord, take the Lord's Supper, and do any Christian work proper for a devout and consecrated woman, for which you may be prepared and equipped.

"Here is what Jesus said in Matthew 19:9, 'And I say unto you, Whosoever shall put away his wife, except it be for fornication, and shall marry another, committeth adultery; and whoso marrieth her which is put away doth commit adultery.' Deuteronomy 24:1-4 says, 'When a man hath taken a wife, and married her, and it come to pass that she find no favour in his eyes, because he hath found some uncleanness in her: then let him write her a bill of divorcement, and give it in her hand, and send her out of his house. And when she is departed out of his house, she may go and be another man's wife. And if the latter husband hate her, and write her a bill of divorcement, and giveth it in her hand, and sendeth her out of his house; or if the latter husband die, which took her to be his wife; her former husband, which sent her away, may not take her again to be his wife, after that she is defiled; for that is abomination before the Lord: and thou shalt not cause the land to sin, which the Lord thy God giveth thee for an inheritance.'

"Note the following facts from the above Scripture:

"1. Divorce meant exactly the same in both the Old Testament and the New Testament. But in the New Testament Christ gives the clear law that divorce is wrong for any cause except for fornication (or continued adultery). Comparing these two passages, then, fornication breaks the vows of marriage and gives a right for divorce. When divorce has taken place on this Bible ground, the first marriage is broken entirely, and the parties are free to marry again. In such a case, a woman who has been divorced and is remarried does not have two husbands, as people sometimes say. The husband of a second marriage is her husband, and the husband of the first marriage is her 'former husband,' the Bible says.

"2. It is equally clear, specially from Deuteronomy 24:4, that when a marriage has been broken, and one of the parties has married again and lived with another mate, the wife may not go back to the husband of her first marriage, or the husband could not go back to the wife of his first marriage, 'for that is abomination before the Lord,' we are told.

"3. One who gets a divorce on any other ground besides fornication, and marries again, commits adultery, said Jesus in Matthew 19:9. If your husband got his divorce not because of fornication, then when he married you and started living with you as your husband, he was guilty of fornication. If his first marriage was not broken before, then it was broken after he married you and lived with you. In either case, he is not now bound to his first wife. God forbids that he should go back and marry her again.

"It would do no good for you to leave your husband. It would simply bring more reproach on the cause of Christ and cause more unhappiness.

"In conclusion, you have only one husband, the man you are living with, and he has only one wife, yourself. You should live together according to the clear scriptural rule of I Corinthians 7:3-5. Note in verses 5 and 6 that even to be apart, one from the other, for a season of fasting and prayer is not commanded. Paul spoke what he did by permission, not as a command. God does not require husband and wife to live apart, and no preacher should give any such instructions.

"Divorce is a terrible thing. It brings always much heartbreak. Sin always brings trouble. Some sins we cannot undo. We can only confess them to God and have them forgiven. If your husband had a scriptural right for divorce before he married you, then he should not be blamed. It he did not have a scriptural right for divorce, he did wrong and he should confess his sin to God and have it forgiven. But he cannot undo it, and he should not break his present home and marriage."

V. Should Divorced People Marry Again?

It is certain that when possible, divorce should be prevented. There should never be a divorce except for the cause of fornication. When the erring mate can be won back to faithfulness, the home should remain intact, even though there has been the scarlet sin. Divorce is a terrible thing and should be avoided. Our principal aim is to prevent divorce and keep the home intact. But we ought to answer honestly from the Scripture the oft-repeated question as to whether it is sometimes right or always right for divorced people to remarry. Several facts are taught by the Scripture.

1. *Scriptural divorce gives a right to remarry; one who has a right to a divorce has a right to remarry.* The modern idea of some Christians that one has a right to a divorce, but should remain single thereafter and never remarry, has no warrant in the Scriptures. In the Bible it is everywhere taken for granted that a right to a divorce means a right to remarry. A divorce, on Bible grounds, means that the former marriage is no longer binding. The former husband is no longer a husband. The former wife is no longer a wife. Those who are divorced on Bible grounds are really divorced, are single, unmarried, unbound.

In the Old Testament, Moses, because of the hardness of the people's hearts, permitted divorce on other grounds than that required for divorce by the Saviour Himself in the New

Testament. Nevertheless, divorce meant the same thing in the Old Testament that it means in the New. In Deuteronomy 24:1, 2 is this plain statement: "When a man hath taken a wife, and married her, and it come to pass that she find no favour in his eyes, because he hath found some uncleanness in her: then let him write her a bill of divorcement, and give it in her hand, and send her out of his house. And when she is departed out of his house, she may go and be another man's wife." Here it is clear that divorce meant the right to remarry. A divorce, if it be scriptural, breaks a marriage, breaks the ties between husband and wife and frees them from one another.

2. *No person should marry a second time if his former marriage has not been broken by fornication (continued adultery).* Those who are divorced on other than scriptural grounds are still married in God's sight, as we have shown above. Of course, when the marriage was broken by fornication, they are free and the divorce is scriptural. Or if one of the parties to a divorce has remarried, then that second marriage, by its adultery, breaks the former marriage. But one whose former marriage has not been broken by fornication certainly should not marry again. In such cases I Corinthians 7:10, 11 says: "And unto the married I command, yet not I, but the Lord, Let not the wife depart from her husband: But and if she depart, let her remain unmarried, or be reconciled to her husband; and let not the husband put away his wife." If a home is broken, with husband and wife separated or divorced, but has not been broken by fornication, then let the woman remain unmarried or be reconciled to her husband. Let the husband remain unmarried or be reconciled to his wife. One has no right to remarry if the former marriage has not been broken by fornication.

3. *Those scripturally divorced have a right to remarry.* This was necessarily involved in the first point above. When a person's former marriage was broken by fornication, and he gets a divorce, then he has a right to remarry. Or when a divorce has been secured and one of the mates has remarried, thus being guilty of adultery or fornication and breaking the marriage, the remaining mate has a right to remarry.

Some people feel that the innocent party has a right to remarry but that the guilty party ought to be barred from remarriage. But what they have in mind is punishment of the guilty one, and they are not basing that contention upon the

Scripture. It is true that one who breaks a marriage is guilty of great sin, particularly one who is guilty of fornication, thus violating the marriage vows and all the decencies of love and marriage and home. He has grievously dishonored himself and sinned against God. But there is no law that a murderer cannot marry, or that a drunkard cannot marry, or that a blasphemer or a thief cannot marry. Men have no right to put a law where God did not put one, and to say that even though a marriage is broken completely, broken in the scriptural sense because there has been fornication, the one who sins should not marry. Certainly one who was guilty of fornication and broke a former marriage would be a very poor marriage risk. If the first wife found him untrustworthy, the second would not likely find him faithful. But when the marriage is broken, it is broken for both parties; and the divorce is in effect. The Scriptures do not require those who are now unmarried to remain single.

If the fornicator had no respect for the law of God while he was married before, who would expect him to remain single now in deference to the Word of God? But God has no command for one to remain single after a marriage is broken by fornication.

4. *Divorced people are not good marriage risks, and should go slow about remarrying.* Anybody should be slow to marry, should weigh well the responsibilities of marriage and the dangers involved. A divorced person should be doubly slow to marry. In nearly every case where a home is broken, both mates are partially responsible. It is rare, if ever, that a marriage fails when one party did all that he or she ought to have done to keep the marriage intact and to make the home happy and successful. So every divorced person may as well accept it as a fact that he has failed to prove himself adequate to hold the respect and love and loyalty of a mate. He took a solemn vow "until death do us part," but in some fashion failed to live up to that vow. He had love and happiness in his grasp and let them slip through his fingers. One who is divorced ought to realize, and anyone who thinks of marrying a divorced person ought to realize that one who has failed once in the marriage relationship is a poor risk. Those who have had one divorce are likely to have another. The woman who fails to make one man happy is likely to fail to make another man happy. The man who fails to be the head of his home, to earn the respect and loyalty of one

wife, is likely to fail with a second wife. Any woman who marries a divorced man, or any man who marries a divorced woman, enters a marriage that is definitely handicapped. Only after prayer and resolution, and perhaps repentance, should a divorced person enter marriage.

There are other problems to consider in the marriage of a person who has been divorced. First, there is often the problem of children of a former marriage. Such children are a source of strife and unhappiness in many homes. Second, there is necessarily, and even properly, shame connected with divorce. Do not think you can flaunt the opinions of a civilized world and not feel it. Do not think that you can discard your mate and appear guiltless before the world after having made solemn vows to take that mate for better or for worse until death do you part. Even the so-called "innocent party" to a divorce necessarily inherits part of the blame. People properly feel that if the wife had honorably loved and obeyed her husband and made him happy, he would not have gone after other women. If among Christian people, there is no such thing as having a divorce and not feeling some odium attached to it. Particularly is this true in the churches. In many, many denominations preachers feel that a divorced person has no right to active participation in church affairs. Some preachers who earnestly contend against divorce, but who do not think through the problem from the scriptural viewpoint perhaps, may say that those who have married divorced persons are "living in adultery," though the Scripture does not say that. So let anyone who is divorced and is thinking of remarrying, or anyone who plans to marry a divorced person, seriously consider the odium and the dangers involved in such a marriage. One had better go slow and prayerfully consider. In many cases one would be much happier to remain single and find God's blessing wonderfully adequate to fill the heart and mind with love and joy and service, without entering again the bonds of marriage wherein one had once suffered failure and shame.

Those who have married the second time should not break the marriage, but those who consider marrying the second time should go slow and make sure they have evidence of God's blessing and that they are not going contrary to His will.

VI. Weighty Human Reasons Back Up God's Command to Avoid Divorce

The Bible never gives a command without good reason. It is always safe to follow the Bible because there are always weighty reasons why one's own happiness will be promoted by doing what God said. God loves His children. God provided everything good for mankind. When the Scripture says, "Thou shalt not," then one had *better* not. One will be happier not to do it. When God says to do a certain thing, you may be sure that your own happiness and joy will be greatly increased by doing what God commanded. So, if any feel that, despite the Word of God, they will never be happy without a divorce, I bring to your mind some important reasons why everyone should hesitate before even considering a divorce.

1. *If there are children in the family, consider their welfare and happiness.* God's plan is that each child should have one father and one mother. A serious wound is made in the personality of any child who does not have both a father and a mother, particularly if this lack is connected in his own mind with something shameful or hateful. By the divorce of his parents a child's happiness is greatly impaired, and often his character as well. Delinquent children usually come from broken homes. The woman who divorces her husband is more likely to see her children turn out to be harlots and criminals, more likely to see them grow up without Christ and live in sin and die away from God, than the woman who is not divorced. Children need a happy home. They need the security, the love, the peace and the contentment that go with a happy marriage and a happy home. Any woman had better swallow her pride, take back her bitter words, forgive and be reconciled to her husband, if that be at all possible, rather than that the children should grow up without a father. I speak particularly to women, since ordinarily about six out of seven divorces are obtained by women.

Now in the immediate aftermath of the war, about three divorces out of four are obtained by women. In most cases of divorce the children go with their mothers. So mother, think what a serious responsibility you take upon yourself and what a sin against your children you commit when you break the home and divorce your husband.

2. *Economic disaster often follows divorce.* Any woman who looks forward to her future security and that of her children should avoid a divorce at almost any cost. It is true that the securing of alimony has become a wicked and conscienceless racket. No doubt the divorce evil has greatly increased because of the shameless demands for alimony that are now often granted by divorce courts. Nevertheless, women had better realize that in most cases divorced men pay alimony very reluctantly, and as soon as possible the alimony is reduced or dropped. Rarely does any man pay alimony except under legal compulsion. Often the man whose home is broken by divorce fails in business or loses his job, and his character deteriorates until he cannot, if he would, continue the payment of alimony to support his former wife in the manner in which he had been accustomed. Usually the divorced husband remarries and cannot well support two households. It is a foolish woman who thinks that she can be secure, demanding that a former husband, whom she now hates, support her with regular payments while she goes on her way and accepts no responsibility for his happiness. Men are not made that way, and the disillusionment, the unhappiness, the deterioration of character that goes with divorce will often make it impossible for the husband to support his former wife, and it makes it certain that he will not want to do so. Women who want to be able to give their children a decent home and education and the comforts and opportunities of life should swallow their pride, should learn to love their husbands again, be good wives, and avoid divorce. A divorce is economic disaster both for wife and husband, and certainly is a grave economic loss to the nation.

3. *Consider the public disgrace of divorce.* A woman often feels that she can divorce her husband and marry more fortunately a second time. A man often feels that he can divorce his wife and marry again and be happy. But such people forget to take into account a serious fact. Many times one who is divorced will not marry in the same class of society as one who has not been divorced. Decent mothers do not want their daughters to marry divorced men. Men do not want to have the odium of marrying a divorced woman. Everybody with good sense knows that a divorced person is a poor risk. The temper, the instability of character, the selfishness that made marriage a failure before are likely to make a second marriage a failure. Hence it often happens that a divorced

person marries in a lower plane of society the second time. You cannot escape the odium of divorce.

I still remember how people in the rural district where I lived as a boy looked with mingled pity and scorn on a "grass widow," a divorced woman. Many nice people would not invite her to their homes. It was more or less taken for granted that she was somehow lacking in character. That was usually true then, and is only less true now, but still partly true. Divorce means that a tragic sin has taken place, and that one who is divorced necessarily had a part, at least some part, in that sin. One who is divorced is regarded as one who does not keep his solemn vows, as one who is not true to his commitments, or at the very best, as one who could not retain the love and respect of the dearest and most intimate companion he or she ever had, the wife or husband.

If you get a divorce, many churches would hesitate about giving you a place of responsibility and leadership.

There is a shame and a sense of tragedy that hangs about a person who has been divorced. I beg you in Jesus' name and for your own happiness, to be reconciled to your companion and avoid divorce.

4. *Consider the shameful reproach on Christianity which the divorce of Christians involves.* This subject needs only to be mentioned to have its weight felt. Christian people particularly are expected to love one another, to get along in the home, to keep their solemn obligations and vows. If Christians cannot live together in peace, then Christians are no better than heathen people, no better than lost people. Every Christian whose home life turns out to be a failure has brought reproach on his own profession of faith, and has brought shame on his own Lord and Saviour. Everywhere it is acknowledged that divorce is largely a church problem. Catholics stand staunchly against divorce, and there is less of divorce among them than among Protestants who sometimes know their Bibles better but are not as loyal to their Bibles as Catholics are to their church decrees. Everywhere it is recognized that earnest Bible Christianity, with a joyful adherence to the commands of Christ and the doctrines of the Scripture, tends to eliminate divorce. So when Christians have their home broken by divorce, there is everywhere shame on the part of the people of God and reproach on the church and on the name of Christ. If you love the Lord Jesus, then at all

events be reconciled to your wife or your husband and do not allow your home to be broken.

5. *Divorce is the wreck of your own love and happiness.* You may think that when you cease to love your mate that he has suffered great loss, and he has. But what about your own loss? How bitter, bitter, is the loss of one who has lost his love or her love! Francis William Bourdillon said:

> The night has a thousand eyes,
>   And the day but one;
> Yet the light of the bright world dies
>   With the dying sun.

> The mind has a thousand eyes,
>   And the heart but one;
> Yet the light of a whole life dies
>   When love is done.

Suppose you keep your pride intact! Suppose you say, "I am not going to stand it! I will get even!" Suppose that you let your hot anger uphold your resolution and you break the marriage ties and renounce your holy vows, and give up all the sweet contacts and rewards of love. You have made a bad, bad bargain. You have bought yourself bitterness and unhappiness and a sense of frustration and failure that will follow you until you die. Far better to swallow your pride and beg forgiveness—far better to forgive others, no matter how bad the sin, as long as love can be revived and home can be safeguarded and marriage maintained.

I knew a man and woman, both Christians, who got a divorce after seventeen years together. Each soon remarried. But to each of them it was a tragedy. The man told me with tears and bitterness of heart, "When you have given seventeen years of your life to one woman; when you have loved, saved together, watched over each other in sickness, gone to church together, eaten your meals together, reared your children together, you never get over it." In all my years of ministry many, many people have told me that, though divorced, they could never quite get over a sense of sadness at the loss they had suffered. It may be that love had turned almost to hate, and that even the presence of the offending mate had seemed insufferable, but after time had cooled the temper and a sad and disillusioned heart had let its yearnings be felt, they realized that the divorce was a mistake. In nearly every case there is a better way, a happier way, than divorce. To at least nine out of ten men and women who seek a divorce, I could safely say, "You will live to regret this hasty and wicked breaking of marriage vows and ties. It will lead to misery and unhappiness that can be avoided if you are willing to be unselfish and forgiving and reasonable and loving again and for the sake of God and the children and your own happiness to avoid the breaking up of the home."

VII. How to Restore Lost Love and Happiness in Marriage

There is an alternative to divorce. If love has grown cold between husband and wife, if disagreement has taken the place of the sweet harmony they expected, and if there is such conflict between mates that the future seems to promise only misery and insufferable contention, divorce is not the remedy. I promise you faithfully, and will prove my point by the Word of God, that there is a way to restore love and happiness in the home.

The Bible commands, "Husbands, love your wives, even as Christ also loved the church, and gave himself for it" (Eph. 5:25). And again the Scripture says, "So ought men to love their wives as their own bodies. He that loveth his wife loveth himself" (Eph. 5:28). It is the plain duty of husbands to love their wives. Not to do so is a sin. If God *requires* husbands to love their wives as a solemn duty, then husbands *can* love their wives, always. God never requires what He does not make possible. God never commands the impossible. Husbands *ought* to love their wives, so husbands *can* love their wives. And the startling thing about God's command is that a husband's love for his wife is to be like Christ's love for the church, an unselfish and holy love even for those who do not deserve it! God's people are so frail and weak and sinful that it is only God's mercy, God's goodness that makes Him love us. And the Scripture commands that husbands are to love their wives like that, "Even as Christ also loved the church, and gave himself for it." Every husband who does right will find that God will help him love his wife, even if she has grieved him, even if she is disobedient and rebellious and unlovely in her attitude. Husbands need not break the marriage nor give up the home since God will help them to love their wives.

Likewise, aged women are commanded "that they may teach the young women to be sober, to love their husbands" (Titus 2:4). Wives ought to love their husbands. Wives who do not love their husbands may be *taught* to love their husbands! So no wife need think that divorce or continued unhappiness together is inevitable. She can *learn* to love her husband again. Oftentimes wives whose lives have been made bitter by a husband's sin and abuse and neglect have learned to love their husbands with a deeper, more abiding love than that which thrilled their hearts in courtship days. God never commands the impossible. If God says that women are to love their husbands, says that older women should teach younger women to love their husbands, then wives can learn again to love their husbands who have grieved them. Lack of love is no reason for divorce. People who ought to love one another can learn to love one another.

The Scripture plainly forbids the breaking of marriage. First Corinthians 7:39 says, "The wife is bound by the law as long as her husband liveth." First Corinthians 7:10 says, "And unto the married I command, yet not I, but the Lord, Let not the wife depart from her husband." Even to a woman who has an unsaved husband, God's Word says, "If he be pleased to dwell with her, let her not leave him" (I Cor. 7:13). If God insists that the home must go on, then a loving God will give grace for the problems of the home, and give grace to meet the temptations and troubles that married life brings. Since God refuses the right of divorce to Christians, surely He knows how to restore the happiness and joy of marriage.

Paul had a 'thorn in the flesh.' I do not know what it was, but it must have been as bad as the irritations and distress which Christians often suffer in an unhappy marriage. To Paul God said, "My grace is sufficient for thee: for my strength is made perfect in weakness" (II Cor. 12:9). God has grace enough for troubled Christians. God can help people do right in times of temptations. If God does not have grace enough to help a Christian to repair his unhappy home relationships; if God does not have grace enough to help a Christian wife love her husband, and a Christian husband love his wife, and to help them both maintain their marriage and their happiness in some respect, and the security and welfare of their children by avoiding divorce, then Christianity is not the all-sufficient answer to man's problems that it claims to be and that others have found it to be. Christians can have grace and help from God to meet their problems and to make home happy. Let me suggest some ways to restore happiness and love in the home, and avoid divorce.

1. *Let husband and wife both determine that the home shall be kept inviolate; that they will maintain love and keep their marriage vows and ties at any cost in the world.* Love has much to do with maintaining a happy home. But a Christian's love for God ought to be greater than his love for wife or husband. And love for God involves another word that, for the happiness of the home, is greater. Love for God means *duty,* and duty in the home is a greater safeguard of happiness than is sex attraction and the fluctuating selfish love of a husband and wife one for the other. Does some young couple think that they love one another so much that they will always be happy? Do they think that their love is so great that there will never be a cross word, never a bitter difference of opinion, never wounded pride nor flaming anger? If so, they are mistaken. The people who get divorces were once just as earnest in their love as other people. Love by itself is not a sufficient basis for marriage. Real character has more to do with the happiness of marriage than love. Blessed is the woman who has a husband who owns that he has a duty to God and who steadfastly and unflinchingly determines that he will do right, whether he is happy or not; that he will do right whether he feels like doing right or not. When a husband and wife decide that this marriage has to last, that they are bound by solemn vows in the sight of God and men, and that character and reputation and their welfare through life and the welfare of their children are involved, then the happiness and success of married life can be maintained.

We were young, my bride and I, and very happy. But she was an only daughter, and I an opinionated young preacher with strong convictions and, no doubt, with many selfish ways. Inevitably there were clashes of opinion and of wills. True love does not make people more than human, and does not take away all temptation.

Once my wife said to me, "I am going to tell your father on you, see if I don't!" Once she sadly said, "I am afraid we will never make a go of it. There are just too many things on which we don't agree."

I answered, "Whether we get along or not, we are going to make a go of it. We are married, and we are going to stay married, and we are going to love one another and adjust ourselves to one another, come what may. We took solemn vows to do that, and we owe it to our God to do that, and that is what we are going to do."

I was young, but I knew that marriage is for better or for worse and until death parts those who take one another as husband and wife. And I thank God we have found out as every other man and woman can find out, that love can come out victorious, and duty can make any marriage happy, if husband and wife will simply have character enough to do right and try to get along.

2. *Both husband and wife should get right with God, trusting Christ as Saviour and Lord.* Regeneration, a new heart given from God to a penitent sinner who trusts Christ for salvation, will do more than everything else in the world can do to make a happy home. All over America I have found cases, literally thousands of them, where the home was unhappy and miserable until husband and wife accepted Christ as Saviour and set out to live for Him. Then character was made stable and strong. Then moral standards were such as would please any wife in her husband, and please any husband in his wife. When Christ comes in, happiness comes in. Dissension, selfishness, quarreling can be conquered when one has Christ in the heart and follows the leading of the sweet Spirit of God who abides in every Christian. If one reads this who is having trouble in the home, consider earnestly that your first need is to have your heart made right. If the husband is saved, and the wife is not, let the husband set out to win his wife to Christ. If she will learn to trust her husband's Saviour, and give her heart to God and live for Him, then she will have the grace to love her husband and make the home happy. If the wife be saved, and the husband be unsaved, let her earnestly seek to help him know the Saviour with forgiveness and peace in his heart. That will help cure his drunkenness, his selfishness, his unloveliness. A new convert will not be automatically cured of all faults, but he will have a heart that wants to do right. How many, many homes have been made happy when Christ came in to dwell in the hearts of the husband and wife!

This one point is more important than everything else in the making of a happy home. So I suggest if husbands and

wives have trouble, they should ask some man of God to
show them the way to trust in Christ from the Scriptures;
and each should definitely set out to live for God, depending
on Him for forgiveness and salvation, and following His will
as revealed in the Word of God.

3. *The unhappy home should turn to the Word of God and
prayer.* After people have trusted Christ for salvation, they
need to read the Word of God, to learn what God would
have them do. There is life and happiness and blessing in the
Word of God. A family altar set up in the home (that is, a
regular season of worship with prayer and Scripture) will do
much to iron out the difficulties and to establish a basis of
mutual confidence and respect and singleness of heart. Then
if husband and wife pray together, confess their sins and
failings to each other and to God, and pray one for another,
it will help them to love one another and to be patient one
with the other. God answers prayer and will make Himself
felt in the home. God gives blessings to the home where
prayer is wont to be made and where the Word of God is
read and followed.

4. *The troubled home can often find sweet happiness when
God sends little children. Plan for children to make the home
happy.* It is God's appointed plan that marriage should produce children. If for selfish reasons a husband and wife have
not been willing to have children, I warn you that your
childlessness may lead to dissatisfaction, selfishness, a sense of
frustration and emptiness that may ruin your marriage. So if
you can, have children. Pray God to give little ones. Open
your hearts to the love they will bring and give the love they
will call for. The mutual love of a husband and wife for each
other and their children will hold them together when many
other things would fail. Oftentimes a husband and wife who
cannot have children should adopt one or two children and
unite in the love and care of the little ones. More often, perhaps, if they earnestly pray, God will give children to the
hungry hearts and arms of a husband and wife, and God will
thus unite them more completely in a bond that will not be
broken on earth.

5. *Let the husband set out to be the godly example and
head of the home.* I do not mean that a husband should suddenly determine to be the boss, without checking up on his
own character and making holy resolves about his own du-

ties. Let a man set out to be what God wants a husband and father to be. Let him prove to the wife and children and to the world that he is God's good man, holy and clean in his life, devout and prayerful and humble and loving in his contacts with others. Then let him guide the home in prayer, in Bible study and churchgoing, and in loving-kindness, as well as in discipline. The man who takes upon him lovingly and with trembling humility the place of leadership in the home will usually find that God will help him. It will not always be easy for a wife to obey him, but at least she will respect him, and God will give him the leadership, in most cases, to maintain a happy home and marriage.

6. *Wives who want happy homes should set out to be subject to their husbands, obey them, reverence them.* Elsewhere in this book we have discussed the plain commands of God that a wife should be subject to her husband, submit to her husband, be obedient to her husband, and reverence her husband. I will not repeat the Scriptures nor the argument that make it essential for a godly wife to so submit herself to her husband in humble obedience. Here I only want to say that this is the way to renewed love. This is the way to restored happiness. This is the way to harmony.

Yesterday a letter came to me from a woman with an unsaved husband. She told me of the bitter years of rebellion against her husband. She told me how her husband had gone into deep sin, how he had more and more interfered with her worship and service for God, and how at last he had definitely planned to leave her, his wife, and children. Then she told me how my book, *Bobbed Hair, Bossy Wives, and Women Preachers,* had fallen into her hands and how on reading the Scriptures contained therein she had seen her mistake and failure, had confessed her sin to God and to her husband, and had set out to please him. Now she writes me to say that her husband feels so drawn to her that he cannot leave though he had planned to. And strangely enough she says, "I find that the more I submit myself to my husband and try to make him happy and please him, the more liberty I have, the more he wants me to have my way." The husband has now made full confession of his sins against the marriage. He has not yet been saved, but fellowship between the husband and wife has been restored, and his respect for her, his dependence on her has steadily grown. Meantime she finds that her love is warm and unselfish and tender, and she has a holy yearning for her unsaved husband. She not only loves him, but she longs to see him saved. She prays for him with confidence and faith. God is restoring the happiness, and I believe will eventually save that poor, unconverted husband, and make the home perfectly happy.

A year ago I got a similar letter from another woman in another state. Her story was much the same. For many years she had beaten the rebellious wings of her will against the orders of her husband. Life had grown more bitter. Her son had grown up to be rebellious, disrespectful, and appeared headed for disaster. She came to see that she was sinning against God. She humbled herself to obey her husband, set out to please him daily. She had been an ardent churchgoer, running hither and yonder to services night after night, despite her husband's pleas to keep the home.

Now, at last, seeing her mistake, she turned to keep her marriage vow of obedience. She spent more time with her husband and her son. The home became happy. As mutual respect and love and joy grew between the husband and wife, the son's attitude became more normal, and he became more obedient and respectful. God's peace began to come in the home. Oh, dear wife with a rebellious spirit, I plead with you to humble your heart and be subject to your husband as God has commanded. That is the way to happiness, the way to restored love, the way to fullness of joy in marriage.

Normally some eighty-six percent of all divorces in America are gotten by wives, with not over fourteen percent gotten by husbands, according to recent news releases. Now, with service men returning from overseas, and having their first chance to be freed from unfaithful wives, or sometimes from faithful ones, seventy-five percent of divorces are still gotten by women. It seems certain that the greatest single cause of unhappiness in homes and of divorce is rebellion on the part of the wife. Many a husband turns to drink, keeps company with lewd women, breaks his marriage vows, because he feels that he has been cheated. The woman who promised to love and honor and obey him till death should part them has not put him first. She has insisted on her own will and way. Many a man would not put it into words perhaps, but he feels that he is no more breaking his marriage vows in being a whoremonger than his wife breaks the marriage vows in refusing to obey him. Wives cannot win their husbands either for the Lord or for themselves if they do not learn to submit to their husbands and to obey them. Real godliness in a Christian woman will enable her to do what God has required of her, yielding submission and loving obedience to her husband.

It is true that the Scripture commands that older women are to teach younger women to love their husbands (Titus 2:4). But the Bible does not say much about wives loving their husbands. It says a great deal about wives submitting themselves to their husbands, about obedience and humility on the part of wives. You may be sure that the dear God who commands a woman to obey her husband will teach her heart to love the one whom she really makes her lord. Sarah obeyed her husband, calling him lord, we are told in I Peter 3:6. So there was never any doubt of Sarah's love. Where the will goes, the heart will follow. God will help any woman's heart to love her husband if she will turn her will to the obedience which God commands.

It was rebellion that took the archangel Lucifer out of Heaven and made him into Satan, the enemy of God. Rebellion has broken most of the homes ever broken by failing love and divorce. Wives, love your husbands; and if that seem hard, obey them, and let God put love in your hearts.

7. *Let wives and husbands woo one another and continually express their love.* In Ephesians 5:22-33 God discusses the duties of husbands and wives to each other. Those are strong counsels and commands, and they should be earnestly learned and followed by those who want a happy home. But we should remember that the passage is prefaced by these words: "Submitting yourselves one to another in the fear of God." So I suggest that every husband woo his wife. Continually set out to make her happy. Continually try to delight her heart, to show your love. You may not have money for the gifts that other men bring. The candy, the flowers, the pictures, the jewels that you would like to bring, perhaps you cannot afford. But the one thing your wife would delight in most, you can give. You can tell her that you love her. Caresses are cheap, and yet a little love-making, a little time for fellowship and courtship between husband and wife will do much to maintain the happiness of the home. Let the flower of love be watered with true courtesy, with loving-kindness, with words of praise, and it will bloom beautifully. This is Christian and right, but it is also wonderfully effective and happy.

Let the wife see that she makes home happy. What God requires is not a cold and austere obedience. What husbands want is not the meticulous service of a slave. A husband wants devotion, wants sincere heart desire to please and make him happy. The wife whose love is often spoken and always shown by her service, the normal and proper need of admiration and praise and deference to the head of the home, will find her cares richly repaid. Let husbands and wives woo one another.

Wife, is it hard to love your husband? You loved him once! You found then certain qualities of mind, certain attractive ways that seemed to you irresistible. And if you let him go, some other woman will find him just as attractive and brave and wonderful as once you thought him. Why not let him be your lover? Why not forgive the wrong, forget the past, and set out to love where you ought to love? God will make home sweet, and love will blossom again, when Christians do right.

8. *Ask God for a holy love toward the mate you ought to love.* It may seem that human measures cannot restore the shattered love. It may be that sin has made all that once seemed so fine and beautiful and sweet into a shambles, into wreck and ruin. Can a woman love a bleary-eyed drunkard as she loved the strong, happy young man who won her years ago? Can a man love the profane, nagging shrew with bitter face as he loved the same woman when she was a fair-faced girl with loving words and kind heart? I answer back that God will help people to love those they ought to love. Go to God in prayer and ask Him for a loving heart!

As I dictated this chapter, my daughter said, "Can there be love when there is not respect?" I answered, "God loves sinners who do not and cannot deserve His respect. Many a mother loves a drunken, profane son, loves him all the more passionately because he has broken her heart so many times. Love that is unselfish, love that is godly, can be deep and powerful even where there is not much room for respect."

Unselfish love, love that longs to bless, love that holds on when it is spurned and despised, is the kind that God can give and maintain, when the unity of husband and wife has been broken by sin. So I say to husband and wife in the home where the happiness is threatened, go to God in earnest prayer. Ask God to give you the loving heart that will love those you ought to love however far short they have come of your ideal, however much they have abused your kindness and have broken your heart.

If God can put into a refined woman's heart a deep love for heathen savages so that she is willing to leave her native land and live in a far country without conveniences or comforts and die and be buried among savages, in order that she might win a few precious souls to the Saviour, could He not help a woman to love an unworthy husband? Or could not God who helps Christian workers to love loathsome lepers with misshapen bodies and stinking sores, teach a husband to love his unlovely wife? Jesus commanded, "But I say unto you, Love your enemies, bless them that curse you, do good to them that hate you, and pray for them which despitefully use you, and persecute you" (Matt. 5:44). If every Christian is so commanded to love his enemies and pray for them, and if he can do it by God's grace, don't you know that God can give grace to a wife to love her husband who has beaten her, or for a husband to love his wife who has failed him and nagged him and made his home a hell on earth? So go to God in prayer, in Jesus' name, and beseech Him to put in your heart the love that a Christian wife ought to have for her husband, and that a Christian husband ought to have for his wife.

Always God can restore the love and happiness of marriage if men and women are willing to come God's way and maintain the marriage instead of taking the cowardly way out by divorce.

CHAPTER XXII

Making Christ Head of the Home

"And when Jesus came to the place, he looked up, and saw him, and said unto him, Zacchaeus, make haste, and come down; for to day I must abide at thy house. And he made haste, and came down, and received him joyfully."—Luke 19:5, 6.

"Whether therefore ye eat, or drink, or whatsoever ye do, do all to the glory of God."—I Cor. 10:31.

"Let all bitterness, and wrath, and anger, and clamour, and evil speaking, be put away from you, with all malice: And be ye kind one to another, tenderhearted, forgiving one another, even as God for Christ's sake hath forgiven you."—Eph. 4:31, 32.

"Be ye therefore followers of God, as dear children; And walk in love, as Christ also hath loved us, and hath given himself for us an offering and a sacrifice to God for a sweet-smelling savour."—Eph. 5:1, 2.

Outside my front door was a cast metal knocker, given by a friend, with these words, "God dwells within." That motto ought to be manifestly true of every home where Christians live. Christ should be the head of the home.

When Jesus saw the hungry-hearted but unconverted Zacchaeus in a tree where he had climbed in order to see Jesus, our Saviour said to him, "Zacchaeus, make haste, and come down; for to day I must abide at thy house." It was only for a day that Jesus stayed in the house of Zacchaeus. But Zacchaeus "made haste, and came down, and received him joyfully." By the instant change in the life of Zacchaeus, we know that his home was a different home. Immediately Zacchaeus resolved to give half of his goods to feed the poor and to restore fourfold anything he, as a Roman tax collector, had taken by false accusation. It was a happy day when Jesus came into the home of Zacchaeus. Though physically the Lord Jesus soon went on His way down the dusty roads of Palestine, still He abode in the heart and home of Zacchaeus through His blessed Spirit. Of all the things a home needs, nothing is so essential as to have Christ as a living Presence to be the Head and comfort and wisdom and Lord of the home. Does the Lord Jesus live at your house?

I.   First, He Must Be Saviour

It is well and good to talk about Jesus as an indwelling Presence, as a Guide and Friend and Lord. But nobody can have Jesus for anything unless he has Him first of all as a Saviour.

Let the mother and father first turn to Christ in penitence for their sins and trust Him as Saviour. If some man or woman reads this who has not yet accepted Christ as Saviour, who does not yet know the joy of having his sins all forgiven, I beg you to stop just now and confess to Him, in your heart, that you are a sinner and need salvation. Turn in trusting faith to Him! Take Him into your heart and depend upon Him to forgive your sins and save your soul! He will do it.

Let us never forget that what Jesus really came to do was "to seek and to save that which was lost" (Luke 19:10). Remember this faithful saying, "Christ Jesus came into the world to save sinners" (I Tim 1:15). It would be foolish and insincere to ask the Lord Jesus to live in the home and to rule the home if first those who are in charge in the home do not trust Him as their own personal Saviour, accepting Him and depending on Him and claiming Him.

Let me remind you of that blessed promise, the most popular one in the whole Bible, given to us in John 3:16: "For God so loved the world, that he gave his only begotten Son, that whosoever believeth in him should not perish, but have everlasting life." God loves you. Jesus died for you. Now if you will depend upon Him, risk Him to save you, you will not perish, but you will have everlasting life. This is the blessed promise.

Never mind how bad a sinner you are. If you are honest in your repentance, if you really want to turn your heart from your sins and want Jesus to forgive your sins and save your soul, He will do it. The moment you trust Him, Christ is yours. Then you may talk and plan with Him about His being the Head of the home. But Christ can never live in the home if He does not live in the heart. So take Him as Saviour today!

In central West Texas I was preaching in revival services. I longed to get into a certain home to talk to the husband and wife. It had seemed impossible. Their hearts were hardened and denominational prejudice kept their hearts closed. But God sent a little baby boy into the home, and I called on them to see the baby. I said to the father who met me at the door, "I hear you have a new baby two or three days old. May I see the baby?"

His face brightened, and he proudly led me to the bedroom and introduced me to his wife who was still confined to her bed. The mother beamed when I said, "I came to see the baby." He was wrapped in a little blue blanket and lay beside her on the bed. She unfolded the blanket and showed me the little red, wrinkled face.

Thinking of all the potentialities in this little human soul, this little one who had come out of the unknown into time and into a home and would someday go on into eternity, doomed in Hell or happy with the Lord; I said to the mother, "Isn't he wonderful? How lovely to have a baby boy!"

Her eyes were misty and her smile was tremulous as she told me how happy she was to have her baby. "We wanted a boy and we got just what we wanted!" she said.

After a little talk I said, "Well, I should like to pray for the baby. Wouldn't you like for me to pray that he will be a good man, pray that God will help you rear him, train him and educate him?"

With deep seriousness she answered, "Yes!"

"Then, shall I pray that he will be a Christian man and live for the Lord and that when he dies he will go to Heaven? Or shall I pray that he will grow up a moral fellow, but not a Christian, will turn down Christ and go to Hell? Which shall we pray for?" I asked.

Startled, she said quickly, "Oh, of course, he must be a Christian. I want him to be a Christian and live right and go to Heaven."

"But how will he be a Christian if his mother and father are not Christians? Are you a Christian yourself? Can you teach him how to trust Jesus and love Him and serve Him if you are not saved yourself? Don't you think I had better pray for you, too, and ask God to help you to be a Christian so you can teach the little one and help him to come to Christ?"

By this time she was weeping. Tearfully she said, "Oh, yes, I hadn't thought about that. I couldn't teach him right if I am not right myself. You had better pray for me, too, that I may be saved so I can lead my boy right and teach him to be a Christian and serve God."

I agreed to pray that she would be saved when I prayed for the baby. Then I turned to the father.

"Are you a Christian?" I asked.

"No, I'm not."

I had understood that he was not a Christian; but I saw over the doorway a motto that said, "Christ is the Head of this house, the unseen Guest at every meal, the silent Listener to every conversation." So I said to him, "Then if you are not a Christian, why do you have that motto on the wall? It is not true if you are not a Christian. You cannot have Christ as the Head of the home if He is not Head of your own heart. How can you have a Christian home without having Christ as your own Saviour?"

"I never thought of that," he said. "I saw the motto and I thought it was so pretty that I bought it for my wife and hung it on the wall for her. I see now that it is a lie, it is not true. I guess I will have to take it down," he said sadly.

"I know something you can do better than that," I said. "You can make it true. You can let Jesus come into your heart today and trust Him to save you, and ask Him to be the Head of your house. I am going to pray for the baby and ask God to make him a good boy, to keep him well, to help him to turn to Christ when he is old enough to know his need of a Saviour. I am going to ask the dear Lord to help your wife to trust Jesus today and to let Him come into her heart and make her a Christian so she can help rear the boy aright. Now don't you want me to pray for you, too?"

The father sat with his head in his hands, and tears dripped between his fingers. With deep emotion he said, "Yes, you had better pray for me, too! You had better ask the Lord to forgive my sins and come into my heart so He can be the Head of the house."

What a blessed time of prayer we had! I think the angels of Heaven leaned down to see the mother's tears, to see how she held the little one on her arm tightly and how she whispered a prayer for the Lord to come into her heart and make her fit to be a mother and make her a Christian. I think they rejoiced to see the tears of that man who came to realize that he needed Christ in his heart and needed Christ to be the Head of his home! When the prayer was done, the father and mother were each ready to trust Christ for forgiveness and to

take Him as Saviour. I left that home that day, but the Lord
Jesus did not leave. He stayed there! Christ had come in to
be the Head of the home and to help the man and wife rear
their baby.

No home is ever much of a home, surely, until the Lord
Jesus is taken in as Saviour in the hearts of the father and
mother. And I beseech you who read, if you have not already taken Christ, then do so today. Let Him be your Saviour. He is the best guarantee for happiness and blessing and
prosperity in the home when you have Him in your own
hearts.

Let there be no secret about it. Husband, if you take
Christ as your Saviour today, tell your companion, your
sweetheart, your wife, about it. Let her share in the joy and
let her share in the decision. Wife, if you trust Christ as your
Saviour today, be sure to tell your husband. Tell him that
you have seen your need of Christ to make you a good wife
and mother and that you want him to join you in that happy
decision for eternity and take Christ as his own Saviour, too.

And let mother and father tell the children how Christ has
come into their hearts and how they plan to make Jesus the
Lord and Head and Master of the home.

II. Christian Attitudes in the Home

I have been fearful, as I have written these pages, that
some would try to have a godly Christian home by mechani-
cally setting up certain rules. The husband might set out to
take the responsibility for the home and to be the boss; the
wife might, with however much heart resentment, resolve to
obey her husband; the children might be disciplined and
taught obedience; and there might be the regular form of
family worship with Bible reading and prayer; and yet the
home might be miserable and unhappy and unchristian. So I
beg you in Jesus' name that the home may glorify Christ.
"Whether therefore ye eat, or drink, or whatsoever ye do, do
all to the glory of God" (I Cor. 10:31). How blessed it will
be if Christians who read this will put away all bitterness and
wrath and anger and clamor and evil speaking and all malice,
and, as Ephesians 4:32 commands, will "be ye kind one to
another, tenderhearted, forgiving one another, even as God
for Christ's sake hath forgiven you." And again the following
verses in Ephesians 5:1, 2 command us, "Be ye therefore fol-

lowers of God, as dear children; And walk in love, as Christ also hath loved us, and hath given himself for us an offering and a sacrifice to God for a sweetsmelling savour." If Christians walk in love as Christ loved us, then home will be a bit of Heaven on earth. That is what it ought to be. But let us never forget that a meticulous carrying out of certain forms and the outward obedience to commands of the Bible are not enough to make home what God wants it to be. The love of Christ must dwell there richly. Christians must manifest the blessedness of the Holy Spirit in their lives and show the fruits of love, joy, peace, long-suffering, gentleness, goodness, faith, meekness, and temperance.

We have before quoted Ephesians 5:22-33 showing how wives are to submit themselves to their husbands. But we ought to remember that this passage which begins to give the duties of wives and husbands, and continues in the sixth chapter commanding children to obey their parents and telling how fathers are to rear their children and how servants are to be obedient to their masters and how masters are to treat their servants—I say this passage all begins with a preparatory command of Ephesians 5:18-21. That command is: "And be not drunk with wine, wherein is excess; but be filled with the Spirit; Speaking to yourselves in psalms and hymns and spiritual songs, singing and making melody in your heart to the Lord; Giving thanks always for all things unto God and the Father in the name of our Lord Jesus Christ; Submitting yourselves one to another in the fear of God." I think it would not be so hard for a wife to submit herself to her husband if she was in a home where people were filled with the Spirit, where people were speaking to themselves and singing in psalms and hymns and spiritual songs with real melody in the heart. You see, the heart attitude is more important than the outward observance. Let us do both, but let us begin where God commands us to begin, by having happy, Spirit-filled hearts in the home.

1. *Let the husband maintain a tender love for his wife.* "Husbands, love your wives, even as Christ also loved the church, and gave himself for it," says Ephesians 5:25. My heart trembles as I read that verse. How can I love with the compassion that Christ has for us poor sinners? How far short I have fallen! How much God demands of a husband! While it is true that God intends a man should provide for his family and that a man should be the head of his home,

this other is a far higher requirement and men ought prayerfully and with deep concern to try to bear the love of Christ toward their wives.

Men often do not understand their wives very well. What man ever understood all about a woman! Perhaps he thought he did until he was married, and then he discovered that he did not understand her as well as he thought. Women do not have to have reasons for doing things. They do things "just because." They jump to conclusions, often accurate conclusions, without being able to tell their process of reasoning. Perhaps it is womanly intuition. Perhaps sometimes it is a lack of logic, but the presence of instinctive common sense. I do not know, and what man does? Women are not like men. What man would wear the dinky little things that women pin on their heads as hats? Men may be irritated by the changeableness of women's opinions. Sometimes women are childish in the use of money, and sometimes wives interfere in the discipline of children, and sometimes they weep for no reason at all! I am simply saying that women are not like men, and men often are almost in despair in trying to understand women and get along with them. I do not mean that women are any worse than men at all. But men, being more logical and more businesslike sometimes, and feeling their superiority as they often do, are sometimes bitter towards their wives. So God gives the plain command in Colossians 3:19, "Husbands, love your wives, and be not bitter against them." Mr. Husband, if you are so superior, here is a good chance to prove it: have the forbearing, tender and forgiving spirit, the compassion that Christ has for us poor erring sinners! Do not be bitter against your wife. Let no grudge, no unforgiveness mar the sweet fellowship of husband and wife. The husband must always be ready to forgive and must take the more responsibility for harmony and peace, since God has made him the head of the wife and has made the wife the weaker vessel. A Christian husband will show his Christianity, to be sure, in taking the responsibility for leadership in the home, and the rule of his children, and the provision of the needs of the home. But more than that, he will prove his Christianity by the tender and loving forbearance which Christ has for the church and which husbands are commanded to have for their wives!

"Likewise, ye husbands, dwell with them according to knowledge, giving honour unto the wife, as unto the weaker

vessel, and as being heirs together of the grace of life; that
your prayers be not hindered" is the command of God in I
Peter 3:7. The husband who does not dwell with the wife according to knowledge, giving honour to her as the weaker
vessel, who does not recognize that she, along with him, is an
heir of the grace of life, will find that his prayer is hindered.

Certainly a husband will sometimes need to give definite
orders and insist on seeing them carried out. Christ has all
authority over the church. But husbands need the courtesy
and gentleness and long-suffering of Christ, and thus they can
make home a joy.

2. *Happiness in the home depends largely on the Christian
and unselfish love of wife and mother.*

The wife has many duties in the home. There are meals
to prepare and serve, there are beds to make, floors to sweep,
and a hundred other duties in a day. But does any woman believe that she has done her duty as a wife and mother when
she toils at the stove or dishpan or at housekeeping tasks? A
man can get meals at a boardinghouse or hotel. A hired girl
can do housework and prepare meals. The best cooks in the
world are often men. A man does not need a wife simply
for the labor she can perform. It is true that the wife and
mother ought to carry her end of the load. There is no reason
why a woman should not work, in her own sphere, as a man
should work in his. But, oh, how much more a woman needs
to do than to work!

When colonists from England came to Jamestown in the
wilds of Virginia and founded that settlement, eventually the
bachelors felt they must have wives, and a hundred maidens
came from England to make homes for men in the new
country. One such girl married a colonist and years later
when she died he had put on her tombstone these words:
"Her little foot touched the wilderness of Virginia, and it became a home." Millions of other men have found that a
woman's tender ministrations made a house into a home. The
bare, unfriendly shelter came to have a soul when a woman
with loving hands came to care for the man she loved.

I lost my mother before I was six years old. I had a good
stepmother, but always I missed my mother. When I was
about fifteen I began to make my own way in the world
much of the time and was away from home long years. I
worked my way through college, was in the army in the first
World War, finished university and then taught for a year in

junior college, before I married. When I married at twenty-five and took my bride to our little apartment in Fort Worth where we entered the seminary together, I learned what it was to have a wife and a home! In dire poverty I had worked my way through long years of schooling. I had darned my own socks, had washed my own underwear, had eaten at hamburger stands and cheap restaurants and dormitories. Now I had someone to cook what I wanted to eat, some-one who longed to please me and make me happy, some-one who asked my opinion and deferred to my judgment. Two and a half months after we were married my birthday came around and I had a birthday cake of my own. It seemed to me the first time in long years that anyone had made a birthday cake just in my honor! We lived very cheaply in the little two-room apartment, and many would have thought our fare very plain and meager. But what a light of Heaven dwelt in those two little rooms! All the furni-ture in the apartment cost less than a hundred dollars, and we bought that, secondhand, on installment payments. There were three chairs, I remember, a rocking chair and two straight chairs, but usually we needed only one of them! A woman's love and care and devotion and faithfulness do something to make a home that is indescribably blessed and indispensable.

Do you say that not all women can marry heroes? Then any woman who cannot marry a hero ought not to marry. For no woman can have the reverence for her husband, the loving devotion to his happiness that she should have if he is not in some sense a hero to her. "Sarah obeyed Abraham, calling him lord," we are told (I Pet. 3:6). I think that was not hard for Sarah. How happy is the wife who can give her-self unreservedly to loving ministration to the needs of her husband and his home, to bearing his children and rearing them, and all for Jesus' sake!

God knew what He was doing when He made a woman's tongue nimble. Many a home is brighter for the happy and harmless chatter of a spirited wife. But let wives be sure that this same nimble tongue is a blessing and not a curse. A nag-ging, complaining wife is a burden that ought never to be given to any husband. In Proverbs 31:10-31 is a wonderful description of a virtuous woman. There we are told "her price is far above rubies. The heart of her husband doth safely trust in her." We are told, "She will do him good and not evil all the days of her life." Much is said about the thrift, the hard work, the handiwork and energy of a godly woman. Such a woman, we are told, stretches out her hand to the poor and needy and sees that those of her household are well clothed. But the finest thing said about the godly, virtuous wife is in Proverbs 31:26: "She openeth her mouth with wisdom; and *in her tongue is the law of kindness.*" Oh, wife, see that the law of kindness dwells in your tongue! As you want mercy from God, then be merciful to your husband in the use of your tongue. A nagging tongue has broken many homes and broken countless hearts. The Scripture says, "It is better to dwell in a corner of the housetop, than with a brawling woman in a wide house" (Prov. 21:9). And Proverbs 27:15 says, "A continual dropping in a very rainy day and a contentious woman are alike." Oh, Christian woman, let God put the law of kindness in your tongue!

3. *Let the father and mother exalt one another before the children.* The discipline of a home is not difficult if the husband and wife will stand together. I knew a preacher's son in his early teens who turned out to be a thief, a problem child in school, a ne'er-do-well. I talked sharply but lovingly to the father and told him that he must take responsibility for his son, must see that he went to school, that he did his work, that he obeyed, and grew into strong manhood. With shame and some bitterness the father told me how he had been unable to whip the boy without a tirade of abuse from the wife in the presence of the children, and sometimes she had interfered with physical violence. Mother-love is great, and it is normal for a mother to have anguish of soul in seeing one of her dear children punished. But she will suffer far more if she does not back up her husband to maintain the integrity and discipline and order and godliness in the home.

Sometimes the situation is reversed, and a husband interferes with his wife who, being with the children more than a father, must necessarily take a great deal of responsibility for the discipline and rearing of the children.

In either case, if the authority of one parent over the children is broken down by disagreement and quarreling and objections on the part of the other parent, the effect on the child is certain to be disastrous, and the effect on the joy of the home equally so.

I well remember what my father often said to us children in the home, "You children may quarrel anytime you hear

Mama and me quarreling." My father and my stepmother may have had their disagreements, but I never knew of it. If they talked things out, they did it in private. Each always thought the other was right. Each backed up the other. The result was that not a child in our home ever entertained a thought of open rebellion. I think it would have seemed like sacrilege to the rest of us children if one of us had ever thought our father was wrong on any important point in the world, so carefully was the unity between my father and my stepmother maintained, and so carefully did each exalt the other and praise the other and demand the proper deference for the other.

Certainly one parent will sometimes see that the other is not wise in some decision. But it would be far better to back up the parent before the children than to encourage disobedience and disrespect. There is not any kind of mistake in a father's judgment, for example, I believe, which justifies a wife in breaking down the confidence of a child in his father and the child's sense of duty to obey.

4. *Children must have love.* I pity any child born into a home where he was not wanted. A letter last night from the president of a college where my daughter is now enrolled, said, "She always has a smile on her face." In the same mail came a letter from my wife saying she had just remembered what a neighbor lady said when this same child, our first-born, was a baby. "She must be a 'wanted' child, she seems so happy all the time," said the neighbor. Thank God she was wanted! All ours were wanted. I had a letter not long ago from a mother rejoicing over an article I had published in *The Sword of the Lord* discouraging birth control. This woman told how she has six lovely children. "Another is on the way," she said, "and I will be just as happy over the seventh one as I was over the first!" Oh, little children have a right to be loved and wanted!

Perhaps I think of it more than some men do since I am away from home so much in revival campaigns all over America; but with every one of my children, the first connected sentence each one learned was "Daddy, I love you!" or "I love Daddy." I had them say it over and over again!

For many years it was a custom in our household at the breakfast table that I should ask them one by one around the table, including Mrs. Rice, "Whose girl are you?" The inevitable reply was, "I am Daddy's girl!" My children knew that

I loved them. They know it now. If I ever get a letter from one of them and they do not tell me that they love me, I will certainly be surprised and grieved!

I never write to them without saying that I love them and that I pray for them, as, of course, I do daily, and often many times a day.

Years ago I was home from a revival campaign, and Joy, then about six, perhaps seven years old, passed her plate to me and said, "Daddy, will you cut up my meat?"

Mother said, "Let me cut your meat, dear. Let Daddy eat his dinner in peace."

But she said, "No, Daddy likes to do it," and passed the plate on to me. And I did like to do it! Through the years my children have known that I was glad to dress them, to bathe them, to tie their ribbons, to answer their questions, and that always I wanted their caresses.

I am a very poor father, I know, but by this personal testimony I hope to illustrate the fact that God intended little children to be loved and taught to give love and express love. It is a poor home where people do not say, "I love you!" It is a poor home where the letters going from one member of the home to another are not ended with cross marks for kisses and circles for hugs!

How blessed it is for a mother's love to be expressed in her fervent prayer. Thousands of young people all over the world have been kept straight because they knew mother prayed for them. A poem called "Prayer Time" tells how a mother's prayers can rise day and night for her children.

The while she darns her children's socks,
    She prays for little stumbling feet,
Each folded pair within the box
    Fits faith's bright sandals, sure and fleet.

While washing out, with mother pains,
    Small, dusty suits and frocks and slips,
She prays that God may cleanse the stains
    From little hearts and hands and lips.

And when she breaks the fragrant bread,
    Or pours each portion in its cup,

For grace to keep their spirits fed,
 Her mother-heart is lifted up.

Oh, busy ones, whose souls grow faint,
 Whose tasks seem longer than the day,
It doesn't take a cloistered saint
 To find a little time to pray!
                    —Ruby Weyburn Tobias
    Used by permission of *The Sunday School Times*

Children must often be punished for their wrongdoings, but the punishment must always be followed with forgiveness. Love must prevail. There must be mercy as well as justice.

In Cleveland, Ohio, a devoted Christian man, after I had preached on the home and the godly discipline there required, told me of the last whipping his father gave him. "He whipped me with a horsewhip," he said. "Long marks were made across my back, and blood trickled down my legs. But when he had whipped me, then he threw the whip down and put his arms around me and wept and told me how he loved me. That was the last whipping I ever needed!" He wept as he told me about it, and thanked God for a father who was Christian enough to punish sin and rear his boy aright, and yet Christian enough to love the boy and never let love be broken. Oh, whatever else you do, let home be a place of love. "And be ye kind one to another, tenderhearted, forgiving one another, even as God for Christ's sake hath forgiven you" (Eph. 4:32).

5. *Children must be taught to love one another and live in Christian peace.* If children see the example of mother and father who live in peace, who work out their difficulties quietly and stand by one another, and if mother and father speak with restrained and Christian tongues, children will be more apt to learn patience and forbearance. Children should be taught to confess and ask forgiveness when they have wronged one another. They should be taught to pray about their sins and to ask God to help them to do right. Children should be taught that showing one's Christianity is not primarily going to church on Sunday, but is living right for God in the home every day.

III. Develop the Christian Grace of Hospitality

"Be not forgetful to entertain strangers: for thereby some have entertained angels unawares" (Heb. 13:2). Christians are to be "given to hospitality," says Romans 12:13. The warm welcome for friend or stranger, the open heart and hand to the needy, are marks of the Christian home.

A bishop or a pastor of a church is particularly commanded to be "given to hospitality" (I Tim. 3:2) and "a lover of hospitality" (Titus 1:8). You see, hospitality is a particularly important mark of a Christian home.

The impact of a Christian home on a community cannot be felt largely unless the doors are opened many times to others. So have people in your home. Other Christians should share the fellowship of the home. Unsaved people should see the sweet joy of a Christian home, should bow their heads for thanks at the table, should be present at the family worship, should see the Christian standards and ideals of a Bible kind of home. It is good to have an extra bedroom for guests. Many homes cannot do that, but someone can sleep on the divan or a day bed, or on a folding cot or a pallet and make room for a guest.

Children with a hospitable father and mother are always proud of their home, and are glad to bring their friends home. In our own home it has turned out especially happy for us that our children select their best friends to bring to the house, and that the young people usually prefer to gather in our home than to go elsewhere. With a number of children, with a rather happy home, and with a welcome for their friends, we have had little trouble in keeping our children off the streets or from bad company.

Many Christian parents tell their children they are *not* to go to dances, they are *not* to attend movies, and they are *not* to go to this place or that; but they do not make their own homes a haven and a center of happy fellowship for their children. Have the young people as guests! An innocent party with games and perhaps some gospel songs and inexpensive refreshments will do more to keep young people happy and loving their homes than many a lecture. If parents love company, meet the young people and know them by name, join in their conversation and sometimes in their games, they will be taken into the hearts and confidences of the young people.

Mothers and fathers ought not to let their young people grow out of touch and out of fellowship with the home. Sometimes parents must know when to let the young people have their good times alone, but a happy fellowship will mean that very rarely are the parents not welcome in the fun. Let us make the home happy for young people. Musical instruments, a radio, some good phonograph records, interesting pictures and games are proper equipment for a home. And mothers and fathers, if they are really happy Christians and if their own children are properly reared, can have prayer or testimony at a party without its seeming dull or out of place.

Lot, the righteous man who vexed his soul with the men of Sodom where he lived, insisted that the two angels come into his home to spend the night. I do not know whether Lot knew that these were angels. They looked like men and were called men. But in the destruction of the wicked city, these same angels saved Lot's life and that of his wife and that of his two daughters. Hospitality is a great virtue, but it is also a great blessing.

In II Kings 4:8-17 is told a beautiful and remarkable story of hospitality and its rewards.

"And it fell on a day, that Elisha passed to Shunem, where was a great woman; and she constrained him to eat bread. And so it was, that as oft as he passed by, he turned in thither to eat bread. And she said unto her husband, Behold now, I perceive that this is an holy man of God, which passeth by us continually. Let us make a little chamber, I pray thee, on the wall; and let us set for him there a bed, and a table, and a stool, and a candlestick: and it shall be, when he cometh to us, that he shall turn in thither. And it fell on a day, that he came thither, and he turned into the chamber, and lay there. And he said to Gehazi his servant, Call this Shunammite. And when he had called her, she stood before him. And he said unto him, Say now unto her, Behold, thou hast been careful for us with all this care; what is to be done for thee? wouldest thou be spoken for to the king, or to the captain of the host? And she answered, I dwell among mine own people. And he said, What then is to be done for her? And Gehazi answered, Verily she hath no child, and her husband is old. And he said, Call her. And when he had called her, she stood in the door. And he said, About this season, according to the time of life, thou shalt embrace a son. And

she said, Nay, my lord, thou man of God, do not lie unto thine handmaid. And the woman conceived, and bare a son at that season that Elisha had said unto her, according to the time of life."

The "great woman" of Shunem loved to have the prophet of God visit her home. She had made a little chamber on the wall and had set there a bed and a table and a stool and a candlestick. There Elisha, the lonely man of God, bowed down with the spiritual burdens of the nation, came to rest, with his servant, as often as he passed that way. Through this same man of God the woman of Shunem was given the desire of her heart, a son. Later, through this same man of God, the child was restored to life after he had died. How great are the blessings of those who open their homes to the ministers of God!

The children who grow up in a preacher's home, on the average, show more vision and character and leadership than children of other homes. Part of this, no doubt, is because of the influence of their own father, the high moral standards, the reverence, the Word of God in the home. But part of it also must be the result of frequent contact with great men who visit in a pastor's home.

It was always the pride of my father's family that his home was a home for every passing man of God. When some earnest preacher came to preach in our town, he was often invited to have dinner or spend the night in our home. The rural missionary turned his horse into our gate without any question of the welcome which would be offered him. As a result I was accustomed from my boyhood to conversation about revivals, about Bible doctrine, testimonies of conversions, to talk of Christian colleges and of foreign missions. Many a time I sat on the floor, very quietly, long past my usual bedtime, and heard my father and visiting preachers tell of wonderful conversions they had witnessed, of answers to prayer they had received, of great sermons they had heard, and of the work of God. Did not my heart burn within me? From the preacher-colporteur we got Christian books that helped to mold my life. I longed to be like those men that I respected and loved: the fervent, compassionate cowboy preacher, Perry Harmonson; the saintly John Longan; the lovable R. H. Gibson, and others. And I could never get away from the fact that I was named for two preachers, dear friends of my father's, John Power and R. R. Gaines, who had often visited our home and with whom my father had labored in a useful rural ministry.

A Christian home should throw wide its doors to the minister and the missionary as well as others who need the haven and the fellowship, the restful bed and the refreshing meal of a Christian home.

IV. Give God the Children!

David Livingstone, the African missionary and explorer who suffered much for Christ, is quoted as saying, "The word 'sacrifice' is not in my vocabulary." Anything a Christian can give to God already belongs to God. In Romans 12:1 is this earnest entreaty: "I beseech you therefore, brethren, by the mercies of God, that ye present your bodies a living sacrifice, holy, acceptable unto God, which is your reasonable service." It is your "reasonable service" if you give yourself up to live or to die, if you lay yourself wholly on the altar for God. Certainly a Christian home wants to put Christ first.

That will mean that Christ is first in the property of the home. Christians, of course, will want to tithe. Any Christian who cannot give God ten percent of his income, plus freewill offerings as God leads him, certainly does not love God as he ought, nor trust Him as much as he might. Christians ought to give tithes and offerings. How blessed it is to seek first "the kingdom of God, and his righteousness" and to know that food and drink and clothing and shelter, "all these things shall be added unto you" (Matt. 6:33). So the Saviour promised, and so, thank God, I, with thousands of others, have found that He fulfills His promise.

I well remember the first car I owned, a secondhand model T Ford touring car. We dedicated the car to God, and my wife and I prayed that God would help us to use it to serve Him. We picked up many a hitchhiker, and a number of souls were won to Christ in that battered old touring car. And with every car we have owned, we have had a dedicatory prayer, and have solemnly and earnestly given it to God and begged God to use it for His glory. All that a Christian has belongs to God.

Sometimes people argue about the Christian's money. There is no such thing as a Christian's money. It is God's money in the hands of the Christian, as are all the other things that God lets us have in trusteeship for a season.

Giving of money and serving God in public services have been discussed elsewhere in this book. Here let me lay on your heart the honest duty to give your children to God. God wants your children. He wants them given to Him in prayerful dedication, wants them reared for His glory, wants them to be surrendered for His service and trained for it.

In Luke 10:2 Jesus said, "Therefore said he unto them, The harvest truly is great, but the labourers are few: pray ye therefore the Lord of the harvest, that he would send forth labourers into his harvest." Do you pray the Lord of the harvest "that he would send forth labourers into his harvest"? If any honest Christian prays that God will lay His hand upon laborers, call them, fit them, anoint them and press them into the harvest field, how can he withhold his own children from God? How can any Christian pray, "Send some other mother's boy, some other's beloved son to preach the Gospel"?

How can any Christian claim to love God with all his heart and mind and soul unless he be willing for his children to serve the Lord, too?

My mother went to Heaven when I was five years old, nearly six. Nineteen years later I, a young college instructor, was visiting my aunt, my mother's sister in Amarillo, Texas. As we looked through some old books a letter fell out, and Aunt Essie said, "John, do you want to read that letter? Do you know who wrote it?"

"Yes, I want to read it. It looks like my mother's handwriting." I had seen some old love letters of my mother's written to my father before they were married. So with eager fingers I took up this letter, written more than twenty years before from my mother to her sister.

It came from a dry Texas farm south of San Antonio. It ran something like this:

"It is very hot here. We need a rain very badly. Willie [my father] is not very well, working in the heat." The letter continued and my dear mother wrote, as a young mother would, about her children. "The baby, Porter, is mighty sweet. Gertrude [my older sister] is so good to help me take care of the baby and to dry the dishes and 'help mother.' And Ruth [my younger sister] is the quietest little thing you ever saw. George [my younger brother] is into mischief from morning till night and yet you can't help but love him. And my little preacher boy is getting along fine. Let me tell you what he said. . . !"

Suddenly I stopped reading. Mother had mentioned all the other children. Nobody else could be her preacher boy but me! I said to Aunt Essie, "Did she call *me* her preacher boy?"

"She never called you anything else!" said Aunt Essie.

So my mother thought of me as her preacher boy! I now remembered that when I was four years old, when visitors would ask me, "What is your name, little man?" I was taught to answer them, "I am John the Baptist preacher!"

Not long after I read mother's letter which had lain away so many years since she had written it with loving fingers, I went to Decatur, Texas, and there saw my father and talked to him. I said, "Dad, I read a letter of Mama's in which she called me her preacher boy. Tell me about it."

My father said, "Son, when you were born, we gave you to God and asked God to make you a preacher. Your mother was so glad she had a boy so he could preach the Gospel. We always planned for you to be a preacher and prayed that God would take you for that purpose."

"Why didn't you tell me, Dad?" I asked.

"We wanted God to tell you," he said.

And God did tell me. It wasn't long until I had given way to that inner urge, that constant longing and hunger of my heart to preach the Gospel, and had stepped out by faith, giving up my college teaching, giving up my contract and some bright hopes for the future, in order to preach the Gospel of the grace of God for poor wicked sinners!

I know now that before I was born I was destined to be a preacher of the Gospel. I know that my mind and heart were colored and controlled very largely by the Lord in answer to my mother's devoted prayer. I know that to this end God protected me. I know that all the lonely years after my mother was taken away, all the hardship and poverty, all the years of preparation were to this end. I had thought I would be a college teacher and then a college president, and perhaps later a senator, who knows? I had beautiful dreams and built air castles. But one June night in 1921 when I was doing graduate work in the University of Chicago, I visited the Pacific Garden Mission to sing and do personal work. There my mother's prayers caught up with me, and I saw that I could never have any joy, any peace, any really adequate occupation except in winning souls. I was called to preach, dedicated to preach, and preaching must be my life work, my passion, my joy, my labor, and my destiny.

In a great class in the theological seminary I remember that there was a poll of the ministerial students. How many were saved before ten years old? A large percentage of them. How many were given to God by their fathers and mothers? Most of the preachers there who turned out to be real soul winners, greatly used men of God, were. They grew up in an atmosphere of prayer. They were educated and trained with holy thoughts and aspirations of mothers and fathers who pleaded that God would see fit to take what they offered, their dearest and best gifts, their boys.

My own six daughters were given to God at birth. I had longed for a son that he might preach the Gospel. If I had ten sons, I would be grieved and disappointed if every one of them did not spend his life in some full-time service for Christ. But God saw fit to give me daughters, and I gave them to God. Their mother joined me in the happy dedication and in the earnest prayer that God would take them and would use them.

There was a time when I felt, "If God wants one of my girls to be a foreign missionary, I will surrender to it. It may be I will weep, as other fathers weep to see their girls go to a far-off land from whence they may never return in this world. I may fear the sleeping sickness of Africa or the communist bandits of China, or the other dangers that beset a missionary, but I will be resigned. I will surrender to God's will and dry my tears the best I can." So I thought once. But at last I saw that that was not the way a Christian ought to feel. *Rsigned* to see one of my daughters go as a missionary? No, not *resigned,* but gloriously *grateful!* If God can use one of mine, or all of mine, oh, praise His name, what a joy that is! At the breakfast table sometime later I told my six daughters, "If any of you marry a man who does not spend his life in full-time service for God, then either you will have married the wrong man, or he will be out of the will of God." I told them that so many prayers, so many tears, such labor, such expense, and so much of holy surrender and dedication and pleading had gone into their birth and training and education, that no one had a right to all the fruits of it but God! So if God will take mine, He may have them. If

God should see fit to use them at home, where they can be near me and I can see them, I will be humbly grateful. If God sees fit to use them in a far-off country telling the Gospel, I will praise the Lord. One of them married a young missionary student, and they hoped to spend their lives on "the roof of the world" as missionaries in Tibet. Well and good, had it proved to be God's will. God has done so much for me that I could not, I would not withhold from Him my lovely daughters.

Oh, let me plead with mothers and fathers that you give your children to Christ! Make sure that the best happiness they will ever have will be as they serve the Lord Jesus, as they win precious souls for Him and as they lay up treasures in Heaven that no one else can ever have but those who give themselves full time to the Master's service. My daughters all married preachers and I praise the Lord! God deserves all we have. No one gives God very much who is not willing also to give his own sons and daughters.

One who gives his children to Christ must rear them for Him. Better lay on the lash, better have stripes, and tears, and heartbreak and a rigid insistence on a godly standard of living, than to let the dear child miss his destiny as a man of God! Better withhold your young folk from the sins and dangers of worldly amusements than let them have the fleeting joys of the present and miss the eternal rewards of soul winners.

If you expect God to use your children, you should set out to see that they are educated for the Lord. That is one reason for a Christian college instead of a secular and Christ-rejecting, Bible-denying university. If Christ is to be first in the home, then see that He is given the children.

Conclusion: Accept Christ Today!

Now we come to a close in this tender exhortation that you make Christ the Head of your home. Would you not like to put yourself on record, each member of the family who has accepted Christ or who will now accept Christ, and sign your names together as trusting Him for forgiveness and salvation, surrendering your hearts and lives to Him and giving Him the reins, making Him the Lord of the home? If so, will you not sign this statement today, particularly those of you who have not heretofore accepted Christ as your Saviour. I suggest that you then copy the statement and send it to me with your signatures. How glad I will be to receive it! How happy your home will be if you do it and mean it.

Evangelist John R. Rice
Box 1099
Murfreesboro, Tennessee 37130

Dear Dr. Rice:

Having read the above chapter on "Making Christ Head of the Home," we, the undersigned members of our family, do here and now decide that we will take Christ as our own Saviour, that we will let Him be Lord of our lives and Lord of our home. Realizing that we are sinners, and depending on Christ to forgive our sins and save our souls, we here and now claim Him and receive Him and trust Him. We will try to live for Him from this day forth.

(Signed) ....Father

....Mother

....

....

....

....

I trust that many of you will write me that you have accepted Christ as your Saviour and have won your family to join you in this holy decision to make Christ the Head of your home and Lord of your lives.

If one reads this who has not accepted Christ, or who is not sure about the matter, I will be glad to send further help on receiving your inquiry.

And now may God bless your home and mine!